"The School on the Hill"

A History of The Woodroffe School and its Pupils

by
Gilly Warr

Copyright © 2007 Woodroffe Association

The author asserts her moral right to be
identified as the author of the work

Published 2007 by Woodroffe Associaiton
c/o The Woodroffe School
Uplyme Road
Lyme Regis
Dorset DT7 3LX

British Library Cataloguing in Publication Data.
A catalogue record for this book is available
from the British Library.

All rights reserved.
No part of this publication may be reproduced,
stored in a retrieval system or transmitted,
in any form or by any means, electronic, mechanical,
photocopying, recording or otherwise, without the
prior permission of the publishers.

ISBN: 978-0-9555519-0-1

Printed from client produced artwork by
Creeds the Printers
Broadoak, Bridport, Dorset DT6 5NL

INTRODUCTION

Memories are precious things, particularly shared memories. During the eight years I have edited the ex-students' newsletter I have become aware of the need to record these memories and the history of the school for posterity. It is debatable whether school days are the best days of your life but for the vast majority of pupils lucky enough to have attended LRGS/Woodroffe this would seem to have been the case. As I have carried out research for this book, I have been struck by several factors.

The **willingness of pupils** through the years to put something back into the school; **the dedication of the staff** who are, and have always been, the backbone of the school. A lot of staff have remained at the school for most of their teaching career, providing both continuity and support for pupils across decades; **the family feeling** engendered by the school as demonstrated by the close communication between ex-pupils and staff during the war years, the existence of a thriving ex-pupils' association which holds regular reunions, and the efforts of the Parent Teacher Association who work tirelessly not only to raise funds for the school but to support the staff and pupils in so many ways; and finally **the commitment of governors**, as epitomised by the founder, Alban Woodroffe, which exists to this day. Governors from all walks of life have served on the Governing Body, sometimes for many decades, taking important and sometimes difficult decisions and giving of their time and expertise freely and without question.

The secret of Woodroffe is that it has always been able to move with the times. It has kept up with the many changes in education and has used them to its advantage. The introduction of boarding to raise the academic standards at the school, the change from grammar school to comprehensive school which enabled the school to grow and survive; the acquisition of grant maintained status - a bold move which served the school well in the long term; the achievement of specialist school status as an Arts College - another initiative that has been of enormous benefit not only to the school but also to the wider community which it serves.

Woodroffe is a shining example of pupils, staff, governors and parents working together towards a common goal – to provide the best education and opportunities for young people in the area. Long may it continue! This book has attempted to capture and demonstrate all of the above. Every effort has been made to ensure the accuracy of information contained within it but it must be stressed that it is the work of a well-meaning amateur. It has not been possible to include every detail but it is hoped that the book accurately reflects the true spirit of the school.

Acknowledgements

My sincere thanks to the following:

- Nicola Steward for proof-reading the final draft – a mammoth task
- Ex-Bursar Peter Rickard for his advice, guidance and encouragement which was invaluable and greatly appreciated
- Richard Steward, John Haylock and Ken Gollop for reading the penultimate draft
- Scott Robson for enhancing many of the old photographs included in the book and his design of the front and back cover
- Richard Vine for his assistance
- Brian Neesam for the excellent colour photos on the back and front inside covers
- Gillian and Carolyn Pearn for allowing the score of the School Song and the Lord's Prayer to be included in the book.
- Sarah Haslam née Rodwell and her family for their tribute to her twin brother, Simon.
- Pat Lomax née Wilkins, niece of James Van Allen, for her input
- Carol Robson, niece of Ken Halliday, for the loan of press cuttings
- Mary Delves niece of Frank Moore for the loan of his photograph
- David Cozens for his contribution re former student Simon Hill
- Cecil Quick for his invaluable help regarding the pupils whose names appear on the school war memorial
- Keith Wiscombe for access to his extensive collection of photographs
- Richard Bateman, Kate Butterworth, Carol Davis née Holbrook, Alistair Kennaugh, Simon Tidswell and Paul Vittle for the loan of school magazines, speech day programmes, press cuttings, etc.
- Neil Adams, David Badman, Gaye Baulch née Raison, Jean Bennett née Austin, Rod Boyce, Ed Bowditch, Norman Bowditch, Alan Brown, Graham Brown, Jean Butterworth, Shirley Caunt, Gwen Chessell, Wilfrid Clark, David Coates, Roy Crabbe, Gillian Dunstan née Pearn, John Ennals, Betty Harrad née March, Reggie Jones, Malcolm Kennaugh, George Lloyd-Jones, Brian Manners, Robert McKenzie, Dick Nute, Ron Price, Mollie Raison née Wiscombe, Kerrigan Redman, Bill Short, Paul Vittle, Brian Wood and Eddie Woodbridge for sharing their memories.
- Guy Bryan for access to his research notes re Gerald Gylde, shared with the kind permission of Gerald's widow, Mrs Joan Gylde.
- Editors of Lyme Regis News and Pulman's Weekly for permission to use extracts from their newspapers.
- Last but not least, I would like to thank my husband, John, for his support and encouragement. I could not have written this book without him.

CONTENTS

Chapter 1 – A Brief History of Education in Lyme Regis		7
Chapter 2 – 1923 to 1932:	The Hill Road site	9
Chapter 3 – 1932 to 1938:	Pre-War Years	22
Chapter 4 – 1939 to 1945:	The War Years	27
Chapter 5 – 1946 to 1949:	The Post-War Years	47
Chapter 6 – 1950 to 1959:	The Fifties	59
Chapter 7 – 1960 to 1969:	The Sixties	75
Chapter 8 – 1970 to 1979:	The Seventies	89
Chapter 9 – 1980 to 1989:	The Eighties	104
Chapter 10 – 1990 to1999:	The Nineties	130
Chapter 11 – 2000 to date:	The Twenty First Century	157
Chapter 12 – Alban J Woodroffe		181
Chapter 13 – Headmasters		184
Chapter 14 – Grant Maintained Status		204
Chapter 15 – The War Memorial		213
Chapter 16 – History of Boarding		222
Chapter 17 – St Andrews		228
Chapter 18 – Harcombe House		234
Chapter 19 – Rhode Hill		242
Chapter 20 – The Madrigal Group		249
Chapter 21 – Nine Decades of Drama		256
Chapter 22 – School Song & Lord's Prayer		292
Chapter 23 – Combined Cadet Force		298
Chapter 24 – Duke of Edinburgh Award		303
Chapter 25 – Ten Tors		305
Appendix 1:	Staff List – Teaching	306
Appendix 2:	Staff List – Support Staff	315
Appendix 3:	Head Boys and Head Girls	316
Appendix 4:	List of ex-pupils who served in the 2nd World War	317
Appendix 5:	Trophy Winners	321
Appendix 6:	List of Governors	325
Appendix 7:	Chairmen of Governors	329
Appendix 8	List of Ten Tors Teams	330
Appendix 9:	Pupil Numbers	333
Appendix 10:	Time Line	334
Appendix 11:	Staff Photograph 2007 and key	338
Appendix 12:	The School Site	340
Appendix 13	Education Terminology	345
Bibliography		349

CHAPTER 1 - A BRIEF HISTORY OF EDUCATION IN LYME REGIS

At the turn of the century, the population of Lyme Regis was 2,095, much less than it is today in 2007. The occupations of the townspeople, as listed in the 1872 nominal roll, were largely manual. Although tourism contributed considerably to the local economy it was not the significant source of local income that it is today. In general, housing conditions were poor and transport links were precarious, mainly due to the fact that the steep hills into the town caused major difficulties for horse drawn vehicles. The coming of the railway to Axminster led to the introduction of a horse bus which went from Lyme Regis to Axminster on a regular basis. The situation was vastly improved when the Lyme branch line was opened in 1903 giving the population access to the main line which ran from Exeter to Waterloo.

In terms of schooling for local children, the 1902 Education Act heralded a new chapter in education, with the creation of 300 new Local Authorities empowered to co-ordinate elementary and higher education. The Act made possible the provision of secondary schools to which children could be sent on payment of moderate fees. The 1918 Education Act extended the powers given to Local Authorities and made it their duty to provide for the progressive development and comprehensive organisation of education in their areas. This Act also made full time attendance at school compulsory from the age of five to fourteen and amended the laws regarding the employment of children. In addition, all school fees in elementary schools were finally abolished.

In 1922 there was a major re-organisation of education in Lyme Regis. The local school, opposite the Parish Church, formerly accommodated a Girls Department on the top floor and a Boys Department on the lower floor. From September 1922 a Senior Mixed Department, catering for fifty boys and thirty eight girls, was formed on the lower floor of the school and a Junior Mixed Department on the upper floor.

It was in 1923 that Alban Woodroffe decided that there should be a Grammar School in Lyme Regis, separate from the Senior Mixed Department in Church Street. At that time he was Chairman of Dorset Education Committee, Vice Chairman of the County Council and Chairman of the Finance Committee, so his opinion carried a lot of weight. The Board of Education declared that there were insufficient numbers to justify a Grammar School in the town but Mr Woodroffe was keen to have one and it is alleged that he visited every house in the town where there was a child eligible to take the entrance exam, often arriving in his chauffeur-driven car. It is said that he then personally invigilated the exam behind closed doors. Curiously enough every child passed which must have created a national record for any selection examination!! Alban Woodroffe's original intention had been that the Grammar School would be for boys only but in the end he needed girls to make up the numbers so the new school was co-educational.

Strangely the new school, established in 1923, was not initially named Lyme Regis Grammar School but was referred to as the Lyme Regis County Secondary School and it remained so until 1927 when Dorset Education Committee decided to put an end to the confusion that existed as to the status of secondary schools in the county, some of which were referred to as "secondary" schools and others as "grammar" schools. In May 1927 the Education Committee passed a resolution that all existing secondary schools would be re-named grammar schools and from that moment on the school was referred to as Lyme Regis Grammar School (LRGS) and it remained so until September 1964 when it ceased to be a grammar school, became a comprehensive and was re-named The Woodroffe School.

Grammar Schools in Dorchester, Bridport and Beaminster also gradually lost their grammar school status. Hardye's School in Dorchester (now The Thomas Hardye School) became a comprehensive in 1979 and a mixed comprehensive in 1993. Bridport Grammar School held its final assembly at the Palace Cinema in July 1956 and in September 1956 the newly built Colfox School opened as the first bi-lateral school in Dorset. Beaminster ceased to be a grammar school in 1963 when it moved to a new site and became one of the early comprehensive schools.

When the new school was established in September 1923 it was situated in Hill Road where the Woodmead Halls are now sited. At that time, the Senior Mixed School was re-classified as a Modern School and a number of pupils from it were promoted to the new school. The Modern School, continued to operate alongside the Grammar School, which subsequently moved to its present site in Uplyme Road in 1932.

In their original development plan the Dorset County Council envisaged a new Secondary Modern School in Lyme Regis but following full consultation with the Governing Body the proposal was amended by the Education Committee in January 1957, when it was decided to enlarge the Grammar School and create a Grammar/Modern School. This suggestion provoked a great deal of discussion in the town and a public meeting was held in the Woodmead Halls, attended by some 300 members of the public. At this meeting, by a small majority, it was decided to recommend to the Local Authority that a bilateral school should be created on the site of the Lyme Regis Grammar School.

In September 1962 the transfer of a number of pupils from the Junior School to the Senior School ceased, with these pupils being accommodated at the Grammar School within a newly-built temporary classroom. These were pupils who had narrowly failed their 11+ examination. In 1963 a further eleven pupils, to form the nucleus of another class, accompanied Ernest Wellings, a teacher from the Senior School, also transferred to the Grammar School from the Senior School. The final transfer of children from the Senior School to the Grammar School, together with remaining staff, took place in September 1964, thus leaving the premises in Church Street for the exclusive use of the Junior School.

In 1964 the Lyme Regis Grammar School was officially re-named. The choice of name for the new school was not straightforward however. In May 1959 the Governing Body proposed that the new school should be called The Alban Woodroffe School but at the suggestion of the local authority in May 1962 this name was amended to The Woodroffe School. It is interesting to note that in October 1962 the governors received representations from the Parents Association, staff and the pupil body, who expressed a strong preference for naming the school "The Lyme Regis School" but after careful consideration the governors decided to adhere to the previous recommendation and the name of the school was confirmed as The Woodroffe School.

CHAPTER 2 - 1923 TO 1932 THE HILL ROAD SITE

How Lyme Regis Grammar School came into being is described in a report written by Mr Woodroffe.[1]

"The late Clement Bone, then Director of Education, said to me 'that far off corner of West Dorset including the Borough of Lyme Regis had been quite forgotten from the educational point of view' and, as this area was represented by me on the County Council, if I wished to move in the matter he would do all he could to help me, to get better opportunities of Higher Education for the area.

I accepted his offer at once as I knew, from experience, that Clement Bone's help meant success and we decided to get permission to start an entirely new type of school. The pupils would remain at school until fifteen years of age and, at the yearly entry exam, there would be a number of scholarships or free places given. Those who did not qualify for a free place could, with their parents' consent, join the school if they passed an entry exam and their parents would agree to the extra year at school and to pay the school fee of £4 per term.

The outline of the school was passed by the Education Committee and, whilst being favourably considered by them, they stated that no bricks would be available for at least two years (this period was just after the 1914 – 1918 war). They advised that there were some Army Huts and Officers Mess buildings at Swanage and, if we thought we could use the material from these buildings with which to construct a temporary school, we could submit plans of the buildings for their further consideration. With at least two years waiting for bricks, plus the erection, it would have meant more children being deprived of Further Education, so we wisely decided, as it turned out, to use the material from the Army Huts from Swanage.

The building soon got started and then came the appointment of the Governors, when I was appointed as Chairman of Governors, and the Governors soon had the most important matter to attend to viz the appointment of the first Headmaster, and then the staff. The appointment of the Headmaster could not have been a better one. He was just the Head to start a new type of school, with so many innovations parents were not accustomed to, such as boys and girls being taught in the same classroom; boy and girl prefects; houses; school colours; girls in uniform; an extra year at school; scholarships or free places and then there was organised football and other matters which made this the first secondary school in the county.

The school was now ready for the official opening. This was performed in May 1923 by the late Lord Shaftesbury, a good friend of the school. During the opening ceremony the late Canon Goodden, the Chairman of the Education Committee, told us that Lord Shaftesbury had graciously allowed his illustrious name to be used for one of the school houses.. After the applause had ceased the Chairman suggested that the other house might be called Woodroffe, which honour I have always appreciated".

---

[1] Report written by Mr Woodroffe in 1961

The governors' minutes at this time reflect an extremely busy period with major decisions to be made about how the school would operate. The first meeting of the Governing Body, at which Alban Woodroffe was unanimously elected as Chairman of Governors, took place in the Guildhall at Lyme Regis on 4th April 1923. At this meeting it was agreed to advertise for a Clerk to the Governors as soon as possible. The arrangement of the new Secondary School was agreed including the constitution of the Governing Body and its powers and duties. It was also decided that the colours of the school would be those of the Borough of Lyme Regis namely "Azure and Scarlet with a Lion in Gold."

Fees were set at £12 per annum for Dorset pupils and £15 per annum for other pupils with 25% of free places to be allocated ie five to be awarded in each year group. It was agreed that, provided Devon paid the required capitation fee of £3, the number of free places awarded to Devon and Dorset children should be proportional to the number of children attending the school but the number of free places to Devon children should not exceed that for Dorset children.

The curriculum was organised as follows: English 2, Languages (French and/or Latin) 9, Science 6, History 2, Geography 2, Mathematics 6, Drawing 2, Scripture 1, Music 1, Practical Instruction (Domestic Science & Handicrafts) 2 and Physical Training 3 – a total of 35 lessons. Periods were forty five minutes each, four in the morning and three in the afternoon. It was agreed that the premises the school would require were:

5 Class Rooms	Head's Room	Boys & Girls Cloakroom &
Hall and Gymnasium	Senior Mistress' Room	Lavatory (sufficient for a
Science Laboratory	Assistant Mistresses' Room	locker for each child for
Handicraft Room	Assistant Masters' Room	shoes, etc)
Domestic Subjects Room	Caretaker's Room	Store Rooms

The clearing and preparation of the site in Hill Road, which was carried out by unemployed labour, involved the removal of trees on the orchard part of the site and two acres were sown with grass. The advertisement for a Head attracted 217 applications. Five were shortlisted to meet the Governors on 12th April 1923 and Mr A W Greenfield, aged thirty three, was appointed at a salary of £500 per annum. It was agreed that Mr Sharley should be employed as Clerk to the Governors and shortly afterwards Mr Bridgeman was engaged as Assistant Master. The next appointment was that of Senior Mistress. This important role was defined as being responsible for the studies, health, well-being and discipline of all female pupils, and liaison with parents as necessary, as well as all issues relating to Assistant Mistresses. The Governors made two attempts to fill this vacancy and in June 1923 Miss Jessie Carson was appointed as Senior Mistress. Another important appointment was that of Caretaker. Fourteen applications were received and Mr Broome, of Lyme Regis, aged twenty seven years, was appointed at a weekly wage of £2 15s 0d for himself and his wife.

(View of the school from Hill Road - 1923)

(View of the school from the back of View Road - 1923)

Woodwork Shop – Hill Road site

Science Laboratory – Hill Road site

At this time it was also resolved that *"any outfitter in the town be allowed to supply caps and colours provided that they are of the quality and colours as the sample approved by the Governors"*. Subsequently two tenders were received for caps – Mr Haddon at 3/6 per cap and Mr Bosence at 3/11 – and the lowest tender was accepted. It was decided that the school badge be purchased by the Governors for sale to pupils by the Head.

The first day of term preceded the opening ceremony by one week. Lord Shaftesbury officially opened the school on 29th September 1923. This was a major event in the town and, in addition to Alban Woodroffe and the Head, other dignitaries present included Canon Goodden (Chairman of the Dorset County Education Committee), Clement Bone (Director of Education for Dorset), Mr Matthews (County Architect), Major Colfox (MP for West Dorset), the Rev Willson (Vicar of Lyme Regis), and newly appointed Governors. Also in attendance were members of the teaching staff, the Caretaker and fifty one pupils including fifteen girls.

On arrival, the first duty of Lord Shaftesbury was to "break" the school flag which, as well as the flagpole were the gifts of Mr Woodroffe. Forming a square in the gravelled space at the front of the school buildings were Boy Scouts from Lyme Regis, Axminster, Uplyme and Wootton Fitzpaine. An inspection of the new buildings took place, followed by numerous speeches from many of the honoured guests present. However, the speaker who received the warmest reception was Mr Woodroffe, as everyone recognised that without his drive, energy and commitment, the new school would not have been created. In handing over the school to the care of staff and pupils, Mr Woodroffre advised the latter that they were *"to uphold the honour of that cap and badge and to pass them on not only unsullied, but with an enhanced reputation"*.

The opening ceremony concluded with the singing of the National Anthem and even more cheering for Mr Woodroffe. Later, the Earl of Shaftesbury presented a silver shield to the school for competition between Shaftesbury and Woodroffe. This magnificent trophy, which fell out of use in about 1960, is still held in the school archive and is polished up and displayed at school reunions.

From 10th November 1923, *"hot dinners consisting of meat and two vegetables and a pudding"* were provided at a charge of 9d. Pupil numbers increased to fifty six by December 1923, divided into three forms – Form 1 with fourteen pupils, Form 2 with twenty two and Form 3 with twenty pupils. Two male and one female prefects were appointed. By the start of the Spring Term 1924, numbers had reached sixty five. *(Photographs provided by Keith Wiscombe)*

Dining Room – Hill Road site

The School on the Hill

In March 1924, the governors asked the Head to arrange for the renting of a piece of land west of the Cobb, at a cost of not more than £10, on which was to be built a hut using scrap timber and corrugated iron left over from building the school. This hut was for the use of pupils who were to be taught to swim. So the school acquired a beach hut, a highly desirable asset these days with huts on Monmouth Beach now changing hands at a staggering £17,000!

During 1924 pupils from the school visited the Wembley Exhibition. The Medical Officer examined all pupils declaring that the great majority were in good health. To give an idea of what it was like to be a pupil at the school at this time Molly Raison née Wiscombe, who attended the school when it was located at the Woodmead Halls site, has provided the following insight.

"I joined the school in 1924 when I was twelve years old, one year after it opened. Previous to this she attended a private school but it had to close when a lot of its pupils transferred to the Grammar School. My twin brother, George (Juby), joined the school in 1923 and was therefore a founder member. My brother had gone to the Grammar School a year ahead of me as at that time the education of male children was felt to be a higher priority than for female children.

The school was accommodated in buildings best described as pre-fabricated. The main buildings ran adjacent to Hill Road down as far as what was then the fire station. This block housed the Senior Mistress' office and cloakroom, the Girls cloakroom, and there was a long corridor that ran the length of the building off which were all the classrooms. There were steps down into the main hall where there was a small stage. There were glass and wood partitions which could divide the space into three large classrooms. A playing field was located on the opposite side to the road, and there were tennis courts on the sloped land treated with tarmac. At right angles to the main building, at the lower end of the school site, were more buildings that accommodated a scout hut, cookery room and chemistry laboratory.

The Head was a tall, handsome and quite a young man being only in his thirties. He wore his gown at all times, as did the other members of staff, and he wore a mortar board on formal occasions. The Girls uniform comprised a navy mop cap, a bit like that worn by District Nurses, with the school badge on the front. Girls also wore white blouses with round collars, gym slips with red and blue sashes worn around the waist and thick silkestra stockings with flat shoes. For hockey girls changed into red and blue socks and their hockey boots but they kept their gym slips on – there was no special kit. The Boys uniform at this time was navy blue blazers, white shirts, grey trousers and the school tie and they also wore caps. School hockey and football matches were played at the sports field which was located on the Sidmouth Road and pupils had to make their way there on foot, although Miss Carson drove up there. I remember the Glyde family[2], who came from Wootton Fitzpaine, who took it in turns to ride a horse to school."

Fellow ex-pupil, Gordon Hunt, shares this memory with Molly.

---

[2] Local author, Guy Bryan interviewed Gerald Gylde before his recent death and his research notes also confirm that Gerald used to ride to school every day on his pony, which was stabled at the London Inn whilst he was at school.

Molly was Chairman of the Old Girls Association in 1951 and her brother served in the Second World War. He was an air gunner and was shot down in the North Sea. Molly later married and had two children, Nick and Gaye, who followed her to the Grammar School. Gaye was Major Pearn's secretary for eight years taking over from Mrs Jackson".[3]

Girls Hockey Team - 1927

*Freda Childs   Margaret Rooke   Christine Langford   Rennie Phillips   Peggy Warren   Hilda Spiller
Vera Bass   Molly Wiscombe   Dorothy State   Queenie Wyatt   Jean McDonnell
(Photograph courtesy of Keith Wiscombe)*

In May 1926 the Governors decided that pupils should have the whole of Saturday off and relinquish the half day off on Wednesday afternoons. Later that year, in December, Lyme Regis suffered a major trauma when a large section of Marine Parade fell into the sea due to a combination of sodden clay and a lively sea.

About this time the Governors, on the recommendation of Exeter University College, decided to make certain amendments to the curriculum including the omission of Latin for a trial period. It was also agreed that the County Adviser for Art should visit the school and a more extended domestic subjects course should be provided for girls remaining at school after sixteen years of age.

---

[3] Notes taken during an interview with Molly Raison in February 2006

The School on the Hill

Sadly in a letter to the Governors, Mr Greenfield resigned as Head, with effect from 1st September 1927, having been appointed as Head of Poole Secondary School. He apologised for the fact that he was leaving so soon and paid tribute to the support he had received from Governors, particularly the Chairman, Alban Woodroffe. The Governing Body were extremely sorry to lose him and recorded their appreciation of his efforts in their minutes. In January 1927 the post of Head was advertised and 162 applications were received. Following interviews in February, Mr Watton was appointed at the age of forty three. He was a linguist who had obtained his degree and teaching qualification at Manchester.

The Old Boys Association was formed in March 1927 with the object of keeping ex-pupils in touch with the school and it was decided to start a school magazine. There is no copy of the first magazine in the school archive; the earliest copy is dated 1929 and is incomplete. However, the following extracts from the first school magazine, dated May 1927, were included in the twenty fifth edition produced twenty one years later. Unfortunately the names of the contributors are not shown.

"On the first Saturday after school was opened we formed a football club and had our first practice on the school ground near Sidmouth Road. We looked a motley crowd, but a very few weeks saw us all wearing the now familiar red shirt.... We owe a great deal to the kindly help and good sportsmanship of our neighbours at Colyton Grammar School. At a time when we had no big boys they played against us very weakened teams.... until we managed to beat them.....When we first went to the field, only two of all the girls in the whole school had ever held a hockey stick in their hands. We lost our first match 9 – 0 and the second was even more disastrous. We lost 13 – 0."......"Our first season of Girls cricket was something to smile at, but later (1925) we beat Colyton by 148 – 34." [4]

The number of pupils attending the school continued to grow steadily, and by September 1927, when Mr Watton took over as Head, there were 129 pupils on roll and the number of staff required to teach them had increased accordingly.

Dick Nute was a pupil at the school at this time and he recalls that a distraction for pupils was the building of the Police Station opposite the Hill Road site. Ironically this has only just been demolished to make way for a housing development and a new police, fire and ambulance headquarters has been built adjacent to the new Woodmead Halls.

In January 1928, it was agreed that the services of Gale Brothers for winding the school clock should be dispensed with and that a member of staff or a pupil should take over this task.

By April 1928 a Reading Circle, Dramatic Society and Scientific Society had been founded. Heavy seas had damaged the bathing hut but the Governors agreed to its repair at a cost of £5. On 8th May 1928 the Board of Education carried out an inspection of the school. A previous inspection in November 1927 had revealed that the teaching of Art was below the required standard and various strategies were put in place to bring about an improvement.

---

[4] Extracts from the School Magazine dated July 1948 headed "Looking Back"

Concern was being expressed at this time at the poor facilities available at the school for sports and the County Inspector was asked to visit the school to inspect both the school buildings and the playing field with a view to submitting a quote for the necessary improvements.

In June 1928 the Governors discussed the recent inspection report and as a direct outcome decided to re-instate Latin. The establishment of a reference library and the provision of a fully equipped gymnasium for physical exercise were also identified as high priorities, subject to funding being made available. At a later date the school received a letter from the Department of Education congratulating all concerned on the outcome of the inspection.

The following principles outlined at Speech Day in October 1928 were highlighted by Mr Watton and described by him as *"worth treasuring by everyone"*. *"What you are is more important than what you possess"* and *"Try to acquire a sense of humour and a sense of proportion"*. The speaker was Mr Thomas Loveday, Vice-Chancellor of Bristol University, and in conclusion he expressed his hope that the school would soon develop a Sixth Form and would some day possess accommodation for boarders.

In December 1928 the County Medical Officer voiced his concern in relation to the school's cross country course. The Head was asked to find a flat course and subsequently a route avoiding Timber Hill was introduced. This satisfied the Medical Officer, as the starting point, to which competitors walked, was now higher and the actual running was all downhill or on the level.

A school photograph was taken by Messrs. Panorama in 1929 and it was felt that *"most of us came out wonderfully well!"*.[5] In addition boys were corresponding with pupils at the Lycée Ampere, Lyon and for the girls efforts were being made to establish an entente cordiale with girls at a school in Chartres. Plans were also in hand to acquire a board on which would be inscribed the names of all prefects for posterity. This does not appear to have been achieved but the idea might have been developed into the provision of an Honours Board.

The school magazine included extensive reports on cricket, football, hockey, cross country, tennis and netball with school teams playing against teams from King's School at Ottery, Beaminster Grammar School, Ilminster Grammar School, Colyton Grammar School and Bridport Grammar School to name but a few.

The Cross Country Run held on 20th March 1929 was the fifth of the school's history. This featured the new course with a different starting point at the top of Charmouth Road, as suggested earlier in the year by the County Medical Officer. The course followed the old Charmouth Road to the end of the Golf Links, struck across the fields to Penn Cross then followed the by-road to the Charmouth Tunnel. The slope down into the valley was accessed via Alban Woodroffe's estate and the runners then ran on to the Old Mill via Sleech Wood.

---

[5] Extracts from School Magazine dated July 1929

Start of the Cross Country Run at Charmouth Road – March 1929
(Photograph courtesy of Keith Wiscombe)

Following the General Election, a mock election was held in school and was fiercely contested. The majority of pupils cast a vote on polling day, 30th May 1929, and two members of staff acted as polling clerks during the dinner hour. The outcome was a win for the Conservative candidate with a majority of twenty nine.

A feature of school life at this time were House Feasts which were greatly enjoyed by pupils. These included a trip to Gittisham Common by char-a-banc with a picnic tea followed by games for pupils in Woodroffe House and, for those in Shaftesbury House, a "splendid tea" followed by a social evening. Pupils were encouraged to *"Do your utmost always, but when you are beaten look on the occasion as an opportunity for developing that spirit for which our nation is so admired. No matter what the odds against you, never give up, give your opponents a good clean game to the finish; they will respect you for it, and after all it is sport in the real meaning of the word"*[6].

By now major changes were taking place in Lyme Regis. In 1929 the Assembly Rooms and Victoria Hall at Cobb Gate were demolished to make way for a more profitable car park, and the first twenty council houses, built in Corporation Terrace in 1911, were increased by a further eight.[7] It was at this time that the housing estate at Colway Mead

---

[6] Extract from the School Magazine dated July 1929 – Report on Shaftesbury House by Mr W E Taylor.
[7] Corporation Terrace renamed Lym Close in 1974

was established. Over a relatively short period of time the estate grew from an initial build of twenty four houses to a total of seventy four.

It was during July 1929 that discussions began with the County Council about a possible new site for the school and a special meeting of the Governing Body was held to consider the matter. Various site meetings took place and it was finally agreed that the field known as "Shelves", situated on the main road near the Railway Station and previously used for grazing cattle, was the best choice. It was close to the present playing fields and also had sufficient space for practice pitches adjacent to the school building. The County Education Committee was therefore asked to enter into negotiations with the trustees of the land to secure it for the school. Once again Alban Woodroffe was instrumental in achieving a new site and buildings for the school and in January 1931 the Governors recorded a vote of thanks to him for his efforts.

The foundation stone for the new school was laid on 29th April 1931 by Mr Woodroffe and he presented the trowel used for this purpose, suitably inscribed, to the school. It is now held in the school archive.

Thus the first years of Lyme Regis Grammar School drew to a close and a new era began with the relocation from Hill Road to the site at Uplyme Road.

(Photograph courtesy of Keith Wiscombe)
Pupils, staff and parents attending the laying of the foundation stone ceremony. Alban Woodroffe is in the left foreground and on the right is the builder, Charles Hallett. It is understood that Mr Woodroffe presented Mr Hallett with an inscribed silver cigarette box as a mark of appreciation for his efforts.

The Mayor of Lyme Regis, Mr Baker, addressing the people

The Chairman of the Dorset Education Committee, A J Woodroffe, laying the Foundation Stone

(Photographs from School Archive)

The Director of Education for Dorset, Clement Bone, addressing the school and people
(Note: in the foreground the Mayor and a Macebearer in ceremonial robes, the Head in gown and mortar board, Charles Hallett, the builder, and Alban Woodroffe, in tail coat)

View across to Timber Hill showing the construction of the Gable Ends
(Photograph courtesy of Ken Gollop)

CHAPTER 3 – 1932 TO 1938: THE PRE-WAR YEARS

An early picture of the school – approximately 1932

Possibly the Opening Ceremony –
Alban Woodroffe on the left   School Flagpole in the background
(Photographs from School archive)

The move to the new school was carried out smoothly thanks largely to the assistance of Alban Woodroffe and his son, Rex, who provided transport. The opening ceremony, conducted by Lord Shaftesbury and held on 23rd May 1932, was a low key affair and nothing as grand as the opening ceremony in 1923 By September there were 144 pupils on roll and consideration was being given to the formation of a Preparatory Department.

Wilfrid Clark, now aged eighty eight years old, writes:

"I joined the school in 1933. The new building had just been opened at the top of the hill. It consisted of two wings and the central portion. The right wing housed the classrooms; the left wing contained on the ground floor the Science laboratory and the upper floor the Domestic Science room; the central portion contained the main hall. The latter was used for the morning religious assembly – a short service consisting of a hymn, the Lord's Prayer and the Headmaster's instructions. It was also used for PE lessons and Friday afternoon singing. Music per se was not taught.

The timetable consisted of Mathematics – Arithmetic, Algebra, Geometry, Trigonometry; English – Grammar and Literature; French; Latin; History; Geography; Scripture up to School Certificate. The VIth form Mathematics course concentrated on Calculus, Pure Maths, Applied Maths, Hydrostatics, etc. Forms I to V concentrated on the course of instruction for the School Certificate which was taken in the Vth Form.

The VIth Form was orientated towards the Higher School Certificate and this was divided into two parts or courses (A) the Arts, and (B) the Sciences. The Sciences included Maths and the Arts course consisted of English Literature, French, Latin and History. The number of pupils in the school was 150 boys and girls, the girls being slightly more numerous. The VIth Form usually consisted of ten pupils, divided into the Upper Sixth and the Lower Sixth. The majority of pupils left school at the end of the fifth year or sooner. VIth Form pupils were prepared for University Entrance

Games were not neglected. I remember Edwin Lillington, a Thorncombe boy, played cricket for the County Colts as a bowler and took three wickets for sixty and he also passed his Higher Certificate with flying colours. W E Sweetland, an Axminster boy and a magnificent all round athlete, made several centuries in the first XI cricket matches and had a trial for Somerset and played Wellard and Andrews, the county fast bowlers, with supreme confidence.

There were no school buses. Pupils travelled by train from Axminster and public transport buses to Charmouth. There was a small boarding house run by a Master and his wife in Pound Road. I remember that the two "houses", Shaftesbury and Woodroffe, had annual outings known as "house feasts". One year Shaftesbury House went to Exeter to see Exeter City play. The Woodroffe House went to Taunton in 1934 to see Somerset playing the touring Australians. The 1934

Australian touring team included the following famous players – Bradman, Ponsford, Woodfull, Grimmet and O'Reilly.

There were three trips abroad during the 1930s. These consisted of visits to the chief cities of Scandinavia – Oslo, Bergen, Helsinki – and day trips included visits to the celebrated fjords. During the 1934 trip 2,000 schoolboys from Grammar Schools all over England, including LRGS, were aboard the troopship SS Neuralia, normally used to convey troops to India. We returned home by the Kiel Canal and we sailed past the Fuhrer's private yacht which was anchored in the Canal. It is interesting to recall that shortly before we sailed past, Hitler had summoned the Army Chiefs aboard the yacht to plot (for political reasons) the destruction of the SA (Sturm Abteilung), the organisation through which he had risen to power. The machinations on board the yacht resulted in the "Night of the Long Knives" in which thousands of the Storm Troopers were massacred and the power of the SA completely destroyed."[1]

During the summer term of 1933 an inspector visited the school. Also during this year the medical officer reported on the state of the health of pupils who were "*on the whole healthy, well cared for and of normal intelligence*". Pupils were not doing that well at games but this was attributed to the fact that they were somewhat younger than their counterparts from other schools.

A Parents' Day took place on 30th November 1933 and about fifty attended to inspect the new school and visit the classrooms. Concern was expressed by governors that boys had been observed doing physical training in braces. It was decided that in future they were to wear suitable gymnasium clothing. The Head advised governors that some of the senior boys had asked for permission to wear straw hats. Permission was granted but to pupils in the Upper Sixth only.

To mark the death of King George, the Head, staff and pupil representatives attended a memorial service in the Parish Church. Subsequently the governing body granted a Coronation Holiday for three days from 12th to 14th May 1937. Representatives from the school also attended the Mayor's procession and service for the Coronation and pupils J E Harvey and M J Lane went to the Empire Youth Rally at the Albert Hall and the Abbey Service.

Following the installation of a telephone in the Head's office in 1934, a typewriter was purchased for his use in 1937. It was about this time that Allhallows School, formerly located at Honiton, took over Rousdon Mansion as their new premises. This huge property had been built by tea tycoon, Sir Henry Peek, in the 1870s at a cost of £240,000. The school was to remain at this location until its closure in 1998.

In terms of extra-curricular activities, Miss Carson started a new society, confined to the girls, called the "Jam Pot Club". Its object was to make a collection of all the

---

[1] Taken from handwritten notes provided by Wilfrid dated March 2006

wild flowers in the neighbourhood and learn their names and habitats. Forty varieties were collected and were displayed in the Art Room.

In December 1938, an honours board was established. As names were added, eventually three honours boards were installed on the wall in the school hall. Sadly these were not preserved when over the years alterations were made to the hall. However, ex-pupil, Roy Crabbe, believes that the first Honours Board bore the following information.

1930	A G Short	College Exhibition, University College London
1938	Phyllis Joan Staples	State Scholarship
	Mary Joyce Lane	Dorset County Senior Scholarship
1939	M J Lane	State Scholarship, Bedford College London
	P J Staples	County Senior Scholarship, Lady Margaret Hall Oxford
1941	M E Stark	County Senior Scholarship, Westfield College London
1942	G C Hollingsworth	Admiralty Scholarship, Royal Naval College Dartmouth
	M E Stark	State Scholarship
	M S C Russell	County Senior Scholarship
1944	G G Baker	County Senior Scholarship, University College London
1945	K W Lisle Smith	Devon County Exhibition, University College London

Ex-pupil, Ed Bowditch, has kindly provided this photograph taken around about 1949/1950, showing the honours board on the wall in the school hall. The hall was also doubling up as a dining room at this time.

The School on the Hill

Joy Britten   Paddy Hunt   Beattie Wrexford   Joan Cozens   Mary Mac   Myrtle Loveridge
Betty Matthews   Joan Staples   Joyce Lane   Rachel Childs   Jean Wiscombe   **1939**
(Photographs courtesy of Keith Wiscombe)

Pat Kemp   Mary Watton   Peggy Goddard   Daphne Shave   Rosemary ??   Paddy Hunt   Phyllis Samways
Betty King   Betty Wrexford   Joan Staples   Rachael Childs   Mary MacGillivray   Jean Wiscombe   Marjorie Bartlett
Joan Potter   Cec Sweetland   Una Hitchcock   Jean Tyrell   **1939**

CHAPTER 4 – 1939 TO 1945: THE WAR YEARS

When war was declared in 1939, the beach in Lyme Regis was cordoned off for the duration and two 4.7 guns, disguised as haystacks, were installed by the Royal Artillery below the golf links and near to the football club on Charmouth Road. During the war the town suffered no bomb damage but there was an incident when Coombe Street was strafed.

Although only a small community, in 1941, during War Weapons Week, the town raised the amazing sum of £40,000. In June of that year it was announced that the town had contributed £69,222 in war savings *"towards sending another ship to fight in His Majesty's Navy for the freedom of mankind from the Nazi thrall"*. This amounted to £25.10s per head from the 2,700 inhabitants. More was to follow as the following year a further £45,528 was donated to the war effort. It is also worth noting that in 1941 Lyme Regis was included in Hitler's invasion plan "Operation Sealion". During the winter of 1943 tens of thousands of American soldiers poured into Dorset with equipment and stores that covered hundreds of acres. Lyme hosted the 16th Infantry Regiment of the United States 1st Infantry Division. Tented camps sprang up around the town for the soldiers who were billeted in Lyme prior to the D-Day landings. The Marine Theatre was used as their NAAFI and they eventually sailed to France from Weymouth harbour.

During the period 1939 to 1945 thirteen air-raid warnings were sounded during school hours. Life at LRGS carried on as best it could with the number of pupils on roll increasing periodically with the arrival of evacuees. Staff and many ex-pupils joined the armed forces, some of whom never returned. Chapter 15 includes information on those who lost their lives in the Second World War. All ex-pupils who served in the armed forces are listed in Appendix 4.

The School Magazine dated July 1939 contained adverts from local businesses who obviously provided sponsorship towards printing costs. These included an advertisement for S Bosence of Broad Street, Lyme Regis who were the local suppliers of school uniform and also the sole agent for the Old Boys blazers and ties. Other advertisers were J Baker (Hairdresser and Chiropodist), E M Watson (Motor Engineer, Broad Street), Cloverdale Garage, Lyme Regis, The Cosy Café, Lyme Regis, Bradford and Sons (Coal Merchants), L D Haddon (outfitters), R J Stratton (Ironmongers), Dunsters of Lyme (Photographers) and Ye Olde Tobbaco Shoppe (Proprietor: A Case). The latter included the phrase "Come and meet your old pals when buying your Tobacco and cigarettes at Ye Olde Tobbaco Shoppe"!!

In school Mr G A Taylor and a working party were busy moving and renovating the school pavilion and Miss Carson had visited the USA which had resulted in an exchange of ideas with an American school.

At Speech Day, held on 19th July 1939, the speaker was Sir Percival Sharp, LLD who advised pupils that *"You may make mistakes but if you don't make your own judgments you just become a unit of a huge unthinking mob of people"*. He continued *"The School exists to make you think…..The most important part of your education is the training you get for your life and the duties of your life to come. You are learning here your duty to each other, to your masters, to your school and country and, lastly, I hope, you are learning your duty to your parents".*[1]

The Old Boys Association was thriving with Alban Woodroffe as President and Mr H F Searle as Chairman. They had some fifty members and their proud boast was that there was not a single old boy unemployed. The AGM of the Old Boys Association was held at the Royal Lion Hotel on 29th October 1938 followed by the Annual Dinner.

The school's Dramatic Society was still functioning at this time, presenting three short plays. Boxing was proving to be a popular sport and the R J Woodroffe Boxing Cup was won by Woodroffe House in the Inter-house Boxing Contest. This was watched by the whole school and several visitors and included a contest for heavyweight, middleweight, lightweight and flyweight.

Sports fixtures were taking place as usual although ex-pupil Robert McKenzie remembers being selected, with fellow thirteen year old Alan Halliday, to play in the school's 1st XI football team which was depleted due to older pupils having volunteered to join the armed forces. The school was thrashed by Ilminster Grammar School by 16 – 0, largely due to the fact that Ilminster's team was augmented by a number of eighteen year old Spanish boys, who were refugees from the Spanish Civil War.

By December 1939 it was estimated that there were between forty and fifty old boys on active service and a list of names was on display in school. 1940 saw 180 pupils on roll with twenty eight in the preparatory department. In May twenty three voluntary evacuees joined the school (five boys and eighteen girls) and many of them stayed for the duration of the war. In addition, forty girls from James Allen's Girls School, Dulwich arrived at the school and fourteen of them also stayed on.

In September 1939, at the request of parents, a preparatory form was introduced for approximately thirty pupils.

Shirley Caunt recalls *"At the outbreak of war in September 1939 my mother and I were invited to Combpyne. I was six years old. To reach Combpyne we travelled on the steam train which, in those days, ran between Axminster and Lyme Regis. There was no immediate vacancy for me in a school so I had private lessons. Then, for a short time I attended Uplyme School. My mother returned to Surrey to be with my father whilst I was looked after by a Combpyne family and their Yugoslavian nanny. I was not too happy at Uplyme and especially disliked the gasmask drill! Also, I was "picked on" as a townie.*

---

[1] Extract from the School Magazine dated July 1939

The School on the Hill

*Preparatory Class 1939 – Lyme Regis Grammar School
(Photograph courtesy of Keith Wiscombe)*

Things changed early in 1942 when I started in the Lower Preparatory at Lyme Regis Grammar School. The school was co-educational with roughly equal numbers of boys and girls. The girls sat on the left hand side near the window facing the blackboard, the boys on the right. We each had our own desk set in rows. School dinners were provided which I thought were good. From the beginning I was very happy at the school and enjoyed all the lessons. After two terms I moved up to the Upper Preparatory. The system of marking provided a real incentive to pupils to try to do well. Marks were given out of ten and on the notice board was a chart listing all our names. At, I believe, the end of each week we were given a coloured star. Three red stars merited a gold star. The highest number of gold stars was reflected in the position in the class at the end of term. I was very proud to have a Form Prize and when asked to choose a book, I selected "Bambi's Children" by Felix Salten. The label, signed by Mr Watton, inside the front cover indicates that the prize was awarded in 1943.

I do not recall any particular punishment for the girls, but the boys certainly had the cane. Discipline in the school was good and it was a happy place to be. Sometimes we were able to go to the beach, but we had to keep a look out for "butterfly" bombs. The war had little impact on Lyme Regis, although the nearby landslip was mined. Lyme Regis station was almost opposite the school and at the end of the day I returned to Combpyne on the train, which usually comprised the engine and a single coach. It was exciting to hear the different noise it made when crossing the Cannington Viaduct. From Combpyne station it was a mile's walk to the village, which I sometimes took across the fields. Farming was done in the traditional way; cows were milked by hand and the milk cooled in the dairy. Tractors were used and fun to ride on but crops were transported by horse and cart.

In September 1943 I went into Form 1 of the main school. After VE Day on 8th May 1945 we returned home, leaving behind what had been my life for over five years. It would be in years to come that I would look back on those wartime experiences and appreciate what they meant and realise that it was then that my deep love of the countryside, animals and all wildlife had been born."[2]

Ex-pupil, Brian Wood, also joined the Preparatory School shortly after it opened and recalls: *"1940 found me as an eight year old at Uplyme Village School. Father disappeared over the hill for five years to fight the enemy in the Merchant Navy but he always wanted No.1 son to have a good education. I was therefore enrolled in the Prep and Transition Department (run by Miss Burchall who lived in the bungalow opposite the school main gates.) There was great excitement during these early war years as there were large demonstrations, laid on by the Army in the main, to attract volunteers from the Sixth Form. Many bangs, and tanks everywhere – top fields provided the venue. During Air Raids in prep days we retired to the basement beside the boiler room; later we had slit trenches all round the fields and alongside the main road. It must have been bedlam for the staff as we sang "John Brown's Body", etc. for hours on end!"*[3]

Brian was a pupil at LRGS from 1940 to 1950. A contemporary of his was Betty Harrad née March (1939 to 1942). Betty has vivid memories of attending LRGS during the early months of the Second World War. She recalls her parents purchasing uniforms for her and her sister at Haddons shop in Broad Street, Lyme Regis. This included navy woollen football socks in winter, for playing hockey and netball, and white ankle socks in summer with gymslips. Betty describes the school as a *"beautifully placed new red brick building with a commanding view of Lyme Bay"*. She remembers that the school coped well with the advent of war time when numbers increased from 150 to well over 200.

Betty was particularly impressed with the discipline at the school: *"We had to walk single file in the corridors, no hurrying and no noise. There had to be silence as the teachers entered the classroom and greeted us. There were sometimes desk inspections and woe betide those boys (never the girls) who had a half eaten banana or orange peel in theirs. Punishments in those days included doing lines and being sent out of the classroom, where the offending pupil would most likely be reprimanded by another member of staff. Very occasionally the slipper or even the cane was administered to the boys, and the girls would receive a verbal dressing down from Miss Carson that they would remember for the rest of their days!"* Betty remembers the letters sent home to parents detailing the newly enforced air-raid

---

[2] Correspondence between Shirley Caunt and author – December 2006
[3] Extract from ex-pupils' magazine "Dispatches".

precautions and she adds that after several weeks of drilling "*Mr. Watton was able to tell the Officials that we could evacuate the entire school to safety in less than ten minutes*"[4]. She also remembers watching, from her classroom window, aeroplanes exercising over Lyme Bay and occasionally enemy action.

Another pupil who attended LRGS during the war years was Jean Bennett née Austin who recalls a field, beyond the hockey field, surrounded by high unkempt hedges. It was to this field that pupils had to hurry and keep hidden under the overhanging branches when the air raid siren sounded. Jean explains that "*not many enemy aircraft were seen over Lyme Bay during daylight hours and I only remember one occasion when we grabbed our coats and fled to the ditch under the hedge accompanied by our teacher, Miss Slaney. It must have been half an hour before the "all clear" sounded and we returned to our classroom – in time for the next lesson*".[5]

A further wartime memory comes from ex-pupil, Norman Bowditch, who was fourteen years old when the Second World War started in 1939. He remembers a number of boys, including himself, being sent up to Lyme Regis Golf Club to help dig holes all over the golf course in order to plant posts intended to frustrate a German landing of aircraft or gliders. He also recalls helping to apply clear varnish or something similar to the glass in the windows in the hall to prevent flying fragments in the event of a bomb shattering the windows.[6]

Robert McKenzie was an evacuee at LRGS from 1939 to 1943, living with the Brown family, who were farmers at Rocombe Farm above Uplyme. Their son, Graham, was also a pupil at LRGS. Robert remembers the introduction of double summertime which meant haymaking and harvesting could go on until 10.00 pm. He also recalls the entire third, fourth and fifth forms being bussed out to Rousdon for potato harvesting, supervised by gumbooted teachers. Robert was in one of the classes requisitioned to pull flax. He remembers the arrival of the JAGS (from James Allen Girls School), school dinners served on the top floor of the north wing and fellow pupil Herbert Bonfield (Bonso) cycling to and from school from Thorncombe in all weathers.

Robert was a member of the school based Air Training Corps commanded by Fl Lt W E Taylor. The annual week away at an RAF base in 1942 was at RAF Coastal Command Base at Mountbatten, Plymouth Sound. His first flying experience was in a Sunderland on routine gunnery practice, flying up and down the Cornish coast. Two days after his visit, the same plane and crew failed to return from a mission. Fifty years later, Robert managed to acquire a copy of the sole survivor's log and finally learned how the crew had perished whilst trying to save other airmen who had been shot down in the Bay of Biscay. Robert's abiding memory of LRGS is "*gazing out of the fifth form window to Golden Cap and Portland Bill beyond and*

---

[4] Correspondence between Betty Harrad and author dated November 2006
[5] Correspondence between Jean Bennett and author dated November 2006
[6] Correspondence between Norman Bowditch and author dated November 2006

realising even then that I was lucky to be receiving a first class education in such a wonderful place".[7]

Norman Bowditch, who lived in Uplyme, was also a member of the school's Air Training Corps. He can recall going down to the RAF Air Sea Rescue Base at the Cobb and being taken out in one of the launches, as well as his first flight from Warmwell. Norman also remembers a German plane being shot down over Lyme Bay and cycling down to the Cobb with his brother to see the rescued German pilot being brought ashore by the RAF Air Sea Rescue craft.

As part of the war effort, the Chief Education Officer enquired whether local fire watching parties could be organised at the school to protect the premises. The response from the governors was that this was the responsibility of the County Council. In the meantime, one stirrup pump was provided. The Head advised that parents were not prepared to take on fire-watching duties. Subsequently lady teachers and the caretaker offered to carry out this work.

The school magazine of July 1941 reported that owing to exceptional pressure of work and a lack of black-out facilities, dramatic performances and boxing competitions had to be cancelled. Sports were also cancelled but this was due to the poor state of health of pupils following various epidemics during the previous term. Numbers in the Preparatory Department were such that part of the preparatory form had overflowed into the hall. The school was continually raising funds and contributed to Red Cross Funds, the War Weapons campaign, the Mayor's Ambulance Appeal, the Cottage Hospital and Mrs Churchill's "Aid to Russia Fund". For the latter a personal letter of thanks was received from Mrs Churchill.

The school was delighted to learn that ex-governor, Major D H Ramage RE had won the George Medal for gallantry. Other governors on active service included Lt Col Greenshield, Major Allhusen and Pilot Officer R J Woodroffe. Captain Pass was in the Home Guard. Over 100 ex-pupils were now on active service and were constantly in the thoughts and prayers of all those at school. A list of names was kept up to date and a copy hung in the corridor for pupils to examine. The school's interest in the old boys was a mixture of pride in their achievements and anxiety for their welfare and safety. All old boys were left in no doubt that their school was immensely proud of them. The school magazines at this time included many snippets of information about ex-pupils serving overseas such as

"To the Prisoners of War: John Watton (Lieut. 4th Border Regiment), now an artist famous for his studies of Prison Camp life, and Juby Wiscombe (Serg. Royal Air Force) – our thoughts go out and we trust that their lot is not "too bad": We can be sure that they are keeping their chins up."

---

[7] Correspondence between ex-pupil Robert McKenzie and Author dated October 2006

"John Loosemore was severely wounded in Rangoon, but is gradually recovering his health. We are extremely glad to learn of his progress and trust that he will soon be quite fit again.....Peter Padbury, who held a commission in the Royal Engineers, has been invalided out of the Army but we are glad to say that he is not incapacitated from following a civilian career....W Dring, who was wounded during the Dunkirk evacuation, is invalided out of the Army. At present he is attached to the RAF in a civilian capacity: he is hoping to be allowed to rejoin his regiment."[8]

"Lieutenant John Watton is not wasting his time in a prison camp: he has made himself a famous artist. In an exhibition of work by war artists held in London recently, John's drawings and paintings were the main feature. By way of a change he, now and again, has a shot at escaping! We offer him our whole-hearted congratulations and admiration."[9]

Drawing by John Watton – Caption: "British Officer Touring in Germany (A prisoner's caricature of escape attempt")[10]

"News has just reached us of John Windsor. John held the rank of Captain in Lord Strathcona's Horse (RC). We are extremely sorry to learn that he was blinded in the Hitler Line in Italy in May, 1944, when his tank was knocked out by a German anti-tank gun. He is back at his mother's home in Canada with his wife and daughter."[11]

---

[8] Extracts from School Magazine dated July 1942
[9] Extract from School Magazine dated July 1943
[10] Taken from the School Magazine dated July 1944
[11] Extract from School Magazine dated July 1945

The School on the Hill

John Watton wrote to the school on several occasions, firstly describing an unsuccessful escape attempt and secondly his life back in a prison camp:

"A week ago I and eleven others were moved from Oflag IV C (Colditz) to IX A (Spangenberg, near Kassel)…..On the way I left the rest and managed to get on to another train. This took me about twenty miles but not having been able to buy a ticket I was picked up by the ticket collector and guards….An hour later, thanks to the efficient German control system, I was returned to my own guards. IX A is a worse camp to get out of than IV C. General Fortune (of the Highland Division) is here, along with other senior officers. There are about ten commando officers from St. Nazaire, a grand crowd. I'm delighted to be in the same mess with them. They have their anniversary on Sunday and I'm designing a large menu card for the occasion. I look forward to getting through some work while in the quiet of the cells (for escape attempt). I hear the "cooler" here is not too bad………."

"No doubt you have heard I've come back to IV C. The three months holiday was OK. I've met a lot of new people, did a number of drawings, had a change. I'm glad to be back, however, with the French and the old familiar faces of the English. The Dutch have moved, a new batch of English orderlies has arrived and we are expecting a new lot of English officers. We brought with us Lieut. C. Purdon, Commando and Dicky Morgan, Commando. They tried to escape from IV C but were caught after having been out for ten days. I've sent from IX A/H two batches of drawings and some oil paintings. Four of the drawings are of commandos. They are all of St. Nazaire survivors. I did their Colonel Charles Newman, too, but will send that from here…". (Col. Newman is the "posthumous " VC).[12]

Another frequent correspondent was Capt J F Dawson MC RA who wrote from North Africa: *"Mr Kemp may have told you that I'd got mixed up in this North African business. Having been out here since the beginning I've seen a lot of very interesting things and done some strange things. My knowledge of French has proved extremely useful in dealing with the French colonists in the large farms out here, who in most cases are very friendly. Naturally, they don't care for their orange trees being cut down for purposes of camouflage but we aren't guilty of that!*

We get very good food out here but it's all "comp" or tinned ration, already cooked in England. Tinned bacon or sausage with eggs which we buy from the Arabs makes a jolly good breakfast. We can also get oranges, tangerines and lemons in plenty, although not so many as in the earlier days. We used to get stacks of them showered on us. I remember the column going through a certain town on the way up and the population were lining the streets. It was the first British column they had seen and they simply flung dozens of oranges and things into our vehicles and flowers on to the guns………Must close now and see how the war is going!...."

---

[12] Extracts from the School Magazine dated July 1943

When he moved on to Italy he wrote again: *"As the BBC keeps telling you we are pushing along in Italy, but it is quite different fighting from both Tunisia and Sicily. The country is far more interesting, possibly because it reminds me so much of England. I could imagine myself round Mr Woodroffe's former place, except that, even at its worst, the Old Mill never had such mud…… It's very cold at night and in the early morning, and the mountains are always snow covered. After being used to blazing North African and Sicilian heat this cold strikes us harder than it would if we'd been in it all year round. I remember our latter days in shorts were very chilly and now battledress seems hardly adequate at times!......*

I hope all goes well at School and that you had a good winter term. Also, I hope that you had a good Christmas. Please give my kindest regards to John (Watton) *when you next write. Tell him I often think of him even if I can't write; and that I'm looking forward to the days when he and I can once more take a stick in our hands and hike over the hills and far away, talking of the good old days when the Fifth Form was a Fifth, and thinking of the days when we had such fun. But until then, as Monty has often told us, we must all together "see this thing through to the end". My kind regards to the staff and, as always, my very best wishes to the School."*

K Northcott gave a vivid account of his war service as follows*".... I joined the Navy in 1937, since when my duties have taken me some thousands of miles in home and foreign waters. I have served on an aircraft carrier, two destroyers and a corvette. The period of the corvette was the happiest, I think. She was a happy ship and an excellent sea boat. It was in her that we spent ten months on the Gold Coast. Here I was able to study the people, their customs and life. Malaria played havoc with all on board the boats; half of our people went under with it. On return to England I, too, went under, and spent nearly ten weeks in Liverpool Hospital getting over it.*

The most dramatic occurrence took place whilst serving aboard HMS--------. On 8th November it was our job to crash the boom at Algiers, thereby making it possible for the troopships to go in. As you probably know, we succeeded and landed three hundred Americans. Also a number of our own stoker commandos for boarding the ships in the harbour. The project came off, but owing to lack of support, the enemy forced us to beat a hasty retreat after sticking it for five hours. The enemy guns were too much for us and soon it was clear that we were done for. For thirty hours we tried to save the ship, without avail. One hour after HMS------- saved us from a cold bath, this grand old lady went under for ever.

So in due course we arrived back in England for fourteen days' leave. Our casualties amounted to eleven killed and twelve wounded. There are many heroes in that action who will never be known. High praise to an American RAMC who saved at least two lives by emergency operations. Since then we have been training in certain classes of engines for future combined ops."[13]

---

[13] Extracts from the School Magazine dated July 1943 and 1944

Back at school, due to increased numbers, the governors took pity on the Head and agreed that a part-time secretary should be engaged to assist with his paperwork and Mrs Hampson took up this post in December 1941. One case of polio was reported but it was noted that the patient was making good progress. With over 200 pupils now on roll, including thirty six in the preparatory department, it was agreed to create an additional form to cope with increasing numbers.

Major D H Ramage GM, returned to the school to give an interesting lecture on Bomb Disposal. A small bomb that was displayed gave pupils some idea of the type of bomb being sent to Germany at that time. Lieutenant Colonel Pass, a member of the Governing Body, presented the school with a new flag, the previous flag having been presented to the school by Mr Woodroffe nineteen years earlier in 1923. The school in turn agreed to purchase a new flag rope.

The School Magazine for July 1942 contained an article entitled "These I have loved….." written by a pupil identified as "M.S." It would seem that this pupil was about to leave and the following extracts describe his/her lasting memories of the school:

"I can see then the terrace clustered with hydrangeas on a cloudless day in high summer, with familiar coastline rising above the almost startling blue of the bay – the drive in spring-time splashed with yellow daffodils – the exam-room with my fellow-sufferers alternatively chewing their pens or scribbling bravely – grey November afternoons when the hill-top school is shrouded in a clinging mist and the lights are on at three o'clock – lazy cricket at Uplyme with an unforgettable setting of blue sky, green grass and white flannels. I recall the glorious mud and bruises of hockey and football on the top-field on a raw and gusty day. I stand once again in the usual drizzling rain to watch the Cross Country, the red and white-shirted boys coming in to Horn Bridge, scratched, torn, bespattered with mud, often shoeless, but invariably grinning. And most vividly of all I can see the faces of all whom I have known during these years, for my memories are theirs too, and no pleasure is so full of joy as that which is shared. I remember – so many things. Happiness is not a possession to be bought, it is a quality of thought, a state of mind. There has inevitably been some sadness, but these years have been happy ones for me, whatever may lie ahead. "Et ego in Arcadia vixi".[14]

In September 1942 the governors received a report on an inspection of the school canteen that had taken place. The outcome of the report was the re-equipping of this facility, leading to improved school meals and a more efficient service. Later on, in June 1944, a new school kitchen was under construction, Cook Supervisor was appointed and meals were being served in the school hall.

Also on the food front, the governors were directed by the Dorset War Agricultural Committee to plough and plant one and a half acres of the school fields adjoining the school. To avoid costly fencing the Chairman suggested that one acre should

---

[14] Extract from School Magazine dated July 1942.

be provided on land above the school as an alternative. It was suggested that when it was no longer required it could be left broken up and used as a permanent school allotment. The potatoes were eventually sold for £15. Still on the subject of potatoes, the Head reported that pupils did not like eating potatoes in their jackets and a potato peeling machine had therefore been purchased. However the governors felt that potatoes in their jackets should remain on the school menu.

The school magazine provided an insight into the everyday life of the school at this point. It included a standing invitation to all Old Pupils to attend school events such as Speech Days, Sports Days, etc. A welcome was extended to Mr John L Longland, the new County Education Officer. Mr Longland was a first-class Cambridge graduate, an athletic blue and was a member of the 1933 Everest Expedition. During the year the Services kept in touch with the school and representatives from the Army, Navy, Air Force, ATS and the Women's Land Army visited. Reference was also made to "*That grand old soldier, Sir Reginald Pinney*" who died in 1943. He had been an original Governor of the school and the school's Speech Day in 1942 had been the last public function he had attended.

Thanks were extended to the County for the "*overhead weather protection to our ARP trenches. Small girls would doubtless welcome an invention for the extermination of stinging nettles but the boys do fairly good service with their garden hooks.*" It was noted that "*There has been a regrettable tendency to nonchalance lately in proceeding to these shelters*"[15].

At Speech Day prizes were presented by Mr Longland. Mr Woodroffe presided and it was noted that he was about to enter his twenty first year as Chairman of Governors. The key note of Mr Longland's speech had been "*Keep on keeping on*" ie never stagnate, never rust, always strive for something better.

A huge amount of correspondence was continuing between school and ex-pupils serving overseas, which clearly reflects the close family feeling which has always been a feature of the school. By now ex-pupils were losing their lives and in the school magazines the Head and Mr Thomas were writing words of encouragement and admiration which are quite moving.

From the Head – "*We at your old School, a bit of England, are proud of your fine service, and send you our thanks. We also thank you for your letters, and those who come this way, for your visits. I have over forty names in my Old Boys and Girls Visitors' book for the past year. Considering where most of you are, this is excellent. John Dawson must have done some gallant work to be awarded the MC. Of course, he is as close as an oyster about it, and probably thinks it came by accident. We are most relieved to hear that Lillington is alive, though a prisoner. I have just heard from George Wiscombe that he has a job in his prison camp post office. He is, of course, very pleased to have a useful occupation.*

---

[15] Extract from the School Magazine dated July 1943

John Hussey and my boy, David, have joined those who have given their lives for their country. John had the sad misfortune to be killed in an air-raid. David was one of the gallant band of parachutists who, fighting as infantry, did such fine work in Tunisia last winter. He fell in German territory somewhere between Beja and Mateur. I wish I could make so fine an end. At least five of you have now gone from us (including John Goodfellow, Kenneth Blackmore and Sidney Henderson). We salute them, and will remember them. May the rest of you return safely and with honour. The new and inspired England will need you."

From Mr Thomas – "By the time these notes are printed we shall have had four years of bitter struggle: a struggle which is testing courage and endurance to the full. The continued successes of our arms today are a glorious tribute to the noble way in which you, and other brave fellows like you, are facing up to the test. Thank you again for all your letters and for coming to see us when on leave. Cheery and full of confidence, I have not heard a single grouse from one of you. Life in prison camps must leave a lot to be desired, but even conditions such as those fail to dampen such spirits. Yours is indeed a high courage.

In thinking of you we are stirred also by the "grit" of your parents, wives and sweethearts who, in spite of their anxiety, keep a brave and cheerful front and 'carry on'……The Headmaster has had his full share of anxiety and loss and has, as you would expect, borne it with stoical courage: how keen he is for news of you… Now boys, hurry up and finish the job. Your old friends keep you in their thoughts and prayers. God bless you."[16]

The routine at school continued throughout the war years and Bill Short, who was a pupil at LRGS from 1943 until 1950, recalls:

"We travelled to school in crowded public buses and boys were expected to stand for adults and girls……. I remember well a grim-faced Mr Watton announcing the sad deaths of former pupils (including his son) in the war and all of us keeping a minute's silence……..The prefects picked us out to be in either Woodroffe or Shaftesbury Houses and also had freedom of discretion to give us lines or sometimes three whacks with the PT slippers for seemingly trivial misconduct….Boxing gloves were occasionally handed out for two boys to settle their differences and others would gather round to watch…….Sometimes, for new boys, there were head duckings in the wash basins before "being accepted" ……

The years from 1945 until about 1949 were seemingly a "golden" age for sport, both at LRGS and also nationally with the first Olympic Games post-war held at Wembley Stadium with huge crowds watching so many sports, starved of so much in the war years and still no TV to distract….. Memories of well-organised sports days, cross country runs, but only for the boys in those days, the rest of the school would make their way down beside the station and Victoria Hotel to the River Lym,

---

[16] Extracts from School Magazines dated July 1943

the finish for junior and senior boys…….. Little food was ever wasted at school meals, first in the DS room and later in the main hall – we were too hungry…….

Of girls, mostly the boys were somewhat shy of them – we kept apart, not taking that much notice. They were even rivals at lesson time! Sex education? We had none! Swearing? I heard no swear words, apart from occasional mild ones, ever, until the Army and National Service – what a shock!......I remember that awful high dentist's chair in the prefects' room and drilling teeth that didn't need drilling! Our teeth were good in the war – strict rationing of sugar and sweets!......We would tie two or sometimes three pencils together for writing lines, to speed it up! We would also place an exercise book in the seat of our trousers before prefects delivered three of the best, leaning over a table or chair."[17]

The school magazine of July 1944 advised that, when the first US Army Unit was posted to Lyme Regis Lieutenant Milotta had been invited to the school for a talk and discussion about his country. In February Major Wallis, British Army Liaison, also gave a very interesting lecture and demonstration.

As 1944 was the 21st anniversary of the school, staff and pupils were honoured with a visit to Speech Day by the Earl and Countess of Shaftesbury. Lord Shaftesbury gave an absorbing address which stressed the importance of a Christian basis for education. He also said that the chief aim of education was to teach pupils *how* to think rather than *what* to think and he urged young men and women to consider teaching as a future career.

The school magazine contained the following verse entitled "Alma Mater":

*"What are the Voices pulsating here, Within these walls, familiar, dear?
Treasures of knowledge, elusive, deep; Waiting upon the minds that leap
To the quest, - and persevere.*

*What is the Charm encircling all, On Playing Field, in Class, in Hall?
Grace of manner; Unwritten laws; Kindly ambition and Fairplay's cause;
Comradeship worth recall.*

*What of the Vision that years unfold, Trusted by each young heart of gold?
Something to Do on the world's high flood: Something to Be in the Light of God:
For Posterity to hold!*

*Hand clasping hand let the chorus soar! Hearts shall thrill to the old School song!
Alma Mater! Evermore, Thy memories live strong!"*[18]

The only indication of the author's identity are the initials CCC but its worth noting that there was a Governor at that time with those initials, ie Canon Carew Cox…..

---

[17] Correspondence between Bill Short and the Author dated October 2006
[18] Extract from the School Magazine dated July 1944

The School on the Hill

The editor of the School Magazine enquired whether anyone could write good music for these verses – was this perhaps the start of the quest for a School Song?

The school continued to receive regular reports on the progress of the war from ex-pupils serving all over the world. Lieutenant W S Prescott wrote from India in July 1944 *"I've been back in Delhi for about a fortnight after a most enjoyable couple of months spent with the 14th Army, a very fine and very tough crowd; probably the best British Army there is or ever has been. I was congratulating myself on escaping the monsoon but I found that I'd come back here just in time for the hot weather. The thermometer is well over the hundred mark now and it goes up a couple of degrees every day. Work is now done in a sort of daze, with hourly intervals of terrific activity, during which we slay flies by the hundred. The heat, the dust, the smells, the dirt, all these things I'm becoming used to; but the flies – they're found everywhere.*

This has been the first leave I have had out here; I spent it in Kashmir. I shall go there again in the next hot weather, if I have recovered sufficient courage to face up to forty hours in an Indian train each way. Indian railways I am sure are creations of the devil……Of Kashmir I can say little except that it is the only place I have seen, so far, in India, that lives up to its reputation. It is cool, clean and green. The only disappointment is Shalamar – the song must have been written because Shalamar was the only word that rhymed. Beside some of our English gardens it is a poor tawdry effort."

R Gage RN wrote: *"… A day before D day we sailed with quite a number of other LCTs all loaded with tanks. We knew we were going to France and approximately where we could land the tanks. We picked up more ships on the way, and also an escort of destroyers, etc….. We ploughed on, and nothing happened, and we only saw our own planes, so I began to feel better and not so nervous as I did when we started….At last we saw the French coast and also the gunfire and bombs. The first assault troops had gone in a good few hours before we arrived. We anchored for that night just off the beach. We had one plane dive on us just before anchoring. It was a Jerry but we did not see it soon enough in the growing dark to fire at it. I supposed he dropped about three bombs which missed us, and was then up and gone in a flash. We opened up several times in the night but no bombs dropped near us.*

Next morning we went in to land our tanks, and we caught a five cwt lorry on the edge of our boat in doing so. Then as we were beaching we noticed we had mines all around us, but, as luck would have it, we did not hit one. We beached at high tide and then the tide went out, leaving us high and dry. We were then able to get out on the beach and walk about. We cut the lorry free from us and removed the mines so that we could get out all right. Then we had a walk around the beach and saw the men clearing the dead and wounded. There were no Jerry planes that day and only a few in the next night.

When the tide came in we came out and returned to England to get another load. We have done this five times now but the things are organised and work runs on a timetable. I managed to get ashore in France again a few days later and saw a lot of Jerry prisoners being marched back to enclosures. I don't think I have ever seen so many ships, both Merchant and Royal Navy, British and American, in my life before!"[19]

Pilot Officer R C Nute, serving with the British Pacific Fleet, wrote: *"My first trip to sea was in a small cargo boat plying through the Bay of Biscay in 1934. Incidentally this co-incided with my first good bout of sea-sickness; unfortunately it was not my last. I look back on happy days on the French and Italian millionaires' paradise, sunbathing on the Lido at Venice, on a camel to the Pyramids, making merry in Malta, sailing down through the numerous islands off the Dalmatian coast and the "call of the East" smell of the North Africa ports.*

I then turn to the day at the beginning of 1940 when I sailed on my first mine-laying operation. What a difference, that dull, sinking feeling one gets sitting over hundreds of tons of high explosives with U-boats and hostile aircraft in the vicinity. Later on we took these operations in a matter of fact sort of way, although we had several lucky escapes. One of the luckiest was when a torpedo found its mark a few hours after the last mine had been laid. It's a peculiar sensation to feel the ship shuddering as the torpedo hits, and then there is the waiting period, wondering how bad the damage is and if it will be necessary to take a plunge in the 'drink'. Fortunately this was not the case and we were able to bring the ship back for repairs amid an occasional air raid.

Even war time brought some pleasant experiences. The Arctic in summer time with the ice breaking up and floating past with polar bears on it, the cold, clear air and midnight sun, all help to relieve the monotony. As a contrast to this I have pleasant memories of swimming in the blue waters of the Bermudas, visiting cities in the eastern states of America before Pearl Harbour, not forgetting the cricket match at Washington where I played for England against America, my first and last Test Match. These spells from the combat zones were very refreshing while they lasted and when I look back after three or four years, the pleasant times are easier to recall than most of the unpleasant incidents."[20]

Lance Corporal C W Searle, 4th Dorset Regt. (BLA) wrote in March 1945 "Now we learn that Winston himself is here with us; what a man, what a leader. To think that a man of his age should choose to be with his troops at such a time. I can think of no finer feeling than to see the 'boss' just before crossing the Rhine: if he couldn't give one confidence, then nothing can" and in April 1945 "We've also had the pleasure to help in the liberation of part of Holland and it's been nice to see friendly faces and see the flags again. These people went wild with excitement, hardly knowing how to show their gratitude."

---

[19] Extracts from the School Magazine dated July 1944
[20] Extract from the School Magazine dated July 1945

As the war drew to a close Mr Watton wrote: *"On VE Day I found myself in conversation with a young Flight Lieutenant, DFC. He asked me what I thought was the chief civilian reaction to the end of the German war. On the spur of the moment I replied that firstly came a profound thankfulness that at least one section of the casualty list had closed down. Then there are other things; thanks for the deliverance of England, for the cessation of bombing in the home counties, gratitude to our fighting men, and hopes for a speedy and equitable re-settlement of the country. Believe it or not, we schoolmasters feel ourselves in a peculiar kind of kinship with our Old Boys, and every time we lose one of them there is a sense of personal bereavement......."* [21]

Mr Thomas echoed these sentiments as follows – *"The end of the war in Europe has relieved us of a great anxiety and we should like to express to you Old Boys our praise and thanks for the gallant part you have played in destroying a ruthless and vile enemy. Some of you are still battling against those fanatics in the Far East: our thoughts are with you. Let us have news when you can.*

It was a tremendous joy to welcome home from prison camps John Watton and Juby Wiscombe, both of whom looked wonderfully well in spite of the hardships they had endured. And how glad we shall be when "Birdie" Lillington, Frank Moore and Daniel Rowe, who are in Jap hands, are free once again. The death of Eric Britton in a bombing raid and of Ken Halliday in a flying accident were tragic events: those boys will live in our memories with the other brave souls whose names will be engraved on our Roll of Honour." [22]

Returning to school matters the governors were informed in March 1945 that when the new intake of fifty five pupils had been absorbed in September that year, the school would definitely be a "two stream" school and that additional accommodation was therefore essential. Plans were submitted for a gymnasium with changing rooms and showers, of the size required for a two form entry school. It was agreed to adopt the plans as submitted and to recommend that the County Education Committee approach the Ministry for permission to proceed with the planning of the work for a two stream school.

172 pupils were expected in September, with six forms in the junior part of the school and four forms for seniors, and there were concerns about accommodation. At this time the school comprised six classrooms, an art room, a domestic science room, laboratory and workshops. Workshops could not be counted and the Head strongly disapproved of the laboratory being used as a classroom. The hall could not be used either as it was used for PT and as the dining room. In conclusion the Head pointed out that to work efficiently the school needed two additional classrooms.

---

[21] Extract from the School Magazine dated July 1945
[22] Extracts from School Magazines dated July 1945

Cricket Team 1944

Brian   Sidney   Michael   Derek   Francis   Tony   Alan   Ernest   Ron
Hallett Watton (Head)Kemp   Kirkland   Foxwell   Harris   Batten   Lovering Turner
         John Grant   Donald Hoare   Bob Trueman   Daniel Hallett   Michael De-Lotz
                (Photographs courtesy of Keith Wiscombe)

Football First XI: 1945 1946

Ernest Lovering   Ron Turner   Bob Truman   Harold Lanfear   Francis Foxwell   Alan Batten
   Michael Kemp   John Grant   David Hallett   Ira Pidgeon   Bob Huckle
                David Trueman   George Rutter

The School on the Hill

By June 1945 a meeting took place between the Chairman of Governors, Mr Firkin (HMI), and the Head regarding further accommodation that was required. The County Architect was asked to prepare plans for a prefabricated unit comprising two classrooms to be erected at the rear of the school in such a position that it would form part of any further extension to the school. Once again the subject of potatoes was raised with a decision made to construct a potato storage shed near to the school by converting the ARP shelters, this work to be undertaken by senior pupils.

In July 1945 Mr G A Taylor returned to the school. Mr Taylor was a very popular member of staff and ex-pupil Ken Peach, who was a pupil at the school from 1942 to 1950 recalls a day on route to school with his old friend, fellow ex-pupil, Brian Wood. *"We would always be passed by G A Taylor, the woodwork master in his BSA sports car. We would raise our caps politely as we did in those days. Imagine our horror one day to see him approaching and flames coming from under the car. No polite raising of caps this time – frantic waving. GAT smiled, stopped just ahead, saw the trouble, put out the flames with his gloves and carried on driving to school."*[23]

Another ex-pupil with fond memories of GAT is Reggie Jones, who was a pupil at LRGS from 1948 to 1953. He recalls that *"One lunch hour Tim Bosence, Brian Turvey, Malcolm Bowditch and I wandered downstairs and, finding GAT's workshop unlocked, we went inside to "look around". We were very soon "found" by Roy Sansom and, to deny him entrance, we wedged the door from inside. Since Roy persisted in trying to get in and was peering in through the glass panel in the door, Tim ignited an oxygen gas flame used for brazing and began to apply heat to the inside door handle. The idea was that the outer handle would soon be too hot for Roy to grasp and turn and then he might leave.*

After three of four minutes of this, we were suddenly alarmed to hear the sound of GAT's voice. I have no idea how hot the door handle was by this time, but in any event GAT's attempts to enter were also futile..... Suddenly GAT left the door and retreated down the corridor..... we then heard the sound of pounding feet, approaching at great speed. A very irate GAT was obviously intent on barging through the door.....If the door held firm the "g" loading on GAT would be rather high! Fortunately for him – and us – the door flew open and GAT proceeded to tell us what he thought of us – none of it complimentary. GAT stories are legion, but on the serious side, I believe he was among the best staff members at LRGS. He was a very competent teacher who invariably treated pupils with respect. The "slogans" on the workshop wall are memorable – and useful. "Think twice – cut once"; "Trifles make perfection but perfection is no trifle"[24].

In addition to welcoming Mr G A Taylor back to the school, the school wished Alban Woodroffe a pleasant and successful journey to the Argentine and

---

[23] Extract from ex-pupils' magazine – "Dispatches".
[24] Extract from ex-pupils' magazine – "Dispatches".

congratulations were expressed to Flight Lieutenant Rex Woodroffe who had been mentioned in despatches. After a lapse of five years the school Dramatic Society was revived and presented scenes from "1066 and all that", a musical comedy.

On 28th February 1945 Radio Officer J E Harvey of the Merchant Navy gave a talk on the war at sea. Mr Harvey had attended the school as a pupil six years previously and had been Head Prefect. He gave an interesting description of life in the Merchant Navy, its advantages and disadvantages. His chief grumble was that owing to the presence of U-Boats he was unable to sleep in his pyjamas! His audience was enthralled to hear all about life in the convoys and U-boat warfare.

To conclude this chapter in the school's history it is fitting to include extracts of letters from two ex-pupils, both of whom had suffered in prisoner of war camps but who had thankfully returned safely to their families.

Warrant Officer G Wiscombe, RAF wrote: *"On 14th December 1941 I set foot in Germany for the first time, being landed at Cuxhaven by a German convoy, and after one night in the German Naval Hospital, I was transported to Marlag and Milag hard, near Hamburg. Here I found naval and merchant naval prisoners, men from such famous ships as HMS Voltaire, Rawalpindi, Glorious and many of our submariners captured early in the war.*

My next move in March 1942 was to Dulag Luft in Frankfurt-on-Main, where all air crew POW's are interrogated by the German authorities. The idea generally was to squeeze information from new prisoners by various crafty means such as bogus Red Cross forms and many other ideas only Germans could think of.

In April I moved to Lowsdorf or Stalag VIIIB, which was situated between Oppeln and Neisse and not far from the Czechoslovakian border. In July 1943 I got to Stalag Luft III and occupied my time by working in the camp hospital in a section of the camp called 'Belaria'. January of this year saw the Russians only some thirty miles from us, and in a terrific panic the Germans moved us to Nurenburg. Here we received the full effect of Allied bombing as the POW camp was barely four miles from one of the main railway sidings. Again panic by the Germans as the Allies in the west were drawing near to us, and so my next move took me to Mossburg, an American POW camp near Munich.

On 29th April I was released by the American 7th Army, a truly happy day. I was in England on 7th June, having flown from Frankfurt-on-Main, where I really learnt the true significance of "the green fields of England". My sincere wishes to "my school" and all success to the school mag."[25]

Bangkok to Moulmein – an account by the late E D Lillington, who died in 1991, by kind permission of his family - *"We were taken off the train just outside Bangkok and the order came "All men marchee!" and we started on one of the hardest and*

---

[25] Extracts from School Magazine dated July 1945

eeriest marches of the war – a march which in twenty nights was to take us over two hundred miles into the heart of the jungle on the Thai-Burma border – more than a hundred miles from civilisation.

The first stage took us through mile after mile of banana plantations loaded with fruit. Siamese villages were dotted here and there. The second night brought us to Kaulmi, the capital of Siam and from there we struck off along a narrow jungle path – a long winding column in single file with Japanese guards at intervals. All our marching was done at night and we rested in jungle clearings by day. Only those who have been in the jungle at night can know how uncanny it is. On either side of the path giant bamboos reared hundreds of feet high closing overhead to a complete canopy through which an occasional glimpse of the night sky could be seen. Around the bamboos twined thick creepers, so thick as to form a complete barrier on either side.

Each of the guards carried a flaming torch which helped to lighten the gloom. The noise was incessant – millions of crickets chatting their loudest and one particular variety which makes a noise just like the whine of a large cross cut saw. Bull frogs barked loudly and every so often could be heard the roar of tigers and the trumpeting of elephants. Chattering excitedly above were hundreds of monkeys. Perhaps the most striking picture of all were the trees covered with fireflies – a mass of brilliant twinkling lights.

The going was very heavy and mosquitoes a great trial but perhaps the worst of all were sand flies which made sleep almost impossible during the brief halts. Our lot was worsened when the monsoon broke when we had about half covered our journey. It just pelted continuously day and night and the whole place became a morass and often we were wading up to our hips. Always we had to carry a certain number of our company who had become exhausted and on several occasions one of the guards! Finally, however, we reached the jungle clearing which was to be our base for the next six months but it was a very depleted and exhausted company who finally straggled into the camp.

Sonkurai, as it was called, was just a clearing with no shelter at first, although after about a month bamboo huts were built for us. Day after day we worked in pretty grim conditions on the railway which finally was to link Bangkok and Moulmein. Life was far from pleasant and they are days best forgotten.

It was a great day when at the end of 1943 the small remnant of us who were left was put on one of the first trains to run over the line and brought back to Kaulmi – and glad indeed we were to get there as the railway was a crazy affair and we knew full well how bad some of the workmanship in it was! It took us six days to cover 250 miles with several derailments and innumerable hold-ups. From Kaulmi we were brought back to Chanji Goal, Singapore where we were until VJ Day."[26]

---

[26] Extract from School Magazine dated July 1946

CHAPTER 5 – 1946 TO 1949: THE POST WAR YEARS

The end of the war coincided with the Head's decision to retire at the end of the summer term. The governors recorded their appreciation of the valuable work carried out by Mr Watton during his headship. In June 1946 it was announced that Major T B Pearn MC had been appointed as the new Head with effect from September 1946.

Speech Day in July 1946 was preceded by the unveiling by Major Wingfield Digby, MP for West Dorset, of the memorial tablet which recorded the names of old boys who had died in the war. The tablet, located in the school hall, was dedicated by the Rev Carew Cox following which the Reveille was sounded in the distance by a trumpeter of the 17/21st Lancers.

The Head Boy at this time, A H Beaven, described his mixed emotions at leaving the school. A day anticipated for so long was now tinged with regret. He recalled *"the long vista of polished corridor floors and laboratory benches which have always welcomed me on my return at the beginning of each term……,the corridors congested with children who, forgetful of single file, hurry to roll-call,… from the windows of the Domestic Science room, I view the familiar sight of terrace steps and well-trimmed hedges, of drive and footpath, crowded with departing children, and of the great fir tree that stands out against the blue back-cloth of the sea. I see for the last time, the tiny green bus crawling down the hill road opposite,…… I pass through the now deserted building …. and depart by the battered but well-remembered green door. Goodbye the School; my best wishes will always remain with you."*[1]

Pupils at work in the Domestic Science Room, which is still used today as such but the subject is now referred to as Food Technology (Photograph courtesy of Keith Wiscombe)

Upon his return from war service Mr G A Taylor wrote an article on "The Purpose of Handicrafts in School" in which he outlined the merits of the various crafts now included in the school curriculum. His message was that real education did not consist of teaching subjects but in teaching children and he advocated a balance between academic and practical subjects. He warned against making the assumption that practical tasks required a lesser degree of intelligence and he urged a return to the days when a craftsman could be proud of his skills and the work he produced. Mr Taylor concluded

---

[1] Extract from School Magazine dated July 1946.

that handicrafts at school encouraged the natural instincts of the child – to make – and to develop such vital attributes as inventiveness, industry, patience, accuracy and above all an admiration for that which is good.

It is interesting to note that ex-pupils returning from the war were now resuming their careers eg: *"Cuthbert Powell has restarted his publishing business in Lyme Regis, Victor Homyer, a qualified boat builder, is in partnership with his father at the Cobb, Ben and Jack Case have returned to their father's business, Pat Crate is apprenticed to Boots the Chemist, Lyme Regis, Cecil Searle has returned to his post as manager of Bradford Sons, Lyme Regis branch, 'Birdie' Lillington is now a full partner in A Paul and Son, Estate Agents in Lyme Regis and, after a refresher course at the Slade School of Art, John Watton, who made a name for himself with his illustrations of life in POW camps and his life-like sketches of prisoners, is now on the staff of a film editing company".*[2]

September 1946 marked the return of Major Evans from war service and the appointment of Dennis Ellis (Art) and George Shaw (Modern Languages). Alban Woodroffe was welcomed back from his trip to Argentina. He was congratulated on being made a County Alderman and on his appointment as Chairman of the Dorset Education Committee for the second time. It was noted that the Vice Chairman of Governors, Col Pass, had recently been awarded an OBE and had been appointed as Chairman of Dorset County Council. Another Governor, Major Allhusen, had been appointed as High Sheriff and Alderman of the County of Devon and Rex Woodroffe, who had recently returned to the Governing Body following his war service, had been re-elected as a Dorset County Councillor.

The arrival of the new Head, Major Pearn, led to a burst of activity. His first report to governors highlighted a number of deficiencies in terms of equipment, which were immediately rectified. The Head proposed the formation of a Parents Association and he also suggested that it would be extremely useful if the two new classrooms were divided into three by means of a partition. The third classroom could then be used by the preparatory form, releasing their existing accommodation to be used as a library. Additionally the Head reported that Mr Taylor was prepared to design and make a pavilion for the Sports Field if the governors would supply the wood. The governors agreed to do this and suggested that a small garden should also be established in front of the pavilion.

The Head also turned his attention to more mundane matters noting that on occasions the milk supplied had not been up to standard and he advised that he had been in touch with the Railway Company and the Omnibus Company to see whether any adjustments could be made to the times of the trains and buses bringing children to school. This would enable them to put in a full day at school and would also allow all lessons to be lengthened by five minutes. The governors in turn asked the new Head to look into the possibility of introducing a Pre-nursing course in the Sixth Form for following year.

---

[2] Extract from School Magazine dated July 1946.

By December the Head advised that two periods per week had been allocated in the Sixth Form to a formal study of current events. The focus of these periods was based on reading The Times, The Manchester Guardian, The Times Educational Supplement, The Times Literary Supplement, The Listener and Picture Post. In addition, to broaden the pupils' horizon, experts from outside had been invited to give lectures on such subjects as "The Problems of South Africa" and "Astronomy". Music concerts had been arranged and a large scale map of the world was to be painted on one wall of the Geography room, by senior pupils under the direction of Dennis Ellis.

The pace at school now appeared to be unrelenting, with the Head reporting to governors that an Art Society had been formed by Mr Ellis. A Choral Society had also been established in which it was hoped four part unaccompanied work would be sung. In addition, a craft section was now carrying out experimental work in plastics. The Head reported that a Parents Association had been formed and already had a membership of over 150 with numbers increasing weekly. The first meeting had taken place and there were plans for two lecture evenings on "The purpose and curriculum of the Grammar School" and "Careers for Grammar School pupils". Turning his mind to the future development of the school, the Head emphasized the need for a Sixth Form, more playing field space and better transport links for pupils from outlying areas. It was felt that the school would benefit from a new prefabricated classroom to be used by the Sixth Form and as a Biology Laboratory.   The Head also began to develop technology as a subject for those pupils who were not of an academic frame of mind to accommodate their needs.

Transport problems were still limiting the length of the school day. It was felt that it would help if all Axminster children travelled by bus so that school could commence at 9.00 am instead of 9.10 am. However, the bus company refused to agree to the school's suggestion that afternoon buses should leave at 4.20 pm instead of 4.00 pm.

Other matters under review of a more general nature were that various firms were being contacted with a view to supplying school caps. The severe weather in January and February had put the school as a whole approximately three weeks behind schedule. A school song had been written by Dennis Ellis and set to music by the Head. This had been taught to various classes as an experiment and members of the governors were invited to hear it to consider whether to adopt it.

The Head remained concerned about the needs of pupils who were not of academic grammar school standard and he felt very strongly that a curriculum must be designed to fit them rather than that they should be required to fit the traditional curriculum. A new timetable was subsequently drawn up which focussed initially on the basic subjects of English and Mathematics. This included a common curriculum for the first two years to enable staff to assess potential, following which there would be differentiation to ensure that the needs of each child were met. The new scheme also included provision to enlarge the scope of Sixth Form work by adding to the normal curriculum; engineering drawing, metal work and woodwork for boys and household science for girls. The plan necessitated extra accommodation and to solve this problem the Head suggested that an extra half hut be added to the present temporary building.

As Major Pearn's first year of headship drew to a close, in the school magazine dated July 1947 he clearly laid out his hopes and aspirations for the school. He referred to the need for the school to have a flag, a charter of purpose as defined in its motto, and a school song. It was at this time that the school adopted the motto "Audacia Constantiaque" which means "by courage and constancy". The Head explained that this was chosen, after a great deal of discussion, for its simplicity, and he urged pupils to live their lives according to it. Staff changes were many but most notable was the departure of Mr Evans and the appointment of Joan Green, who would be joining the school in January 1948. Miss Green subsequently remained at the school for over thirty years.

The school magazine of July 1947 noted that the school had now been largely re-decorated in "*pastel shades of green, pleasant primrose and dignified brown*". Reference was made to a rumour that Speech Day in July 1947 was to be held in the cinema that year. This remained a rumour as Speech Day took place at the school as usual. It was pointed out that the hall "*flower bedecked and packed to overflowing with the school, parents and Old Pupils, had an intangible atmosphere which any outside building would inevitably have lacked*".

Grant wins Senior Cross Country, Middle Mill 1947(Photograph courtesy of Ken Gollop)

The Speaker at Speech Day was Lady Digby who reassured all those who had not won prizes that not everyone could be a prize winner. She stressed the importance of working hard and trying one's best. She also urged pupils to go out into the world and be good citizens. In his speech the Head alluded to proposed developments within the school ie an enlarged curriculum, more facilities for the development of the individual pupil, and the possibility of a longer school day. He also advocated close co-operation between parents and staff. Speech Day ended with the first public performance of the School Song.

It was not only pupils who submitted articles for inclusion in the school magazine – the School Secretary, Miss Partridge, wrote an amusing account of a typical day in the school office which seemed to include everything from removing splinters from the rear end of pupils to greeting important visitors, counting dinner money and making sure that the Head had his supply of tobacco!

The Old Boys and the Old Girls Associations continued to thrive with reports on activities by Mr Thomas and Miss Carson. Many sporting and social events had been organised and well attended. Reference was made to the fact that Alban Woodroffe had resigned from his presidency of the Old Boys Association and it was noted that he would be succeeded by Cecil Hodges. Mr Thomas also reminded Old Boys of their motto "Sursum Semper" – meaning "Ever Upwards".

1947 saw the closure of the Preparatory Department and the formation of a full-scale Sixth Form offering a variety of specialised courses. It was anticipated that September 1948 would see increased numbers and the scope of work enlarged.

Roy Crabbe was a pupil at LRGS from 1946 to 1951 and he recalls "*Most people entering the LRGS in September 1946 were scholarship pupils garnered from a wide rural area across three counties, but not all. Don't forget that the war had only ended the previous year and that the local, yokel population had been leavened with the evacuees, many of whose families had taken a fancy to rural life and never returned to London….There were not many pupils at that time which meant that there were few teachers as well and thus a narrow selection of subjects…..*

This year's intake was the first to take the new 'O' levels taking over from the old School Cert. Two things went wrong for the first wave of us: we were ill-prepared by the staff and we were limited to some very silly choices of subjects which affected us throughout our lives. The 'O' levels were covering the same subjects as the old School Cert. and to the same standard, the difference being that we need not take the fixed raft of subjects at one sitting and we could add passes in any subjects at a later date. Thus we were reliant on the teachers to prepare us properly and while some did, some didn't.

We were not allowed to choose many subjects for ourselves. I think there was a core of subjects, History and English for example, that everybody took. Others were in pairs: you took one or the other. I remember that we were stunned to be given either Latin or Geography and Maths or French. Maths and Geography were my two best subjects which left me with no foreign language which was essential for a University Degree. If you took Maths then you had to take Latin as your foreign language if you ever aspired to university. The thing was: we were not being prepared for university entrance like today. However, two of us at least did get scholarships. The staff at that time had very low expectations for us.

Mr Pearn was a sort of war hero to some: a major with the Military Cross. He had a lot of drive and enthusiasm. This was his first year and he was very young for headmastership. Unfortunately he made very few changes for the better while I was there, I think he was just feeling his way. There were so many silly things about the place that he could have changed. There was a tennis court which was out-of-bounds to the boys, thus no boys learned to play tennis. There was segregation of the sexes everywhere at all times: in the classroom and during the play times and in the hall and during meals: even a staircase reserved for girls. There was a forge in the workshops but this was never used because Mr Woodroffe objected to smoke appearing from the chimney…..

There were many children from very poor families. This meant that a lot of us had to work to help the family finances. As with many other families, my father was a farm labourer earning the minimum wage. Some children were suffering at home from abuse or just ignorant parents not appreciating the learning of languages for instance or the need for homework – parents just could not see any advantage and could not justify the added expense. Unfortunately, a number of very good prospects had to leave school to start earning money for the family and could not stay in the Sixth Form….

The school had no playing field(s) in 1946 and the Uplyme Cricket field was used a lot. After a few years the land at High Knapps was bought and later extended……Along the top of the school boundary was a rather overgrown hedge and one year a group of boys made a sort of camp in it, used at play times. One day a very serious Head called the boys to a dressing down meeting in the hall. Apparently a neighbour of the school had complained about us. Thinking it was just about noise we were informed that the complainant was ex-army who told Mr Pearn that in all his service he had not heard such foul language as ours!"

By the end of the school year it was reported that the general health and attendance of pupils was good, remedial exercises had been incorporated into the time table and three classrooms had been equipped with wirelesses. The curriculum had been completely revised with the following changes made – the Sixth Form had a complete curriculum and many could choose groups of subjects from the fifteen on offer; Spanish had been introduced into the Vith Form as an optional fourth subject; the amount of time allocated for RE had been increased in all senior forms; normal teaching in RE, English, History, Science and French was augmented in certain forms by wireless lessons; and finally the school day now ended at 4.10 pm instead of 3.45 pm.

Transport was still proving a problem that was not completely resolved. After a great deal of difficulty, buses for Dorset children had been arranged to leave the school at 4.20 pm rather than 3.55 pm. As Devon had not yet approved an alternative time, Devon children were catching the 5.00 pm bus doing homework under supervision in school instead of at home. However, seven children to whom this would cause hardship due to the distance they had to travel had been given permission to leave at 3.50 pm to catch the earlier bus.

In an effort to combat the inertia of many children, and to give them an "active" interest in some hobby, it was agreed to make all periods on Wednesdays thirty five minutes in length and to use the forty minutes thus gained, plus twenty extra minutes, as a "hobby" period wherein "no pupil may study a subject already within his/her normal curriculum". As a result of this initiative, enthusiastic groups of boys for example, wishing to do cookery, and of girls, who wished to study light crafts and plastic work had already been formed.

Boys' caps, ordered from Messrs D H Evans of London, were available for purchase and the school made a ten inch record featuring the School Song and "Let us now praise Famous Men" by Vaughan Williams at a sale price of 7/- per record.

At this time, as the school only had half the acreage of land that it should have for playing field purposes, the County Council was asked to provide an additional playing field. The Head looked into the possibility of engaging sappers, under a training scheme, to help with the construction of a new practice games pitch but it was later noted that the Royal Engineers could not help with this work. The feasibility of using a piece of land adjoining the school as school allotments was being considered. The Head reported that the County organiser for PE and the Planning Organiser had inspected the school's playing field and recommended that a second playing field be rented as soon as possible, namely the field immediately opposite the present one on the opposite side of the dividing lane.

The standard of school meals in terms of quality and quantity was generally very good with approximately 230 served daily. The Parents Association held their AGM in November and it was decided that the third meeting of the term would be a lecture by the Head on "Grammar School Education and the part of the parents". Caps had now arrived and in spite of a cost of 10/- almost every boy purchased one.

In February 1948, as it had been impossible for Devon to provide the bus service requested, adjustments were made to the timing of the school day. School now started five minutes earlier, the lunch hour had been reduced by ten minutes, and the afternoon shortened by ten minutes. This new arrangement enabled all pupils to catch buses and trains at 4.00 pm and at the same time retain most of the extra time gained under the scheme inaugurated the previous term.

At a special meeting in April 1948 the governors met to consider the future status of the school, particularly in view of the decision of Devon Education Committee to enlarge Colyton Grammar School, which would result in the withdrawal of Devon children from LRGS, and also the intention of the Dorset Education Committee to build a modern school on the Charmouth Road, on the opposite side of the valley. The Chief Education Officer favoured a multi-lateral school with a new building erected by the side of the present school. It was envisaged that this school would accommodate 450 pupils, under one Head. There was some doubt as to whether a new school could be built on the existing site due to problems with levels and also the fact that there was insufficient space for the additional playing fields that would be required.

The Chairman the Governors put forward the view that the school should continue as a grammar school with a boarding house to balance the loss of numbers on the possible withdrawal of Devon children. However, it was agreed that a new additional school building be built in due course, on adjacent land, and that the school should be bilateral.

In May 1948 it was announced that the acquisition of a new hut had at last been approved and it would be erected as quickly as possible, ready for occupation by September, owing to the growth of the school and the expansion of the curriculum.

By now there was a small but steady demand for a Sixth Form course for girls wishing to become State Registered Nurses. A one year Sixth Form course for such girls was offered which, while continuing their general education, would contain a bias towards biology, hygiene, practical nursing (in conjunction with the Lyme Regis Hospital) dietetics and similar studies.

The governors gave further consideration to the establishment of a boarding house and the Chairman proposed that suitable premises in Lyme Regis be purchased and adapted for the purpose to accommodate between thirty to fifty boys. The governors also continued to press the Local Authority for the immediate acquisition of additional playing field accommodation and investigations began into the possible utilisation of the space in the roof above the Head's Room which at that time was adjacent to the Domestic Science room.

The School on the Hill

The school magazine published in July 1948 was described as a special issue as it was twenty five years since the school was founded. There was an introduction from Alban Woodroffe referring to the school's small and difficult beginnings. He felt that the success of a school could be measured by the character of the pupils. He praised the traditions that had been established in a comparatively short time and he wished the school well for the future.

The County Education Officer echoed the sentiments expressed by Alban Woodroffe and he referred to the many changes that had taken place at the school over its first twenty five years. He highlighted the excellent reputation of the school which had grown steadily and was now widely recognised. He also praised in particular the huge contribution Mr Woodroffe had made to the success of the school, from its founding to the present day, and he referred to the great affection and respect in which he was held by its pupils. The school magazine also contained messages from former Heads, Mr Greenfield (1923 – 1927) and Mr Watton (1927 – 1946). Staff now totalled sixteen, sharing between them responsibility for eighteen subjects. It was noted that Miss Carson was the only member of staff who had been in post since the day the school opened in 1923.

School societies were thriving and girls now enjoyed lessons in carpentry, plastic work and were achieving skills with hammer, saw and plane, whereas boys in retaliation had demanded to be taught cookery. Many school visits had taken place – to the Bath Assembly, to the Art Gallery at Poole and to Westland Aircraft Limited to name but a few.

Sixth Form 1948/49 (Photograph from School Archive)

The original members of the Sixth Form in 1948/49 were: Mr W H Thomas, BA, Form Master, J W Grant, School Captain and Woodroffe House Capt, Jillian Ramage, Senior Girl and Woodroffe House Capt, F G Foxwell, Shaftesbury House Capt, Patricia Gladding, Shaftebury House Capt, B J Hallet (left 31st March 1948), A Broom, D Hore, M Kemp, P Parkhurst, C Wilson, J Wiscombe, Margaret McNeil, Molly Smith, Pamela Taylor, Rita Turner, Janet Worth.

With regard to school uniform, boys now wore school ties and caps and the proposed grey flannel suits were steadily gaining ground as coupons permitted and the need for replacements occurred. The standard of uniform amongst the girls was very good and it was noted that they, too, were fitted out with the new school hat. The most important innovation had been the introduction of the coveted gold tassel on the prefects' hats – girls and boys alike – thus doing away with the undignified metal label worn in the past.

Ed Bowditch recalls his experience of this spectacular addition to school uniform - *"Blue caps with red rings were worn by boys as an essential part of school uniform. But who was it who decided that boy prefects should have a golden tassel hanging from theirs?"* Ed recalls a day trip, organised by Mr G A Taylor, to the Vickers Armstrong works at Wyke Regis. *"School uniform had to be worn including those caps. I don't remember much about the manufacturing processes for the Vickers torpedoes but when we were taken around part of the works by a foreman our vocabulary was certainly broadened by some shop floor language about fairies with tassels and we were whistled on our way."*[3]

For the first time in its history, the school held a formal Open Day for parents and other visitors during the afternoon and early evening 22nd July 1948 which attracted nearly 800 people. Efforts were made to ensure that everyone saw a fair cross-section of school activities. The day was so successful that some visitors did the tour twice and even staff, pupils, the Chairman of Governors and the Head discovered things about the school and how it operated of which they had not been previously aware!

The Old Girls Association was flourishing and the Old Boys Association had been in operation for twenty one years. As a mark of their gratitude for his twenty years' endeavour on their behalf, and as a token of their affection, the Old Boys Association presented Alban Woodroffe with an oil painting of the school.

The County Education Committee indicated that it favoured the suggestion of the governors for the establishment of a boarding house and that no action would be taken with reference to the possible change in the future of the status of LRGS from that shown on the Development Plan. It was pointed out that when the time came to proceed with the building scheme for a new Secondary Modern School at Lyme Regis, the governors would be asked to consider the position afresh, with reference to the school becoming a bilateral school ie one that catered for both grammar and non-grammar school pupils.

Two pupils, both holding School Certificate, were following the pre-nursing course. Their studies included English, Domestic Science, General Science, Hygiene, Physiology,

---

[3] Extract from ex-pupils' magazine "Dispatches".

General Psychology and First Aid. They also spent two afternoons a week at the hospital under the tuition of the Matron and an afternoon at the Child Welfare Centre where they received practical instruction. They also undertook normal periods of RE, PT, Games and Music.

Mr MacNamara BA from the Glebe Collegiate Institute of Ottawa, visited the school in February 1949 for three weeks and in the school magazine he described how in the bad winter of 1946 – 1947 coal trucks could not climb Lyme's icy steep hills and the school was about to close for lack of heat. Not to be beaten the boys, using improvised hand-sleighs, dragged enough coal up the 300 foot slope to keep the school going. They did this twice a day for two weeks. He also mentioned that the previous Spring there had been a bus strike. Although half the children at the school came in by bus no-one missed a day's school while the strike was on. Apparently they walked, hitch-hiked and cycled and although many were late, they always got there in the end. The teacher's final comment sums up his admiration for the school and its pupils – *"To teach children as eager as this is a pleasure"*[4].

Great emphasis was being placed on the teaching of French at this time. Senior pupils had been to Bournemouth to see a group of plays performed by a French Company and a similar trip was being organised to Bridport. Two Sixth Form boys were planning to attend a short course in Paris during the Easter holidays and George Shaw, the French master, was arranging for a group of twenty to thirty pupils to visit France during the summer holidays.

The Fifth Form at work in the new Physic Lab
(Photograph from School Archive)

By May 1949 the new laboratory was finished. The pre-nursing course had been successful with both girls accepted by training hospitals who had congratulated them on the advanced state of their work. A questionnaire was circulated to pupils and as a result the Deputy County Medical Officer visited the school on 10th May to discuss various psychological and health problems arising from answers given by pupils. In particular he gave most helpful advice concerning sex education.

---

[4] Extract from the School Magazine dated July 1949

Subsequently the Head advised that he had met with the County Medical Officer and a syllabus had been agreed to cover hygiene, physiology and sex education. Meanwhile the governors received from the LEA the suggestion that LRGS and the modern school in Lyme Regis should be combined into a single three form entry school with one grammar and two modern streams.

It was reported that Mr G A Taylor and a small team of boys had agreed to give an hour a week for the welfare of the school, carrying out minor repairs. The main object was not to economise but to give pupils a pride in their working environment. The theme of self-help was reflected in the editorial of the school magazine of July 1949 when reference was made to the dilemma facing the school in terms of what it could expect from the Local Authority and what it must expect to provide itself. It was suggested that a lot could be achieved if everyone gave up an hour of their own time to the service of the school.

The Head advised that if the school was to survive it must strengthen itself numerically and academically. To this end Alban Woodroffe had worked tirelessly over a long period to secure the acquisition of St Andrew's Hotel, which was to be modified and extended to provide first class boarding facilities.

The school magazine containing articles on such diverse subjects as yacht racing at Lyme, the sixth form visit to Dorchester, a day with the Culmstock Otter Hounds and a visit to Whitehead's Torpedo Factory at Portland. A report on the new forge was particularly graphic. Much had been expected of this new piece of equipment which had a rotary pump and therefore did not require pumping by hand. Apparently when lit the forge produced copious amounts of thick smoke and was likened to *"the Atlantic Fleet laying a smoke screen"*.

Many clubs and societies were now flourishing within the school, alongside a full programme of games, athletics and outside interests. Craft for girls had been developed and Boys Cookery Club was now firmly established. A Model Aeroplane Club had been organised, there was an enthusiastic group of cyclists, the Music Group and the Art Society were thriving and a Chess Club had recently started. It was suggested that a Stamp Club might be next and possibly a Debating Society. It was noted that the school community was divided into two halves – those interested in nothing and those curious about everything. The trick was how to encourage the former and restrain the enthusiasm of the latter.

When the Chief Examiner in Handicraft, from the University of London, visited the school to examine candidates for Higher School Certificate he was impressed by the work done but highlighted shortcomings in terms of equipment. Reference was made to the complete re-classification of the school curriculum which had taken place in 1947 – 1948. Attempts were now being made to make the curriculum even more elastic and tailored to the needs of the individual pupil.

By now the Ministry of Education had authorised the purchase of St Andrews Hotel as a boarding house for the school and it was anticipated that the purchase of this property would be completed by the end of October. The County Council also proposed to buy the field adjoining St Andrews.

In order to take the fullest advantage of the regulations for the new General Certificate of Education, a system of sets was devised for the middle school which enabled more individual attention to be paid to the varying aptitudes of the pupils. The subjects immediately concerned were Mathematics, French, History, Geography and Science and it was hoped that this arrangement would enable each pupil to follow his/her natural bent whilst at the same time continuing a broad education.

Inspectors who visited the school during the Autumn Term 1949 were very impressed and remarked particularly upon the syllabus adopted for the A and B streams and also upon the interest shown in out of school activities. When the written report by HM Inspectors was published it was outstandingly good and the LEA congratulated the governors, Head and staff on the school's achievement.

The Inspectors' report highlighted a need for additional space for the expanding Sixth Form, possibly by utilising the area over the Head's room. The Library needed revision and the number of books increased to 5,000. It was also noted that further workshop space was required.

A corner of the Library 1949 - Now the Staff Room
(Photograph from School Archive)

It was anticipated that the Boarding House would be opened in September 1950, by which time the necessary adaptations and alterations, estimated to cost £7,500, would be complete. Accommodation for thirty boys would be provided and arrangements were in hand for the appointment of house staff and the necessary furnishings, etc.

The final page of the school magazine dated July 1949 carried an announcement that in the early part of the Summer Term the school had been greatly saddened to learn of the early death in the Argentine, of Rex Woodroffe at the age of forty five. As a governor and friend of the school for many years he would be greatly missed. Deepest sympathy was expressed to his wife, the former Miss Aileen Allan, whom he had married in 1938, and to his father.

CHAPTER 6 – 1950 TO 1959: THE FIFTIES

One of the major features of school life during this decade was the introduction of boarding. In early 1950 preparations were well underway in respect of the new boarding house, which it was decided would retain the name St Andrews. The Head was appointed as Housemaster thus vacating a house named "Highways", owned by the LEA, which was adjacent to the school's boundary with Sidmouth Road. This was subsequently leased by two mistresses and when they vacated it at a later date, George Lloyd-Jones and his family took over the tenancy. It was agreed that St Andrews would open in September 1950 for approximately eighteen boys, hopefully increasing to thirty by January 1951. Fees were set at £135 per annum.

In February 1950 a letter of congratulation was received from the County Education Officer commending the school's Higher School Certificate results in handicrafts. The course had been wholly designed and directed by Mr G A Taylor. Don Cameron was also commended for his efforts in the PE Department which had increased a keenness for sport throughout the school.

The school magazine dated July 1950 featured an editorial on the importance of uniform and it observed that those pupils who did not wear their uniform with pride were, more often than not, those in whom the school had little pride. It was pointed out that to any school a uniform was the outward expression of an inner unity and corporate pride on which it was suggested a school could flourish.

In terms of the school curriculum, Mr W E Taylor and Ernest Lovering were developing an experimental course in Science which was proving to be most successful and Mr G A Taylor was working on a course for pupils who found academic mathematics (eg analytical Geometry) difficult. This practical course, was based on mechanical drawing and was being developed in conjunction with an approach devised by Mr Thomas and Miss Green. Mr Edridge had also been experimenting with the teaching of Poetry to younger pupils.

The first exchange visit between pupils at LRGS and a school at Valenciennes took place in July 1950 when twenty one French children and two masters arrived in Lyme to spend ten days staying with pupils. The return visit to France, Belgium and Switzerland, which had taken place in August, was a great success with the pupils involved spending three weeks abroad and travelling nearly two thousand miles at a cost of just £14 per head. Mr Shaw was commended for his efforts in organising and leading this very ambitious tour. Thanks were also expressed to Mrs Shaw who had ably assisted her husband and to the two County drivers for their patience and driving skills.

The party spent ten days staying with host families in Valenciennes and for the remainder of the holiday accommodation was provided in French Boarding Schools. Mr Shaw felt that all involved would long remember *"the night coach journey to Dover, the first impact of French family life, the language and the food; Paris from Sacre Coeur, a glimpse of Mont Blanc in the sunset glow; the River Arondine looking a mere ribbon in the depths of its gorge a thousand feet below; the variety of bathing scenes they enjoyed;*

sandwiches; and our coach christened Bonaparte or just "Boney" at more trying moments". He paid particular tribute to the spirit of camaraderie which had pervaded the entire trip and had *"transformed what might have been an onerous duty into a very pleasant holiday"*[1].

The school magazine of July 1950 also included comprehensive reports on the many sports fixtures and matches that had taken place, both inter-house and against other schools. Reference was made to a change that had been made to the system by which the Victor Ludorum trophy had been awarded. For the first time, instead of passing to the pupil who amassed the greatest number of points on Sports Day, a different system had been adopted. Senior Boys were marked over ten events, scored on Decathlon lines, whilst senior girls, and junior boys and girls were tested over four events. It was felt that this system was fairer.

Football Team 1950

Les   Terry   Malcolm   Ronald   Lawerence   Don   Desmond
Loveridge   Broome   Bowditch   Dampier   Sercombe   Cameron   Taylor
Keith Wiscombe   Michael Gold   Brian Wheller   David Govier   David Cozens
(Photograph courtesy of Keith Wiscombe)

---

[1] Extract from the School Magazine dated July 1951.

Dorset Schools Championships held at LRGS on 18th February 1950

Bill Short has provided the above photograph; he is on the right, jumping the stile, with Tom Lodge third from the right. Both represented LRGS in the race and Bill came third, having been passed at the finish line by the winner, No. 11 in the dark shirt. The photograph was taken as the runners came off the golf links in Charmouth Road and the boy with the bike is Roger Bosence.

Swimming had been introduced into the PE curriculum at this time, which involved hordes of excited children going *"beachwards on afternoons of alternate weeks (depending on high tides) some to learn and some to become more practised in the aquatic art"*.

A pupil about to leave the school recalled her early days as a first form pupil at the school six years previously, in 1944. Many pupils were meeting up for the first time and some found the experience terrifying although they soon made friends but in some cases, only just! *"... the girls all got to know each other's names upon the first day and immediately took sides to play Wild Indians and Mounted Police in the lunch hour. Broadly speaking this was Lyme against Axminster and everyone entered into the game (which was resumed each day) as if their lives depended upon it, although when the "fight" was not actually in progress we were good friends. I do, however, remember one phrase in which the enmity became real and the Axminster section then turned into the "Perm-headed Piggy-breads" while the Lyme-ites were known as the "Fish faced Baboons!....But now, after six years of Grammar School life we all seem to get on well together"*.[2]

---

[2] Extract from the School Magazine date July 1950.

The school magazine included a report by Mr Taylor on the newly formed Friday evening dancing class for senior pupils. Olive Stainton, assisted by Don Cameron, took pupils through such delights as the Moonlight Saunter, the Square Tango and the Pride of Erin Waltz, followed by the more boisterous Gay Gordons and the Lancers. In a brief article on the Boys Cookery Class, run by Ernestine Jowett on Thursday afternoons after school, it was noted that two boys had entered sponges in a cake competition and produced some highly commended work. It was also revealed that one boy had got this braces caught in the mangle. No further information was provided on this unfortunate incident which seemed to have little to do with cookery so the exact circumstances will forever remain a mystery!

In 1951 Mr Squance, the father of a pupil, presented the school with a handsome handmade antependium and dust cover for the memorial lectern, in black silk with the school crest embroidered upon it. Also Dennis Ellis, the author of the words of the School Song, left the school to be replaced in the Art Department by George Lloyd-Jones, a talented artist and a noted clock and watch maker.

A commercial course was introduced in the Sixth Form in May, particularly for girls who were leaving school at the age of fifteen, in order to encourage them to remain at school for a post-certificate course. The typewriters were already available in school for Evening Institute work. The course covered not only shorthand and typing but English, French, Spanish, Geography, Book Keeping and Elementary Office Routine as well as the general subjects of RI, PE, Music and Current Events.

The Head was given permission by governors to purchase flowering trees for planting on school premises to commemorate the Festival of Britain Year. The governors also agreed to the Head's suggestion in February 1952 that an avenue of trees or flowering shrubs should be planted on either side of the footpath leading from the school to the caretaker's bungalow.

The spirit of self-help continued to thrive at the school, with the school pavilion on top pitch, which had been blown down in a gale, entirely re-built by senior boys during weekends and a party of boys volunteering to re-decorate one of the rooms of the pre-fabricated hut during their evenings. The furnishing of the Art Room was largely carried out within school by making easels, etc. from out-worn desks and special equipment such as hinges, etc. manufactured in the metalwork room under the guidance of George Lloyd-Jones, Dick Richards and Mr G A Taylor. Also Don Cameron and a party of boys had begun the construction of pits for high jump, long jump and shot, and the enlargement of the run up of the long jump, etc. This group also proposed to lay a concrete practice cricket wicket. Later on a small printing machine was purchased enabling minor printing work to be carried out by a voluntary group of boys and girls, and the library was completely re-classified under the direction of Ernest Lovering. George Lloyd-Jones formed a book-binding group which was supplied with the necessary equipment to re-bind and repair both library and text books. Besides learning a useful hobby, this group effected a substantial saving for the school.

In terms of extra-curricular activities the Dancing Club was thriving and the LRGS Road Club (the Cyclists) was extremely active. Regrettably the Model Club had suffered a little when the Government had put a Purchase Tax on Model Aircraft kits and accessories. However, there had been a resurgence of interest with the introduction of radio control. A School Sailing Club had been established but, as it owned no boats, it had become affiliated to the Lyme Regis Sailing Club as a juvenile section. A total of fourteen pupils had joined the club and two of them had been presented with the "kipper" for capsizing.

A Conjuring Club had also been formed under the leadership of Mr G A Taylor. It comprised four founder members named as M Thomas, M Rule, J McGinley and G Llewelyn. At the first meeting each member demonstrated several tricks and there was mutual surprise at the standard of magic. Over a period of time the boys felt they had progressed beyond the novice stage and were so confident they staged their first show before Mr Thomas. Initially sceptical, he went away praising their efforts. However, plans to stage a show for the whole school fell by the wayside due to pressure from other activities.

The Fifth Form July 1952 on the Terrace (Photograph courtesy of Ken Gollop)

Increased emphasis was now being placed on music at the school. Music lessons in the curriculum had been increased and the school choir, which numbered approximately thirty pupils, was making encouraging progress. A string class had been introduced and many children were now taking piano lessons. Pupils were also heavily into sport including football, hockey, cricket, tennis and netball, plus Cross Country and Athletics, and ten ardent tennis fans had visited Wimbledon.

School Fete – 1952 (Photograph from School Archive)

There were many expenses incurred by the school for which there were no county funds available and in order to raise monies to meet these costs a school fete was held at the end of the Summer Term in 1952. This was opened by Alban Woodroffe, and attracted nearly 1,000 people who enjoyed gymnastic displays, exhibitions of dancing, a punch and judy show and various sideshows, stalls and amusements. Afternoon tea was served and a good time was had by all with the day rounded off by the first performance of the operetta "The Idea" with music by Gustav Holst. Unfortunately towards the end of the day the sky clouded over and rain brought proceedings to an end.

George Shaw had organised two further foreign trips. In July 1952 there had been a trip to the Pyrenees, when unfortunately he managed to fall some twenty feet whilst poised to photograph his fellow travellers as they toiled up a mountainside, breaking his leg. The previous year a journey had been taken through Belgium, France, Switzerland and Italy, then over the French Alps to Cannes. Mr Shaw described the trip as follows –

"The chief highlight was during the two days from Annecy to Cannes by way of six Alpine passes, including the col de l'Iseran, the highest motor road in Europe. These gave us many thrills, with their hair-pin bends and ever changing viewpoints. In Cannes we spent some lazy days on the beach; took a sea trip to the Iles de Lerins where the Man in the Iron Mask was imprisoned; saw Nice and Monte Carlo; visited a perfume factory in Grasse after going up the Gorges du Loup; bathed near "St Raphael" where we actually had "tea and cakes"; and saw the Roman arena and aqueduct at Frejus. We returned to Avignon, famed for its bridge, and the Palace of the Popes, up the Rhone Valley to Lyons and thence via Chatillon-sur-Seine and Rheims to Valenciennes where we willingly returned as we liked the food and the company. We went thence on our now well-known route to Ostend and back to dear old England."[3]

By now Reg Pocock had joined the teaching staff, as Head of Music. George Lloyd-Jones had suffered a serious injury to his eye in a gardening accident but was back in school albeit in dark glasses. He was joined by George Shaw who was on crutches following his accident in France.

Boarding at the school was now developing rapidly. The LEA took over the lease of Harcombe House in August 1952 and Mr and Mrs Jowett were appointed as the first Houseparents. Twenty girl boarders took up residence in September and boarding fees at this time for both boys and girls were £132 per annum.

The Mayor, Mrs Staples, visited the school on Tuesday, 26th May 1953 to present to local children the gifts of the Borough in commemoration of the Coronation. The Head assisted by Mr Upjohn of Messrs Cox and Humphries arranged for the temporary installation of a number of television sets throughout the school. All local children were invited to view the scenes in London and Westminster and a huge number of children and staff were accommodated, taking home with them memories that would remain with them all their lives.

In July 1953, for the first time, editorship of the school magazine was taken over by a committee of pupils. The editorial referred to the impression that the school made on its pupils and the memories of it they took with them when they left. It explained that the spirit and tradition of a school were inseparable and became ingrained in the personality.

---

[3] Extract from the School Magazine dated July 1952.

It was suggested that the magazine, with its accounts of the busy life in school and the varied lives of those who had left, reflected that spirit and tradition. The school magazine contained a variety of interesting articles from pupils past and present. A Second Former, who was a boarding pupil from the Falklands Islands, gave an interesting account of his first impressions of Great Britain and also an insight to life on the Islands. Old Girls wrote from Malta, Munich and Singapore and Old Boys sent interesting reports on their travels to such far-flung places as Singapore, Mauritius, Kuwait and Korea. The Old Girls Association had made Mrs Staples, the Mayor of Lyme Regis, an Honorary Life Member and had introduced an Old Girls Blazer of black cloth, single breasted with bone buttons at a cost of three guineas. The badge was "a really handsome affair" being made in gold thread by hand at a cost of 45/-.

Speech Day took place at the Regent Cinema on 27th October 1953 during which Alban Woodroffe was presented with a book in recognition of his thirty years' work as Chairman of governors. The book had been made in the school, illuminated by the Art Department and bore the signatures of the staff, pupils and all the others who worked at the school. Mr Woodroffe said he would treasure it and all it represented and he congratulated the school on the progress it had made over the thirty years, particularly under the leadership of Mr Pearn.

The Staff 1953
Mr Pocock, Mr Lovering, Mr Cameron, Mr Lloyd-Jones, Mr Shaw, Mr Adams,
Miss Money, Miss Male, Miss Partridge, Miss Green, Miss Satterley, Mrs Cameron
Miss Gordon, Miss Slaney, Miss Carson, Major Pearn, Mr Thomas, Mr W E Taylor, Mr G A Taylor
(Photograph from School Archive)

The Head passed to governors his suggestions for developing the curriculum for pupils in the B stream, some of whom were leaving as they considered that they had failed by not reaching the A stream. He also advised that an experiment had commenced which made a four year course rather than a five year course available for the few really intelligent pupils in the A stream which would stretch them intellectually, provide for a third year in the Sixth Form and increase their chances of University scholarships. It was considered that this arrangement worked well alongside the efforts to develop the curriculum for disenchanted pupils in the B stream.

Neil Adams took over as editor of the school magazine in July 1954, assisted by a committee of pupils. His editorial pondered on the value of the arts to the individual and the important part they played in the education of children.

The Music Department enjoyed another successful year, under the leadership of Reg Pocock, including winning six cups at the West Dorset Schools Music Festival, the Senior Choir was invited to sing at the annual Youth Carol Service at St. George's Church, Fordington, Dorchester and the Senior Choir carried off the main trophy at the Dorset Music Festival at Weymouth. The school orchestra gave its first performance at the school fete, excellent individual results were achieved at the Associated Board of the Royal School of Music exams and visits had been arranged to various concerts.

As ever the school excelled at sports and in the West Dorset Championships several records were broken. Two pupils had qualified for the All England Squad and the school had supplied eight out of the ten runners for West Dorset in the County Schools Championship for Cross Country. Cricket was benefiting for the first time from a concrete practice wicket and consequently the school's batting had improved greatly. To stimulate greater house spirit it was decided in September 1954 to make a third house specifically for boarders, to be known as School House.

The editorial in the school magazine of July 1955 focused on the magnificent views enjoyed by the school and how easy it was to get used to such beauty. The reader was reminded that environment played a very great part in the formation of character and it pointed out how well served pupils at the school were by the space and beauty that surrounded them.

View from the Terrace 1955 by George Lloyd-Jones

Miss Carson announced her intention to retire in July 1955 and the governors wrote to thank her for her outstanding service during her thirty two years at the school as Senior Mistress. It was estimated that since it opened in 1923, 1,546 pupils had passed through the school and all had benefited greatly from Miss Carson's care.

In the Music Department more successes were achieved at the Dorset Schools' Music Festival and the South West of England Music Festival. Reference was also made to a BBC audition and recording, performances at various Carol Services and Concerts both in the community and at the school. More and more pupils were learning an instrument and a record player had been purchased with funds raised by the school fete.

By now Neil Adams had started elocution classes which proved very popular and there had been an inter-house debate, chaired by the Head. Visits were organised to Poole Potteries, London, Maiden Castle and Dorchester Museum and the enrolment of the Harcombe Guides took place which resulted in twenty two new recruits to the guide movement.

At Sports Day the new School House put up a very creditable performance coming a close second to Woodroffe, despite having fewer members than the other two houses, which led to speculation that in future years School House would be a force with which to be reckoned. Of particular note was the performance of David Cozens who obtained five first places in the Senior Boys events.

At the Annual Meeting of the Old Girls Association permission was given to the Old Boys Association to use the Old Girls Association Badge, which had originally been designed by Miss Carson, provided the Old Boys allowed the Old Girls the use of their striped blazer! In amongst various articles relating to the Old Boys Association was a letter from the House of Commons from John Harvey, thanking the Old Boys for their congratulations on his election to Parliàment. Reference was also made to the new Old Boys badge which was in stock at Norman Bosence's shop.

An article and a poem were included in the school magazine following the passing of Quin, the school cat, who had been put to sleep by the vet on 23rd May 1955, aged ten years. Quin lived at the school bungalow with Mr and Mrs Stocker and five years previously he had been seriously ill. When he recovered a photograph was taken of him and copies sold to cover the cost of the vet's bill. Quin was laid to rest under the silver birch trees.

In May 1956 the Head expressed his concern at the lack of accommodation for a school fully organised in two streams with an unusually wide range of subjects. The Library and certain specialist rooms were being used on occasions for other than their main purpose. Four spare rooms had been created by adaptations but they were all very small. All possible space at the school had been used and additional main classroom accommodation was now urgently required.

By now Miss Partridge had resigned as School Secretary after twelve years, as she was moving out of the area. Her replacement was Mrs Jackson, formerly of the Town Clerk's Office. During the summer term it was felt that it was time for a change in relation to the summer dresses for girls which were blue and white check. It was decided that girls should be given the option of two different designs, in either blue or red stripes. Mr R J Stratton presented the school with a flag in school colours – navy blue with a broad maroon stripe through the centre. It was noted that in future the Union Jack would be flown on all national occasions, with the school flag flown on days of school importance.

The school fete in 1956 was even more ambitious and successful than its predecessors and raised £367 for school funds. There had been raffles, a lucky dip, side shows, jumble, teas and various stalls selling cakes, books, garden produce, etc. Pupils had been busy making pottery animals and ashtrays for sale and the Art Department had arranged an exhibition of paintings, pottery and printing as well as creating portrait silhouettes of the many visitors to their Department. There were even pony rides, a fortune teller's tent, and a coconut shy where one first form boy won no less than thirty seven coconuts!

In the school magazine George Shaw gave an interesting account of another tour to France undertaken by staff and pupils which had lasted sixteen days. They visited Reims Cathedral and the famous champagne factory at Epernay. Having journeyed over the Jura Mountains the party arrived in Annecy, and then travelled onwards to Briancon and Grasse. They were glad to leave the mountains behind them *"as travelling at six miles an hour for most of the day can be very tiring. We went up to a height of about nine thousand feet and little "Boney" did very well"*.[4] Seven days were spent in Grasse with visits to Monte Carlo, Menton near the Italian frontier, Nice, Cannes and St. Raphael. The journey home included a stop in Paris.

The Art Department bought a new kiln with proceeds from the school fete and consequently this craft flourished with many new glazes being used. The printing press purchased four years previously was doing sterling work producing leaflets, tickets, programmes, etc. for school events although it was noted that for the recent revue and fete the press had been abandoned and the cricket roller had been used in its place as the heaviest implement available for the purpose. The Art Department also used its many skills to make props for school productions and it was noted that for "The Pied Piper" the art room curtains had been used to make a dead cat! Reference was made to the success of the portrait silhouettes produced at the fete which had proved to be an excellent money-raising activity.

LRGS 1956
(Photography courtesy of Ken Gollop)

In October 1956 the governors congratulated Alban Woodroffe on being appointed a Knight Commander of the order of St Gregory. At this time the long term future of LRGS was again being considered by the Governing Body. The Chairman was adamant that the school should not lose its "special spirit" and he advocated that LRGS should not become bilateral (ie accommodating both grammar and non-grammar school pupils). However this view was

---

[4] Extract from the School Magazine dated July 1956

not shared by all his fellow governors. The matter was fully debated with all points of view taken into consideration. Finally the governors agreed that provision be made for the enlargement of the LRGS to allow it to become a three form entry bilateral (Grammar-Modern) school serving the Lyme Regis catchment area.

Views of Lyme Regis Grammar School 1957
(Photographs courtesy of Ken Gollop)

In terms of sport the annual hockey match between boys and girls and staff ended in a draw, and only one match played against the Old Girls, which the school won. A boys hockey club had been formed under the guidance of Neil Adams. Efforts in tennis, football and cricket had been a bit disappointing but in cross country the school won all three shields at the West Dorset championships and provided the first runner home in each event.

In May 1957 the governors received plans prepared in outline by the county architect for additional classrooms. It was explained that there would be enormous difficulties in making additions to the main school building which would also have to fit in with any future extensions when the school became a grammar-modern school. The site for the additional classrooms, on the bank behind the school, had been chosen so as not to interfere with any future buildings and when the school was enlarged could be used in connection with either Rural Science work or Art and Craft.

Articles in the school magazine included one on the plight of girl boarders who had to wear panama hats during the summer term. Apart from the fact that it was impossible to find a hat that fitted, by far the worst part was the walk up the school drive when the weary girls were greeted with cruel jeers by their male counterparts. Consequently they all looked forward to the winter when they could return to their shabby but insignificant berets! Another pupil remembered doing trolley duty ie transporting school dinners from the kitchen to the school hall. His difficulty was that he was smaller than his fellow second form pupils and could not see over the trolley. However, he developed some sort of radar and managed to negotiate his loaded trolley into the hall and back again without mishap.

The Old Girls Association were very much against the proposal to make the school bilateral. The Old Boys had discussed the proposal but unlike the Old Girls had not made a final decision and their response was to urge their members to give the matter some serious thought.

In terms of the curriculum and timetable the Head reported that the re-organisation of the school from the third form upwards, into "groups" following various courses rather than streams, seemed to have had the desired result of erasing the notorious "B stream" mentality. There was not the slightest doubt that more work was being done. In addition the minor but complicated modification of completing teaching in four and a half days and leaving Tuesday afternoon free for pupils to carry out individual work in a chosen subject or group of subjects had given further impetus. Staff were unanimous that Tuesday afternoon was the hardest worked period of the week!

By February 1958 work on the additional classrooms had started and it was hoped they would be completed and ready for occupation by May. Equipment had been ordered and it was intended that the classroom would be used chiefly for Biology, Engineering Drawing and as an Engineering Laboratory.

May 1958 saw some changes in uniform when grey flannel suits for boys were phased out in favour of blazers and grey flannel trousers. Gym slips for girls were replaced by blouses and skirts.

Following the departure of Neil Adams, Brian Earnshaw took over the editorship of the school magazine in July 1958, assisted by J Porter and R Harris as secretaries. In his first editorial he bemoaned the fact that the majority of clubs and societies at the school only thrived due to the input of staff rather than pupils. His hope was that in the future more pupils would come forward and share the workload.

Reference was made to "*a prefabricated building of conventional Scandinavian appearance*" which had been "*perched upon the steep slope above the school*". These two new rooms were to be used for Biology and Technical Drawing and their décor was described as "*a pleasing symphony of plum, grey and yellow*"[5]. The view from them was, and still is, one of the finest along the south coast.

These classrooms are still in use today for Environmental Science
(Picture by kind permission of George Lloyd-Jones)

In the school magazine the Head wrote a moving tribute to Mr Thomas upon his retirement in 1958 after thirty two years loyal service. The feelings of everyone could probably best be summed up by the first paragraph of his tribute: "*The years bring change to all schools. The buildings grow, the curriculum develops, children and staff come and go, but up to now, whatever changes have befallen us, we have always had Mr Thomas – unobtrusively efficient, imperturbable and unfailingly kind.*" Reference was made to the elegant and splendid lectern of oak which Mr Thomas had presented to the school on his last day at the school. It is pleasing to note that this lectern is still in regular service at the school and remains as handsome as the day Mr Thomas gave it to the school – a fitting tribute to a lovely man.

With the introduction of two new form rooms, the Art Department now had more room to expand. This included the little room known as the "Black Hole". This was a small room along the top corridor used as study room for the Sixth Form and later a prefects' room. Ex-pupil Reggie Jones recalls that at his previous school the boy prefects' room was a windowless "cubbyhole" where mediaeval torture on seemingly randomly selected unfortunate boys was administered. When the small upstairs room was made available,

---

[5] Extracts from the School Magazine dated 1958

Reggie named it the "Black Hole" and the name stuck. Another ex-pupil can remember someone locking members of the Sixth Form in the "Black Hole" during a staff meeting. This escapade resulted in their trip to the Festival of Britain being cancelled and the confiscation of their prized tassels for a week!

1958 saw the start of The Field Society which carried out three expeditions in total, all taking place on Saturday mornings remarkable for bleak east winds and chilly rains. The first expedition was a long tramp to Colyton and back; the second began at Bridport, moved on to Punknowle then on to Chesil Beach and Burton Bradstock and the third was undertaken in the teeth of an easterly gale and included a tour of the prehistoric remains above Abbotsbury.

Malcolm Kennaugh, an ex-pupil who now lives in New Zealand, was a keen member of the Field Society and recalls *"Its immediate appeal was to be in the company of other pupils for a day of walking through the wonderful history and backdrop of the local district. Brian Earnshaw was the teacher who had initiated the group and for six years it grew from strength to strength. Distances were not for the faint hearted. My first walk (with a group of about twenty others) was to Maiden Castle near Dorchester. Blisters and limps were commonplace. Mr Earnshaw feared for my roman-sandal footwear but we made it, and on another trip (via Chesil Beach) I remember John May throwing his shoes into West Bay Harbour. Some archaeologist may verify that one day! Mr. Coates took over leadership in 1960 and some mischievous pupils took advantage of this to get some serious private time on the cliff walk to Axmouth.*

Later on, in around 1963, in the build-up to the Vietnamese war, newspapers reported that American soldiers (probably with heavy packs) weren't managing their fifty mile training walks very well. Mr Pearn seized the moment to advise the world that the Field Society would show the way (without packs!). For the next few years the society became quite famous for carving into some impressive distances. I had the role of helping plan the routes (safety was just starting to be a concern in those days) so it was with acute embarrassment that one year I took four or five trusting souls five miles off the route . Sadly, in later years, the Field Society lost its own way and was reduced to an annual sponsored walk. When I revisit England (from New Zealand) I still check out some of my favourite paths from this memorable era."[6]

Sports Day was postponed owing to rain and this was the year when there was controversy over the number of laps completed in the mile race. The pace had been so slow no-one was quite sure and with uncertainty all round the matter was never resolved! This year the finish for Cross Country was in the meadow by Middle Mill. There were some splendid finishes with the runners bursting out of the trees by the footbridge and battling towards the finish line in tight groups.

At the District Athletics Meeting the school won all available shields and at the County Sports won two events. Two pupils from the school were chosen to represent Dorset in

---

[6] Information provided by Malcolm Kennaugh in New Zealand by e-mail dated 27th November 2006

the Western Counties final, gaining 2nd and 4th place respectively. Not to be outdone the School Choir took part, with other selected choirs, in a final concert at the Albert Hall for the BBC programme "Let the People Sing".

The Old Girls Association were strongly opposed to the proposal for the school to go bi-lateral and in fact Mrs Geary, the previous year's President, was serving on the Bi-lateral Protest Committee. The Old Boys Association was very much taken up with the retirement of Mr Thomas, who was to be succeeded by Mr G A Taylor. It was noted that Mr Thomas would be remaining in Lyme Regis for the time being and would therefore continue to attend school functions. Many tributes were paid to him at the Old Boys AGM. and their Annual Dinner.

By February 1959 the LEA announced that in the building programme for 1960/61 it had included a proposal for providing the necessary extensions to the school. A preliminary estimate prepared by the county architect put the cost of these extensions at £151,000. For the first time in ten years, the school was inspected from 26th to 28th May 1959. The Inspector was Dr Arnold. By now there were 286 pupils on roll and both boarding houses were full with a total of eighty five boarders.

The school's hockey, football and tennis teams did not fare well this year but cricket was much improved. A strong team had represented the school at the West Dorset meeting and had carried off five of the six available shields. With regard to cross country the usual high standard was maintained at West Dorset and the All Dorset Championships. The course for the school cross country had had to be modified due to the fact that part of the senior course had slipped into the sea! This meant that the competitors had to start by grinding up Timber Hill.

The Field Society had enjoyed a memorable year with vastly increased numbers. The first trip had involved a *"jolly romp around the rocks and brambles of the Landslip"* and had been followed by what was described as "The Great Weymouth to Lyme Regis Trek, October 1958". The intention was to walk from Weymouth to Lyme Regis via Chesil Bank. As usual the weather was dismal and the going was tough. Everyone eventually reached Bridport safely where the majority took taxis. Some staggered as far as Charmouth and then took a bus home, and a few finally trudged into Lyme well past midnight.

The next expedition, in February, attracted only five hardy souls who caught a bus to Sidmouth. The party visited Salcombe Regis Church, accessed the beach through the grounds of Dunscombe Manor and then "crunched gloomily" along to Branscombe Cliff. Having negotiated the headlands of Branscombe and Beer, the party reached Seaton by nightfall and, fortified by fish and chips, they undertook the most exciting stage of their journey – a night passage right through the Landslip. They eventually reached St Andrews at 8.25 pm, having left Sidmouth at midday. The final expedition aimed to prove that Roman Legionaries could have walked from their port at Axmouth to Dorchester in one day. Along the way various people dropped out and in the end only a few completed the route and triumphantly reached a bus-stop on the Weymouth road, thus proving the Roman theory beyond a shadow of doubt.

Discussion was now taking place on a name for the school. Initially it was decided that the school would be known as The Alban Woodroffe School but eventually this was amended to The Woodroffe School.

Sixth Form pupil, Donald Pitman, took the courageous decision to go whaling in the Antarctic for seven months and he wrote about his exploits in the school magazine giving a vivid account of his experiences as follows: *"I remember particularly how fine the weather was on Monday, 10th November 1958 for it was on that day that I saw the last of England for over five months. With hardly a thought for the labour that lay ahead I had signed on as a member of the crew of H.F. Balaena to do whatever work I was ordered during whatever hours I was ordered for the seven month contract period. A life on the ocean wave! You can keep it, thanks. I only entered one port during twenty two weeks of hard graft. During the trip to Capetown I was a mess-boy; half an hour after reporting for duty on the first morning …there was I, with ashen face, leaning over the rails, feeling very much like a first tripper.*

We docked at Capetown, took on some stores and headed south, leaving behind a mate stabbed to death in a Capetown back-street by a pickpocket. Within a week we were smashing against our first icepacks. Christmas and the New Year came and passed in a couple of drunken stupors. Then came the novelty of the open season with catches of up to seventy-two whales a day. These days between January and February earned one between ten and fifteen pounds a week. By the end of January people were beginning to get fed up, the novel situation was fast becoming tedious. The men, instead of thinking of the money ahead were now thinking of their families 8,000 miles away. By now we had had two more fatalities – the first mate of a catcher went missing on New Year's Eve, presumed drunk and drowned. A deckboy was swept from the heaving decks of a tanker during a near hurricane.

At length the signal for the end of the shooting came. By now, with the prospect of soon being home, the men were in a happy mood. However much we had looked forward to the Southampton docking it was a sad moment when as our tender headed away from Balaena we heard the hooter send us off with the same signal we had listened to so impassively at Las Palmas when the last catcher left the parent ship."[7] Upon his return Donald was interviewed by ITV and quite understandably was known as Moby Dick.

Mr G A Taylor, who had taken over responsibility for the Old Boys Association, advised that Mr Thomas was enjoying retired life. Apparently he looked very fit and his garden was a show piece with onions four inches in diameter! As the year and the decade drew to a close, Alban Woodroffe indicated that he would be resigning as Chairman of the Governing Body after Speech Day. He subsequently vacated the chair and Sir Bertram Rowcroft was appointed in his place temporarily. Sir Bertram paid tribute to the long and devoted service of Mr Woodroffe and his remarks were endorsed by the whole of the Governing Body.

---

[7] Extract from the School Magazine dated July 1959

CHAPTER 7 - 1960 to 1969: THE SIXTIES

The swinging sixties were an important decade for the school not least because during this period it lost its grammar school status and became a new grammar/modern school. Also a major building programme was undertaken to accommodate the growing number of pupils which was expected to reach 500. In this connection, in early 1960, governors and the Head examined plans for the extension and re-modelling of the school buildings. A deputation of governors also met with LEA representative to emphasize the need to continue to attract sufficiently talented boarders to the school in order to maintain and develop its academic standard. At this meeting the governors pointed out to the LEA that a number of staff might resign if there was a decline in academic standards. The Head also referred to the fears of the Parent/Teachers Association, which was particularly concerned at the possible resignation of existing teaching staff. The authority was reminded again that the school's high academic standards depended very heavily on boarders and it gave assurances that it would do its best to maintain the quality of the boarding entry at LRGS.

By now there were 306 pupils on roll, with thirty five boy boarders and forty eight girl boarders. In February it was announced that Mr W E Taylor would be retiring as Deputy Head/Head of Science with effect from August 1961 and the governors expressed their appreciation and thanks for his long service. Governors noted with dismay that the production of a school magazine had been discontinued as it had been running at a loss. Alban Woodroffe asked if the school magazine could be re-instated. It was agreed that publication should recommence with any deficit being met from the Tuck Shop Account.

In September 1961 the school started to consider the idea of building a learners' swimming pool. It was established that a pool of the required size could be built at an approximate cost of £3,000, but only if contractors were generous with their terms and part of the work was carried out by voluntary labour. The LEA subsequently advised that it would only provide a grant of £300 towards the cost and that the school would be responsible for the remainder. At this point a sub-committee was formed to look at ways of raising the necessary funds, by direct contributions, a covenant scheme and various money-making activities. The sub-committee discovered that early indications were that £1,200 could be guaranteed (by two Governors, Commander Eyre and Mr Awford) which suggested that the target of £3,000 was achievable.

On two occasions during a four month period, the school choir was invited by the BBC to broadcast. One broadcast involved a trip to Weymouth to record three songs for the programme "Let the People Sing". The other was called "Musical Round-Up". Warm thanks were extended to Reg Pocock who had trained the choir to such a high standard. His departure in 1961, after eight years at the school, was a cause of great sadness to the choir who had had so much fun singing with him.

The Head felt that it was time for pupils to give something back to the school that had given them so much, thus mirroring the continuing generosity of Commander Eyre, who had recently given the concrete steps and path up to the games field. How many have dragged ourselves up those steps and been grateful to Commander Eyre for the pleasure!

On the sporting front the 1st XI soccer team in 1961/1962 was the best fielded by the school in its history. The team remained undefeated throughout the season and the crowning glory was that the Old Boys Cup was returned to the school after an absence of several seasons. The junior Boys team was not so successful but they managed to retain the Kenway Cup. The staff hockey match was a lively affair with the staff forward line, comprising Brian Earnshaw, Timothy Cock, George Shaw and Stan Arrowsmith, turning in particularly sparkling performances.

The Music Society mused on the large number of smaller groups that formed up within its ranks whilst they listened to the music ie the knitters, the readers and some just waiting for the rain to stop. It was noted that the music blasted out to such a level that it reached Derek, sitting in his bus at the bottom of the drive waiting for the Harcombe boarders.

The School Cross Country featured a new course which started at the station. There were scenes of chaos at the start of the junior race when the boys at the front tended to get knocked down by the surge from the rest but apart from that it all went well, with everyone arriving home safely.

Speech Day this year, held at the Regent Cinema, was quite a lively affair with the Head's address appearing in the national press. This was because he suggested that many school children were working too hard and would therefore benefit from a four term year with four three week holidays. Reports appeared in The Daily Mail, The Sketch, The Telegraph and The Express, the majority of which got the Head's name wrong. The item even appeared on the ITV news that evening.

Sadly, by now both the Old Boys and the Old Girls Associations were in a critical position owing to the fact that over 70% of children in the school now left the area to embark on a career. The associations were very aware that the structure of their constitution might have to be radically changed in order to meet the new situation and a series of committee meetings were held to consider future policy. Eventually, after the Old Boys had got over their initial misgivings, the decision was made to amalgamate and in September 1963 the Woodroffe School Association was formed.

By September 1962 the transfer of certain children from the Junior School to the Senior School ceased, with these pupils being accommodated at LRGS within a newly built temporary classroom. The Head reported that the additional children had settled in very quickly. Tributes were paid to the sterling efforts of Joan Green who had put in many hours of work during the school holidays to ensure that the new term started smoothly.

This year the editors of the school magazine were Rosemary Knight, Amanda-Sue Silburn and Brian Earnshaw and the magazine was entitled "School and After". They explained that they intended to focus on what happened to pupils when they left the school. It was felt that if the school had a fault it was that it did too much for its pupils, it coaxed the best out of them, flattered their talents and subsequently left them surprised by the unappreciative world into which they ventured out.

The view of the editors was that the new school buildings, currently under construction, would be spacious and adequate in a functional way but they pondered on the decorations that would give it character, just as the gables and terrace had given the old school its character. Ideas were being discussed for the bare south wall in the new hall and various suggestions had been made by both staff and pupils – a large clock in the centre, two massive gilt eagles, a ceramic mural depicting school activities and a huge symbolic hour glass in bronze and crystal were just some of the ideas put forward.

More ambitious ideas for other parts of the school featured imposing statues and included the siting at the entrance to the hall of a soldier riding a rearing stallion with his spear and shield made of copper to catch the light, a large bronze statue on the roof of the hall featuring a Chinese Dragon, a glass statue with hidden lights making prisms and even a reclining lion drowsily guarding the entrance steps. Ideas were not restricted to the new buildings – a large bronze bell for the main entrance was one suggestion, a Michael-angelo type "David" on the front grass to be visible from the road was another, as were handsomely carved flag poles outside both the old and the new buildings from which flags could be flown on special days.

The Head suggested that the school arms could be emblazoned in a stained glass window. The ideas flowed freely but sadly very few got incorporated into the buildings. The general feeling was that the massive new walls would tower into the sky and would be a visible reminder that the school was beginning a big and new adventure. It was hoped to keep this spirit in the decoration of the buildings and to create something of which everyone could be proud.

The school magazine included a letter from W H Auden, one of our greatest living poets, in response to an enquiry by senior pupil, Cheryl Reynolds née Turner, about the nature of love as expressed in a poem of his which was being studied at O level. The letter, from an address in New York, was two pages long and provided a very detailed reply to the question put. Cheryl also received a reply to a letter she wrote to Sir John Betjeman. Her granddaughter is now a pupil at Woodroffe and Cheryl pays tribute to her English teacher, Brian Earnshaw, who inspired in her a great love of the subject.[1]

In November, Speech Day was held at the Marine Theatre, rather than the cinema, and due to increased numbers for the first time juniors received their awards in the afternoon and seniors in the evening.

This winter bad weather caused severe difficulties both at school and at the boarding houses. Site staff at St Andrews worked as a team with school site staff to keep things going. St Andrews received all mail and supplies, which it then distributed to school and Harcombe. Attendance at school was badly affected, mainly due to transport difficulties, and fluctuated between 60% and 95%.

During the Christmas holidays a party of twenty seven boys and girls went to Pontresine, Switzerland for a skiing holiday accompanied by Brian Earnshaw, Mr and Mrs Arrowsmith and Miss Duckham. This was a remarkably successful venture, greatly enjoyed by everyone concerned although one senior girl broke her leg. The party left on the first day of the great snow and parents faced severe difficulties getting pupils to Axminster in order to catch the 7.00 am train. To get round this, just before midnight the night before, the Head and Mr Arrowsmith toured the area asking all parents to get their children to St

---

[1] Information provided by Mrs Cheryl Reynolds née Turner

Andrews by 5.45 am. At 6.15 am the party set off for Axminster in a breakdown lorry and boarded the train on time with the exception of three people who were snowbound. However, arrangements were made for these unfortunate souls to meet up with the party later on.

By 1963 work on the new buildings was proceeding. A competition was held in school to encourage pupils to make suggestions for new amenities and a number of worthwhile ideas were submitted. To enable the money to be found for larger projects, the Parents' Association, Old Pupils and the school decided to hold a Fete on 18th July 1963.

Discussion took place on the need for an additional house to accommodate the extra number of pupils now attending the school. The purpose of the house system was to give pupils a small unit to which they could give their immediate loyalty within the large framework of the school. The unit also had to be small enough to ensure that a majority of children could take part in representative games and activities. After lengthy discussion, Coram House came into being, alongside Woodroffe, Shaftesbury and School House and pupils were redistributed across all four houses. All boarders remained in School House which was augmented with some day pupils to even the numbers up.

At this time, in Lyme Regis a debate was raging as to possible changes being put forward by the Boundary Commission which would result in Lyme Regis being located in Devon. There was fierce opposition to this proposal as had been the case when boundary changes had previously been mooted the previous century, in 1888. At a special meeting in July 1963 the governors resolved that the future of the school was secure as long as it remained under Dorset LEA. It was agreed that the Vice Chairman should represent the Governing Body at a forthcoming Public Enquiry, the outcome of which was that Lyme Regis remained in Dorset. The LEA subsequently thanked the governors for their support.

In October 1963 the school was officially renamed. The front cover of the school magazine this year not only bore the new school title "The Woodroffe School", it also included the phrase "A Building of Spirit" which summed up the great changes that were taking place at this time.

The Editors, Rosemary Knight, Catriona Macdonald and someone mysteriously referred to as GBP, began by describing the trials and tribulations endured by both staff and pupils during the extensive building programme that had begun the previous Spring. The sounds of men at work, ie drilling, hammers and transistor radios, interrupted many a lesson but all had soldiered on and the end was now in sight

It was anticipated that by Easter 1964 the new Art and Craft rooms, three new laboratories and three prep rooms would be ready for use, with the new Assembly Hall, the Gymnasium, the Workshops and the Games Room completed during August and September. By Easter 1965 it was envisaged that the old school hall would become the new Library, the Music Room would be enlarged and the Domestic Science Department would have a whole wing to itself.

Efforts had been made to gauge the reactions of new pupils joining the school from smaller primary schools. Although many had been over-awed by the size of the school buildings, the number of fellow pupils and the fact that the teachers wore black gowns, the majority had been pleasantly surprised by how kind and helpful everyone had been to them and how quickly they had started to feel at home.

The famous fifty mile walk which took place on 10th March 1963 was a huge event in the life of the school and for all those associated with it, and the report in the school magazine of 1963 illustrated the tremendous efforts of all those who took part whether they completed the full gruelling course or part of it. Extracts from the article give a glimpse of what it was like on that memorable day – the camaraderie, the sense of achievement but above all the pride in being part of such a huge and exciting adventure.

"Climbing up Timber Hill I was quite convinced I would never walk fifty miles; the television camera-car crawled slowly behind us, as we walked through the lanes towards Whitchurch; My memory is rather hazy on the road, but I remember sheltering under that huge black umbrella on the way up that unending hill before Eype; at Swyre, snowdrops grew where we sat like grumpy bears, surveying the remains of our toes; then the rain again and the Headmaster to make us feel jollier, at that bleak point. People got into his car, worn out.

We walked through Toller Fratrum and Toller Porcorum, hilly and golden against the spring sky; we reached Beaminster Square as dusk fell, and threw chocolate peanuts into our mouths in a last desperate attempt to gain energy; we did not realise that just behind us others were trying to convince themselves that they were going to do it; many times we longed to sit down and sleep and dream. But we kept on going keeping our legs moving, our feet moving, our brains awake.

We heard the familiar growl of the school bus bearing up on us, its round eyes glaring into our tired eyes, tempting us into the dim interior, whispering into our limp minds. What comfort to drop quietly and unnoticeably into a seat, perhaps to dream. Shouts from the hypocrites inside and Derek asked for the last time "Sure you're sure?" "No thanks, we're walking" and we watched the red rear lights flickering into the darkness; the roar of the exhaust was swallowed up into the night; Mr Pearn drove by at intervals; by now time was going too slow to judge the intervals of hours and minutes. When Mr Pearn stopped, our sagging wills we poked and prodded into refusing a lift.

Our first awakening from the blackness of the countryside was just after Birdsmoorgate when a car approached us. As it saw us, it stopped; without a word a man got out, took our photograph and speeded off into the darkness again; The way past the station was made really splendid by the blinding illuminations of the television spotlights. The lights of Harcombe came into view with Mrs Jowett and her retinue standing at the white gates. She hugged the girls. At last we reached the end. "Audacia Constantiaque!"[2]

---

[2] Extract from the School Magazine dated 1963 "A Building of Spirit"

The School on the Hill

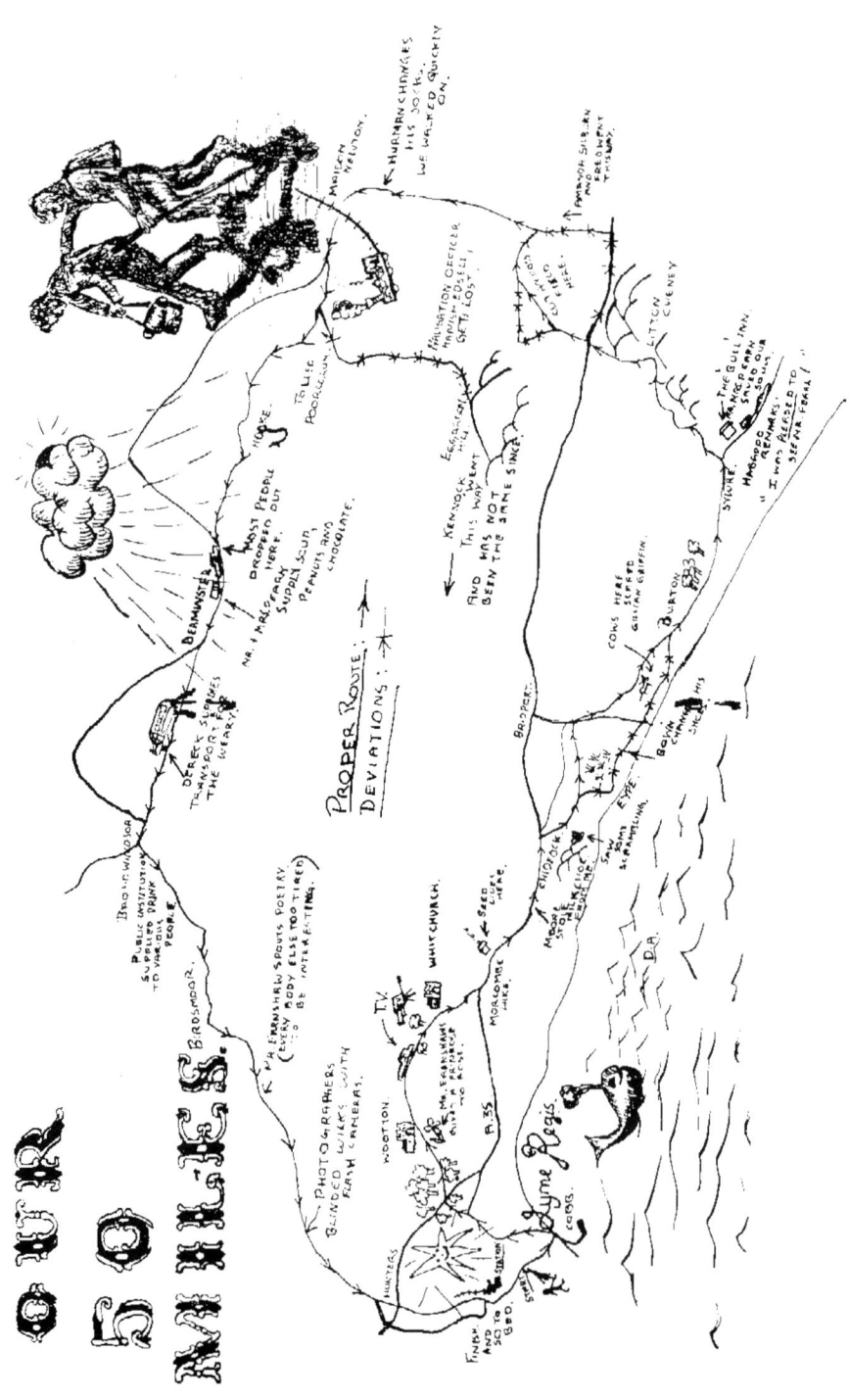

In the school magazine it was noted that the Chemistry Club provided an opportunity for 4th, 5th and 6th formers to perform experiments excluding the practical study of pyrotechnics, ballistics and similar fool-hardy pursuits. In addition their efforts succeeded in proving that the flooring in the new science laboratories rapidly softened to a "gooey mess" when hot and then became inflammable! The Sixth Form biologists contemplated the forthcoming move to their new laboratory with mixed feelings. Although they welcomed the thought of this well-equipped and purpose built facility they lamented the loss of the spectacular views from the window of their former laboratory and the "Heath Robinson" nature of their studies in that classroom.

The school now boasted a total of nineteen societies of which fourteen were for senior pupils. An Operatic Society had been formed, under the leadership of David Coates, and a small band of dedicated members met regularly to perform scenes from "Don Giovanni", "I Pagliacci", "The Tales of Hoffman", "The Mikado", "The Gondoliers", "The Pirates of Penzance", "Bitter Sweet", "Merrie England", etc. The Musical Appreciation Society was entertained by David Coates' choice of Desert Island Discs, Brian Manners gave three piano recitals and a session of "Jukebox Jury" also took place. The knitters amongst this group were still going strong and they swore by Bach, as the regular rhythm of his music seemed to produce three more stitches to the minute than any other composer, whereas Beethoven created unexplainable holes in their handiwork.

A trip to see "Much Ado About Nothing" at Bristol was greatly enlivened by the fact that pupils did not have to wear uniform. The inside of the Theatre Royal greatly impressed the party who thoroughly enjoyed the production, especially Ernestine Jowett who was pleased to discover that Nero was played by her favourite character from the TV series "Compact"! An article in the school magazine on the school's annual cross country event opened with the lines *"There's an old mill by the stream, push him in, hear the scream"* and this tended to sum up the feelings of one or two athletes forced to endure this gruelling event.

The school magazine for 1963 concluded on a sad note with an obituary notice for Major General Sir Bertram Rowcroft, KBE, CBE and also that of his wife, Lady Rowcroft. Sir Bertram had been a Governor and great friend of the school for many years and had died in office as Chairman of Governors. Commander Eyre was appointed as Chairman for the remaining part of the year.

Progress was being made with regard to the building of a swimming pool at the school. The Head estimated the cost of a 25 metre pool would be approximately £4,800. The LEA approved the swimming pool project but were unable to assist with funding until 1965/66. However, the Education Committee agreed to support the application made by the governors for a loan of £2,000. It was expected that the first £2,000 could be raised quite rapidly by voluntary efforts. Two governors, Commander Eyre and Mr Awford kindly agreed to act as guarantors.

The title of the school magazine for this year was "Phoenix '64" which epitomised the rising of the new school from the ashes of the old school. The editorial explained that 1964 had seen the death of two schools – St Michael's Church of England School and Lyme Regis Grammar School – and from their ashes had sprung the new Woodroffe School which offered new possibilities, new problems and a new outlook. With the imminent departure of the builders, the future of the new school was now being contemplated. It was hoped that the best of the traditions of both schools, would all contribute to the success of the new school.

The annual 50 mile walk took place on Saturday 7th March 1964 in bitterly cold weather. The route covered tracks and lanes between Lyme Regis and Taunton. There were forty nine starters, roughly divided between boys and girls, of whom thirty nine completed the course. The youngest competitor was twelve years old. No one gave up under thirty seven miles. The biggest enemy was the cold. Two points were noted – the comradeship amongst all those taking part and an extraordinary good spirit. (*Photo courtesy of David Coates*)

Stephen Evemy, Michael Groves and David Coates stepping out

The Swimming Pool Committee was making good progress. The Head challenged the school on the last day of the Easter Term to see if it could earn some money for the Fund and as a result of this single appeal a cheque for £100 was received. Both the Parents' Association and old pupils worked very hard throughout the summer selling tickets for the Car-for-a-Bob scheme and it was revealed that the Appeals Committee had raised £2,000 towards the cost of the pool, in spite of the fact that no official appeal had yet been issued. A Ball was being planned in the new Hall in November featuring the dance orchestra of the Royal Berkshire Regiment and the Victor Sylvester Orchestra. In the meantime the school fete in July raised £166.

Commander Eyre was elected as Chairman of Governors and Douglas Fortnam as Vice Chairman in May 1964. It was agreed that Mr Davies, Mrs Giles, Mrs Pocock, Mr Way, Mr Wellings and Mr Richards should transfer from the Lyme Regis Senior School in Church Street to the staff of the Woodroffe School with effect from 1st September 1964.

Sadly Ernestine Jowett announced her resignation as housemistress at Harcombe after twelve years in charge. This was accepted with regret by the governors who expressed warm thanks to her for her past services. In the school magazine dated 1964 there was a tribute to Mrs Jowett and reference was made to the fact that she and Mr Jowett had done much to make Harcombe a temporary home for many of the female pupils of the old Grammar School and the present Woodroffe School.

By now the new school buildings, with the exception of the Hall, the Gym and Workshops were in use. It was hoped to use the Workshop after Whitsun and the metalwork shop in early July, with the hall and gym ready for the Autumn Term.

The Debating Society held ten meetings throughout the year and discussed such topics as Corporal Punishment in Schools, Insularity in Politics, Charm versus Talent, Equality among Men and The Superiority of Woman, the last proving to be one of the most amusing debates. An invitation had also been made to two members of staff, Miss Lloyd-Evans and Mr Reeks to speak against each other on the subject of narrow-mindedness which had been particularly entertaining.

| Ann | Sally | Sarah | Catherine | Marilyn | Patsy | Jane | Celia |
| Douglas | Collier | Jackson | Thorrington | Hodder | Scott | Austin | Ridgewell |

First day of term for pupils from St Michael's Junior School, Lyme Regis – 1964
(Photograph courtesy of Keith Wiscombe)

Membership of the Musical Appreciation Society now stood at sixty with the group listening to records varying from Bach sung by "Les Swingle Singers" to Honegger's "Pacific 231". Mr Manners gave further piano recitals and had also given an organ recital. As the school organ was not yet completed, this had been recorded at the Parish Church and replayed to the Society. Further Jukebox Juries took place and the most popular record of the year proved to be Rachmaninoff's "Piano Concerto".

Both Junior and Senior drama pupils entered the Dorset Festival. The Seniors' contribution was based on Puccini's "Turandot", set in old Peking, but the Juniors outshone their elders with David Coates' adaptation of Browning's poem "The Pied Piper", which received a very high score from the judges. However, the Seniors, not to be outdone, were excellent in their production of "None Shall Sleep" at the annual Fete in July, with excellent performances by all those who took part.

The Art Department now had two spacious, well-equipped art and craft rooms and was a hive of activity. George Lloyd-Jones had been joined by Mrs Pocock and Mr Seale. An art exhibition raised £8 in sixpences and attracted no less than 480 visitors. The Art Appreciation Society was proving to be extremely popular with two joint projects completed, both featuring painted friezes. One of these illustrated the infamous cross-country and everyone had been running in the same direction!

Mr Reeks started a Jazz Club. The initial idea created a huge response with nearly all members having one thing in common – they knew nothing about jazz!! Numbers dwindled a bit when it was made clear that the "Stones" were not classified as jazz, but membership settled down to an enthusiastic thirty.

The Cross-Country Club "*not so much a sport, more a way of life*" which described itself as "*the brave, Spartan, long-vested, short-panted souls*" met at the bottom of the drive most Mondays and Thursday to pursue their sport. Not for the faint-hearted, this group of enthusiastic athletes was able to boast a win against Weymouth Harriers in a handicap race and a narrow defeat by Axminster Secondary. A Rugby Society had also been formed and Mr Arrowsmith started a Gym Club. Another new activity was the Woodwork Club supervised by Mr Richards.

The Head reported to governors in September 1964 on the problems which had beset the school at the start of term. Apart from the usual complications of the first few days of a new school year, staff and pupils had been faced with the noise, dirt and distractions of builders actually working both in the corridors and in classrooms, often while lessons were proceeding. The fact that there has been no discipline trouble of any significance and that the teaching programme had not been disrupted, reflected considerable credit on the staff and pupils. It was hoped that work on the original building would be completed by January, with the grounds cleared and prepared for use by March 1965. Gratitude was also expressed to the catering staff for operating the new canteen and dining arrangements so efficiently. A check by the Head had revealed that meals were being served at the rate of seventy five a minute!

In February 1965 it was announced that both Mr G A Taylor (31 years service) and Miss Slaney (37 years service) would retire in August. Both members of staff were thanked by the governors for their many years of loyal service.

An electronic organ which had been slowly built over the last three years by staff and pupils was now complete and in use daily. Work was to begin shortly on a second manual which would greatly enhance its performance. The long building period had been due to the fact that in order to make the organ fully polyphonic new techniques had to be employed, which meant that the organ was a prototype.

In February 1965 a contract was signed with the Blue Lagoon Swimming Bath Construction Company for the provision of the swimming pool. By now the tennis courts were complete. The school was also a lot cleaner thanks to the efforts of the caretakers and cleaners.

The annual 50 mile walk this year followed a route between Lyme Regis and Ottery St Mary. The majority of walkers finished the course and the weather was a lot better than in previous years. The first boy home averaged nearly five and a half miles per hour and the first girl five miles per hour. Thanks were expressed to governors, parents and friends of the school who had covered parts of the route to help the stragglers or to deliver food and drink to scattered groups.

Senior Speech Day was held in April 1965 and for the first time it was decided that Junior Speech day would be held at the end of the summer term, to co-incide with the School Fete and Open Day in July.

Col Charrington (President of the Lyme Regis Water Polo Club) enquired if the club might use the new swimming pool one night a week and it was agreed that the facility should be made available to them. The pool was officially opened in June by the Mayor, and Mr W E Taylor donated two garden seats for the verge by the swimming pool.

By the Summer Term, the greenhouse had been erected, a lot of work had been carried out in the grounds and the road at the northeast end of the school had been completed to provide access to the hutted classrooms. A performance of "The Magic Flute" took place and the Madrigal Group won the Weymouth Festival Madrigal Cup for the third year in succession. The comment of the adjudicator (a Professor at the Royal College of Music) was that the Choir's singing was "the finest performance of a madrigal I have ever had the pleasure of hearing".

The governors indicated in January 1967 that they would like closer liaison with members of staff and to this end it was suggested that staff might like to join them for tea after the next governors' meeting. A new form of report was produced in September whereby parents were asked to add their comments to those of staff. This proved to be valuable, as a number of parents took advantage of the opportunity to make constructive and useful comments.

During 1967 the new Lifeboat Station was opened in Lyme Regis by the Mayor, Councillor Eric Price. The dedication was performed by the local vicar, Rev Hugo Charles, and pupils from Woodroffe under the direction of Brian Manners led the singing of hymns.

In October the school was informed that provision had been made in the draft 1968/1969 capital estimates for a unit of accommodation for ninety pupils, in relation to the raising of the school leaving age. This proposal was welcomed but there were concerns at the lack of appropriate accommodation for the existing Sixth Form and the LEA was pressed to provide additional facilities as a matter of urgency.

A review of prizes awarded at Speech Day was carried out and it was decided to make a few changes. It was agreed that prizes would be divided into three groups – those awarded by subject or form for academic excellence, a "credit" prize whereby a child working to a standard above his/her normal standard achieves a credit and then gains a prize for twenty credits, which meant that the child was working in competition with him/herself, and finally a group prize, chosen by a vote of staff, to decide which form had been the most energetic and generally co-operative through the year. For the latter the whole form would be given a full day's outing paid for from the prize fund. Initiative prizes were also considered by staff for individuals who had clearly done something on their own initiative, completely away from normal school activities and work.

In February 1968 the governors became concerned at the proposed deferment of the raising of the school leaving age. When the school became a comprehensive in 1964 it had encouraged pupils to stay on beyond the minimum leaving age. The national average for remaining at school was about 42% but at Woodroffe from 1965 to 1968 this had risen from 65% to 80%+. A school of the size of Woodroffe would normally expect a Sixth Form of forty eight to fifty five but the Sixth Form now numbered 102. On the assumption that the overall national decision to defer the leaving of the school age was irrevocable, a request was made to the LEA for temporary accommodation to be provided. It was pointed out that the school could find time, manufacture equipment and produce its own texts but it could not build accommodation! In the meantime, a re-distribution of accommodation within the school was carried out in an effort to ease the situation until something more permanent could be organised.

The sponsored walk, held in May 1968, raised a little over £400, and the 50 – 50 sale sold goods to the value of £500, with half of this sum going to school funds. The cost of the pool was therefore cleared by the end of the Summer Term. The governors expressed gratitude and admiration at the amount of work carried out by parents, old pupils and staff in clearing a debt of almost £6,000 in less than four years.

In October 1968 the Head and representatives from the LEA examined the need for additional accommodation in the light of the decision to allow all 11+ transfers in the Uplyme area to come to Woodroffe in September 1969. Consideration was being given to the introduction of correspondence courses for the academic year 1970/1971 as it was felt that such courses could offer pupils a wide range of opportunities. Joan Green and Dr Goldsmith were preparing a scheme to meet the needs of pupils in terms of sex instruction and it was agreed that parents should be briefed before this was delivered to their children.

Governors were also considering the problem of pupil unrest but felt that this problem was unlikely to rear its ugly head at Woodroffe. The Head explained that there were regular meetings between Form Masters/Mistresses and their forms and that he met prefects on a regular basis. There were also set times when any child in the school could discuss anything privately with the Head or Deputy Head. In addition there was a school committee which considered problems and all pupils were encouraged to discuss difficulties or make suggestions as freely as possible. In short, children were encouraged to revolt but in a constructive and co-operative manner!

It was confirmed in February 1969 that the space under the hall was to be converted for use as additional teaching units. Concern was being expressed at the dangerous situation at the school exits both for traffic using the main road and for pupils crossing the road. It was felt that a crossing patrol might ease the latter.

In March 1969 Mrs E Duncan donated the sum of £8,000 to the school for the establishment of a Welfare Fund. The gift was approved by the Charity Commissions and the income was therefore tax free. The Trustees were Mrs Duncan or a family nominee, the Chairman of Governors and the Head with the latter acting as secretary of the Trust which was to be known as the Hope Wright Fund. This Trust is still in existence and many pupils have benefited over the years from the generosity of Mrs Duncan.

Sports Days were greatly enjoyed with fierce competition between not only the pupils, but staff versus pupils and even staff versus staff. The first picture shows the Head of English (David Coates) beating the Head of PE (John Hobson) in the annual staff race. On another occasion both were beaten by Doc Goldsmith, a well-loved member of the teaching staff who was over eighty years. Admittedly he had been given a head start of some 80 yards, one for each year of his age!

The second picture features the winning staff relay team who won the 4 x 100 metres in 49 seconds. Members of the winning team were David Coates, Richard Brooks, Ian Franks and Paul, a pupil PE teacher. *(Photographs courtesy of David Coates)*

By now the LEA was considering the possible purchase of Rhode Hill for additional boarding accommodation and it was decided to go ahead with the appointment of a House Master-designate so no time would be lost if the negotiations for the purchase were satisfactorily completed. The purchase was completed in June and arrangements were made for the new boarding house to open in September 1969. It was agreed that St Andrews would provide accommodation for senior boys with Mr and Mrs Pearn in charge, Mr and Mrs Roy Deasey would run Rhode Hill as an all girl boarding house and Harcombe would accommodate junior boys who would be looked after by Mr and Mrs David Badman.

At school new methods of teaching continued to be developed. It was hoped to create a Resources Centre in September and the SRA Reading Laboratory was proving highly successful throughout the whole ability range. In addition Ron Price, in conjunction with the University of Exeter, was planning a new method of teaching junior Geography.

The School on the Hill

By September 1969 the new boarding house was in full operation and the two new rooms under the hall were completed and in use. Numbers in school had increased to over 600 for the first time and this led to a review of the house system. With the influx of boarders it was apparent School House would be overwhelmingly the most powerful house and genuine competition would be lacking. After full discussion it was decided to form three new houses which would include a mixture of day and boarding pupils. These were named as Blake, Lister and Somers, all of whom had direct connections with Lyme Regis.

The school magazine for 1969 had a completely new look, and a new name, "Lyme Juice". It was published in November 1969, sold for 13p per copy and advertisements were included. The magazine took on a completely different flavour. There was no editorial and no information about staff changes, etc. The content of the magazine did, however, reflect what was going on in the school. For the first time the school entered two girls teams and two boys teams in Ten Tors.

The sixties were without doubt an important decade for the school and a great deal was achieved. The numbers on roll doubled from just over 300 to 600 and consequently the number of staff increased substantially. The major building programme although disruptive, provided the school with much needed accommodation and excellent new facilities. The school lost its grammar school status, becoming a mixed comprehensive, and with this change came a new name. Due to the huge effort of parents, staff, pupils and ex-pupils a huge amount of money was raised to build the swimming pool. Sadly Mr Woodroffe, the founder of the school, died and many long-time members of the teaching staff retired, making way for younger staff to take their place. Boarding was flourishing and with the opening of a third boarding house at Rhode Hill its future seemed assured. On all fronts the school was doing well and it faced the next decade with optimism.

Sketch by George Lloyd-Jones featured in the school magazines of 1961 & 1964

CHAPTER 8 – 1970 TO 1979: THE SEVENTIES

1970 began with a parents meeting in January when the various new methods of teaching were explained. In school attention was focussed on methods used for assessing and recording pupil progress and a sub-committee of staff under the chairmanship of Mr Davies came up with a system of assessment involving a new record card.

The Governing Body was concerned at the ramifications of proposed changes to the examination structure. The initial aim had been to produce a more balanced curriculum and to improve the quality of sixth form work through a broader range of study and yet the proposed structure suggested that choices would be constrained and subject areas for study carefully prescribed. Governors felt that this approach would reduce the scope for individuality and have an adverse effect on the growth and development of secondary education.

Road safety outside the school was continuing to be a problem. At this time a builders' yard (Bradfords) was established across the road from the school and the increased traffic, particularly large lorries loading and unloading, was creating an additional traffic hazard. To alleviate the situation it was agreed that, subject to agreement with British Rail, school buses and parents should park in the station yard. Investigations were also taking place as to the possibility of providing a protected lay-by at the bottom of the main drive which would also be widened so that it could be incorporated into the lay-by. The need to resolve this problem was clearly demonstrated when a motorist was killed in a road accident at the entrance to the school drive.

When considering the salary levels for staff employed at the three boarding houses the governors received from the Head a report outlining the main problems for the Housemaster and Housemistress which could be roughly summarised as follows:

Small boys – dirty, naughty and destructive
Middle boys – the same, but more so!
Senior boys – career problems, occasional but sometimes serious wildness, motor vehicles and a casual approach to life
Girls – tantrums, emotional upheaval, physical problems, the permanent time bomb of possible pregnancy. Not an enviable job for anyone!

September saw modifications underway at St Andrews and Rhode Hill. Complications had arisen at the latter which led to seven girls being accommodated temporarily at Marven House, a guest house in Uplyme. As soon as the work at St Andrews was completed these girls were moved into the top wing of the house under the care of Matron, returning to Rhode Hill by half term.

Joan Green, assisted by two lady governors, was given the unenviable task of deciding whether girls should be allowed to wear trousers. After a great deal of discussion no decision was made and the matter was left in abeyance.

The School on the Hill

A Remembrance Service was held at the school on the evening of 11th November 1970 and a very successful Opera "Amahl and the Night Visitors", preceded by a mystery play performed by Juniors, was presented on 10th, 11th and 12th December 1970. The school under fifteen XI won the Dorset Schools Football Championship for the second year in succession and were to represent Dorset in the All-England competition. The Madrigal Group was invited to sing at the Anglo-German Festival to be held at the Fairfield Halls, Croydon and a party of sixth form pupils undertook responsibility for the Christmas decorations at the Lyme Regis Hospital.

In February 1971 changes were made to the prefect system, which had operated for over twenty years. Although this was efficient and successful, because of the growth of the sixth form, there were some deserving individuals who did not have the opportunity to take part. Following discussions with the sixth form a new system was devised, to run for an experimental period. This involved every member of the Sixth Form and therefore the number of duties per prefect was considerably reduced.

It was announced that work on the ROSLA block would be completed by 28th July. This long awaited accommodation would provide a Sixth Form Common Room, History Room and Technical Drawing Room. In addition the third room on the top floor would become a specialist room for Religious Instruction. Prior to the opening of the new ROSLA block, which eventually came into use in October, a sub committee was set up to consider the curriculum for the pupils who would shortly be staying on for a further year.

With the number of pupils on roll now standing at 650, the Head was becoming increasingly concerned at the problem of keeping in touch personally with all children. The wide range of options in the school meant that there would be some pupils in almost every form who were never taught by their own form master/mistress and thus they might well find that they had no-one to whom they could turn in case of difficulty. It was therefore hoped to introduce a tutor system.

In September 1971 a presentation was made to Major Pearn in appreciation of twenty five years' service as Head of the school. Mr and Mrs Roy Deasey left Rhode Hill and were replaced by Mr and Mrs Rod Boyce.

Largely due to the efforts of Roger Draper in particular, a new timetable was designed specifically to integrate into the main school programme pupils who were staying on due to the raising of the school leaving age. It was anticipated that this would also increase the amount of choice available and would cut down on movement around the school. The new timetable was brought into use for the last two weeks of the summer term to allow for teething problems to be ironed out. The formal timetable for the academic year 1972/1973 was written during the summer holidays. Several refinements were made to the new tutorial system which had also helped to solve the problem of integration of "ROSLA" pupils.

It was about this time that Mick Mawer and his wife, Annie, joined the teaching staff. Mick recalls "*I think both Annie and I can safely say that our few years at Woodroffe, between 1971 and 1974, were the happiest of our lives in teaching. I took on a one year contract (always a risk) in my second year of teaching but the previous occupant didn't return after his course so the Head offered me the post of Head of Department. I arrived at Woodroffe with lots of "big ideas" and a clear philosophy of what I wanted a PE Department to achieve. Primarily my aim was to offer every child, regardless of ability, the opportunity to experience and learn an active leisure pursuit to take into life after school. I was also keen to provide pupils with a particular aptitude towards any sport, the opportunity to develop their skills and enjoy a higher level of competition…. Participation in the Duke of Edinburgh Award Scheme was introduced to encourage those who were less team sports inclined to develop a healthy outdoor leisure pursuit and practice expeditions were conducted in West Dorset, Abbotsbury, Portland, Durdle Door, Dartmoor, etc. at weekends. It was a great time and I have fond memories of staff and pupils at the school. The whole experience at Woodroffe moulded my career, helped develop my teaching philosophy and influenced what I did in teacher training for the twenty eight years following Woodroffe (at Trent Poly and Hull University)".*

In October 1972 the Head resigned from his post as Housemaster at St Andrews and shortly afterwards Fred Middleton was appointed to replace him. In December, due to a shortage of cleaners Sixth Formers were employed to clean the school on a temporary basis. It was also decided that female pupils could wear trousers of a standard pattern and colour in the winter term as an alternative to navy blue skirts and that the present policy of making school summer dresses optional would remain.

Plans were made for a formal dinner to mark the 50th anniversary of the founding of the school. By this time two of the three classrooms promised had been erected but not finished and the matter of accommodation was again becoming pressing.

In October 1973 the Head was turning his attention to the strengths and weaknesses of careers education at Woodroffe. He was concerned at the lack of provision at the school which was largely due to staffing and accommodation shortages. He pointed out that as the local area suffered from a lack of opportunity, both occupationally and geographically, it was imperative for the school to be proactive in terms of careers as part of its responsibility for the individual welfare of every pupil in its care. This is still the case today, of course.

With regard to the timetable it was clear that more accommodation, especially specialist accommodation, was urgently required. As this provision was unlikely to come from the LEA, which was facing proposed cuts of £70 million in school buildings, the only solution was to "make" additional accommodation by "organisational" means. To this end a timetable was designed to ease the situation. The aim was to combine the maximum opportunity for flexible expansion with the minimum of expenditure.

Concern remained for the safety of children entering the site from the main road on foot and the school was relieved that the LEA's minor works programme for 1973/1974 indicated provision for a bus lay-by with work to commence in the Spring Term 1974. Several changes were proposed to the curriculum in October including the introduction of a Child Development course for fourth and sixth formers. The Head also suggested the introduction of a course on thinking which was now being recognised as a subject in its own right.

In November 1974 it was reported that entrants to university from the school in September had been 8.1% of the age group, considerably exceeding the national average of 5.9%.

Road safety was a continuing headache. The new coach lay-by had been constructed and was being used, but parents were now parking on the opposite side of the road on a fast bend and this was proving hazardous. Yellow lines in this area were therefore called for as a matter of urgency.

The question of the validity of physical punishment was raised by governors. The Head explained that a punishment book was kept but that physical punishment by caning was extremely rare and did not amount to more than one or two occasions in a year. In addition to the Head, Mr Lloyd-Jones had delegated responsibility to administer the cane.

The last weeks of the summer term in 1975 were a hive of activity with pupils under the leadership of David Badman converting the two rather dank rooms under the hall into one and a team of boys under George Lloyd-Jones converting the unnecessarily large boys' cloakroom behind the school hall into two changing rooms for swimmers. This work was completed by old pupils and parents in the summer holidays. Members of the English Department, under David Coates, redecorated three classrooms, staying behind during the holidays to complete the work, and a group of pupils altered two store rooms to form an office for Ernest Wellings and an interview room for the use of visitors. Thanks were expressed to Ewart Watts, the Caretaker, for his patience and very hard work. As a skilled craftsman he was invariably available for advice and during the holidays he had brought the school up to a high standard of cleanliness.

In September Commander Eyre resigned as Chairman of Governors. The school was tremendously indebted to him for his enormous help and support and his unfailing interest in both staff and pupils. He had been a tower of strength in any crisis and had always been keenly interested in the running of the school and the welfare of everyone connected with it.

A team of HMIs visited the school in December 1975 to observe the teaching of Languages, Maths and Science for 4th and 5th year pupils. The team also looked at the general welfare services provided by the school across all age groups and in the report they submitted after their visit they praised the amount of care given to less able children and the work they achieved.

At Easter Mr Pearn retired after thirty years as Head. His period of outstanding service to the school was marked by a series of events and presentations. Mr David Butterworth was appointed to succeed Mr Pearn and in May 1976 he attended his first meeting of the Governing Body. To co-incide with the arrival of the new Head, July saw the launch of a regular newsletter to parents, edited by Mr Pengelly, which was introduced as a means of communication between the school, parents, governors, feeder schools, the local authority, etc. On a fashion note, this was the seventies after all, parents were urged to discourage their children from wearing platform shoes which were both dangerous on stairs and slopes and caused posture difficulties and backache.

The School on the Hill

The school moved from a seven period day to an eight period day to accommodate all the necessary subjects in the lower school and to create more contact periods in the upper school. Lessons were therefore reduced to thirty five minutes with a morning and an afternoon break. School began at 8.50 am with the admittance bell and lunch was taken at 12.00 pm until 1.15 pm.

Rod Boyce was appointed as Director of Sixth Form and a Sixth Form induction course was introduced by the Head, led by Mr Middleton. This included a series of visits to Exeter University, South Dorset Technical College, Bridport Gundry, Herrison Hospital, Dorchester Hospital and the Cheshire Home in Lyme Regis. Guest Speakers were also invited into school to address pupils on the need for personal commitment in every aspect of living.

GCE examinations in Woodwork and Metalwork were now no longer available with both subjects amalgamated into Design and Technology. Science was taught as three separate subjects ie Biology, Chemistry and Physics.

Extra-curricular activities included a Stamp Club, Chess Club, Bridge Club, Dramatic Society, Boys' Tennis Club, Fossils Club and a Girls' Junior Madrigal Choir, who had won the Chichester Shield at the Devon and Exeter Festival of Music for the second year in succession. The School Sailing Club was able to function thanks to the generosity of the Adventure Centre. The school repaid the favour by assisting the Centre with its annual boat maintenance. In between painting and varnishing sessions, pupils also learned about coastal navigation and general seamanship.

Ron Rice organised a TV Club, which met at lunchtime, to view programmes previously recorded. Mr Rice also ran the Pets Club which started in 1970 and was very popular with pupils. Due to the increased cost of food prices the normal breeding programme was curtailed to keep down the number of animals – it is unclear how this was achieved!

(*Ron Rice with members of the Pets Club*)

Richard Bland was running a Fencing Club and with his wife was organising training for the Duke of Edinburgh's Award Group. Michael Newman was the first member of this particular group to achieve a Gold Award, which he was to receive at Buckingham Palace, and at the Mayor's Presentation in February two Silver Awards and nine Bronze Awards were presented.

The PE Department had a very busy year with Wendy Van Der Plank selected as a member of the County Under 13 Gymnastics Squad; the first year girls' swimming relay team beating the rest of the schools in South and West Dorset in the relay event; Mark

The School on the Hill

Perry selected to play for the Dorset and Wilts XV; the U16 Boys Basketball team winning the West Dorset and South Dorset Basketball League; Dominic Burkhalter and Nigel Knight playing for the South West England team and Peter Jones the first Dorset boy home in the Intermediate Age Group at the National Cross-Country Championships.

The Orchestra now had forty two members and gave its first concert at the local Parish Church which raised funds for the Princess Elizabeth Orthopaedic Hospital in Exeter. The purchase of instruments was always a problem but the orchestra now owned three cellos and a double bass and was saving to buy a French Horn and a Bassoon.

In October 1976 a report appeared in the local paper advising that staff in the Modern Languages Department had assisted Lyme Regis Town Council with checking and re-writing translations for their overseas publicity brochure. Translations commissioned by the Council had proved unacceptable and so the staff had been asked to help out, producing text in French, German and Dutch.

George Lloyd-Jones included in the parents newsletter a puzzler for pupils as follows:

"Woodroffe Wonders No. 1 – at the bottom of the school drive, by the gateway, can be seen a concrete slab, with odd bolts sticking out. Before its reason for existence fades from human memory, let me record it for you, and for posterity. Before the school's water supply came from its present source at Pinhay, there was insufficient pressure to supply the tanks which were then in use. The concrete slab was the site of the wooden hut which housed a hand pump (fitted to the bolts which you see sticking up).

Everyday the caretaker walked down to the hut and pumped up, by hand lever, enough water for the day's needs…. This was a tremendous labour, which went on for years and the caretaker was overjoyed when the new supply was introduced. The old pump was taken out and slumbered for years in the boiler house: in those days, too, the boilers were coal fired, and after hours of pumping the caretaker shovelled coal for most of the rest of the day. The pump was made of thick brass and parts of it ended up in the Art Department built into two home-made potter's wheels."[1]

Mr Lloyd-Jones concluded his puzzler by asking pupils to see if they could find the gauge, "in plain view", that told the caretaker how much water was in the tank so that he knew when to pump.

In early 1977 consideration was given to the introduction of a new style summer dress for the girls' summer uniform to replace that with blue and white stripes worn for many years. However the Governing Body felt that the cost to parents could not be justified in the current economic climate and it was decided that the summer uniform, which had always been optional, would remain unchanged for the time being.

The school was sad to hear of the death of ex-pupil Lt William James Turner of the Royal Marines who had died during a submarine diving exercise in Loch Long on 15th January

---

[1] Extract from the Newsletter dated December 1976

1977, leaving a widow and baby son. Jim joined Woodroffe in 1964 as a boarder at St Andrews and a sixth form pupil. He had captained the first XV, achieved the Duke of Edinburgh Gold Award and left school with A levels and a Royal Marine Scholarship.

The Parents Association announced an interesting programme of speakers including Mr Bill Foy on alcoholism; Lawrence Whistler who showed an enthralling collection of slides on glass engraving; Bill Hoskyns, the fencer, who represented the UK in three Olympics and won a silver medal; Sergeant Day spoke about police work in relation to young people and Freddie French entertained parents with his experiences as a famous London hairdresser.

In March 1977 there was a new development in the close working relationship between the school and the Governing Body, which involved a series of informal "teach-ins" for the mutual enrichment of both parties. The budget remained tight but every economy was being made with £200/£300 saved on exercise books and an amnesty for the return of missing library books.

Tributes were paid to Ernest Wellings who retired at Easter. He was the first member of staff to transfer in 1963 to prepare the way for the amalgamation of Lyme Regis Senior School with the LRGS and from that time onwards he was in charge of the Remedial Department at Woodroffe. He became Head of the Lower School on the retirement of Mr Davies in 1973. Mr Wellings contributed widely to the work of the school but his particular interest was Music and he trained the Junior Girls Madrigal Choir. A dinner for some eighty members of staff and their wives was given in honour of Mr Wellings during which he received farewell gifts from staff and pupils.

On the retirement of Mr Wellings it was announced Joan Bareham would take over temporarily as the Head of the Lower School until December 1977 when she would assume responsibility as Head of Middle School (Years 4 and 5), with David Badman taking over as Head of Lower School.

For the first time girls took part in the annual cross country event. The boys were busy playing rugby, football and basketball, with the girls activities centred around gymnastics. A party of forty five girls travelled to Wembley to watch the annual international hockey match between England and New Zealand. The trip was now established as a tradition and this year, for the third year running, the long journey to London had been livened up with a request played on the Ed Stewart radio programme.

In the parents' newsletter the importance of school uniform was highlighted and it was pointed out that whenever pupils were out of school on trips and visits they were complimented on their appearance, manners and behaviour. There was a strong tradition of uniform at Woodroffe and it was emphasized that uniform brought a sense of unity, and a sense of belonging to a community with a common purpose. It also set a standard and it removed invidious competition in terms of dress and took the pressure off parents to provide the ever-changing latest fashions.

George Lloyd-Jones issued "Woodroffe Wonders No.2" as follows:

"At the back of the old school building, between the needlework room and the staff marking room, you will see high up on the wall a large white triangle surrounded by a black line…...Years go, before any of the new parts of the school were built, we had our dinner in the old hall, which is now divided into the Library and room 8. The food was served from hatches in the corridor almost opposite room 10 and pushed on trolleys to the hall…..As you will have guessed by now, the kitchen was outside the corridor (before the girl's cloakrooms were built) and the white triangle is what remains of the white paint of the inside end wall of the kitchen. The black line is where the roof touched this wall and was sealed by pitch ".[2] For his next teaser Mr Lloyd-Jones asked pupils to seek out the name of the original builder of the school which was clearly engraved somewhere for all to see.

Rod Boyce, the Director of Sixth Form, introduced "talking newspapers" to the local area. Under this scheme Sixth Formers made recordings of items printed in the Lyme Regis News. The local branch of the Round Table provided four cassette recorders and the tapes were distributed to ten blind people in the community once a fortnight to enable them to keep up with local news.

Sixth Form students in the late 1970s (Photograph from School Archive)

In July 1977 over 600 pupils tackled a seventeen mile sponsored walk to Seatown and back to raise funds for books and equipment. It was announced that in an effort to absorb its financial cutback, Dorset LEA was increasing the distances between school and home at which children qualified for free transport. Luckily, because of the school's

---

[2] Extract from the School Newsletter dated March 1977.

large catchment area not many families were affected. The cost of a school meal was now 25p.

It was suggested in the local press that young people at Woodroffe might benefit from membership of the Tufty Club as the majority, both seniors and juniors, had no idea of road safety! This suggestion met with a cool response from pupils but there remained grave concerns about their safety on the walk to school, particularly along the road from Uplyme, and the danger they posed to drivers and vice versa.

Unrestricted use of calculators was now allowed in GCE, O and A level exams but they were not allowed in CSE exams. 1st and 2nd formers were only able to use calculators in class for checking answers but with the permission of staff, and calculators were not allowed in school exams.

A new course entitled "Origins" was to be introduced for 1st Formers in September 1977. This consisted mainly of material previously taught under the headings of History, Classics and RE. In September 1977 it was also planned to introduce a new Geology course for Sixth Formers to provide an additional O level qualification.

The Queen's Silver Jubilee provided the opportunity for an exhibition built around two themes – the history of the Royal Family and events of the previous twenty five years. A Silver Jubilee Concert was held at the end of May. The Junior Girls Madrigal Group, taken over by Brian Manners following the retirement of Ernest Wellings, took part and the Wind Band had its first public performance only six weeks after being officially formed. The finale, performed by the combined choirs and orchestra, was "Zadok the Priest" – one of four Coronation anthems by Handel, composed for the coronation of George II in 1727 and performed at every coronation since. The school performance was overwhelming and received a well-earned encore.

Bird watching was a new interest that was emerging in the junior half of the school. The Chess Club was proving so successful that an appeal was made for more chess sets. Inter-house games were played, individual tournaments also took place and there were 6th and 5th form knock-out competitions.

It was announced that from September each pupil would be issued with a Homework Diary, funded by the Parents Association, in which they could record the homework set for each subject each day across the whole academic year. There would be provision for parents to sign the diary at the end of each week with tutors checking that diaries had been signed and noting any comments made by parents. It was intended that the homework diary would become an informal link between home and school. There would also be a section for parents to acknowledge that they had received information sent home by school. This form of communication between home and school is still proving very effective today.

In his Wonders No.3 George Lloyd-Jones explained how, many years ago, a group of mischief makers had let the heavy cricket pitch roller run down from the top bank, narrowly missing fellow pupils on its swift journey to the garden of the end cottage below the drive. Everyone concerned had been badly shaken by this near tragedy, particularly as a baby had been asleep in its pram not two yards from where the roller had landed. Needless to say, the roller was never left unattended again. Mr Lloyd-Jones then went on to reveal the answers to his two previous puzzles. The water tank gauge was located halfway up the stairs from the bottom corridor to the cookery room – it was a weight on a wire emerging from the ceiling which went up an down as the water level in the tank rose and fell. The builder's name was Hallett and it was carved on a block on the bungalow side of the corner by the boys' bicycle shed. Mr Lloyd-Jones set a further puzzle, explaining that the old school was built in a Tudor style and therefore the Tudor rose was much in evidence. Pupils were asked to try and spot them all – there were sixteen altogether.

By now girls were taking part in the South West Dorset Cross Country League. Walter Poole had been assisting with training the senior hockey players and at netball, all the school teams had competed in the SW Dorset Tournament.

A group of pupils visited the Northcott Theatre to see a performance by the Ballet Rambert, which had been specially prepared for schoolgirls. This included an explanation of the history of dance and how modern dance has developed which was of particular interest to the girls who were were looking forward to beginning their dance course at school after Christmas.

On 12th July 1978 the annual school sponsored walk took place. The weather almost led to the cancellation of this important event in the school's calendar but it went ahead and generated the sum of £1,500. The Table Tennis Club, organised by Dennis Applebee and Cyril Keattch, reported a membership of over forty, both boys and girls. Three tables were available and all were in constant use when the Club met every Monday and Wednesday after school. It was reported that a Table Tennis League had recently been started in the town and the school would be entering two teams.

George Lloyd-Jones' Woodroffe Wonders No.4 explained the history of the school, back as far as the 1920's. The puzzle he set this time was to identify an iron staircase in the old school which was in daily use. The answer to the query re Tudor roses was to look at the "rainheads" at the top of the rainwater pipes on the old school buildings.

The acoustic board in the ceiling of the school hall collapsed while workmen were re-painting it in January 1978. Temporary repairs were made pending a long term solution involving roof insulation and new acoustic system which was to be tackled during the first phase of the school's £460,000 redevelopment plan due to commence in 1979.

In March 1978 the Head referred to recent snowfalls and advised that the English Department was encouraging pupils to record their memories of the "Snow of '78" before memories fade. Reference was made to the fact that two of the boarding houses were cut off except by phone. Boarders were rescued by Land Rover from Axminster and St Andrews had temporarily housed both girls and boys. A hectic time was had by all at school and at the boarding house and the Head thanked staff, parents and helpers for their efforts in helping the school through this difficult time.

The activities of the PE Department were restricted by the bad weather – heavy rain and then heavy snow. However in January the school staged the West Dorset Schools Cross-Country and individually pupils achieved some outstanding results. The school's own cross country went ahead despite the cold weather and once again girls participated and did very well. A party of senior boys attended the England v Wales rugby match at Twickenham and a girls hockey team from Canada visited the school for lunch and then played a match against a school team in the afternoon. The U12 Netball Team had a successful year, winning all their matches, and were now South West Dorset Champions.

The Debating Society set up a "Brain of Woodroffe" competition loosely based on "Mastermind". There were five games leading up to the final which generated a lot of work for the organisers in terms of setting questions. The final was tense and exciting and was eventually won by Justin Cozens.

In July 1978 the Head reported that the Academic Board had completed a review of the entire curriculum and by November all Departments would have updated their schemes of work. Financial juggling had taken place to ensure an injection of capital into areas of growth and change. A record number of fifty eight teachers would be in post by September which should lead to smaller teaching groups.

The Chairman of Governors, Douglas Fortnam, outlined the recent workload of the Governing Body which had included lobbying the LEA re boarding finances, examining and discussing with the architects the plans for the new building scheme, investigating complaints and reviewing the records of pupils whose conduct was deemed to be unsatisfactory. They also noted and commended outstanding success or contributions to the life of the school and three governors attached to each of the boarding houses had continued to visit them regularly and informally. Quite a workload for a voluntary body!

Warm tributes were paid to George Lloyd-Jones who was retiring after twenty seven years at the school. Mr Lloyd-Jones' five sons had been born in Lyme and had all attended the school. When Mr Lloyd-Jones joined the school in 1951, Art and Music shared the same room. In 1953 his work was highly commended by the inspection team who had visited the school. A gardening accident had cost him the sight of one eye but diminished in no way his zest for his subject or his sense of humour and many pupils will remember being inspired by his talks on art appreciation.

The traditional "turn" at the senior pupils Dinner/Dance began almost by accident, firstly with Reg Pocock then with Brian Manners. All ex-Woodroffe pupils will remember the familiar strains of "Much Binding in the Marsh". Mr Lloyd-Jones was succeeded as Senior Master by Ian Cook. Mr Cook began his teaching career in Sheffield before taking up the post of Head of English at Blandford Upper School. In 1973/1974 he took part in a year's exchange scheme with Redwood High School in California.

A major part of the Autumn Term in 1978 was spent in preparing for the première of Ann Jellicoe's community play "The Reckoning" which was staged at the school. It was also announced that, at the start of the Summer Term the following year, the builders would move in to begin the re-building, re-wiring and re-decoration contract due for completion by the summer of 1981 at an estimated cost of £600,000.

The School on the Hill

The weather dominated most of the Spring Term in 1979 with an unexpected heavy snow fall leading to staff frantically packing pupils on to an "emergency run" bus which took one and a half hours to get through to Charmouth. Boilers were out of action, pipes froze leading to flooding and in some cases pupils sat examinations in coats and gloves to beat the cold. The Head felt that the adverse weather conditions and the problems they had caused had robbed the school of its momentum in the first half of the term but staff and pupils pulled together and as the end of term approached all activities were back on track.

Although two other major re-building programmes in the County had been stopped at the tendering stage due to economic uncertainty, the building programme at Woodroffe was set to commence in April as planned. However, staffing improvements had been frozen and the capitation allowance (used to purchase books and equipment) represented a reduction in actual purchasing power. To combat these financial constraints the school intended to organise a sponsored walk after the summer exams to supplement funds.

In February 1979 the local press reported that parents, staff and managers at Uplyme School had left Devon County Council in no doubt that they preferred their children to receive a secondary education at Woodroffe and not be transported to a revamped school in Axminster. It was stressed that Uplyme and Lyme Regis were very much united as a community irrespective of the county boundary.

The History Club was busy with a party of pupils visiting Thorncombe Church and bringing back with them some good quality brass rubbings of the Brook Tomb. A display had also been prepared in connection with "The Reckoning" with pictures and posters providing background information on James, Duke of Monmouth, and the rebellion which formed the central event of the play. War games had also been fought regularly featuring the model fleets and armies of David Wickens and Roger Draper. Pupils had been able to witness titanic struggles between Roman Legionaries and Greek Hoplites, French Knights and English Yeomen, Russian T34s and German Panzers. Ron Rice had contributed by tracing the moves in the Atlantic in the hunting of the Bismarck, enlivening the story with some personal reminiscences.

After the success of their Brain of Woodroffe competition, the Senior Debating Society organised a mock election which attracted five candidates and 430 voters. Geoffrey Evemy representing the Uplyme People's Popular Front gained forty seven votes, Becky Parker (the only female candidate) took seventy votes for the Suffragettes but the elected winner was Winchester Cathedral, a sunflower which took 253 votes and relied for its campaign on absurdity, frivolity and pure charm. Pat Baker and Chris Mead represented respectively the Preservationist Party and the Lawnmower's Freedom Fighters. Campaigners took advantage of the fine weather and made speeches both indoors and out, and were pelted with rotten fruit on most occasions. They chained themselves to railings with bicycle locks and forgot combinations, made about 1,000 badges, drew posters and twice resorted to kidnapping Winchester Cathedral!

Concern was expressed about the safety of those walking to school due to the construction of a new footpath opposite the Black Dog Hotel. While building work was in progress pupils were asked to use only the hotel side of the road when walking to school.

It was also reported that the Governing Body had received details of a £17,000 scheme for Dorset County Council to complete a new footpath through to an extended bus bay.

In May 1979 school life was disrupted by industrial action by teaching staff. This was described by unions as a "withdrawal of goodwill" and constituted such actions as a refusal to supervise outside the classroom and strict adherence to "a five hour day, spread across a 190-day working year", which led to the curtailing of many extra-curricular activities.

At the end of the Spring Term the Head gave details of the beginning of the building works. In May the first signs of the re-building scheme were to appear with the setting up of a builder's yard in the field to the north of the school, the creation of a new car parking area in front of the swimming pool and the provision of extra temporary classrooms behind the ROSLA block and possibly in front of the terrace in order to provide the school with extra spaces to move into during the main contract. In the summer holidays Rooms 46, 44 and 45 were to be removed so that the area they occupied could be used for the construction of new buildings for Creative Arts and Music/Modern Languages in 1979/1980. The following year would see major alterations to the existing buildings.

In July 1979 the Head referred to concerns from parents about how the LEA were going to respond to cutbacks by central government on public sector expenditure. He stressed that the Woodroffe re-build was already financed and would continue but at the eleventh hour £64,000 was cut from the total sum of £889,000. This cut meant the loss of three specialist classrooms at the back of the site. However, the school was fortunate that the rest of the re-build was going ahead as planned.

In contrast to the doom and gloom, the Head drew attention to the many good things that had happened in the school ie "The Reckoning" and a school production of "Oliver", a very fine music concert, the Llangollen entry for the Madrigal Group, three television appearances and two of the best Ten Tors teams, to name but a few.

Prize winners at Junior Speech Day – late 1970s
(Photograph from School Archive)

Ian Cook gave a lengthy account of the building programme as follows: *"Bartletts of Yeovil arrived on site early this term to start Woodroffe's re-build at last. So far they have built the largest hole in the ground in West Dorset (see photograph below); they have disembowelled the kitchen and masked men are attacking the walls with compressor-driven hammers….It is unfortunate that building schemes appear to start destructively but during the summer positive things will begin to emerge: the car park should be finished, new buildings will begin to appear where modern languages now are, "temporary" classrooms will appear behind the ROSLA block and in front of the school, and a new path to the ROSLA block will be constructed. In September Mrs Barlow and her team should be able to return from exile at the Primary School, take possession of a refurbished kitchen and inaugurate a cafeteria system in the dining hall.*

The "big hole" begins to emerge

Inevitably there has been some disruption to the school. The PE Department has been very badly hit as it has lost the tennis courts as a temporary car park and the gym as a temporary exam hall. When the school re-convenes in September we shall really be working in the middle of a major construction site.

As well as external building operations, major internal alterations are also taking place…. This summer the oldest part of the school is going to be re-wired. The electrical engineers are sure they can complete the job during the holidays but there are storage problems (where <u>do</u> we put the library while the men are working in the room?); and, for Ewart Watts, there will be a major headache getting the school clean for September….. In 1981, when it's all finished and the school is shining beneath its first coat of paint for fifteen years it will all seem very worthwhile"[3]

Ian Cook conferring with the builders

---

[3] Extract from the School Newsletter dated July 1979

The Head wrote a warm tribute to Joan Green who was retiring in July after thirty one years at the school, having arrived in 1948. Throughout her time at LRGS and latterly Woodroffe, Miss Green had thrown herself into the life of the school. Her formal responsibilities had multiplied – she was made Senior Mistress in 1958, Head of Department in the same year and finally Deputy Head in 1961. As Mr Pearn became known to a wider educational world, Miss Green increasingly deputized for him in school. The Head described her as very patient, very kind and always the true professional and he paid tribute to the fact that through her office had passed the problems, joys and sorrows of two generations of girls. Sylvia Jones was appointed as Senior Mistress to replace Miss Green.

There was also a glowing tribute to David Coates who was also retiring, after sixteen years at the school. Mr Coates had come to the school in January 1963 and within a couple of years was Head of the English Department. His many out-of-school activities were highlighted including fifty mile walks and cross country running.

The Debating and Public Speaking Society was also enjoying a busy term. In March a balloon debate took place with characters fighting to remain in the balloon. These included HM The Queen (Alison Potter), Father Christmas (Roger Draper), St George (Karen Woodbridge), Sir Harold Wilson (Rory Anderson), Wonder Woman (Jenny Alford) and Simon Pipe, as Shakespeare, who eventually won. The Society had decided in future to concentrate more on debating techniques but in the meantime the event had provided forty minutes of hilarious competition featuring misread poems, rhyming couplets, story singing, just-a-minute contests and proverbs. Simon Pipe was the "boss" giving out and removing points as he fancied and after a very close fight the victor was decided by the pronunciation of "Floccinaucinihilipilification". Having discovered the word, Simon was the only one who could pronounce it and therefore carried off the glory!

In October 1979 the new kitchens and servery were opened and the Head thanked the Woodroffe kitchen staff and the catering staff at St Michael's Junior School as from the beginning of June the kitchens at the latter, designed to produce two hundred meals a day, had been used to prepare meals for both schools. The Head also took the opportunity to thank the cleaners at Woodroffe who had cleaned the school following the building works that had taken place during the holidays.

The Chairman of Governors advised that Ron Baker was leaving the Governing Body after ten years sterling service, recently as Vice Chairman of Governors. Cyril Keattch was elected as Vice Chairman in his place and Karl Kolya joined the Governing Body. It is interesting to note that twenty eight individuals applied for the vacancy on the Governing Body at that time.

The 1970s were a period of steady growth for the school marked by the retirement of Mr Pearn, the school's longest serving Head, the raising of the school leaving age and further extensive development of the school site.

CHAPTER 9 – 1980 TO 1989: THE EIGHTIES

In terms of the new buildings, by May a lot of the brickwork was visible above the ground. It was anticipated that the Creative Arts block would be handed over in December and B Block in February.

The buildings start to take shape

Ian Cook and pupils on their way to lessons

1980 saw the start of the gradual introduction of computers into schools and in March a group of senior pupils won a prize for computer programming. The programme submitted by four Sixth Formers was based on a biological experiment involving genetics. The team won the second prize of £20 and decided to put the money aside for the future needs of the computer science department. It was hoped that at some time in the future the school could purchase a micro computer instead of having to link with the ICL2903 mainframe computer in Poole.

The Head referred to the outline of the long term strategy for the school, which he had delivered at Senior Speech Day the previous March. He emphasized the pressure placed on maintained schools to produce academic results. Although Woodroffe could hold its head up high in terms of the achievements of its pupils, the Head suggested that in the future the emphasis should not be solely on exam results but that there should be an expansion and enrichment of studies in schools with pupils learning more about themselves and their potential. The school was already tackling this need with its expanding Human Development course, but budget constraints could hinder progress in this area.

To help the school in its efforts to advance, a new streamlined support organisation was set up, entitled Friends of Woodroffe, under the leadership of Karl Kolya. It was envisaged that this group would be a working organisation, using and co-ordinating the skills, experience, knowledge and energies of anyone who wished to support the school.

Tributes were paid to Ernestine Jowett who was retiring from teaching, having joined the staff of LRGS in 1948 as a Domestic Science teacher. In addition to being the first house parent at Harcombe House and teaching Domestic Science, she was the co-founder of Woodroffe's Human Development Course which went on to become nationally known. She also taught Parentcraft and played a major role in the school's career service. Mrs Jowett would be greatly missed and it was noted that part of Woodroffe's strong tradition of caring had come from her.

A sponsored walk was held in April 1980 when fifty five pupils covered fifteen miles from Hardy's monument to Dagger's Gate at Lulworth Cove. £300 was raised in aid of the Royal Commonwealth Society for the Blind. This event was organised by Fred Middleton who led the party, with the ever faithful Snoopy – from the rear.

Lyme Regis Dramatic Society helped a Woodroffe pupil who was partially-sighted to overcome a major handicap while studying for his GCE examination. He had had difficulty in obtaining some of his set books in sufficiently large print. The society helped out by recording on cassette tapes a number of plays, poetry and prose and some Greek literature. This close association with the Dramatic Society was a good example of the way in which mutual help between the school and the community was encouraged.

Bitterly cold weather forced nearly 300 walkers to drop out of the Ten Tors expedition on Dartmoor. Army helicopters were brought in to evacuate a number of the 2,600 young people taking party. However, both the boys and the girls teams from Woodroffe did well, keeping ahead of their schedules.

The senior basketball team was surpassing itself with a very successful season in the Exeter and District Division III. Their style of play earned them friends as far away as Teignmouth, Exmouth, Crediton and Exeter University, and at the end of the season the team was considered one of the strongest school sides in the South West. Junior Basketball players were also doing well and showed potential for the future as did the junior rugby teams. Athletes from the school were also shining at cross country, achieving successes at the West Dorset Championships, the South and West Dorset Championships and the County and All England Championships. There was also plenty of activity in the girls PE Department. A new activity that was proving particularly popular was circuit training. The demand was such that a girls only session had been organised so that the gym could accommodate all the fitness fanatics.

Careers advice was now focussed on making pupils aware of competition for careers after they leave school. Staff were concentrating on a better understanding of industry, regularly attending school industrial liaison meetings, and local firms were sending representatives to talk to members of the upper school. The Rotary Club was also helping by arranging mock interviews. It was noted that 1979/1980 was the first year of serious school-leaver unemployment in West Dorset but gratifyingly most of the 5th form leavers at Woodroffe appeared to have secured a job.

At a Civic Presentation for the Duke of Edinburgh Awards Scheme, held at the Lyme Regis Adventure Centre, the guest speaker was Squadron Leader Brian Hoskins, leader of the RAF Red Arrows. Twenty Bronze Awards were presented, five Silver Awards and three Gold Awards. The Gold Awards were received by Alison Clegg, Anne Woodman and Caroline Rattenbury.

The Pets Club was celebrating its tenth anniversary. The Canoeing Club had expanded and was enjoying a variety of activities depending on the weather and sea conditions. The Sailing Club announced that many of its members were now competent Topper sailors and had graduated to helming the Wayfarers with pleasing success.

The Wind Ensemble, under the direction of Mark Riddington, had had a good year and the Madrigal Group had also been busy singing at the "Win a Mini" Draw, school assemblies, the Carol Service, the Music Concert and Speech Day. Invites had been received to sing at the Berlin Festival and even the Vienna Festival, but funds were not available for such trips. However, the group was hoping to attend the latter the following year, pointing out that when they had sung there in 1972 it had cost £72 per head – in 1981 the estimated cost was £200 per head.

The Parents' Association had organised a full programme of evening meetings covering such diverse topics as micro-processors, astronomy, careers in craft, pupil grants and the RNLI. The Mini Car Draw was a great success and the Christmas Fair had raised £500. Parents were planning to join together with others in West Dorset to make representations to County Hall about cuts in the education system. Thanks were expressed to Cyril Keattch who had been a hard working and very effective Chairman of the Parents' Association for three years. His successor was Mr Meade.

In June 1980 a party of twenty two physically handicapped youngsters from Martindale School in Hounslow, who were enjoying an educational holiday at the Joseph Allnutt Centre in Lyme Regis, received practical help from Woodroffe pupils. Volunteers from the fourth form upwards provided daily practical help and companionship. A total of seventy offered to help with the project and forty five were selected. They helped the youngsters move around in their wheelchairs and they accompanied the group on visits to places of interest, provided entertainment and chatted informally.

By now parts of Broad Street, the Marine Parade and the Cobb were being transformed back into the 1860's for scenes from "The French Lieutenant's Woman" which was being filmed during the first three weeks of June. Eighteen Woodroffe pupils were selected as extras and when filming was over, the Location Manager in charge of the whole operation visited the school to talk about all aspects of making the film, bringing with him some of the many drawings and designs prepared for the production.

Many residents in the town enjoyed socialising with the film crew, including a number of girl boarders. Unfortunately this involved sneaking out of the boarding house after lights out and returning in the early hours. The local papers and even the national papers had a field day and rumours abounded involving drink, cannabis and even a degree of *sexual activity*". The lurid headline in the Sunday Mirror on 20th July 1980 was "Film men in romp with girls". Eventually four girl boarders had their boarding contracts withdrawn and order was restored.

Computer experts from the school put their new £2,500 OKI Microline 80 through its paces during a public demonstration at the Guildhall in March 1981. The computer, which was paid for through a series of local fund-raising events, was programmed to simulate a failure in a nuclear reactor. Also on show was the paper print-out machine, which cost £400, paid for by Lyme Regis Council through its local lottery profits.

By May 1981 the Head felt that the school was entering the home straight in terms of building works. The two major new buildings "A" and "B" block had been occupied since mid-winter and "A" block was now linked to the back of the school by a spectacularly high corridor. The contractors were about to join the ROSLA block to the rest of the school and were making minor alterations within it. The old school hall was being restored to its former dimensions and half of it was the temporary home for staff whilst the Staff Room was being altered. Portakabins were beginning to disappear from the site and three of the temporary classrooms in front of the school would follow in early July. The contractors were slightly ahead of schedule and the school was starting to think about how to show its new facilities to parents and other interested parties in the late Autumn when the £1 million contract would be completed.

Portakabins in bus bay awaiting removal

Reference was made to forthcoming examination results and an idea being pursued with the LEA and the Manpower Services Commission to organise a locally-based thirteen week full time course for any young men and women not placed in employment by mid autumn.

Staff changes included the retirement of Ron Price, Head of Geography, who had taught at the school for eighteen years, following a distinguished career in West Africa, including a spell of Headmastership. Mr Price had transformed the Geography Department and many generations owed much to his careful and dedicated teaching. James Thomas took over from Mr Price as Head of Geography. It was also announced that due to health problems Mr Sutherland-Graeme would be leaving at the end of the summer term. Since 1970 many Sixth Formers had benefited greatly from his individual knowledge and concern, and his great love of English Literature.

The Music Department had recently moved into its new quarters which meant that practice rooms were available for use during break and lunchtimes. The number of pupils taking instrumental music lessons was increasing and they were taught by six visiting music teachers during school time and a further two after school.

In the PE Department, girls had been selected for the Junior Hockey Trials, and the West Dorset Cross Country Championships were held at Woodroffe, with several girls doing extremely well. In March a party of girls and four members of staff had visited Wembley to watch the Womens' Hockey International – England v Wales. The Queen had made a tour around the stadium before the match, which England eventually won by two goals to one. The high spot of the year was a visit by a hockey team from Brentwood College School of British Columbia, Canada, who had visited the school three years previously.

Continued links with Osnabrück and CES Lavalley in Saint-Lo were being maintained by the Modern Languages Department. Mademoiselle Cecile Bozet, a first year pupil from the teacher training college, the Institut Pedagogique d'Etat in Liège, joined the Sixth Form for two weeks and spent some time observing language classes in the Lower School. It was hoped that in the future arrangements might be made for Sixth Form pupils from Woodroffe to spend a week at the college in Liège.

Due largely to the efforts of John Haylock and a large number of pupils who were "press-ganged" into short sentences of very hard labour, the Library was re-located to its new quarters in the old Art Room (ie on D level in what is now the Sixth Form Common Room). Pupil Librarians were appointed and were working very hard, as was Joan Green who spent many hours voluntarily undertaking clerical and repair work. Mr Haylock pointed out that the greatest asset in the Library was the new carpet which greatly reduced the background noise level and was conducive to the air of quiet.

(Pupils at work in the new Library)

The Music Concert was a triumph, with a huge variety of both solo and group performances. The Wind Ensemble got the concert off to a good start but the first half was dominated by the Madrigal Group. The orchestra opened the second half with "The Entertainer" followed by some polished solo performances. The Senior Choir changed the atmosphere with such favourites as "Gingerbread Man" and "Bridge over Troubled Water" and the combined choirs closed the show with an unusual arrangement of "Clementine", complete with encore, followed by "Land of Hope and Glory".

Friends of Woodroffe reached the end of the first year of operation and had made significant contributions to the school in terms of finance and support. The group was now registered as a charity and as such could benefit from the covenant scheme. Funds raised helped in providing transport, buying new curtains for the hall, video tapes for a number of departments and a new skeleton for the Biology Department. Support had been provided by transporting small groups to exhibitions and university open days, speaking to pupils about jobs and experiences, judging public speaking and debating competitions, and cataloguing in the Library. Assistance had also been given with games coaching, interview techniques, Oxbridge entry and extra work with non-exam groups. The scheme was generally proving to be very beneficial to the school in a number of ways.

An article appeared in the local press concerning the purchase of £300 worth of fabric by The Friends of Woodroffe, to make the new curtains for the school hall. They were appealing for someone brave enough to cut it up into the required lengths. They had a team of volunteer seamstresses poised with sewing machines but no-one had the courage to cut the fabric!

In July 1981 430 pupils from the 1st form to the 4th form took part in a sponsored seventeen mile walk to raise funds for the school Computer Fund and for the Lyme Regis Society's Appeal Fund for £2,500 to help buy land near Charmouth for the National Trust. The walk raised more than £2,000 and from this the school donated £200 to the Lyme Regis Society.

Shapely female pupils were castigated by the Head in October 1981 for looking too feminine. Problems arose when some girls turned up for school with splits up the side of their skirts. They were told by the Head at morning assembly to "Please sew them up". Mini-skirts were also banned and all skirts were required to be on or below the knee.

In December 1981 the Head reported that the school site was blissfully quiet with the £1.25 million rebuilding scheme almost complete. The builders were finally off site and the grass beginning to grow where the contractors' yard had stood. A number of large maintenance jobs had been completed and masons were restoring the terrace and preparing to re-build the gate posts which had been early victims of portakabin-carrying lorries.

Repairs to the school gate posts

Preliminary wood clearing in the railway cutting beyond the bus bay heralded the forthcoming footpath and footbridge extension through to the Devon boundary. A lot of furniture had been delivered and the new curtains made by the Friends of Woodroffe had been hung in the hall. There had been minor teething problems with the new boiler house, the pottery studio which was not yet fully functional and the corridors in B block but generally speaking the school was settling into the new premises and parents and visitors were being given the opportunity to look around at an Open Day.

Now that things were back to normal governors were keen to become more closely involved in the day to day running of the school by making regular visits and by accompanying school parties on outside visits. An open day was arranged for them and many took the opportunity to spend the day in school visiting various departments.

The Head expressed the view that it was no good having fine new buildings if the curriculum taught within them was severely restricted due to budgetary constraints. Recent examinations results were encouraging and it was hoped that by a careful mixture of human and financial resources from within the school, from the local community and from friends and helpers it would be possible to move forward in a positive way.

Mr Sykes, the Head of Computer Studies, referred to the Research Machines Micro Computer now installed at the school and looked forward to the delivery of two new Research machines, under phase two of the Department of Industry's "Micros in Schools" scheme. Under the scheme the Department paid half the cost of the hardware and the remainder was to be paid for from monies raised by the sponsored walk. The Computer Department was also to be equipped with a further BBC Micro to be provided from the school's capitation allowance. Mr Sykes emphasized the efforts being made by the Computer Department to spread the use of the computer as a teaching aid across the curriculum.

Ex-Woodroffe pupil, Erica Roe (24) hit the headlines when she ran topless across the Twickenham turf at the England-Australia match in January 1982, to the amusement of 68,000 spectators and millions of television viewers. The story, with accompanying photos, received national coverage. One particular photograph showed Erica being escorted from the pitch by a smiling policeman who was attempting to spare her blushes with his helmet. Erica had been a boarder at Woodroffe in the 1970s and was remembered as "great fun" and an "extrovert". She had no regrets describing her mad dash as "a marvellous experience". In an article in the Daily Telegraph reporters had tracked down her father, Peter Roe, who said that his daughter had spent her childhood in Africa where bare bosoms were not regarded with any disfavour.

Local journalist, Philip Evans, who was a Town Councillor at the time, remembered when Erica had entered the "Miss Lyme Regis Contest" in 1975, a few years prior to her appearance at Twickenham. He recalled that for the first time the competition was held at the Marine Theatre and initially it had been a disaster with the microphone playing up and the crowd in the bar making far too much noise. However they soon went quiet when Erica came on stage and the evening had been a great success, with Erica placed third in the competition.

The school now had three micro computers and hoped by the end of the school year to have acquired two more. An Open Day took place in March and sixty five parents and friends had toured the school, guided by Upper Sixth pupils.

The new Madrigal Group was hard at work. Only fourteen members remained from the group that visited Vienna but already, the group had returned from their fist appearance at the Bath Music Festival with the Lady Wilkinson Trophy and the highest mark (95%) of the day, awarded by Lady Barbirolli.

The Head reported that the new edition of the Sixth Form Prospectus had just been published by Rod Boyce and Heads of Department. It was hoped to revolutionise the one year Sixth Form by the appointment of a full time Business Studies graduate who would lead a team of teachers offering personal life skills, information technology and business know-how to pupils.

Reference was made to The Simon Hill Leukaemia Fund. Simon, a 4th form pupil at the school, was resolutely battling against leukaemia, and had resolved to set up a fund to help build up a special unit at Westminster Hospital, London for the further development of bone marrow transplants and the tracing of potential donors. The hospital was well known to Simon as he hoped to have a transplant there himself. Simon was planning a sponsored walk and others in the school were finding ways to show their support including Roger Dowle, who was running in the Exeter Marathon.

In April 1982 several ex-Woodroffe pupils serving in the armed forces were setting sail for the Falklands Islands. They included Tony Sexton aboard the aircraft carrier, HMS Hermes; Royal Marine Jeremy Robson (SS Canberra); and Vernon Rattenbury (HMS Avenger). Also David Humphrey was stationed at HMS Excellent, a shore base at Portsmouth.

In May 1982 celebrations took place to mark the fiftieth anniversary of the opening of LRGS, on its current site, by its founder, Alban Woodroffe, in 1932. A major exhibition was mounted featuring old photographs of staff and the buildings, a record of building works, graphs and charts, etc. as well as the old scroll-type school photographs. In September it would be the diamond jubilee of the founding of the old grammar school at Woodmead Halls. The previous year St Andrews had celebrated its thirtieth anniversary and Harcombe House had enjoyed its silver jubilee.

The Head reported that the exam results achieved the previous summer were probably the best in the school's history. Twenty pupils had been accepted for university with one offered a place at Oxford, one at Cambridge and one at the Bristol School of Veterinary Science where it was notoriously difficult to gain entry. In the 5th year 98% of pupils had gained worthwhile qualifications enabling Careers staff to place all but three in full time courses or employment.

Drama at Woodroffe received a considerable boost with the creation of a new Drama Studio in the former library, which was in fact the old school hall. Every class from the 1st to the 3rd form now had regular timetabled drama lessons and there was provision for an hour of improvisation per week for 4th and 5th formers. In December a Junior Drama Festival was held in which every child had the chance to perform in a class play before the rest of his/her year group – a daunting audience of well over one hundred in each case.

In May 1982 TV personality Fern Britton travelled from Cornwall to wish Simon Hill well as he set off on a ten mile sponsored walk from Bridport to Abbotsbury to raise money for the Westminster Hospital's Bone Marrow Transplant Unit. Simon and sixty fellow walkers raised over £1,500.

(BBC Personality Fern Britton gives Simon Hill a hug of encouragement before he sets off on his sponsored walk)

The school's computer hardware situation was improving all the time. However, as yet disk drives were not available for BBC computers and the only storage device was ordinary cassette tapes which were rather fragile. Consequently valuable programmes had been lost due to damaged tapes but pupils were learning fast that they needed to handle their tapes with greater respect.

Ron Rice retired as Senior Technician after fifteen years, having previously been employed at the school as a groundsman and bus driver. The Biology Department paid tribute to his hard work and dedication. It was felt that his interest and enthusiasm had over the years added a richness to the study of Biology that had benefited pupils and staff alike. Ron had been largely responsible for the school pond, the old greenhouse and particularly for the Pets Club which he had run for twelve years. The latter closed down on his departure.

In the Girls PE Department the 1st form netball team won all their inter-school fixtures and qualified for the County finals, finishing second in the South West Tournament held at Beaminster School. 1st formers were also working hard at hockey and were showing great promise. Rounders was proving to be a popular summer activity with all age groups and full use was being made of the swimming pool with early morning and lunchtime training sessions being arranged for the school swimming squad. Several girls were preparing for the South West Dorset Athletics meeting and others were attending volleyball club, circuits and basketball training. Tennis was also proving to be popular as was the new gym club at The Hawkshyde Motel, near Hawkchurch, which members of the school could attend on Friday afternoon after school.

The Photographic Club, under the leadership of Henri Chourot, now had a dark room in full working order and besides an enlarger, it featured a meter to assess the exposure needed for print, an electronic time switch to control the exposure accurately, an automatic print washer and a rotary trimmer. A Pentax ME Super camera was also available for use on various school assignments. The club was concentrating on developing and presenting black and white films but was hoping to move on to taking colour slides which it would process itself.

In January 1983 the school was devastated at the sudden death of Simon Hill after a long and incredibly courageous fight against leukaemia. The full congregation at his funeral was an eloquent tribute to the esteem in which he was held by both young and old alike. In March, the first £15,000 raised by Simon's Leukaemia Fund, was presented to the Bone Marrow Unit at the Westminster Hospital in London and the school vowed to carry on with fund-raising efforts for this good cause in memory of Simon.

Ex-pupil and Governor, David Cozens, who knew Simon and has family very well writes *"If ever a pupil epitomised the essence of the school motto – Audacia Constantiaque, courage and determination – that was Simon Hill. The youngster, whose ambition was to become a Doctor, was diagnosed with leukaemia in 1980 and died three years later at the age of sixteen. He was under no illusions about his chances of survival from the beginning but was determined to help other sufferers. Encouraged by his devoted mother, Wendy, and friends, he set up the Simon Hill Leukaemia Fund and raised £47,000 for Westminster Hospital Bonemarrow Transplant Unit.*

His bravery was recognised with the award of the prestigious BBC Blue Peter Gold Badge, while his cause was taken up by Rotary, stars of radio and television and international artistes. Among those who gave their services at a concert for the fund at Woodroffe School were former BBC Young Musician of the Year, Nicholas Daniel, pupils of the Yehudi Menuhin School, and concert pianist Eileen Minchna, who flew from the USA to appear.

Simon was a truly remarkable and inspirational young man who left all who knew him feeling very much in awe".

Simon's memory lingers on at the school as the Simon Hill Award is presented at Senior Prize-Giving each year to a pupil who has overcome adversity. The presentation of this prize is always particularly poignant and is a fitting tribute to Simon and the courageous battle he fought.

Teams from the school did very well in various annual competitions including the Rotary Public Speaking Competition, the Schools Challenge and the BBC TV South West's Music Quiz. The team comprising Alison Easey, Sarah Kendrick, Susan Marsh and Tom Everett, supported by Brian Manners and Mrs Easey, were among the last eight who had recorded programmes at the Plymouth Studios. They reached the semi-finals and won many friends at the BBC.

In June 1983 John Haylock temporarily left the school to take part in an Anglo-American teacher exchange spending a year at Estacada High School near Milwaukie, Oregon. His opposite number, Ellen Spitaleri, exchanged homes and jobs with him.

The Careers Department drew attention to the difficulties faced by pupils living in rural areas such as Lyme Regis, when it came to finding employment. Youngsters at Woodroffe however were supported by a wide range of careers services and schemes from which they benefited greatly and the Government's Youth Training Scheme (YTS), introduced by the Manpower Services Commission, was also proving to be of great assistance.

In May 1984 Rod Boyce highlighted the fact that young people in the South West in their late teens and early twenties now seemed to be using abortion as a form of contraception. Arrangements were therefore made for a suitably qualified and experienced non-local medical practitioner to meet the Sixth Form to discuss the matter in some detail. Attendance by Sixth Formers would be voluntary and a senior member of staff would be present during the initial talk but would leave at the start of question time.

At the end of the Spring Term the community play "The Western Women" was held at the school. This production opened a season of special events, including a royal visit, held in Lyme Regis to mark the 700th anniversary of the granting of a Charter to the town by Edward 1.

Mr Pearn's setting of "The Lord's Prayer", well known to generations of Woodroffe pupils, had now been published by Novello's and copies were available from the Music Department at 25p per copy.

A plea was made for help in providing the school with a new flagpole. The existing flagpole, which was sited in front of the rebuilt terrace, had been taken off its tabernacle as it had rotted to a dangerous extent and finding a replacement from the already stretched school budget was a problem. It was mentioned that the school had a splendid School Flag and Union Jack and it was a pity not to use them.

Upper Sixth pupils achieved a magnificent twenty A and twenty B grades in the summer exams. At this time the majority of universities required three C grades for entry. Pupils were now leaving Woodroffe to study for a wide range of degrees including Science, Modern Languages, Medicine, Engineering, Law, Sociology, Electronics, Architecture and Business Studies.

In April 1984 thoughts at county hall were turning to future provision for Sixth Formers. With the child population in Dorset falling in number, various scenarios were under consideration, including the rationalisation of existing provision. Parents were urged by the Head to make their views known to the LEA so that a solution could be arrived at based on educational grounds and not on considerations that were solely financial, logistical or political. Subsequently, 250 Woodroffe parents attended a consultation evening and forty two letters were written to the LEA by parents. They were therefore left in no doubt that parents wanted full Sixth Form provision to remain at Woodroffe.

The Head advised that "The Western Women", the community play written by Faye Weldon, had been a complete sell-out with all 3,300 tickets sold for the eleven day run. Taking part had been a demanding but memorable experience for all involved. The promenade production had been visited by enthusiasts from as far afield as Manchester, Cornwall, London and Kent and had been nationally reviewed and covered by Radio 4 (twice) and local television.

In May the Head reported to governors on the effects of teachers' strike action on the operation of the school. This had come about due to the rejection of the 4.5% pay offer by all teachers' associations without exception. The national half day strike by NAS/UWT on 11th April had resulted in fifteen classes being affected and just over 20% of pupils missing school. There was a universal desire to protect public examinations from disruption but most lunchtime and after school activities had ceased.

Also in May 1984 HRH Princess Alexandra visited Lyme Regis to mark Charter 700 year. Space at Cobb Gate car park, which was on the route of the royal walkabout, was reserved for eighty Woodroffe pupils and arrangements were made for the Head, the Head Boy and the Head Girl to be introduced to the royal visitor by the Mayor.

Roger Dowle advised that school athletes had achieved considerable success in both cross country and road running with Sinead Burke, Sue Huey, Becky Owen and Robert Retter running for Dorset in the Southern Counties Championships. Not to be overlooked was the performance of James Thomas and David Chambers in the London and Exeter marathons respectively. 1984 was the twenty fifth anniversary of Ten Tors and the school entered a girls and a boys team.

The School on the Hill

Locally there was concern about a proposed reduction in hospital provision in the town. The Head wrote to the local paper on behalf of the school urging the retention of full hospital facilities.

It was reported in June 1984 that Dennis Geary would be taking early retirement from teaching due to poor health. Mr Geary had taught at the school since 1975 and he would be particularly remembered for his outstanding drawings and diagrams for the school booklet. Roger Draper would also be leaving to take up the post of Deputy Head at the Convent of the Sacred Heart School in Weymouth. Mr Draper had joined the teaching staff at Woodroffe in 1967 and was therefore one of the longest serving members of staff. He and his wife had run Rhode Hill with great understanding and commitment from 1975 to 1982.

Tributes were paid to Douglas Fortnam who was resigning from the Governing Body, after twenty six years, the last eight as Chairman. Mr Fortnam was described as a "fair but very doughty fighter for the school" who had welded the Governing Body into one which was well known and respected at County Hall. The devotion of both Mr Fortnam and his wife was recognised by a reception and presentation by Governors and the Parents' Association held at Colway House, followed by a presentation by staff the following morning. Mr and Mrs Fortnam were particularly appreciative of a performance by the Madrigal Group at the reception. Mr Fortnam was succeeded as Chairman of Governors by Karl Kolya.

Hot on the heels of the Charter 700 celebrations it was reported that in July 1985 there would be another major historical event – the 300th Anniversary of Monmouth's Rebellion against James II, which began in Lyme Regis, ended at the Battle of Sedgmoor and was followed by Judge Jeffrey's Bloody Assizes in Somerset and Dorset. This would provide an opportunity for interested pupils to become involved in commemorative activities, and both the Sealed Knot and the Civil War Society were expected to be involved in the week-long events.

The Madrigal Group was recording items at the Plymouth studios of the BBC for the new television series "The Music Maker" which featured outstanding music in schools. It had provided entertainment at the Cheese and Wine party as part of the Lyme Regis Charter 700 celebrations, competed in the first round of the Choir of the Year competition sponsored by Sainsbury's and BBC television and it was to participate in the "Singing Week" organised by the Federation of European Youth Choirs at Namur, Belgium.

The PE Department advised that the Senior XV had won the majority of their matches, but was narrowly defeated by the President's XV made up of "Old Boys" back from college and university, a few staff members and friends of the school. Many sporting activities had been curtailed by industrial action by the teaching unions. The school running club was now promoting an active interest in running and an increasing number of both staff and pupils were taking part in Fun Run and Road Races up to half and full marathons. It was reported that James Thomas had completed the London Marathon and to date he had raised £650 for the RNLI.

For the first time in March 1984 a party of forty 3rd and 4th formers, accompanied by James Thomas and Julia Lamb, had taken part in the Dorset Schools Ski Course at Santa Caterina in the Italian Alps. They were among 220 pupils from all over Dorset who spent a strenuous week on the slopes.

In May 1984 changes were made to the menu for school meals on an experimental basis including no sale of chocolate bars and biscuits but a daily supply of salads, wholemeal items, yogurts, fresh fruit and natural food bars. Chips, cooked in vegetable oil, would now only be on sale twice a week – and this was before Jamie Oliver came on the scene! These changes were not straightforward, however, as takings in the school cafeteria fell by approximately 10% as a direct result. Kitchen staff were under pressure to produce more homemade items and concern was also being expressed at the lack of choice now that a ready supply of chips was no longer available. This matter was discussed several times by the Governors in later months and the Head was asked to point out to the LEA the inappropriateness of applying purely commercial criteria to feeding and training young people to eat sensibly.

In October 1984 the school was shocked and saddened by the sudden death of teacher Henri Chourot, at the age of just forty. He left a wife and three young children. Colleagues and governors set up a fund in his memory to provide a Bursary Award each year to enable a pupil following European Studies to visit the Continent.

It was reported that a decision had been made on post-16 education in West Dorset which involved a continuing separate Sixth Form at Woodroffe and a combined Beaminster/Colfox Sixth Form at Bridport.

In November 1984 the Head advised governors of current national educational developments including the proposal to introduce the General Certificate of Secondary Education (GCSE) in September 1986 to replace O levels and CSEs and also the possible introduction of AS levels alongside A levels. He explained that an AS level subject would reach the same standard as Advanced Level but in half the study time on a reduced syllabus content. Pupils would be encouraged to take two A levels and two contrasting AS levels. The Head cautioned that although universities had stated that they were willing to accept prospective pupils on either type of result, this proposal was far from being accepted.

In December 1984 TVEI (The Technical and Vocational Education Initiative) was introduced to parents as a means by which the curriculum could be enriched from the 4th form and above, in such areas as Information Technology, Robotics, Biotechnology and the Community and Caring Services. This initiative would attract considerable additional funding for the school and the schemes of work involved new approaches to teaching and learning, with assessment organised in a very imaginative way with a profile for each individual.

It was stressed that TVEI existed alongside the usual curriculum, so that the full range of academic subjects remained. In the first two years the TVEI content would form 30% of the week and in the Sixth Form the proportion would be reversed, with probably part of the week spent at an associated college or on work experience.

December 1984 also saw some minor changes to Sixth Form uniform. It was agreed that blazers could become optional provided a navy blue or grey v-necked jumper was worn and girls could wear brown sandals without socks or stockings in the summer. There was no change to the colour of shoes.

In February 1985 the Head reported to governors on the current situation regarding industrial action by teachers. NUT members of staff were not covering for staff absent through illness after the first day but to date classes had not been affected. NAS/UWT members had withdrawn from organised meetings and functions. So far few extra-curricular activities had been affected but an escalation of industrial action was expected in late February and March. This proved to be the case and in March classes were disrupted when fourteen NAS/UWT members were missing from school in connection with a pay claim.

By now the Head had announced his intention to resign at the end of the academic year and in March the appointment process for a new Head began with 168 applications for the post.

Parents were being bombarded with information about their children's education. In addition to TVEI the Department for Education and Science had circulated a pamphlet advising that with effect from the Summer of 1988 the General Certificate of Secondary Education (GCSE) would replace the O level and CSE exams throughout the country. Following on from that the Head had introduced to parents the Certificate of Pre-Vocational Education (CPVE) which was aimed at the one year Sixth Form and was likely to be introduced in September 1986.

Efforts were now being made to strengthen the school's pastoral structure and to this end Joan Bareham was to retain oversight for the Middle School (ie 4th and 5th forms) but would in future concentrate on the 5th form, with her newly appointed Deputy, Richard Hudson, assuming responsibility for the 4th form. David Badman, Head of the Lower School, was to concentrate on the 3rd form (ie option choices and interviews, etc.) and the 2nd frm, and Mary Swainston, as Deputy Head of the Lower School would take over responsibility for the 1st form and links with primary schools.

The Parents Association were concerned that their role had in recent years been confined solely to fund-raising. Initially this had been for so-called "extras" but of late the Association had been providing funding for essential items and it was likely that this situation would continue in view of the latest LEA education budget. It was felt that it was now time for all parents to let their voice be heard at county level and to call a halt to the erosion of educational standards not only for today's children but for their children.

In May 1985 Lyme Regis Town Council sent a delegation to Dorset County Council pressing hard for more use of local school sports facilities by members of the community. Councillor Jeff Robbins led the group, which was keen for dual use to be established in relation to the school's playing fields and tennis courts. However, at school concerns remained on the security of the school site if it was used by members of the public out of normal hours and also the fact that all overheads had to be fully met by letting fees as monies provided for education could not be used for other purposes.

The School on the Hill

The Friends of Woodroffe managed to accumulate the sum of £2,700 through the Covenant Scheme which was used to purchase the new piano for the Drama Studio.

The school participated in the Centenary Commemorations of the Monmouth Rebellion. On Tuesday, 11th June 1985 a school group, in costume, took banners on the first stage of a March to Sedgmoor and on Saturday, 15th June in the School Hall the Sedgemoor Theatre Company presented a promenade performance of "The King's Justice".

In his final newsletter to parents, in June 1985, the Head welcomed the new Head, Paul Vittle, who he felt would bring to the school his own enthusiasms, expertise and ideas and he wished him well for the future. However, he felt that he could not leave without voicing four deep concerns he had for the national system of education. These concerns included the critical level of under-funding for maintained schools; the low level of maintenance of LEA schools (many of which were falling into a serious state of disrepair); pressure on the curriculum from so many directions, and the need to review the salaries of teaching and support staff.

The Head also referred to the retirement of Mike Fairley, who had taught at the school since 1965 when he joined the school as the first specialist historian. He was therefore largely responsible for creating the subject in school and additionally had built up an impressive archive of the school's growth. His calm, quiet humour would be greatly missed but it was hoped that he would keep in touch, as he only lived across the road from the school.

Mr Fairley in turn noted that the things he would miss included "… *the long brisk walk to school in the morning, meeting all the eager shining faces at the gate; Mr Cook's bellow echoing along the corridor; the receding outline of Mr Watts disappearing at the other end; summer hurricanes on Sports Day on top pitch; pink custard and nutty slack in the canteen; going on visits in the school bus; singing "Morning has Broken". But most of all I shall miss the bell at five to four*".[1]

Roger Dowle pointed out that 1985 was the centenary of the introduction of craft education in schools. He felt that subjects such as Home Economics, Needlework and the Creative Arts should be more prominent within the curriculum and he welcomed the introduction of TVEI, with its input of staff, finance and technology, which should benefit the school as a whole. Mr Dowle expressed the view that there was a need to promote Design and Technology courses to their highest level so that pupils of all abilities would be able to face the modern technological society with confidence.

Despite the sudden and tragic death of Mr Chourot and the inability of the LEA to provide a qualified supply teacher for French/European Studies, with the help of Pascale Dillon who had stepped in at a moment's notice, the Department had managed to deliver the curriculum although some extra-curricular activities had had to be curtailed, in particular the French exchange. However, eleven 6th formers had made a short visit to Paris, three 4th formers had taken part in the Dorset-Osnabruck exchange and thirty one 3rd formers

---

[1] Extract from the School Newsletter dated June 1985

had been on a whirlwind European tour, the first ever European Studies educational visit, which had been an outstanding success. The party had been escorted by Pascale Dillon, John Haylock and Richard Hudson and had visited France, Germany, Holland and Belgium.

The Woodroffe Parents Association had a new Chairman, Mike Davies, and several new committee members. The Association was greatly encouraged by the offer of help from twenty five parents at the AGM. The school was gratified to learn that at 95% the school had the highest attendance rate in the county.

In June 1985 it was reported that the Simon Hill Leukaemia Fund, launched by Simon before his death from the disease in January 1983 stood at £30,000 and investment from it was helping to save lives. Researchers were making significant strides forward in their battle to defeat leukaemia but vast sums were required to conquer the disease, which was why the fund remained open and continued to generate funds. The latest donation was from the proceeds of the two battles being staged by the Sealed Knot as part of the re-enactment of the Siege of Lyme. Prior to his departure from the school Mr Butterworth donated cash from his farewell presentation fund to aid the fight against leukaemia in memory of Simon who had fought so bravely against this disease.

Sadly at this time the school was also mourning the tragic death of another ex-pupil, Lieutenant Simon Rodwell who died in the South Atlantic where he was serving in Her Majesty's Forces. Simon's family has kindly provided this tribute to him

"Simon and his twin sister, Sarah, were pupils at Woodroffe from 1976 to 1978. Whilst at the school, he was a senior prefect and a talented sportsman. He played for the 1st XV at rugby and the 1st X1 at soccer and cricket. Simon also played tennis and was a proficient sailing dinghy helmsman. One of his favourite outside school activities was gliding.

On leaving Woodroffe, after taking his A levels, Simon joined the Royal Navy. When he passed out from the Royal Naval College, Dartmouth, in 1984 he was nominated as the best overall pupil on the course, having completed his training in just two terms. He was a fun-loving, life-and-soul of the party lad who enjoyed a great sense of humour. Simon lost his life shortly before his 25th birthday. He was declared missing after a mid-air collision in the South

Atlantic. Simon was serving with 826 Squadron, based at Culdrose in Cornwall. He was in a Royal Navy Sea King helicopter in collision with an RAF Hercules north of the Falklands. The Hercules returned to base safely.

On receiving news of the loss of Simon the school flag flew at half mast. Prayers were said at morning assembly and the hymn "For all the saints who from their labours rest" was sung. Mr Butterworth paid tribute to Simon, who always had a burning ambition to fly and travel, stating that he was a young man of outstanding ability who did well at most things to which he turned his hand."

Simon's family donated a tree to the school which they visit regularly. This tree is planted on the front lawn and is a lasting memorial to him.

September saw the arrival of Paul Vittle, who had been appointed in April from a shortlist of twelve candidates. Mr Vittle came to Woodroffe from West Somerset School where he was Acting Headteacher. Originally from Bristol, he trained as a Teacher at Exeter and later gained a Batchelor of Philosophy degree at Exeter University in 1981. A special service was held for the new Head at Lyme Regis Parish Church on 29th October 1985 during which Mr Vittle was welcomed by the Mayor, Councillor Ivor Curtis. Rev Murray Dell conducted the service and prayers were said for the three local schools.

The school immediately reacted to the Mexican Earthquake disaster and collected items for Rotary Emergency Boxes. Sixth Formers with a flair for computers were designing an internal teletext sytem as a kind of electronic noticeboard and in order to expand this they were appealing to members of the community for unwanted and defective television sets. This initiative was pupil-led and it was hoped that it would promote an interest in computers and media studies amongst the school population.

Parents were concerned about the steep, concrete path to the bus bay. The path had a gradient of one in four and became slippery and dangerous in wet or frosty weather. It was felt that steps would be just as dangerous and what was needed was a non-slip surface. Shortly afterwards the school was advised that the re-surfacing of the path was being given a high priority by the Local Education Authority. However, the steepness of this path remains a problem to this day.

The school was closed for one morning as a result of industrial action by members of staff belonging to the NASUWT. Members of NUT and AMMA worked as normal and afternoon lessons were not disrupted. The Head stressed that the strike was not only about the teachers' pay claim but also about the quality of the education service provided at the school. As a result of the industrial action no sporting fixtures were taking place.

The school contributed to a local appeal to make dolls for the comfort of children in Ethiopia affected by the famine there. The town contributed 350 handmade dolls, with 200 produced at Woodroffe. Dolls were also made by Uplyme and Lyme Regis Primary Schools. The national appeal was made by Bob Geldof as part of Band Aid and British Rail kindly allowed the dolls to travel to London free of charge. As a token of appreciation for the effort made local organiser, Miss Frances Stannard presented the school with a gift of frankincense and myrrh all the way from Ethiopia.

Plans were underway for the introduction of Technical, Vocational and Educational Initiative (TVEI) and the Certificate of Pre-vocational Education (CPVE) in September 1986. Deputy Head Ian Cook, was responsible for leading these two initiatives and as a consequence Jo Culham took over temporarily as Deputy Head.

Concern was expressed about the volume of people wishing to attend the school's Annual Carol Service at the local Parish Church. The previous year 700 people, plus 200 members of the school's choirs were squeezed in but this year, due to restriction imposed by fire regulations, numbers would have to be reduced to 400.

A report appeared in the local press stating that a mysterious intruder had been pinching girls blue PE knickers from their kit bags. A policeman advised that four girls had reported the theft, but nothing else had been taken…..

A horizontal pastoral system, rather than a vertical one, had now been introduced with tutor groups comprising pupils of the same age.

At Speech Day in March 1986 the main speaker was Lieutenant-General Sir David Mostyn. The Head in his speech stressed the danger of under-estimating the value of State education. He warned that there would be a high price to pay if the nation continued to under-value, under-fund and generally misunderstand state education and the role it had to play in modern society. The Head challenged Sir Keith Joseph, the Education Secretary, to visit the school and to see for himself how the school managed to function so successfully despite the many problems in education at the present time. Subsequently Chris Patten, the Minister for Education, took up the invitation to visit Woodroffe.

Lyme Regis Town Council allocated the sum of £1,397 to the school to help develop facilities to be shared by the community. Projects under consideration were the installation of two external doors to the changing rooms to allow access to the swimming pool without entry into the building, the conversion of part of the changing rooms into a fitness centre and the possibility of flood lighting and improvements to the tennis courts. As an outcome of a meeting with Councillors Jeff Robbins and Dennis Applebee it was decided to form a Community Association comprising parents, representatives of local organisations, school staff, governors and councillors. Although the Sports Council could not provide grant aid to a school, it was established that it would be possible for the local council to apply for aid on behalf of a community association.

On Sunday, 27th April 1986 the first Lyme Regis Run took place, organised by three members of staff – Roger Dowle, who was the Race Director, assisted by Jo Culham and David Chambers.

The start of the first Lyme Regis Run

The School on the Hill

The event was supported by Lyme Regis Town Council and the Mayor was the official starter for the races. Although organised by the school this was heralded as very much a community event. The main sponsor was Zair and Co, estate agents from Lyme Regis, plus local builders Broom and Evans, A J Wakely and Son and Cloverdale Garage. Bridport Sports also provided prizes worth £150. A total of 603 runners took part, 477 of whom ran in the Fun Run, and the event raised over £2,000 which was to be used for the improvement of facilities at the school for community use. A total of £1,070 was raised in sponsorship, with a huge range of both local and national charities benefiting. The most popular charity proved to be the Simon Hill Leukaemia Fund, which received over £250.

In May 1986 a team of boys from Woodroffe showed tremendous character and resourcefulness by completing the 45 mile route in Ten Tors in atrocious weather conditions. Out of 2,400 competitors taking part only 600 completed the course. A girls team had also entered the event but were forced to give up due to the extreme weather conditions. One of their members had to be lifted off the moor by Army helicopter with medical problems. Mr Middleton, who trained the boys team, stressed that Ten Tors was not a race but a test of team work, leadership and endurance.

The Madrigal Group celebrated its 25th anniversary with a party which was well attended. Sixteen former members came from all over the country to share in the evening of nostalgia. Mr Manners was presented with an engraved salver to mark the occasion.

So many people wanted to attend the Junior Speech Day in July that in order to accommodate them all some would be seated in an overflow area where they would watch the proceedings by close circuit TV.

Four members of the school staff and one pupil organised a 160 mile run to London to demonstrate their belief in young people, in the future and the value of education. Ashley Dowle, Alan Brown, Roger Dowle, Dave Chambers, Stephen Holmes and Sixth Former Toby Pennington (*pictured right*) covered the course in relays, finishing at 10.00 pm, twenty hours after setting off. The event was sponsored by Jim Bolton, Managing Director of J Bolton and Sons, and Bridport firm, Par Acoustics, who provided two support vehicles.

The runners were met at Broadcasting House by Radio One DJ, Tommy Vance, who shared a bottle of champagne with the runners and featured their efforts on his rock show. The Woodroffe team then set off for Downing Street where a letter was handed in for Prime Minister, Margaret Thatcher. Whilst the runners were doing their bit, two other members of the teaching staff, Keith Culham and James Thomas, were attempting to swim 19 miles (ie 1,216 lengths) of the school swimming pool. They both succeeded.

In September the Head floated the idea of creating a careers centre at the school for the use of both the school and the local community. With no job centre available in the town it was felt that there was a need for somewhere where employers could advertise their vacancies, and where individuals could find out about training opportunities. Plans were drawn up by a local builder and architect to extend the school's careers facilities and the idea had the full approval of Dorset County Council. An appeal to raise £6,000 was launched and immediately £1,000 was received. The Head suggested that if every home donated £1 sufficient monies would be raised.

On 27th September 1986 ex-pupils Julie Hicks and Valerie Curtis organised a reunion for fellow ex-pupils at The Royal Standard. Over eighty people turned up and as an outcome it was decided to revive the Old Pupils Association.

The school was shocked to hear of the sudden resignation of Fred Middleton who had been a popular member of staff at the school for seventeen years. He was greatly missed by colleagues and pupils, particularly by boarders at St Andrews where he had been housemaster for many years,

Radio One DJ Gary Davies broadcast from the school on the afternoon of Wednesday, 17th December 1986 as part of his Christmas "Bit in the Middle". Contact was made with Radio One when the five runners from the school ran to London in the summer. The show lasted two and a quarter hours and included a jingle, written and performed by pupils under the direction of Mr Poole, and also featured the Madrigal Group singing Christmas Carols. There was a surprise appearance by top model and singer, Samantha Fox in a fur-lined Father Christmas outfit.

The school was fully immersed in a fund-raising campaign to raise money to buy a new mini-bus. Events organised included a 12-hour non-stop disco, an acting marathon organised by 5th form drama pupils, a music concert, and the annual Christmas Fair and 50/50 auction which raised £2,935.

During 1978 the school was delighted to welcome back to boarding husband and wife team John and Claire Ennals who returned from the Scilly Isles to take over from David and Mary Badman as Acting Houseparents at Harcombe.

By now regular meetings were taking place with Lyme Regis Town Council to discuss community use of school facilities and in the local press the MP Sir James Spicer praised the school's commitment to developing community use of its amenities. In April 1987 a public meeting was held at the school to discuss the matter.

In the summer of 1987 4th Formers joined the Trident Scheme. This scheme was designed to develop self-reliance and responsibility to others. In order to achieve their Trident Certificate, pupils had to gain work experience, undertake some kind of voluntary service and take up a new hobby or physical activity.

The Governing Body was sad to lose the services of Karl Kolya who resigned as Chairman of Governors after eight years as a Governor. He was succeeded by Vice-Chairman, Lt-Col Hugh Gibson.

About fifty members of Woodroffe School's Amnesty International Group took it in turns to sit in a cage at Bell Cliff throughout the day to highlight the plight of prisoners of conscience throughout the world. The Group had adopted a prisoner, an Albanian living in Yugoslavia, who had been detained for protesting about the treatment of Albanians in that country.

Twenty five pupils at the school fasted for twelve hours in order to raise funds to adopt a Third World Child. The cost of doing this was £144 and as they managed to raise £200, surplus funds were passed to the school's mini-bus appeal. Also, seventeen extra keen 3rd formers volunteered to work all night to raise funds to send fellow pupil, Jonathan Whetlor, on a cricket tour to Denmark with a Dorset Schoolboy Team. Teachers volunteered to take lessons throughout the night and the pupils *(pictured right)* even managed to stay awake for lessons the following day.

The Second Lyme Regis Run took place on 5th April 1987 but was marred by the sudden death of one of the competitors in the Fun Run who collapsed at the finish line. As a mark of respect no post-race presentations took place. The event, which attracted over 600 runners, featured a Fun Run over approximately two miles, a five mile race and a more strenuous ten mile race for serious runners.

At the annual Speech Day, the Head highlighted the fact that cuts in the education budget had resulted in leaking roofs, falling plaster and large areas of damp, which was not an environment conducive to learning. He stressed that the money allocated to the school for cleaning, furniture, books and administration amounted to just 2.9p per pupil per lesson. The Head's message to the County Education Officer was that education remained the most valuable investment for the future of the country, but too much central control of schools created a degree of impotence and therefore inhibited growth.

A large and enthusiastic gathering at a public meeting unanimously approved the constitution for the Woodroffe Community Association, bringing town use of the school's facilities much closer. Under the constitution it was intended to form a management committee including representatives of individual users. Further plans included opening up school facilities to members of the community; to make the school a base for local organisations, possibly fostering the formation of new organisations; the opportunity for adults to join A level classes alongside pupils; the possible use of school boarding facilities during the holiday periods for residential courses; the creation of a refreshment lounge for community use and, in the long term, employment of a community tutor to manage and promote the dual use of school facilities.

In the Summer of 1987 Ken Burton retired as Head of Mathematics and Senior Teacher after twenty nine years' service at the school.

The whole school took part in "Worldroffe" subtitled "Beat a Boeing". The idea was to challenge everyone to travel round the world in thirty hours "faster than a Boeing aeroplane". The distance to be covered was a staggering 24,840 miles. Backed by teachers and parents, 650 pupils used an assortment of vehicles to clock up the miles. Participants used skateboards, roller skates, prams, wheelbarrows and sailboards. They walked, swam, and rode horseback. There was even a team pushing a Fiat car around a measured circuit on the school playing field. The challenge was all part of the Woodroffe Challenge, a yearly contest in which the school set out to affirm its belief in young people and the value of education. It was successfully completed in twenty nine and a quarter hours with an amazing 27,000 miles covered. The event was organised by Roger Dowle who congratulated everyone on this magnificent achievement.

During the summer holidays, the school's "O" level results were lost in the post and anxious pupils had to wait an extra week before learning their fate. The A level results arrived on time and were excellent, although not as impressive as the previous year's. At A level there was a pass rate of 81% - the equivalent of 2.1 passes per pupil.

On Saturday, 26th September 1987 a reunion for ex-pupils was held in the drama studio which attracted 200 people, including former pupil, Erica Roe, who was now famous for her exploits at Twickenhan. The following day Ernestine Jowett organised a reunion for ex-girl boarders from Harcombe, to celebrate the 35th anniversary of the establishment of the boarding house. Major Pearn and Brian Manners also attended and among the former boarders present was Stephanie Yates née Baggett, who had travelled all the way from Capetown, South Africa.

The Parents' Association began a fund-raising campaign to raise money for an improved Resources Centre. Events included a Poetry Competition, a non-uniform day, a sponsored walk, even a sponsored water-ski, and parents were sponsored to spend a day in school following a full programme of lessons including economics, social education, art, maths, poetry, physics and music. In total £1,116 was raised.

When addressing the local Chamber of Trade, the Head emphasized that education should be "from the cradle to the grave". In this context he very much hoped that children of pre-school age and their grandparents would be able to use school facilities under the auspices of Woodroffe Community Association. This new group received an injection of cash from the proceeds of the third Lyme Regis Run held in April 1987, which had attracted over 550 runners of all ages. The bulk of sponsorship money raised was donated to Lyme Regis Hospital.

The Head, two members of the teaching staff and four pupils were treated to a trip in a Royal Navy Sea King helicopter from Portland, after the Head had revealed that he had never flown in one before. The helicopter landed on the school tennis courts to pick up the party.

A heated annual meeting saw the former Woodroffe School Parents Association change its constitution to become a parent/teacher association. Some parents felt that they had not received enough information about the change in the constitution. The main concern was that the change would lead to a reduction in the body's influence outside the school, particularly with the LEA. The Head reassured parents that this would not be the case and gave his full support to the new association, emphasizing how hard they worked for the good of the school on a purely voluntary basis.

In March 1988 the Head referred to the pace of education which appeared to be getting faster and faster, with greater demands and pressure placed on everyone involved. For example he had to balance his responsibilities in terms of the management of the school buildings, personnel and a budget in excess of £1 million pounds per annum against his wish to continue to teach, observe classroom activities and to know staff and pupils on a personal level. For the teaching staff there was a need to continually update teaching skills whilst remaining loyal to their present pupils by teaching them regularly, marking their homework and organising extra-curricular activities. The vast majority of pupils was striving to keep up to date with homework, coursework deadlines, exam revision, whilst at the same time they wished to enjoy leisure activities and the company of their friends. Parents needed to have confidence in the school without interfering and yet they needed to understand all the changes that were taking placing in education. It was a difficult balancing act for everyone.

As the school year drew to a close in 1988 the Head introduced a new mentoring scheme entitled "Befriend" to provide guidance with relationships. It involved weekly sessions which attempted to increase the self-awareness of a group of twenty four pupils so that they in turn would become more sensitive to the emotional needs of their contemporaries. The scheme received national acclaim for its innovative approach.

A mystery male streaker was spotted in the grounds of the school. The Head advised that a group of girls was playing netball and when one girl went to retrieve the ball from the tennis courts she saw a naked man fleeing. The matter was reported to the police but the man was not seen again.

Pupils received their Records of Achievement under a new Dorset Education Authority Initiative. This came about because the LEA felt that when young people left school they should take with them far more information about themselves than the usual report or reference. The Records of Achievement were built up over the whole period of a child's school life and detailed all sorts of achievements from music to sport. It also contained a statement about the individual which was put together by negotiation between them and their tutor. The records included samples of work and to give the records status they were verified by a Validation Board.

Three West Dorset Driving Instructors conducted a course at the school for Sixth Formers designed to prepare them for the road. The course consisted of six one-hour sessions. It was part of a campaign to reduce the number of serious car accidents in Dorset involving young people between the ages of 16 to 18. While the Sixth Form was getting to grips with learning to drive, four 5th formers were honing their Tiddlywinks skills and raised £50 for Oxfam with a Tiddlywinks Marathon.

Woodroffe Community Association was moving ahead and appointed a part-time administrative assistant. It was felt that this appointment would help the association to make rapid progress in its efforts to promote community use of school facilities. It was noted that the most popular facility enjoyed by the community was the multi-gym.

Local business woman, Lillie Pettit, was so concerned at the lack of lockers for pupils at the school that she donated £1,000 worth of stock from her bed-linen company, to raise money to buy more. Her particular concern was that many children were carrying heavy books and equipment around school all day.

As all attempts to appoint a Lollipop Patrol at the school had failed, a sixth former, fully trained by the LEA, took over this responsibility ensuring the safety of his fellow pupils crossing the busy road outside the school.

The Head organised an "Any Questions" Evening at the school which was designed to provide a blend of entertainment and education. The panellists were Dorset's Chief Education Officer Peter Gedling, Police Western Division Commander David Trickey, Lyme Regis GP Dr Andrew Llewellyn and Axminster Deacon Doreen Brown.

Textiles teacher, Rebecca Barnes, made a quilt five times the normal size for the National Theatre in London. The quilt, which took her over forty hours to complete by hand, was needed for a play featuring eight old-age pensioners, with all the action taking place in or around the bed.

As part of a fund-raising prank at the end of the Spring Term 1989, the Head was kidnapped at the end of morning assembly by "armed" Sixth Formers dressed in combat jackets and wearing stockings over their heads. He was spirited away to a building site in Yeovil where he was left without any money after being told to make his own way back to school. However, the Head confounded his kidnappers by arriving back at school barely ten minutes after they did! The prank raised £50 for Save the Children, to add to the £235 already raised.

Ross McWhirter, the brains behind the Guinness Book of Records, visited the school to give a talk, including colour slides and to answer questions. The visit was organised by the PTA and Mr McWhirter spoke about how the Guinness Book of Records began. Another famous person also made a visit to the school: actress Wendy Van der Plank, (better known as "Wizadora"), an ex-pupil and former boarder, and a star of the TV series "Forever Green" returned to present the prizes at Junior Speech Day.

Dennis Applebee, Chairman of Woodroffe Association, called for a leisure strategy for Lyme Regis involving the Woodroffe Association, the Swimming Pool Committee, the

PTA, the Lyme Regis Leisure Centre and the Marine Theatre Management Committee. Mr Applebee expressed the view that the town's leisure facilities had an exciting future "if we all get in the same boat".

At the Lyme Regis Run in April 1989, the Wiscombe family did extremely well with all six members winning a place in their various classes. 590 people took part including one pupil suffering from an arthritic condition which prevented him from running who was pushed around the course by his brother and his best friend.

Controversially the Head put forward the suggestion that the Woodroffe School and Axminster Secondary School should be amalgamated to form a major comprehensive on two sites. This was because Woodroffe was suffering badly from over-crowding brought about largely by the number of children from Axminster attending the school. Pupil numbers at Axminster Secondary School however had nearly halved during the 1980s and the school was fast reaching the point of no longer being viable. At Woodroffe numbers stood at a record level with 866 on roll, including 160 in the Sixth Form, which was due to rise to 200 in September. One suggestion was that children aged between eleven and fourteen from both schools would be educated at Axminster, with the older ones educated at Woodroffe.

The Head's merger idea drew a favourable response from Devon education officers and Education Secretary Kenneth Baker indicated that he would back the plan if Devon and Dorset could agree on the arrangements. However, in Dorset there was a certain amount of disquiet, particularly from Woodroffe parents who organised a petition and called a public meeting. Eventually, the merger plan was rejected.

During the Autumn Term 1989 the school held its first Dance Show entitled "Motion Commotion" which comprised twenty four routines on three topics – dance style, movies in motion and dance through the ages. Forty eight pupils from the second form to the sixth form participated.

It was announced that the numbers of boarding places at the school were to be axed by Dorset Education Authority. Of the 179 current boarding places, fifty nine were to go by September 1991 when the authority proposed to provide boarding places for both boys and girls at a purpose built facility within the school grounds. However, following a request from school governors the authority agreed to make provision for the possible expansion of the new accommodation so that it could take up to 140 boarders.

Over 300 people gathered at the school in 1989 to celebrate the 25th anniversary of the school as a comprehensive, with the star guest being former Head, Thornton Pearn, who was welcomed back to the school by Paul Vittle. The gathering included many former pupils of the old grammar school and some members of its teaching staff who enjoyed a performance by the Madrigal Group and an exhibition of photographs and literature recording the school's development and progress over the twenty five year period. One of the most nostalgic interludes came with Mr Pearn playing a rousing version of the School Song on the piano. As part of the celebrations, Mr Vittle and Mr Pearn planted a tree on the front lawn to mark the occasion.

The School on the Hill

"Tristan Harris and Natalie Price bury the time capsule"

In 1989 a time capsule was buried on the school site by Head Boy, Tristan Harris and Head Girl, Natalie Price. The music of pop stars Bros and a video tape of Neighbours were amongst thirty seven items buried which also included instant food packets, exercise books, a test tube containing sea water and an indication of what the uniform at the school looked like.

The trunkful of items included a "letter to the future" written by them in which they expressed their fears for the world in twenty five years time. The time capsule was buried and covered with a stone plaque inviting the same pupils to dig it up in 2014, when they would have reached the grand old age of thirty seven! The project was organised by Head of History, Mr Seabrook, and fellow historian, Mr Wood.

The suggestion of an educational Iron Curtain was mooted, to be drawn across the Devon/Dorset border to prevent unhappy parents "fleeing" to Woodroffe. Dorset LEA proposed to stop Axminster and Seaton children from attending Woodroffe as numbers at the school had exceeded 900 with many pupils housed in temporary classrooms. The authority proposed to hold talks with Woodroffe governors to discuss the possibility of re-defining the catchment area to reduce the annual intake. This proposal followed on from the merger idea which had earlier been rejected. The intention was to reduce the annual intake from 145 to 120.

Eddi Woodbridge took over as Chairman of Governors in September 1989 when Hugh Gibson retired from office. As the mother of five children who had attended the school she felt that she wanted to do something constructive to help it continue to develop its fine record.

At the conclusion of the decade the school hall underwent a much-needed refurbishment funded by the PTA and Dorset County Council. £4,000 was raised for this purpose which was felt to be a top priority as the hall was used for many public and community events as well as for school purposes.

CHAPTER 10 – 1990 TO 1999: THE NINETIES

In early 1990 Dorset Education Sub-Committee announced that there would be no major school building programme at Woodroffe until the outcome of future plans for Axminster School were known. Governors were urging the local authority to replace temporary classrooms with permanent ones but the authority was adamant that there would be no building programme for at least four years.

Consideration was being given to changing the timing of the school day by moving the start time from 8.55 am to 8.45 am, the finish time from 4.05 pm to 3.25 pm and reducing the lunch period by fifteen minutes in an effort to reduce the long school day. It was pointed out that many children had long journeys to and from school which meant that they were often too tired to complete their homework. Lesson time and after school activities would not be affected by the new timings.

In the newsletter to parents dated Spring 1990 the Head advised that the school had entered a new era with the introduction of Local Management of Schools (LMS) on 1st April 1990. This meant that the governors now had more control on how the school was managed, not just in terms of finance, but also the effective use of all resources. The Head welcomed LMS and felt optimistic that the Governing Body would be able to maximise the school's resources for the benefit of its pupils. The Head also pointed out that there was to be a move away from 1st, 2nd, 3rd, 4th and 5th forms to Year 7, Year 8, Year 9, Year 10 and Year 11 as these groupings related directly to the National Curriculum. A whole school, colour photograph was taken on 25th April 1990.

The Music Department announced that the Madrigal Group had successfully auditioned to take part in Harry Secombe's programme "Highways" which was to be televised on 20th May 1990. In the meantime it had competed in the Sainsbury's Choir of the Year competition and had joined forces with twenty other choirs for a "singing day" at Wembley Conference Arena where it had performed Mozart's Requiem, conducted by Brian Kay, an ex-member of the King Singers. Plans were well advanced for the Madrigal Group's visit to two schools in West Germany in the summer.

Pupils in the Design Technology Department were keen to enter a national competition, organised by BP, to build a car or hovercraft. However the most economic estimate indicated that it would cost a minimum of £400 to enter, so an appeal was made for sponsorship, help with materials, etc. Subsequently the Seaton Motor Company Limited, J Bolton Vending Co Ltd and Roper and Roper, Solicitors, came forward as sponsors.

Tony Caffrey, Head of Biology, and two Sixth Formers interested in a career in medicine accepted an invitation from the Senior Theatre Sister at Weymouth and District Hospital to spend a day with her and her staff. They subsequently witnessed a consultant sewing up a patient after a successful operation, which lasted three hours, to correct a compressed fracture of the spine, and also an operation involving the repair of a serious lung wound. The day was rounded off by a visit to the anaesthetic room.

The School on the Hill

Alan Brown reported on the 6th form pupil ski trip that had taken place at Christmas 1989 when fifty pupils and staff had travelled to Zell Am See in Austria. The trip catered for all comers – complete beginners, competents and experts, with a sprinkling of complete maniacs! The group enjoyed glorious sunshine and good snow conditions and were looking forward to the next tour planned for Easter 1991 when a visit would be made to St Gervain in France. The 4th year ski trip to Foppolo in Italy, which had involved forty eight pupils had not been so lucky with the weather but the snow just lasted long enough and by the end of the week all had skied from the top of the mountain.

It was announced that following the success of the two Activity Days at the end of the Summer Term 1989, it had been decided to have a week of activities for the whole school in July 1990. Trips planned included visits to Berlin, Moselle and Paris and more locally based activities would include water sports, athletics, board games, food preparation, photography, cycling, calligraphy, deep-sea fishing, conservation projects, swimming, various coach trips, video-making, computing and drama.

The school was extremely proud that Baroness Warnock had presented prizes at Senior Speech Day in April. Baroness Warnock was Mistress of Girton College, Cambridge and a scholar of Educational and Moral Philosophy. She had been a member of several Government Committees and was the Head of Oxford High School. Baroness Warnock had been on the BBC "Any Questions" panel which had been broadcast from Woodroffe in September 1989.

Five members of the teaching staff – David Chambers, Roger Dowle, James Thomas, Alan Brown and Gary Wells took part in a fifteen hour marathon sponsored cycle to raise funds to buy replacement bikes for two pupils who had had their brand new mountain bikes stolen whilst on a five day cycling trip to Dartmoor organised by the school.

Environmentally friendly pupils in Years 7, 8 and 9 combed eight miles of beach between Pinhay and Seatown for rubbish and collected a staggering amount of litter (including a kitchen sink) in a litter pick organised by David Manners. Once again the Fun Run took place in May with over 500 runners taking part in the Fun Run, the Ten Mile Race and the Five Mile Race. Local participants were joined by competitors from all over the West Country, including fitness fanatic and local MP, Sir James Spicer.

In the Summer of 1990 the Head outlined the vagaries of Local Management of Schools (LMS), the newly introduced system which offered schools greater control and flexibility in terms of the management of funding. However, although there were opportunities for the latter, the whole system fell down due to insufficient funds being available to meet the needs of all pupils. The dilemma was one of balancing the books and yet keeping the educational needs of children central to all decisions.

The Chairman of Governors, Eddie Woodbridge, provided parents with a breakdown of work being undertaken by the Governing Body. Seven sub-committees had been set up to look after boarding, curriculum, finance, public relations, repairs and maintenance, staffing and uniform. The uniform group was looking at ways of improving the standard of dress and the proposal of the PTA to establish a school shop would greatly assist. The introduction of LMS had meant that the school had to make two teachers and one member of the support staff redundant but efforts were being made to continue to run the school on a curriculum basis. The governors were pressing the LEA for the outcome of the Re-appraisal of Boarding which it had instigated in 1986, as the school was keen to build up boarding and was planning to introduce weekly boarding. Mrs Woodbridge paid tribute to the teaching staff who had had to absorb a huge amount of extra work generated by the implementation of the National Curriculum.

The PE Department were looking at ways to modify the PE curriculum in order to comply with the requirement of the National Curriculum. Innovations including the introduction of more teaching in mixed classes, a health related fitness course in Years 10 and 11, gymnastics for boys, orienteering and information packs for school leavers regarding sporting issues. Extra-curricular activities were flourishing, including the recent "Motion Commotion" dance show which had played to packed houses and had raised £850.

The introduction of the National Curriculum meant greater emphasis on practical skills in the Geography Department and for Science, which had become a core subject. All pupils were now required to study Science from age eleven to sixteen. Another recent innovation was the introduction of the GCSE Science in Society Course in the Sixth Form, which enabled those who did not have a particular scientific bent to achieve a qualification in the subject.

The English Department announced that they too had been working hard towards the implementation of the National Curriculum. Year 8 had been given the opportunity to study Desk Top Publishing and it was proposed to start a Desk Top Publishing Lunch Hour Club, with a view to producing a school newspaper.

In Modern Languages there had also been significant changes during the past year. Year 7 were now studying a foreign language, German had disappeared from the Year 9 curriculum but Russian would be available in the Sixth Form to GCSE level by Summer 1991, and there were Spanish GCSE exams and even Dutch tuition.

The national curriculum in the Faculty of Design had seen the introduction of Technology in Year 7 as a foundation subject and compulsory element. The Department had also helped to pilot two major national initiatives – the development of a new Modular Design and Technology A level syllabus for the Associated Examining Board, and the development of SATS (Standard Assessment Tasks) to assess pupil performance for the National Curriculum.

Careers work, or Work Related Education as it was now known, was rapidly changing and broadening. The aim now was to link the work of the classroom with the wider community and industry to ensure that pupils from primary level upwards were aware of the link between the two. The school worked closely with the Dorset Careers Service and the school's Careers Library was an essential resource providing up-to-date information on a wide range of careers and training including degree courses.

The initiative "Technology Through Home Economics", in which Dorset had participated with six other counties from Cornwall to Wiltshire, had allowed the Home Economics Department to contribute to national developments. The initiative, along with TVEI, had provided the Department with several cameras, a video camera, computers and word processors, to be used alongside food processors and wooden spoons.

At Junior Speech Day in July 1990 the Head suggested to pupils that they should mark themselves out of ten to try and gauge their abilities. He referred to the fact that they were the best advertisement for the school and on the whole they lived up to his expectations of them. Reference was made to uniform and the fact that efforts were underway to create a school shop where uniform could be purchased on site. For the first time the Head referred to a recent decision by the Governing Body to seek grant maintained status which would allow the school greater flexibility and more independence.

The guest speaker was former Head, Mr Pearn who referred to the school motto "Audacia Constantiaque" which he had devised some forty years previously. This roughly translated meant "with courage and determination". He advised the audience that at that time there were only 200 pupils, no Sixth Form and no boarders. Thirty years later there were now 900 on roll, over 180 boarders and a large Sixth Form. Mr Pearn suggested a new motto for the school "Cum Misericordia" (with humanity and compassion) and he felt that the efforts by some pupils, who had recently participated in a beach clean, was an excellent example of what could be achieved living by such a motto.

At the end of the Summer Term 1990 Brian Manners, Head of Music, retired after completing almost thirty years at the school. Tributes were paid to him at a special evening attended by former members of the Madrigal Group who had travelled many miles to be there. The event was combined with a cheese and wine party preceding the Madrigal Group's tour to Germany. The evening reached a nostalgic climax when former members of the Madrigal Group joined current singers to swell the ranks to over one hundred for a performance of one of their favourite arrangements of "When I'm 64". Another popular member of staff, Alex Bax, who taught Design and Technology, also retired after eighteen years at the school. Roger Dowle lamented the loss of Mr Bax whose tremendous skill and expertise had been invaluable over many years.

Throughout the Autumn Term there was considerable discussion between governors, parents and staff as to whether the school should "opt out". After a consultation period a parent ballot was held and it was agreed that the school should apply to the Secretary of State for Education for Grant Maintained Status.

Meanwhile school life was proceeding as normal. Year 7 took part in a nationwide sponsored reading event to raise funds for The Malcolm Sargent Cancer Fund for Children, entitled "Readathon 90". The Christmas Fair raised £1,500 towards the cost of establishing a school shop. The school also organised activities relating to Red Nose Day which generated a total of £350.

It was announced that West Dorset District Council had agreed a grant of £4,500 towards the cost of setting up the school shop which would also be available for use out of school hours as a social area and coffee bar for community groups using the school premises. The total estimated cost for this project was £15,000.

Kriss Akabusi, European 400 metres hurdles champion, visited Woodroffe as part of the Superschools Scheme, which encouraged the raising of money to fund exceptionally talented youngsters who required financial help to pursue their sport to the highest level. £1,500 was raised in total, with £500 going to Superschools and the remaining funds being retained in school for new equipment and items for the new library.

Pupils also collected hundreds of small gifts as Christmas presents for children in Romania as part of an appeal organised by local businessman, Adrian Huxon. In another initiative Woodroffe Sixth Formers and their Business Studies teacher, Jan Jaques, raised over £200 for the Crisis in Africa appeal by holding a school disco.

Harriet Marsh and Angharad Williams appealed for the school community and local residents to send letters to former pupils serving in the Gulf War. This followed the receipt of a letter from RAF Pilot officer, Andy Calame, an ex-boarder.

In November 1990 the governors received the news that they had been waiting for, that the school had successfully achieved Grant Maintained status. The Secretary of State for Education had given his approval which meant that from 1st September 1991 the school would no longer come under LEA control. At about this time governors announced that they were considering building a new boarding complex for 140 pupils on land adjacent to the school site. This land was already ear-marked for a housing development and the Governing Body was negotiating with the developer for the site.

After an extensive training period, Sixth Formers, Nicholas Gray and Graham Blackmore *(pictured right),* joined the Lyme Regis lifeboat crew. Nicholas was a full lifeboat crew member and Graham was a launcher. Both were required to be on call at all times and carried their "bleepers" in school.

800 pupils paid 20p each to join an open-air aerobics session on the school tennis courts, organised by Jan Jaques, which raised over £300 for victims of the famine in Africa. The event was filmed by television cameras from the BBC programme, Newsround. A dance show, entitled "Dancing the Alphabet" raised £500. Seventy five pupils took part and costumes were produced under the supervision of textiles teacher, Rebecca Barnes. Each night a member of the teaching staff joined in the fun to make a mystery guest appearance in a highly memorable rendition of "Seven Little Girls".

In March 1991 the Head explained that schools, like families, grow and he advised that several new things were happening at school – the PTA shop and Woodroffe Community Association social area and coffee bar was taking shape and a Combined Cadet Force for all three services was to be introduced in September. In an effort to promote boarding it was proposed to offer a weekly boarding facility whereby boarders returned home for weekends. The governors were also looking into the possibility of arranging daily transport for those living in outlying areas.

Eddie Woodbridge advised that having heard in February that the school's application for Grant Maintained Status had been successful, the governors had not only appointed a new Bursar, Peter Rickard, they had also engaged the services of consultant architects, The Jonathan Ball Partnership, to assist with the school's capital bid. Close liaison was also taking place with the Grant Maintained Trust to determine how best to approach the many other aspects of "opting-out".

In the Design Technology Department individuals and various groups were involved in commissions for outside agencies. These included production runs of screen printed designed T shirts, the complete graphic identity for the prestigious public launch of a newly formed company, and the design for the security code to be used on American Express credit cards. Visitors to the Department had included Artist-in-Residence, Andy Wood and the theatre group Imule, who had worked with Year 8 Technology pupils.

Jan Melvin advised that as an outcome of the school's input into the "Technology Through Home Economics" initiative, she had been invited to take part in a live television programme which had been broadcast via satellite both nationally and across Europe. Examples of pupils' work were exhibited during the programme and video film which was taken on location at Woodroffe was shown as an example of "good practice".

Woodroffe pupils celebrated winning £3,600 in a national competition by taking tea on the terrace of the House of Commons with local MP, Sir James Spicer. Sarah Thomas and Christopher Groom, together with the Head and Head of Art, Dot Page, called on Sir James after Woodroffe's success in the Sainsbury's Award Scheme was announced at the National Gallery. Sainsbury's had called for imaginative educational arts presentations and the school had submitted an inter-departmental project featuring the 1839 landslip which included a five-day music workshop with a local musician who specialised in traditional Dorset folk songs, music and drama. This was to be followed by the writing and presentation of poems and short sketches and songs based on the history of the big slip. More than 340 schools had entered the national competition, twenty had been short-listed and twelve schools, including Woodroffe, had been successful.

Thirty five pupils from Woodroffe enjoyed the most ambitious school trip yet, a week long visit to the Soviet Union. The party was led by languages tutor, Helen Graham, accompanied by History teachers, John Seabrook and Ian Wood. The trip had been organised to improve the understanding of Russian culture and the changes taking place in the country under the then leadership of Mikhail Gorbachov. The tour included visits to the world famous Hermitage Art Gallery at the Winter Palace in Leningrad, to The Kremlin, Lenin's Tomb and to the cathedrals in Moscow. Pupils wrote about their experiences as follows:

"Aeroflot was an experience! The landings were hair-raising, toilets very "Russian" and the planes seemed to be held together with ice! During our three days in Leningrad we visited the Peter and Paul fortress which is situated on an island, the Winter Palace in all its resplendent glory, the Museum of the October Revolution and the graves of those who died in the 900-day siege. Snow-covered graves stretch out on either side, broken by pathways and black, leafless tress. Loudspeakers play solemn music, the nameless graves a poignant reminder of our own fragile peace.

The School on the Hill

The hotel was what you might call "basic" although meals by Russian standards were five-star. Usually breakfast consisted of meat with lots of bread. We had butter most days but it is rationed for the ordinary Russians. Lunch is the Russians' main meal - usually a starter, a soup and then meat. In Russia green vegetables are a thing of the imagination, although the hotel did try to give us at least one piece of fruit a day. We travelled to Moscow on the overnight train, which is an experience in itself.

Arriving in Moscow in the early morning we saw a very different city to Leningrad. Moscow has a stark modern appearance compared with the Tsarist splendour of St Petersburg. The black market is illegal in the USSR but everywhere we went we had stacking dolls and fur hats pushed our way in exchange for hard currency – the rouble seems to be a rude word in Russia! Russia is a country that has great potential. Seeing the queues makes you feel deeply humbled because while we were there we were given two cakes and a box of chocolates which are in short supply. The people are so pleased to help in any way they can. How can a nation with so little give so much?"[1]

At senior speech day in July 1991 the Head again stressed his belief that the school's greatest asset was its young people. He explained that good manners in the classroom, travelling to and from school and activities and conduct within the community were good yardsticks in the assessment of the quality of the school. He urged pupils to have the confidence to condemn and criticise their fellows when they did something to damage the reputation of the school. The Chairman of Governors, Eddie Woodbridge, praised pupils of the school who were getting better examination results than their predecessors yet at the same time were less self-centred when it came to caring for those less well-off than themselves. She hoped pupils would continue to work hard and reap just rewards, reminding them that "*you will make your living from what you earn, but you will make your life from what you give*".

The school began the new school year in September 1991 as a Grant Maintained School, funded directly by the DfES. The governing body now had total responsibility for the management of the school budget, it owned the school buildings and all other assets, it was the employer of all staff and it became the admissions authority for entry into the school.

The Head announced a pass rate of 74.5% at A level, with two pupils taking up places at Oxford and a further fifty three intending to enter higher education. The Head was particularly pleased that a number of individuals, who a few years ago would not have considered studying for A levels, had gone ahead and done so and had achieved their goal.

A dance featuring the Weymouth All Stars was held at the school to celebrate grant maintained status, the opening of the new coffee lounge by Woodroffe Community Association and the opening of the new PTA shop. Woodroffe Community Association launched its "Class 4" series of evening classes which offered a wide range of courses in blocks of four.

---

[1] Extract from the Lyme Regis News undated

In October 1991 a decline in demand for boarding places forced the governors to decide to rationalise boarding provision and Harcombe House was closed, with junior boys transfering to Rhode Hill.

Eddie Woodbridge advised that the transitional grant of £55,170 had been used to set up a workable administration system, complete with computer network and with the new offices, expenditure of the grant had resulted in greater efficiency and economical use of space, time and money. Another tangible result of the decision to opt out was the fact that instead of reducing staff, as would have been the case under LMS, the school was now able to appoint additional staff.

Mrs Woodbridge clarified the funding arrangements for grant maintained schools. She explained that they received the same amount of money as LEA schools, plus currently an additional 10%, soon to be 15%. The extra percentage was to cover the cost of services which the school no longer received free from the LEA, such as catering, cleaning, grounds maintenance, insurance, banking, auditing and general administration. This allowed the school greater flexibility in running the school. Examples were the improvement in school meals and the school grounds now that the governors had been able to appoint their own contractors.

Bids were being placed with the Department of Education and Science for the provision of a new Science and Technology building, and a new Library, and a task group was also looking at ways to improve sporting facilities at the school by pursuing further grants with the intention of providing a sports hall for use by both the school and the community.

The introduction of the national curriculum for PE in the Autumn of 1992 meant that all children between the ages of five and sixteen would be required by law to participate in Physical Education. David Chambers reflected on the general level of fitness, which he felt was deteriorating not only at the school but nationally. This was attributed to excessive viewing of videos and television, a reluctance to walk anywhere and the increased dangers of being on the roads either as a cyclist or pedestrian. He urged parents to encourage their children to participate in sport and to consider carefully before writing a note excusing them from sporting activity.

The school staged two performances of "The Landslip", its winning entry in the Sainsbury's Awards for Arts Education. The production, the culmination of workshops and research by a wide range of departments at Woodroffe over a three month period, was an original study of the Axmouth landslip of 1839. Staff and pupils involved in the project received support from professional musician and singer, Tim Laycock, who adapted children's poems and writing to music.

As part of fund-raising for Children in Need, Deputy Head, Jo Culham challenged pupils to collect enough pennies to match her weight! Roger Dowle, in the Design Technology Department, constructed a see-saw to demonstrate the success of the collection.

Kathy Elliott, organised a Cabaret Evening which featured both staff and pupils. This highly successful event raised a total of £150 which was shared equally between Amnesty International and The Guide Dogs for the Blind Association.

The School on the Hill

A twelve year old Croatian refugee, Igor Glavan, who had fled war-torn Yugoslavia with his mother and sister, spent seven months as a Year 8 pupil at Woodroffe. When he arrived he could not speak English and had to communicate in German, his second language. However, he quickly learned sufficient English to get by and he received a special Woodroffe silver award in recognition of his academic achievements and attitude at a farewell assembly. Igor had proved to be a popular member of his year group and was praised for his courage, diligence and good humour. When he and his family left, they flew to Italy, where they were re-united with Igor's father at his grandmother's home near the Croatia-Italy border just south of Trieste.

There was trouble about the decision by the school to withdraw the sale of tuck in the newly created PTA shop, as this was having an adverse effect on the catering operation run by the school's professional caterers. Some members of the PTA felt that the success of the shop was being undermined, as without the revenue from the sale of tuck there was a danger that it would no longer be financially viable. Although initially the governors had indicated to the PTA that the sale of tuck in the shop would be allowed, they pointed out that their obligation to manage the school under the instrument and articles of government now had a higher priority. Two outlets for the sale of food were proving to be counter-productive and therefore the decision had been made to concentrate all food sales through the school's catering service and to improve the quality of food available to pupils.

Ex-pupil, John Denham, achieved one of the biggest political swings in the country when he ousted Roads Minister Christopher Chope from his Itchen, Southampton seat. The new Labour Member of Parliament took the seat by 600 votes – a swing from the Conservatives of 6.2%.

The school took a strong stand against under-age drinking, advising those over eighteen to obtain proof of age cards and encouraging all licensees in the town to refuse to sell alcohol to youngsters who could not produce proof of their age. The Head pointed out that the dangers of alcohol abuse formed a main part of the school's education programme but little could be achieved without the vigilance of parents and the caution of licensees. The local police and licensees supported the introduction of the proof of age cards.

Design Technology pupils Tim Gibbins and Andrew Squire were awarded maximum possible marks for their Design and Realisation practical projects. Also Vincent Rattenbury, Simon Holt and Paula Hannaford took first, second and third place in the Rotary Club Young Inventors competition. A pneumatic vice for use by handicapped persons, designed by Vincent, was to go forward to the regional final. Roger Dowle advised that the school had benefited indirectly from a break-in at Axminster sports shop "Sport 'n' Gear". The Design Department had received nine very expensive Hi-Tech sports shoes to be used in design studies by Sixth Formers - the other half of each pair had been stolen with their boxes from the stock room.

As the Summer Term drew to a close, concerns began to be raised about a deficit budget and possible staff redundancies. The situation had escalated by the start of the Autumn

Term in 1992 and this difficult period of the school's history is covered in some detail in Chapter 14 on Grant Maintained Status.

At the end of September 1992, after a turbulent few weeks, Paul Vittle stepped down as Head and Eddie Woodbridge also resigned as Chairman of Governors. Ian Cook became Acting Headteacher and Tony Terrett took over leadership of the Governing Body. Mr Vittle resigned in December and Mr Cook remained in post for the remainder of the academic year. Morale within the school was particularly low at this time but Mr Cook and Mr Terrett between them kept the school on an even keel and moving forward.

There was controversy over the school's annual Carol Service. Rev Murray Dell indicated that due to bad feeling in the community, he was not willing for this event to take place in the local parish church. Consequently the Carol Service in December 1992 was held in the school hall for the first and only time in the school's history.

In March 1993 the Dance Show "Box of Tricks" took place and this highly successful event raised £870 for the PE Department. In May a new publication, the Parents' Bulletin, was launched. It was hoped to circulate an issue every half term which would contain all information going home to parents in one document. Also in May the interview process for a new Head began which culminated in the appointment of Mr Kerrigan Redman.

By now the Library was fully computerised and pupils were able to borrow books when the Librarian was present. Refurbishment of this area would be completed by the end of term and new books were being acquired constantly. It was noted with some satisfaction that the Library was re-emerging as a focal point in school life.

Activities Week took place from 12th to 17th July 1993. This week had been introduced four years previously to accommodate various foreign visits by staff and pupils, thus avoiding sporadic disruption of classes and teaching throughout the year. This year activities included hiking, orienteering, fossil-hunting, computing, magazine production, mask making, music workshops and a wide variety of games including swimming. Visits were made to France, Wales, the Lake District, Ireland, Dartmoor and Austria.

Sadly, the decision to close another of the boarding houses was made in July when St Andrews was shut with senior boys transfering to Rhode Hill which became the school's sole boarding facility.

The PTA announced that they had raised £3,000 for the school which would be used to buy equipment on each Department's priority list. This included maps for Humanities, keyboards for Music, cameras for Art, kitchen equipment for Home Economics, molecular models for Chemistry, an ECG interface for Biology, a reading machine for SEN plus equipment for PE, Textiles, RE and Geography. The sums raised by the PTA during the year totalled an amazing £6,000 and the Committee was thanked for their efforts by their new Chairman, Merrie Weldon, who had taken over from Patrick Dixon.

At the end of the Summer Term Ian Cook took early retirement after fifteen years at the school during which he had done sterling work, including the supervision of the major rebuild in 1979 and later the introduction of TVEI in 1988. He will best be remembered for leading the school through an extremely difficult period in its history and ensuring a smooth transition for the new Head, Kerrigan Redman, who took over in September 1993.

Mr Redman came to Woodroffe from Bridlington School, a large mixed comprehensive with boarding. Originally from Swindon, he was married with two grown up daughters both of whom were teachers. For the first few months of his headship he and his wife, Pamela, and their dog, lived in their caravan in the grounds of Rhode Hill. They then took up temporary residence in the flat at St Andrews before moving to their new home in the town.

In the October Parents' Bulletin the new Head advised that he had enjoyed his first half term at the school and had been impressed by the excellent relationships that existed within the school, the range and quality of opportunities available to the pupils and the commitment of his colleagues. He felt that he had inherited a very good foundation on which to build in partnership with parents.

During the autumn term a team of ten Year 9 girls participated in the first ever sports exchange between Woodroffe and Cranbourne School in Basingstoke. Pupils from Cranbourne stayed with girls from Woodroffe and over the weekend friendly hockey and netball matches were held and also a swimming gala. The aim of the exchange was to foster friendly competition and this was definitely achieved. A return visit to Basingstoke was planned.

The closure of the Lyme Regis Outdoor Education Centre in 1993 after twenty five years was greatly regretted, as the school had enjoyed a very close working relationship with staff there. Thankfully, due to a lot of hard work and the goodwill of many people, arrangements were made whereby the school's canoeing and sailing clubs could continue to operate. Four members of the teaching staff, Dot Page, James Thomas, Hugh FitzGerald and Chris Joyner, undertook an intensive instructor's course at the end of term, which ensured that in future there would be sufficiently qualified staff on hand to supervise activities on the water.

The school had recently been allocated the sum of £150,000 by the Department for Education to enhance Science facilities. In addition to the refurbishment of existing facilities, plans were being drawn up to provide a new laboratory and prep room over the flat roof of C26. Work on site was scheduled to commence on 1st November 1993 and it was hoped that the project would be completed by 1st March 1994.

The Sixth Form curriculum had now been revised and included courses for both one year and two year pupils leading to job specific National Vocational Qualifications (NVQs) and General National Vocational Qualifications (GNVQs) alongside more traditional A level and AS level courses. This provided greater choice and widened the range of sixth form opportunities, thus hopefully increasing the staying-on rate.

As a grant maintained school an annual grant of £28,000 was paid to the school for small capital works and consideration was being given to how to use these monies to improve the overall-efficiency of the school.

The Science Department was involved with the setting up of a neighbourhood engineers scheme, and the ICT Department together with the Learning Support Team, was co-operating with a Devon scheme to provide portable computers for pupils with special learning difficulties. It was also noted that computer literacy and IT skills elements were being introduced to Enrichment Programmes for Year 10 and the Sixth Form.

In addition to reports on hockey, rugby, basketball, and cross country, the PE Department advised that the school had entered a team at the Inter-School Show Jumping Competition that had taken place at Clayhidon, near Cullompton. Two teams were entered and performed extremely well with one team reaching the final where it achieved second place.

Design Technology was firing on all cylinders, planning a "Woodroffe Walking Wild Fashion Show" involving A level design pupils, the PTA and the Textiles Department; Les Driver and Dot Page had set up a display of pupils' art work at the new Health Centre; speakers had visited from British Gas, Playgroup Organisations, Social Services and the Health Centre and trips were planned to Barcelona and the Clothes Show in Birmingham.

The new Enrichment Programme for the Lower Sixth was proving very successful with modules being followed including Green Issues, Photography, Word Processing, Geography of Tourism, Survival Cookery and the Youth Awards scheme. The Upper Sixth were working on their personal statements to support Higher Education applications or planning exciting gap years but there was time for social events such as a barbeque, a residential trip to London, and, of course, preparations for the Fifth and Sixth Ball before mocks loomed next term.

In February 1994 it was announced that the Department for Education had released funds to pay for the repair of the flat roofs on a number of school buildings with the work to be completed by March. Work had begun on the new Science laboratory which should be completed by late Spring.

Year 10 under the guidance of Jenny Pearson were working on an edition of The Oracle, the popular school magazine produced by Media Studies pupils. Paul Skelton's Year 10 group had chosen MediActive as the title for their eight page supplement on the Media and Entertainment in Dorset, funded by Dorset TEC, to be printed by the Dorset Evening Echo. Carol Hyde's junior drama group had just produced a very entertaining but updated version of Cinderella for 1994.

The dance show "A Cocktail of Dance" was very well received playing to packed houses on all three nights. Particularly impressive were the opening numbers from Cabaret. Sam Warburton made an admirable host, having remarkable stage presence and Harriet Marsh's rendition of Sally Bowles number "Mein Lieber Herr" was particularly memorable.

In May 1994 the Head advised that in September 1993 the Secretary of State for Education had launched the Technology Colleges initiative for Grant Maintained and Voluntary aided secondary schools. Technology Colleges would benefit from support from business and industry sponsors, both financially and in terms of advice and management support. They would deliver the full requirements of the National Curriculum while emphasizing Technology, Science and Mathematics. Schools wishing to become Technology Colleges had to raise £100,000 in sponsorship, a particularly difficult task in a rural area, although the Department for Education did specify that the sum could be shared between several sponsors and as well as cash, relevant equipment and materials were acceptable. A school successfully bidding for Technology College status would be eligible to receive an annual grant in addition to its normal funding. For a school the size of Woodroffe this would amount to £85,000 which could be used to appoint additional teaching and technical staff, increased in-service training for staff or the updating of specialist equipment. In January 1994 the governors agreed to put in a bid for Technology College status.

A group of Sixth Formers successfully passed the Basic Food Hygiene Certificate, and others had been learning more about photography and computer-aided design. Through a link with Headwey, a local training provider, nine pupils successfully completed their Community Sports Leader Award whereas others had been working with a local management consultant in an objective and target setting project.

Under the Neighbourhood Engineers Scheme a local engineer was visiting the school weekly to help Design A level pupils with their project work and a civil engineer was conducting site visits of the work being undertaken at Leper's Well and a building in Broad Street, Lyme Regis. Both these sites were suffering from structural problems and were of archaeological and historical interest which presented particular difficulties to the engineer.

In June a group of Year 9 girls visited Cranbourne School in Basingstoke to complete the away fixture of their PE exchange programme. Both teams thoroughly enjoyed the experience and friendships were fostered amongst the girls from both schools. The exchange programme proved a huge success and would continue for the Year 9 girls when they moved into Year 10.

Changes were made to the uniform for Sixth Formers as an embroidered school jumper was introduced in the autumn term to be worn with a white fine knit roll necked top or with a plain white shirt and Sixth Form tie. For the summer term an embroidered white polo shirt without a tie was to be an option.

At the start of the autumn term the Head reported excellent A level results including outstanding performances by Anna Labrom and Magnus Frampton which had gained them places at Oxford and Cambridge respectively. At GCSE level 46% of pupils gained at least 5 A – C grades. The gap between the performance of boys and girls had narrowed but was still significant. This was a national issue which the school was actively addressing.

During the summer holidays a substantial area of the school was re-decorated and carpeted and the Music Room was equipped with new console desks containing keyboards and headphones. A computer unit to aid composition and performance was also about to be installed. Much of this work was funded from the formula capital grant which Woodroffe received as a grant maintained school. A proportion of the grant remained to be used in 1994/1995 for the erection of a new store at the rear of the gym.

In an effort to increase "ability setting" the Head reported that in Year 8 pupils were now *set* for English, Mathematics and Modern Languages and in Year 9 Science and Geography were added to these. A new Homework Diary and Personal Log was introduced which it was hoped would increase communication between home and school.

Over 100 girls visited the WISE (Women into Science and Engineering) bus when it came to the school in October 1994. The bus had eight work stations on board and five different activities including building electronic circuits from modules, a computer design package to produce a desk tidy, and automatic door operating system run by pneumatics, a computer controlled greenhouse and a computer controlled conveyor belt which sorted cotton reels by colour.

It was noted that there were currently boarders at the school with families living in a number of countries: Japan, Turkey, France, Germany, Switzerland, South Africa, Ghana, Brunei, Taiwan, Hong Kong, Ascension Island and Slovakia.

Wednesday afternoons were providing Sixth Formers with the opportunity to get more involved in the community and to participate in a very wide range of sports. Two had been successful in obtaining a place on the Project Trust Scheme after arduous selection activities – Simon Ayers would be going to Egypt and Lenny Sheldon (Helen) would be off to Brazil. Five pupils would also be attending a seminar on the European Community in Paris, an exciting event designed to give a firsthand impression of opportunities afforded by the EEC.

In March 1995 the Head announced a proposed visit to South Africa by the Under 15 Rugby team and a possible Madrigal Group tour to Old Lyme, USA. Both these tours required a great deal of fund-raising and sponsorship to make them viable and committees were set up to raise the necessary monies.

The Rugby Tour involved boys from Year 9 and Year 10 and those participating needed to raise £12,000. It was envisaged that the tour would take in five games over a seventeen day period, beginning in Pretoria and finishing in Cape Town. The group would also see two World Cup games as the tour co-incided with the 1995 Rugby World Cup.

A Madrigal Tour was planned for mid-July and formed part of an exchange visit between Woodroffe and the High School Band from Old Lyme, Connecticut. The party from Old Lyme would be in Lyme Regis in late July and would perform at a concert at the school.

Work had also commenced on two projects – the creation of a PE store behind the old gym and the creation of an outside social area for pupils in the quadrangle. New cheque book reports were being introduced for Years 8 and 10 and local writers, Peter Benson and Laurence Anholt, visited school as part of a very successful Book Event in the Library. The school was engaged in the Dorset "Healthy Schools" Project and efforts were being made to improve the dietary information available to pupils in the school dining hall with assistance being provided by the community dietician.

Design Technology pupils were busy working with the Lyme Regis Town Council which had set up a competition for young people of the town to design a new town clock. The clock was to be sited on the impressive development carried out recently on the sea front and would serve as a commemoration of the completion of the new development.

A group of sixteen Year 9 Scientists attended a Science and Technology Day at Beaminster, alongside pupils from Colfox, Beaminster and The Gryphon School in Sherborne. It was a very intensive and rewarding day during which a variety of technology related problem solving exercises were undertaken. An extra dimension was added for the evening session as parents arrived to try their hand at one of the tasks – to design a package which would prevent an egg from breaking after being dropped from a height of 2m using only one piece of A4 paper and some sellotape.

In June 1995 a Year Council was formed to provide a means of consultation. This would enable pupils' views to be included in the various decision-making processes within the school. In addition the governors circulated a questionnaire to parents to assess their feelings about the school.

For the third year in succession a party of thirty five went to the South of France during activities week. They were based at a lakeside camp site south west of Bordeaux where they spent the week sailing, canoeing, windsurfing, swimming and surfing in the Atlantic. This year pupils also took part in the Exmoor Challenge and Ten Tors – in the latter a mixed team successfully completed the forty five mile trek.

The School Sailing Club was temporarily not functioning. However, a group of local people were in the process of setting up a trust to raise finance to maintain and administer a sizeable amount of equipment provided by the LEA, which included Toppers, Wayfarers, canoes, a safety boat and other essential equipment. Arrangements were also being made to use the facilities of the Lyme Regis Sailing Club.

The Rugby Tour of South Africa took place from 18th May to 2nd June 1995 and was an epic event with the party travelling from London to Johannesburg, Pretoria and Cape Town. The tour was described by David Chambers who accompanied the party.

"We trooped into assembly and stood on the stage dressed in green track suit bottoms and claret red training tops with the school crest and the South Africa Springbok embroidered on our chests… we were wished "bon voyage" …..we sang the South Africa National Anthem we had learned with the help of Malcolm Matthews. When we arrived at our first host school in Pretoria we were introduced to our host families. The players were billeted in pairs. Generally speaking the generosity and welcome we received from our host families was overwhelming. More often than not they organised a variety of evening activities for the boys.

The first game we played was against a development XV from Mamelodi, a black township. In this respect Woodroffe was making history as the first foreign school to play in Mamelodi. The game was won by Woodroffe 23 – 13 but the result was incidental as the occasion was so significant. After the game the players from both sides mixed freely at a reception in our honour. Together we sang traditional rugby songs, although in this respect we came a poor second to the wonderful harmonies that our black opponents managed to conjure up.

Perhaps the most vivid memory of Pretoria that the boys will reflect back on was the day that we visited a black school in the Mamelodi township. As we entered the school gates the children were shouting and screaming at the windows hoping to catch a glimpse of their visitors. This reception could have been mistaken for a threatening gesture but in fact it showed sheer enthusiasm. We were shown around the school and taken into a room which they called the "library". The school choir then assembled in front of us and for the next hour and a half sang to us. I cannot begin to describe the quality of the sound they produced, it was magical. At the end the girls danced over to the boys, still singing, took their hands and continued to dance around the room – this was a traditional welcome. Not wishing to be outdone, we in turn sang their National Anthem to them. This received great applause and excitement from the choir who responded by singing it back to us, properly, and I must admit I preferred their version.

We travelled down to Cape Town on the Trans-Lux coach. This was a nineteen hour journey but luckily we were in daylight as we descended from the High Veld through the Karoo down to Cape Town. The scenery at this point of the journey was magnificent. The next day we all got in a cable car and went to the top of Table Mountain. Throughout the tour the quality of the rugby that we played improved but this tour was about more than rugby. I feel sure that the experience that the boys had and the friends that they made will stay in their memories for many years. It was in all respects an outstanding tour!"[2]

The hard-working support team behind the tour party included Patrick Dixon, John Howe, Keith Jenkin, Nigel Powell, John Seabrook and Iain Thomson.

In November 1995 the Head paid tribute to the vast amount of work carried out by both teaching and support staff, during the summer holidays in preparation for the new term. He gave details of a trip he and his wife had made to Trencin in Slovakia. The visit had been at the invitation of the Head of the Gymnasium Ludovita Stura, a selective mixed school with 1,000 young people aged from fifteen to nineteen. The Head Stefan Marcinek, was extremely enthusiastic about twinning with Ludovita Stura and suggested that initially pupils would start writing to each other prior to exchange visits. He felt that there was a strong possibility that a link could be established between the Madrigal Group and Trenchan, the school's folk dancing and singing group, which enjoyed a national reputation, and he felt that sporting and ski-ing trips could also be considered. The Madrigal Group had enjoyed a successful tour to Lyme, Connecticut where they had received two standing ovations at Mystic and Lyme. Upon its return the group received a

---

[2] Extract from Parents' Bulletin dated June 1995

return visit from the Lyme Symphonic Band which gave a combined Concert incorporating the Symphonic Band, the Madrigal Group and the Lyme Regis Junior Band. No sooner had the Head unpacked his bags from Slovakia, the rugby tourists shaken off the dust of South Africa, and the Madrigal Group had got over their jetlag when Sharron Hutchings began to make plans for a squad of twenty five girls, drawn from Year 9 and Year 10, to travel to Canada in May 1996 when they would visit Ottawa and Toronto. The squad was in training and the fundraising was about to commence with a total of £18,000 required to finance the tour.

A new extra-curricular club in Control Technology was formed with a view to entering for a national "Micromouse 2000" competition. Sixteen new Apricot ZEN PC computers, purchased with Formula Capital funds, had been installed in the IT Department and were having a tremendous impact on learning. The new machines ran the same software as the computers in the Sixth Form Common Room thus enabling users to move easily between the two sites and work on the same document in either room. The increase in power of the new computers also meant that pupils were able to work to a higher standard and more quickly.

Some of the rather old and out of date BBC computers formerly used by the IT Department had now been re-located within a new area created in the DT Department by teaching staff and the DT technician, Colin Cockram. These were to be used for Computer Control work including a range of electronic and mechanical projects. The remaining BBC computers had been installed in the Science Department thus allowing much larger groups to work on IT based topics. Plans were being made to replace the old Amstrad PCW machines in Business Studies with personal computers. These would be compatible with the hardware now installed in the Maths Department and would enable the Business Studies Department to run the industry standard software they had wanted to use for several years.

The School Sailing Club was afloat again with a keen, enthusiastic group of sailors from Year 7 to the Upper Sixth. Chris Joyner had qualified as a Senior Instructor, joining the ranks of James Thomas, Dot Page and Hugh FitzGerald. The success of the Club relied very much on a new organisation called "Lyme Regis Sea School Trust", chaired by Jim Bolton, which owned and administered all the equipment. The Trust had gained support from local bodies such as Lyme Regis Town Council and Bumbles Circus but needed to generate an income of around £2,000 a year to cover overheads. A competition was being organised to design a logo for the Trust and pupils were encouraged to enter.

A reunion of ex-pupils of both Lyme Regis Grammar School and the Woodroffe School took place on Saturday, 23rd September 1995, with Thornton Pearn as the guest of honour. Over 270 ex-pupils attended with guests travelling from all parts of the globe to attend including Tim Castle from America, Rodney Jones from Germany and Lesley Santan from Trinidad. By the end of the evening it was discovered that there was at least one former pupil from every year from 1924 to 1987. The highlight of the evening came when Major Pearn played the piano for a lively rendition of the School Song.

February 1996 saw the closure of the last boarding house, when the Head announced the decision to close Rhode Hill with effect from 31st July 1996. This was attributed to changing social patterns and the reduction of the Armed Forces, both factors having led to a major national decline in the demand for boarding places in the state and independent sectors. Arrangements were made for boarders half way through their examinations courses to be accommodated at Allhallows College. It was pointed out that although the loss of boarding was to be regretted as it provided the school with a special dimension, the school no longer depended on boarding to maintain numbers on roll as the popularity of Woodroffe locally was now ensuring full year groups in the main school and a healthy Sixth Form.

A small group of Upper Sixth pupils attended the "Your Future in Europe" Conference in Paris accompanied by Bob Inskip. The party travelled with other sixth formers from The Gryphon School, Beaminster and Colfox. Jayne Barron advised that she and two GNVQ Advanced Level Leisure and Tourism pupils would be visiting Slovakia to investigate the growing Slovakian tourist industry. The visit would build on the link recently established with Gymnazium Ludovita Stura and Woodroffe.

The Humanities Faculty was receiving regular correspondence from Richard Hudson who was on a sabbatical year and was travelling in Nepal and India. Sixth Form environmentalists had been on a guided tour of the new Lyme Regis seafront project and pumping station followed by a visit to the newly completed Sleech Wood sewerage treatment scheme in Uplyme.

James Thomas apologised to parents who might have had their sheds raided whilst Year 7 were working on a homework project requiring them to exercise their technological and inventive skills to produce weather measuring equipment. Some impressive instruments were produced which measured wind speed and direction, rainfall and even air pressure but the most impressive had been an anemometer, cleverly constructed by Kevin Davies, which measured wind speed using a sophisticated set of cogs and incorporating a bicycle speedometer.

In June 1996 it was announced that Roger Dowle, Claire Jones and Mary Swainston were all retiring. Roger had been at the school since 1974 and throughout his time at the school had built up a highly successful and diverse Design Technology Department. Claire joined the school in 1986 as Head of Modern Languages, and had steered the Department through a number of important curricular changes. Mary would be missed for her expertise in German and the foreign trips she had organised over many years. Her role in co-ordinating the arrangements for the transfer of primary school children to Woodrooffe had been particularly outstanding. Mary ensured that they felt at ease and she went out of her way to calm parental concerns as their "babies" entered "big" school.

The Hockey Tour to Canada took place in May. £22,000 had been raised in a very short time due largely to the excellent partnership which existed between the school and parents. The Head congratulated Sharron Hutchings, the tour leader, on the success of the venture. Other staff who joined the trip were Jo Culham, Sheila Bland and student teachers Vicky Castle and Louise Hipkins

Louise gave a comprehensive report on the tour, which had commenced on 17th May 1996. The party visited the Toronto Islands and Ontario Place, a small theme park. They also visited the CN Tower and Skydrome, the home of the Bluejays baskball team. The glass elevator at the tower ascended at fifteen mph and having got over that the next feat for the girls was walking over the glass floor at the top of the tower. Sightseeing was followed by two hockey matches and two training sessions. The party then moved on to spend a weekend at small town called Kincardine where the girls would stay with different families. At Tournament Day at Kincardine High School the teams played four matches in total, winning one, drawing two and losing one. At Hamilton two games were played and during the last game the girls were live on Channel 12 television. A visit to Niagara culminated in a boat trip which passed the America Falls and then the famous Horse Shoe Canadian Falls. The day concluded with a walk through the tunnels under Niagara. The tour finished with a three hour shopping spree in the Eaton Centre in Toronto prior to the long flight home.

In the English Department there was much excitement about the Carlton TV project on Mary Anning which was to be filmed in Lyme Regis in June. Four pupils – Hayley Chapman, Melanie Easton, Graham Renton and Gaeton Beresford – had also been selected to be involved in this scientific docu-drama on fossiling to be shown on Channel 4 programmes.

A twenty-five PC network using Microsoft Windows and Excel was installed in the Business Studies Department and the intention was that after September the Business Studies suite would be available for the use of the whole school. The facility was open at lunchtime and was also used in the evening for Adult Education classes. The Department had recently been given permission by RSA to run NVQ Business Administration at Level III – often only granted to businesses - and three pupils were now studying that course.

Two GCSE pupils, from the Design Technology Department travelled to Brunel University having reached the Southern Regional Final for The Yeda Prize which targeted young electronic designers across the whole of the British Isles. Unfortunately Matthew Wilson, with his device to control prescribed medication, and Nick Grant, who designed an input device for controlling a remote for precision handling of equipment, narrowly missed being selected for the final at the National Science Museum. Not to be outdone, the Micro Mouse Club was getting ready to compete in the World Micro Mouse Championships 1996 to be held at the University of East London.

In Food Techonology Year 10 were involved in "Shopping 2000" a project funded by West Dorset Compact, which involved a tour of the new Safeway Store in Yeovil. Post-16 GNVQ pupils had recently undertaken an extensive range of visits and activities including a visit to West Dorset District Council, where they toured the Pathology Department. They had also attended a First Aid Course, worked with the Diabetic Support Group at the Health Centre, been involved with the No Smoking Day and had worked with a community dietician and with a representative from CADAS in relation to drugs and alcohol.

Sixth Form artists visited both Paris and Amsterdam and had also found time to fit in trips to the Tate to view the Cezanne Exhibition, a workshop at the National Portrait Gallery and a visit to the Victoria and Albert Museum. Pupils were working on banners for the

Lyme Regis Jazz Festival and a group of A level artists, with 30 other Dorset Sixth Formers, were due to spend a residential week in Swanage attending a course run by Dorset LEA which featured two African artists in residence instructing the group in pottery and painting.

The Fashion Show "Hot Stepping", organised by the Textiles Department, was a great success. The show had featured a combination of garments designed and made in school, alongside merchandise from local designers and retailers, all modelled by Woodroffe pupils.

Thanks mainly to the fund-raising efforts of Mike Hankey and Royston Davies, £2,500 had been raised to provide the Woodroffe Cricket Club with new cricket nets. However, the school had made a contribution by raising £400 in sponsorship from the Lyme Regis Run. Merrie Weldon, resigned as Chairman of the PTA and was succeeded by Cora Rawlins. Fund-raising led to a cheque for £5,000 being passed to the Head to be spent by individual Faculties and Departments on items to benefit all pupils.

In November 1996 a new IT room which had been built at the northern end of the quadrangle was opened. This project had been financed by proceeds from the sale of St Andrews and, as a Grant Maintained school, the governors were able to retain these funds for capital expenditure. Remaining funds would be used to further develop the school's administration centre and IT facilities. In the past two years £80,000 had been spent on IT in the school.

By now contracts had been exchanged for the sale of Rhode Hill House, which was due to be converted into residential units. Funds from this source and from the sale of land at the rear of St Andrews were ear-marked for the building of a sports hall and drama studio, but the financing of this ambitious project was dependent on matched funding and grants.

Important curriculum changes were being planned for 1997/1998. In September 1997 the teaching week was to be extended from 23.5 hours to 25 hours, with the timetable organised around 20 seventy-five minute periods per week to allow for flexibility on a two week cycle. There would also be some redistribution of the time allocated to subjects particularly at Key Stage 3 where Drama was to be introduced as a discrete subject in its own right.

A major curriculum innovation was the introduction of a Personal and Social Education (PSE) course for Years 7 to 11 and a General Studies course, leading to an A/S level for Sixth Formers.

Thirty two boarders had now transferred to accommodation at Allhallows College and had settled in well under the care of John Griffith and Anne Philbrick. They were joining in a variety of activities with Allhallows residents.

The new IT facility was now fully operational and was equipped with sixteen PC 486 machines previously located in the Maths Department. Further computers were being purchased to increase this number of PCs to twenty. The intention was to network the machines and to extend the network into the Design Technology area to provide access to up-to-date IT facilities in that Department. Mike Goodrick was now in post as the school's first IT technician and the school also had an e-mail address that parents could use to contact staff.

The PE Department announced that pupils were being encouraged to participate in sport not only through lessons but also via ten different extra-curricular activities. The response had been overwhelming and the school was now able to run teams in every major sport up to U19 level. Year 8 had been involved in an inter-tutor group competition, Jan Williams' tutor group proving to be champions in soccer and Malcolm Matthews' group in hockey. David Chambers reported that as usual rugby was thriving particularly the Saturday morning training sessions which attracted between forty to one hundred boys on a regular basis. Under the auspices of the Three Shires Rugby Club, insurance cover had been obtained to allow parents and friends to assist with training and coaching and it had therefore been possible to extend the fixture list. Hockey was also a firm favourite with over forty girls attending regular training sessions after school on Wednesday evenings.

In his new role as PSE Co-ordinator, Roy Sleigh outlined plans for the new PSE programme which would be delivered by staff to their own tutor groups on issues pertinent to the overall development of the individual. These included such topics as study skills, careers and health issues and plans were also afoot for an Amnesty International Group to meet regularly.

In March 1997 the Head announced that the school Architect, John Howe, had produced plans for the new Sports Hall and a grant application to the Funding Agency for Schools would shortly be made. This body operated a seed capital scheme whereby they would contribute £1 for every £2 raised by the school. The plan was to build the Sports Hall first and then the Drama Studio. The existing PE changing facilities adjacent to the old gym were to be re-modelled to provide workshop and storage facilities for Drama. It was envisaged that the Sports Hall would be completed by the start of the 1998/1999 school year with the Drama Studio ready for the end of that year. However, a new Head of Drama would be appointed in September 1997, as from that date Drama was to be taught as a discrete subject, with Years 7 to 9 enjoying a period of timetabled Drama within their curriculm.

In March 1997 the school put on a production of "My Fair Lady" to much acclaim. The lead part of Eliza Doolittle was taken by Katie Moore and Lizzie Sweetland, performing on alternate nights, and John Haylock took the part of Eliza's father, Alfred. Many pupils were involved on stage and others worked hard backstage constructing scenery, collecting props, and assisting with marketing, etc.

Paul Skelton retired at the end of the Easter Term and grateful thanks were expressed to him for his long and dedicated service to the school over the past eighteen years. During his time at the school he had run a thriving English and Music Faculty and had contributed significantly to extra-curricular activities. Ewart Watts, affectionately known as "Cuddles" also retired after twenty three years' loyal service as the school caretaker.

In June 1997 it was announced that the school's bid to the Funding Agency for Schools for seed capital to build the Sports Hall had been successful. This would be added to the proceeds from the sale of Rhode Hill to provide full funding for the project. It was anticipated that building would start in the Spring of 1998 with completion by September 1998. It was envisaged that the new Drama Studio would be completed and ready for use by the Summer Term 1999.

Further good news was that the Department for Education and Employment had recently advised that the school's Basic Needs bid had been successful and funds were to be made available for a forty three place extension. Plans were being made to provide an additional art room on C level, to extend the existing Textiles Area and to convert B3 to a third Information Technology room. The Head pointed out that by the year 2000 when all work was completed over £1 million would have been re-invested in Woodroffe, mostly from the sales of redundant property.

A new computer room was installed in the Design Technology area housing a network of five PCs with an A3 colour printer and a scanner. This equipment had immediately been put to good use in producing an A3 double-sided full colour brochure to support the school's application for Art College status. Unfortunately the school had been unable to raise sufficient sponsorship to meet the May deadline set by the Department for Education. However, plans were in hand to re-submit the bid in October.

In November 1997 the new Labour Government issued a White Paper on "Excellence in Schools" which indicated that Grant Maintained status was to be abolished, which would have serious financial implications for the school. As the school had made massive strides since it became grant maintained the governors were anxious to retain as much autonomy as possible and therefore were planning to elect to become a Foundation School. As such the LEA would once again play a major role in determining capital spending priorities and it would also be responsible for setting challenging targets for a three year period. However, the governors would retain ownership of land and buildings and would remain the employer of staff.

Peter Dawson, the Head of Modern Languages, took on a new additional role as Co-ordinator of School Improvement. In this capacity he was setting up very significant, detailed monitoring programmes and would be working with Heads of Year to initiate systems for accurately tracking the academic progress of pupils against their potential.

In terms of Drama, up to seventy pupils auditioned for forty parts in the school's production of "A Midsummer Night's Dream" to be performed in July. Plans had now been drawn up for the new Drama Studio which would be a purpose-built flexible theatre space to enable the development of pupils' potential and to create exciting performances. In 1998 A and AS level Theatre Studies would be offered in the Sixth Form for the first time.

Juliana Sims, the new Head of English, advised that the introduction of longer lessons had allowed for the implementation of several new initiatives including the raising of the profile of reading. All lessons now began with fifteen minutes of independent reading for everyone and all pupils at Key Stage 3 and 4 had been given a suggested reading list.

A link had now been established between the school and the Exeter ICE Trust. The Trust was an ecumenical church initiative set up to be a shared church resource for secondary education in Exeter. The ICE Co-ordinator, Colin Piper, met with the Head on a regular basis and he had started to attend school assemblies which were proving very popular with pupils. The initiative had provided funding of a youth worker for the Uplyme committee which also supported young people at Woodroffe.

Work on the sports hall which was to have commenced in March 1998 was delayed due to the need to plan and build a new electricity sub-station and to upgrade water and gas services. It was hoped that work would begin in July 1998 with completion by December 1998. Work on the Drama Studio and the new Art and Design accommodation was now scheduled to start in early 1999. The governors also had plans to build a basic toilet/first aid facility on top pitch and to refurbish some of the Science accommodation depending on how far existing resources could be stretched.

Work begins on the new sports hall

Laying the foundations (above and left)

Preparations begin for the Drama Studio (right)

The School on the Hill

Temporary access road to new sports hall (left)

The walls of the new sports hall begin to emerge (above)

Creating steps to the new drama studio (left)

Following the successful tour of South Africa in 1995, the Three Shires Rugby Club was in the process of organising a tour to China, Japan and New Zealand which would involve a large number of Woodroffe boys. Fund-raising had started for this project and a major event was a performance by the Treorchy Male Voice Choir and the Lyme Regis Town Band at Allhallows.

A dance competition highlighted a wealth of talent, which was underlined when Kathy Elliott advised that nearly a quarter of the school's population had applied to audition for the Christmas Cabaret in December. 112 pupils were eventually selected to take part and acts included not only dance but vocal solos and duets, instrumental items and recitations and dances. Members of staff also performed and £600 was raised which was divided between Shelter and the NSPCC.

Changes were being made to the girls PE uniform. Girls in Year 7 were required to wear a plain red short sleeved polo shirt. Pupils in other years could continue to wear a white polo shirt but when replacing this they were required to switch to a red one.

The School on the Hill

The end of the summer term 1998 marked the departure of several members of staff not least of whom was Peter Rickard, who had been the school's Bursar and Clerk to the Governors for the past eight years. Peter had seen the school through the transition to Grant Maintained Status and he had been responsible for all aspects of financial management and maintenance of the school buildings and grounds. Throughout his period of office there had been many capital building developments which he had overseen, liaising with a wide range of bodies in the process. He had also served the Grant Maintained sector at national level and upon his departure from the school he went on to run the national organisation for school bursars in the maintained sector, which he had founded whilst at Woodroffe, with the support of the Department for Education. In his place, Gill Sleigh was promoted to the post of Finance and Administration Manager and Audrey Coussens was appointed as Clerk to the Governors.

Another departure was Jayne Barron who had been in charge of the Sixth Form for six years, during which time pupils had benefited greatly from the wide range of activities and courses that she had established. Malcolm Matthews, Head of Music was also leaving after eight years, having worked very hard to ensure that the high reputation of music at the school continued.

The English Department announced that from September Year 7 would be banded by ability so that the problem of literacy could be addressed and help directed to where it was needed. Banding allowed support to be given to less confident individuals and would ensure that the more confident were stretched. Another exciting innovation was to explore the possibilities of introducing gender teaching in Year 9. Instead of five mixed groups there would be three boys sets and two girls set. This would allow staff to see whether gender specific material could be produced to increase the performance of boys and stretch the performance of girls. If the experiment was successful, consideration would be given to extending it to other year groups.

The Art Department was delighted to announce that Sixth Former William Howe had been awarded an unconditional place at St Martin's School of Art to study Product Design. A place at St Martin's was considered as prestigious as a place at Oxford or Cambridge to pupils of Art and William's success was even more outstanding as it had been achieved directly from the school's Sixth Form without having to take a Foundation Course, which was the usual route for Sixth Form pupils.

The bid to the Funding Agency for £65,000 to help link the school to the National Grid for Learning had resulted in a grant of just £6,500 which meant that the whole school network would have to wait a little longer. However, these funds would allow for improved internet access for both pupils and staff.

Unfortunately, due to cost factors, the major building programme did not commence in the summer holidays. However, planning permission was now being sought to build both the Sports Hall and the Drama Studio on top bank. It was anticipated that building would start in late February/March 1999 with the Drama Studio completed by September 1999 and the Sports Hall a little later in the Autumn Term. At the same time, a new changing, toilet and first aid facility would be built on top pitch and the Art and Design and Design

Technology facilities in school would be extended and re-furbished. Any remaining funds were to be used to re-model some of the Science laboratories.

The Art Department was very excited about improvements to its facilities which were due to begin in August 1999. This would involve an extension to the Ceramics Room which would double its size. Above it a Print Room for both Textiles and Art would be created, fully equipped with photographic silk screen equipment. The Dark Room would be re-designed and equipped with six enlargers and a totally new Art/Textiles Room was to be built next to the Dark Room on top of the girls' toilets.

The new Art facilities begin to take shape

The Food Technology Department was concerned that a recent national survey had revealed that the majority of eighteen to thirty year olds rarely cooked. Very few had the skills or the time to create their own meals. Woodroffe was very fortunate to have facilities in which pupils could learn the rudiments of food preparation. Efforts were made to encourage them to select a diet which was both healthy and enjoyable. Concern was expressed at the number of young people who left home in the morning without a proper breakfast and others who skimped on lunch either to save their money or to remain slim.

The Year 9 rugby team had undertaken a Summer Tour to China and New Zealand organised by the Three Shires Club. The boys played six fixtures and won four of them. All who went on the tour agreed that it had been a fabulously rewarding experience for everyone. Fixtures were played against a Beijing representative side and in Auckland, Christchurch, Wellington, Wanagnui/Taranaki and Hamilton.

With the arrival of Jon Cullimore in September 1998, the Music Department had undergone several major changes. Plans were being made to construct a fully equipped digital recording studio during half term, which it was hoped would be operational by December 1998. A new ensemble, a Jazz Band, was being formed as well as a small Brass Ensemble. It was also hoped to form a Brass Group, an Orchestra and a Flute Group in the not too distant future.

A committee of parents was set up to raise the £11,000 required to stage the production of "Torchbearers" in October 1999 which would involve sixty pupils from Year 7 to the Upper Sixth working closely with the National Youth Music Theatre. Meanwhile auditions were taking place in the Drama Department for "Grease" which would be performed in July.

In June 1999 the funeral took place of former Head, Major Thornton Pearn, MC, OBE. Right up until his death Major Pearn had retained a great affection for the school and continued to take a positive interest in its development. He had been particularly pleased when the governors decided to name the new Drama Studio after him. Two years previously Major Pearn had been made a Freeman of Lyme Regis, which was a reflection of the esteem in which he was held in the town. He was fondly remembered by colleagues and by thousands of young people for whom he had created an educational environment that had given them an excellent start in life.

It was announced that in September 1999 there would be a change to the organisation of the school day with the introduction of a twenty five one hour period week. This would mean four periods before lunch and an afternoon assembly (Collective Worship) followed by the last period of the day. Starting and finish times would not be affected.

In the English Department, Juliana Sims reported that the Year 9 SATS papers had just been sent off and soon it would be possible to measure how successful the single sex classes had been. One of the boys had remarked that *"We don't have to show off to the girls. I think I am doing more work. I just flirt more at break time!"*

Although it was suffering massive disruption due to the building work, Design Technology felt that there was some compensation as the large scale project gave pupils the opportunity to examine the structures and materials used in the construction and the contractors had offered site visits to demonstrate building methods and the materials employed. Due to the building works, all external exams had taken place at the Lyme Regis Boys Club to provide a peaceful environment at this crucial time.

The start of the autumn term 1999 was delayed due to unfinished building work. For the first week of term both teaching and support staff were fully occupied moving furniture from where it had been stored back into the newly converted spaces. This also involved moving half a Morris Minor which had been on stage for the July production of "Summer Loving".

The ex-pupils' reunion held in October 1999 was a huge success. Approximately 600 people were expected to attend but well over 1,000 filled the hall and the gym to capacity. A Service of Thanksgiving had been held in the school hall on the following day at which tributes were paid to Major Pearn, OBE and David Butterworth, former Heads who had both died recently.

The 1990s were a time of great change for the school. It marked the demise of boarding, and the introduction of Local Management for Schools, followed by Grant Maintained Status. In addition there was a change of leadership and an ambitious building programme which provided the school with state of the art facilities in many areas. It therefore entered the new millennium revitalised and ready to the face the challenges of the future.

CHAPTER 11 2000 TO 2007: THE TWENTY FIRST CENTURY

In February 2000 it was reported that the construction of the Drama Studio and the Sports Hall complex was complete and the new toilet, changing and first aid facility on top pitch was almost finished.

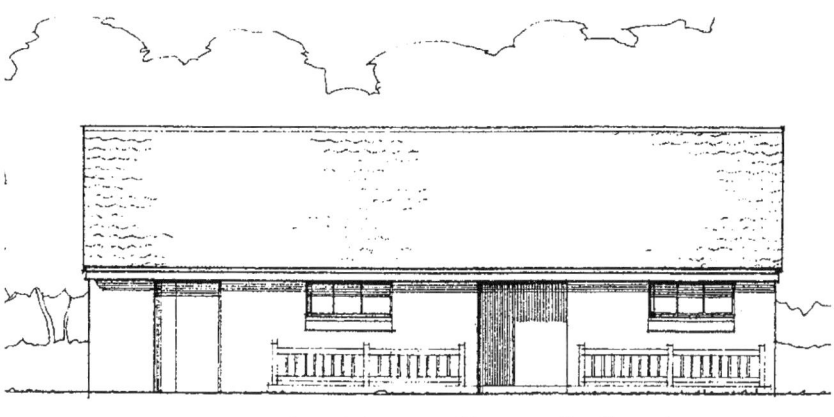

Sports Pavilion (Top Pitch) - South Elevation

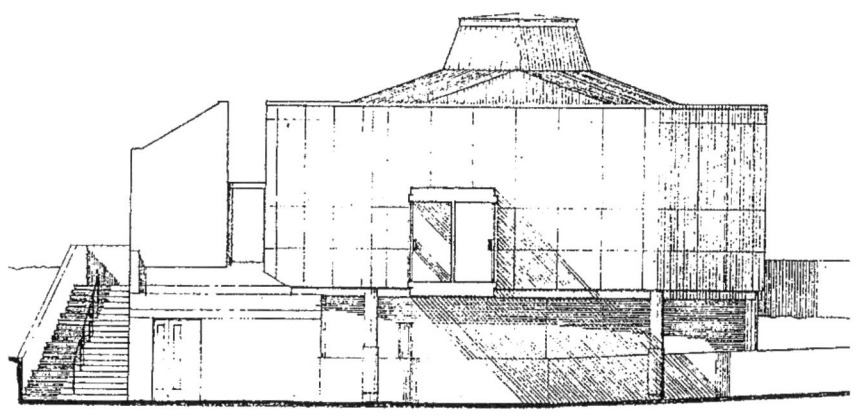

Drama Studio - North East Elevation

The Drama Department was greatly enjoying the new Thornton Pearn Studio which provided a stimulating atmosphere in which to explore a range of theatre forms.

The Mathematics Department was also pleased that its entire suite of rooms had been carpeted which had reduced noise levels considerably. The new print room had been completed and was in use by the Textiles Department. It had been designed with a store, changing room, sewing machine area, display boards, print table and a huge window to gaze out of if all else failed! Refurbishments in relation to Resistant Materials and Systems and Control had also just been completed and a dust extraction system was in the process of being fitted.

The Art Department were getting excited about moving into its new accommodation. The downstairs part of the extension to B3 had made what used to be a very cramped facility into a light, airy, spacious and beautifully proportioned room. The two kilns, a new pug mill and the clay processing were now all re-housed in the new extension, whilst the existing part of the room was now being kept as a clean, dry area for 2D work. Upstairs C12 and C14 now shared a "wet" area to be used for lino printing and photographic silkscreen printing onto paper, fabric painting and dyeing. Again the room had been beautifully designed by John Howe, with a north facing glass roof for maximum light.

The PE Department was thrilled with the new Sports Hall which offered four badminton courts, four cricket nets, one volleyball court, one basketball court, one tennis court, indoor five-a-side pitch, indoor hockey pitch and indoor netball court plus a fully equipped Fitness/Weights Room.

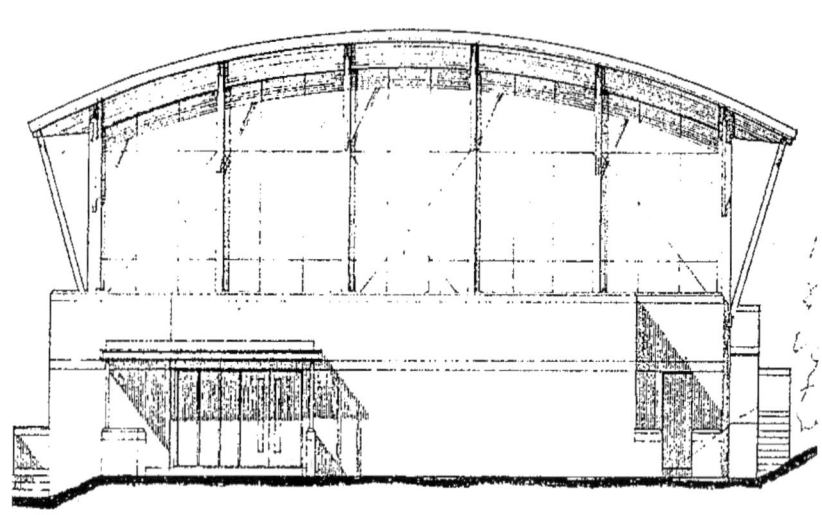

Sports Hall - North West Elevation

In June 2000 the Head reported an excellent outcome to the OFSTED inspection held from 27th to 31st March which had resulted in the clear message that Woodroffe was an effective and high achieving school. The school had also received the good news that it would be receiving additional revenue funding for 2000 – 2001 direct from the central Government amounting to £40,000.

The Science Department was now enjoying the benefits of three fully operational new laboratories. The new preparation room was nearly complete and the technicians were busy computerising the indexing of the equipment and chemical stock. The final part of the refurbishment would be the completion of the new Science office which would be ready shortly.

As part of BBC Music Live on 29th May the Jazz band played in Langmoor Gardens. A joint concert with the Three Counties Jazz band was also planned for June, followed by a barbeque in the quad. The term would finish with a joint concert with Lyme Regis Town Band, The Woodroffe Jazz Band and the Junior Choir.

The Art Department had settled into its new accommodation and pupils were enjoying working with Naomi Vincent, an artist in residence, who had been commissioned to build a floating structure. The finished article would be floated in the pool outside the harbour throughout the whole of August. In the Textiles Department the volume of coursework to be sent away was staggering and one inventive pupil had packed hers in a highly decorated suitcase which contained clothing suitable for travel purposes.

It was announced that following the recent highly successful reunion for ex-pupils, which had taken place in October 1999, an organisation had been set up to be known as Woodroffe Association. All ex-pupils and members of staff of both Lyme Regis Grammar School and Woodroffe School were eligible to join.

In October 2000 the Head reported that at Key Stage 3 results significantly above the national average had been achieved in English, Mathematics and Science. Year 11 pupils equalled the excellent GCSE results of the previous year with 59% gaining at least 5 A* - C grades. A level results had been a little below par but the majority of pupils had gained places at appropriate Higher Education courses.

Looking ahead a large number of overseas visits were being planned, including exchange visits to Germany, France and Slovakia, art trips to Barcelona and New York, a hockey tour to Barbados, a Jazz Band tour in Spain and CCF camps on foreign bases.

The Design Technology Department organised a trip to London's West End for a group from Year 10 to investigate the way in which technology is used in the theatre. Pupils were taken on backstage tours of the Palladium and Drury Lane theatres and attended performances of the new Ben Elton/Andrew Lloyd-Webber musical "Beautiful Game" and a new play called "Copenhagen" about a meeting between two atomic physicists during World War 2. The Drama and Music Departments were also busy preparing for a production of "Bugsy Malone", a whole school production to be staged in July. Auditions had been held with 180 pupils vying for just sixty parts.

A recent trip to Slovakia by a party of fifteen staff and pupils had been a great success with the group travelling by coach across France, through Belgium, Germany and Austria before crossing into Slovakia. Host families had provided accommodation and visits had been made to castles, caves in the Carpathian Mountains and the capital Bratislava, where the party attended a performance of Romeo and Juliet by the National Ballet Company. The adults on the trip also enjoyed a visit to a glass factory and a Turkish Bath high in the Tetra Mountains.

Owen Cooke, a pupil in the Lower Sixth, advised that he had enjoyed himself so much *"meeting new people and finding out about their culture, which is so different to ours"* and fellow pupil, Robert Mandy, wrote *"I chose to go to Slovakia because it's not a place that you hear of many people visiting….. as an ex-communist country it is only in recent years that tourists and cameras have been allowed to cross the borders….. I had a great time learning about Slovakia's culture and history plus some interesting facts such as one Easter day the men whip and soak the women! Overall the exchange was good and I would love to go again."*[1]

---

[1] Extracts from the Parents' Bulletin dated June 2001

Maisie Shannon, the Squad Captain for the forthcoming Barbados hockey tour, described the excitement and anticipation of her team mates and referred to the long build up and the endless fund-raising. She concluded that it was the opportunity of a lifetime and would be a tremendous experience for all concerned. During their tour the girls would not only play eight matches but they would also have the opportunity to enjoy beach parties, an island safari by Land Rover and a catamaran cruise.

The Jazz Band tour to Barcelona had provided another trip of a lifetime for a different group of pupils. The trip had begun with a thirty hour coach journey to get to Calafell. In Barcelona the Band's first concert took place at the Maritime Museum, where they played in the open air under the orange and lemon trees. The tour also included a visit to the Universal Studios "Port Aventura", a massive theme park near to Calafell. The next concert held at the Hotel Palas in Pineda was a huge success, particularly when the band combined with the Okehampton Big Band and really raised the roof. Leisure time in Barcelona included visits to the Neu-Camp Stadium, seating capacity 110,000, home of Barclona FC, and the Templa de la Sagrada, Familia, Gaudi's great temple of the Holy Family. On the way home the party made one final visit, this time to the Olympic Stadium in Barcelona.

The Jazz Band perform on the Marine Parade

Target setting was well-established as part of the school's culture and the intention was to improve the percentage of Year 9 pupils gaining Level 5 and 6 in the three core subjects of the national curriculum. The current Year 11 had been set a very challenging target to achieve a 70% pass rate for 5 A* - Cs in the summer of 2002.

Owing to work commitments Gwen Chessell resigned from the Governing Body in September 2001 and Stephen Hallworth was elected as the new Chairman. Gwen reflects on her role as Chairman of Governors as follows:

"As a professional educationalist with experience in tertiary education I was an active and involved governor. My special interests ranged from the content of the formal school curriculum to work with the sixth form on interview techniques and careers and the compilation of Records of Achievement. The value of the last I considered deserving of much wider recognition, particularly at tertiary level and by employers.

I found my time as Chairman extremely interesting and enjoyable and was impressed by the commitment of staff and their dedication to the school and its pupils. One of Woodroffe's strengths was its potential to offer achievement to pupils of all ability levels. On the minus side, the intervention of central government in school affairs with over-management and untested initiatives was frustrating and irritating and seemed to take little account of the quality and quantity of the dedicated work put in by teaching staff at all levels in the English education system. On a personal level I regretted the prescriptive nature of the national curriculum which I considered constrained the inspiration of many of the gifted staff.

My time as a governor and later Chairman co-incided with two school inspections, both of which confirmed Woodroffe's effectiveness at educational, artistic and pastoral levels. The building of facilities such as the Drama Studio and the much-needed Sports Hall, together with the refurbishment of the science laboratories, was a satisfying project although difficulties which arose during the building process tended to take some of the gloss off the achievement at the time.

To be an effective governor involves a considerable commitment in time and energy. Not all members of the governing body shared this commitment and it was important to try and find meaningful involvement for all governors. But it was a pleasure to work with many governors who were unstinting in their support of the school."

Every curriculum computer was now connected to the school network with full internet access. This meant that pupils could save work on any school PC and access it on any other PC in the school.

In February 2002 the Head reported with great sadness the death of Tony Terrett, who had joined the Governing Body in 1988 and had been Chairman of Governors from 1992 until 1997. Mr Terrett had served the school with great energy and determination and had given the Governors a clear sense of direction. Progress made under his Chairmanship was considerable, including the extensive capital programme which led to the building of the Sports Hall and Pearn Studio and the refurbishment/extension of the Art/Design, Design & Technology and Science facilities.

The Head announced that plans were being made to make an application for Visual Arts College status in October 2002. The application required a huge amount of work and Dot Wood, Head of Art and Design, was undertaking a "community audit" of provision in the visual arts which involved discussions with feeder primary schools and a range of bodies, statutory and voluntary, devoted to arts activities locally. This close liaison was important as the community objectives would form a crucial part of the school's Development Plan and, if the bid was successful, a significant part of the Government funding allocated to the school would be devoted to community development in the visual arts.

Curriculum implications were also being investigated and objectives would need to be identified for school-based activities. The bid would have to show an expansion of visual arts within the school curriculum, particularly at Key Stage 4 and post-16, and targets would need to be set for pupil achievement over a four year period. £50,000 in sponsorship was needed in order to make the bid but, if successful the school would receive a capital grant of £100,000 and a revenue grant over a four year period of around £110,000.

The Head announced that the governors had approved a change to school uniform. All years would now be able to wear a white polo shirt with an embroidered school badge during the summer months. This privilege was already enjoyed by Sixth Form pupils and to protect their distinctiveness they would be given a choice of colour polo shirts to choose from, similarly embroidered. The Head stressed that the wearing of a polo shirt was optional and pupils could still wear their conventional long sleeved white school shirt and school tie during the non-blazer summer period. It was felt that the polo shirt, which did not have to be tucked in, would be a popular choice with pupils.

Ten Tors was back on track after the disappointments of 2001 caused by foot and mouth disease. It was noted that the largest ski trip ever to leave Woodroffe would be departing for Zauchensee in Austria during the first week of the Easter holidays.

Rehearsals were underway for the Dance Show, "Global Groove" to be held in March. The theme of the show was to be based on cultural and traditional dance from around the world and the wide variety of work to be featured ranged from American hip-hop and Russian mazurka to traditional African dance. Even the Sixth Form boys rugby team would be making an appearance.

The Early Music Group, under the leadership of John Seabrook, was working hard preparing for the Cabaret performing two pieces from Tschaikovsky's Swan Lake followed on a lighter note by "Mamba No.5". To demonstrate the versatility of this group of musicians, they had also been invited to play Tudor music to pupils at St Catherine's Primary School in Bridport.

In June 2002 the Head announced his intention to retire with effect from 31st August 2003, having served as a Head for twenty two years, with ten of them at Woodroffe. He did not however intend to sever his links with education completely as he had plans to train as an OFSTED Inspector. The governors had already begun the process to appoint a successor and hoped to appoint a replacement by the end of the autumn term 2002 to enable the new Head to be involved in essential planning, particularly in relation to finance, staffing and curriculum that always takes place in the spring and summer terms ready for the start of the new academic year in September 2003.

Demand for places in Year 7 had led to an additional form of thirty pupils being organised for September 2002 and with Sixth Form numbers estimated at 150 the total number on roll was expected to rise to around 910 to 920 for 2002/2003.

Dorset Careers had now been transformed into "Connexions" as of 1st April 2002 in line with national changes in the provision for young people. The Connexions service in each county was now aimed at providing a unified support system for pupils. There would still be traditional careers advice but there would also be co-ordinated input from a wide spectrum of other outside agencies as and when required ie youth service, health, leisure, cultural, special educational needs, etc, all under the Connexions umbrella.

The School on the Hill

In October 2002 the Head reported a good start to the new school year with numbers on roll the highest they had been for over twenty years. 62% of Year 11 pupils had gained at least 5 A to C grades in their GCSE examinations and the A level pass rate had risen again to a creditable 92%, with most pupils able to take up their chosen places at university.

The autumn term was completely dominated by the final stages of putting the bid together for Arts College status. Sponsorship of £50,000 had been achieved largely by donations of £21,000 from parents through the PTA and £20,000 sponsorship from LymeNet. Other contributions were received from governors, local businesses, local residents and the Friends of Woodroffe. Thanks were expressed to Peter Westoby, the Chairman of the PTA, who had worked tirelessly to achieve such a high level of parental contribution. The bid was passed to the Department for Education and Skills and the outcome was expected in late December 2002/early January 2003.

The whole of Year 8 was involved in a residential visit to Carey Camp where they had enjoyed working together as part of a team in solving all sorts of problems ranging from getting everyone safely through an assault course to piecing together some extremely complex puzzles. In addition to orienteering, the highlight of campcraft skills was learning to build a shelter warm and dry enough to sleep in given just four pegs and one piece of polythene. Culinary skills were also to the fore with 150 pupils cooking their own breakfasts over an open fire.

Joan Bareham retired at the end of the summer term 2002 after thirty six years' devoted service to the school and to its pupils in many guises – as a valued member of the Science Department, as a houseparent when the school had boarding facilities, as a Head of Year and as the school's Examinations Officer to name but a few.

The major investment of funding from the National Grid for Learning during this year had been used to purchase more computers. Thirty new machines had been installed in B12 and all the slower machines in ITL had been replaced bringing the total number of workstations in that area to thirty. A new file server had also been purchased to handle staff and pupil files and at last the benefits of the networking carried out the previous year could be appreciated. The combination of a modern network, up-to-date computers and a broadband Internet connection meant that internet access was now a lot faster. All this work had been carried out during the school summer holidays and thanks were expressed to Mike Goodrick, the school's ICT technician, for the vast amount of work he had undertaken within a very tight time frame.

The Connexions room had been decorated in the summer holidays in a startling combination of vibrant orange, red and purple. It was hoped that pupils would find the area welcoming and also useful, as the intention was to provide information on health, finance, leisure, lifestyles and a wide range of teenage problems as well as the more traditional careers, college and university information. Plans were being made to invite pupils from Years 9 to 12 to take part in a wide range of work-related activities arranged in conjunction with the West Dorset Education Industry Partnership. These included days focusing on construction, engineering, university, business, land-based occupations, catering, mechanics, hairdressing, childcare, art and design, media and health.

Unfortunately, in February 2003 the Head announced that the initial bid for Arts College Status had not been successful which had been disappointing. However the feedback received from the Department for Education and Skills had been encouraging and a revised bid was being submitted in March. The newly appointed Head, Richard Steward, had been able to contribute to the new bid and his input was particularly welcome as he was currently working at a Visual Arts College in Cheltenham.

The Head explained that there would be a major change in September 2003 that would affect the school in that the curriculum at Key Stage 4 ie for Years 10 to 11 would be "freed up". This would mean that the only compulsory subjects at this Key Stage would be English, Mathematics, Science, Religious Education and Games. Woodroffe intended to ensure that all pupils at Key Stage 4 followed a course of Information Communication Technology and Personal and Social Education (including Citizenship) and, when Arts College status was secured, in a Visual Arts subject. The school would also expect most pupils in Year 9 to continue to study French in Years 10 and 11 but all other subjects would form part of the options pool from which pupils would be able to choose two (or three in the case of those not studying French). It was hoped that pupils' choices would lead to individual programmes of study that were broad, balanced and coherent. The Government was also keen for schools to introduce vocationally orientated courses in Key Stage 4 and this was an issue to be considered by the school and governors at a later date.

As part of the revised bid for Arts College Status, negotiations were taking place locally in relation to joint community projects. Ideas under consideration included a Marshwood Vale map, sculpture along the River Lym, a Lyme Web Gallery, fossils and jewellery making workshops, a children's website for the heritage coast, and printing and sculpture workshops – all to take place with partner schools.

The Upper Sixth Drama class put on a stunning production entitled "Friends Re-United" which required each performer to play over twelve different stereotypes as well as their main role. The pupils involved had decided on the theme of a school reunion and had written the play themselves. The meeting between the four so-called friends after fifteen years since leaving school had devastating consequences, as everything was not as it appeared. The Drama Department was also very busy auditioning 100 pupils for the musical "Oliver" to be staged in July 2003.

For the first time the school Cabaret took place on two consecutive nights and was a resounding success with approximately £1,600 raised for charities and buying equipment for future events. Huge thanks were expressed to Kathy Elliott, the driving force behind this very popular annual event.

The PTA committed £1,000 of its hard-earned funds to purchase a new organ/keyboard which would enable future rehearsals and performances to take place at different locations within the school with the minimum of fuss and expense. In January the PTA sponsored an information evening for parents of pupils in Years 7 to 11 who sought clarification of some of the bewildering curriculum choices facing young people and their parents under new Government proposals.

In May 2003, as he prepared to retire, the Head reflected on his time at the school which he had greatly enjoyed. He felt extremely proud of the achievements and attitudes of Woodroffe pupils, both in and out of the classroom, and was extremely grateful to all teaching and support staff for their dedication and hard work. Richard Bland was also retiring in the summer after thirty four years at the school in a number of roles, most recently as Head of Information Communications Technology where he had been at the forefront of the major developments that had taken place in that area.

The Woodroffe team in the European Science Olympiad won the Gold Medal in the final held in Ireland, where the team had had to complete two very difficult practical science tasks, competing against thirteen other teams representing Ireland, Germany, Holland, Belgium, Sweden and Spain. Chris Sweetland reported that throughout the competition the team, comprising Abby Jenkin, Richard Bugler and Ben Moass, had worked together with intelligence and enthusiasm. He felt that there was no praise high enough for their amazing achievement and that they had done both the country and Woodroffe School proud. The team was subsequently invited to County Hall in Dorchester in July where they were presented with the Perpetual Team Trophy - a magnificent piece of Dublin Crystal now on display at the school.

Year 9 had had the opportunity to experience some real Japanese culture as three Sixth Form Japanese pupils, who were studying at Woodroffe, had visited their Geography lessons to talk about their country. They had worn traditional Japanese clothes, described the different cultural aspects of Japan, pop music, housing, school rules, hi-tech industry, the bullet train, life in the cities and the cherry blossom. Japanese writing was explained and demonstrated with all the pupils receiving personal name badges written in Japanese. They were also encouraged to learn some Japanese phrases, use chopsticks to eat noodles and taste traditional green tea. The three pupils – Shinichiro Sunahara, Maasa Tsuchiyama and Yoko Nakada had prepared and practised their presentation as part of their extra-curricular English lessons.

The Fashion Show, organised by the Design Technology Department, had been a huge success involving pupils from Year 6 (Charmouth School) to Upper Sixth. It had demonstrated the huge wealth of talent available at Woodroffe and been a triumph of team work between staff and pupils.

It was announced that in September it was hoped to be able to offer NVQ Catering and Hospitality in the Lower Sixth using a new facility to be funded by a grant of £30,000 from the Learning and Skills Council. Using these monies it was intended to refurbish one food room and to install a catering style kitchen during the summer holidays.

In September 2003 Dr Richard Steward took over as Principal and received a warm welcome not only from staff and pupils but from the wider community.

By now the school had not only heard that its bid for Arts College status had been successful, but from September it had assumed its new status and became a Visual Arts College. This meant a substantial boost in income but more importantly it had led to an exciting and wide-ranging programme of developments both in school and in the community. Visual Arts Status meant that not only the Arts would flourish at Woodroffe but efforts would be made to ensure that its benefits were widely felt in every department in the school.

In addition to more teaching and support staff in the Art Department, other exciting initiatives included plans to create a new Digital Arts area; Maths, RE and Art had embarked on an exciting cross-curricular project entitled "Sacred Geometry"; new evening classes were taking place; there were additional after-school activities for pupils; the school was working closely with feeder Primary Schools in a joint project called "Every Picture tells a Story" and last but not least the school was heavily involved in the local Lyme Regis Arts Festival.

The school now had a new sign and prospectus. Twenty Year 7 pupils had taken part in a weekend workshop making boats out of driftwood with local artist, Hugh Dunford Wood. The splendid results had been displayed in local shops and on the outside of buildings down the main street. Another twenty pupils had taken part in a jazz dance workshop organised for the Lyme Regis Arts Festival and had performed in front of local MP Oliver Letwin, the Mayor and other dignitaries in the opening ceremony. Two Sixth Formers had been enlisted as official film makers to record and make a documentary of the week's activities as part of their AVCE and A level coursework.

Adult Education classes had also taken off with classes available in photography, life drawing, creative textiles and figurative ceramics. Sixth Formers were busy working on decorating ideas for the InSPARation Youth Café, re-designing a logo and letterhead for the Marine Theatre, re-designing graphics for Adsatis, a management consultancy firm based in London, and designing a banner and signposting for the school. It was clear that Arts College status had already made its mark in a very short time and everyone eagerly anticipated its continuing impact on school, its environment and the pupils in a variety of cross-curricular projects over the coming months.

In November 2003, as part of their A2 Drama and Theatre Studies course, pupils had to research and devise, rehearse and then perform an original piece of theatre. They chose to explore the idea of a modern freak show and posed the question "what do we mean by "freak"? The story of John Merrick, the "elephant man" and the theories of theatre practitioner Antonin Artaud inspired the group and they grasped the challenge to shock and confront the audience by posing the question – how do we know who's the freak in society? The production took the form of a Victorian music hall as its inspiration, telling the story of three "freaks" – the drug addict, the anorexic and the woman falsely accused of murdering her husband.

During the year the Greenpower racing car reached the national final at Goodwood. Construction of the car and racing it was not only an exciting extra-curricular activity but also a coursework component for four A level pupils.

In February 2005 the Head reported that Woodroffe's Key Stage 3 test results were the highest in the county and its position in the Government's league tables confirmed the school's reputation as a place where academic success mattered.

A party for sponsors of the Arts College initiative and governors had been held at the annual school exhibition at the Town Mill. Everyone enjoyed the celebratory atmosphere as well as viewing the exciting variety and breadth of work on display. In school the departments had been bidding for funding from £3,000 set aside for the purchase of resources to facilitate the inclusion of visual learning in classes. Other purchases included three digital cameras and a digital video camera as well as the new kiln and a colour photocopier. An after-school "fast track" art club for Year 7 pupils had started and Alison Bowskill, the Community Art Teacher was working on several projects with local primary schools and Mountjoy Special School. A Summer School for Year 6 children from the feeder primary schools was planned, featuring Drama, Art and Music, partly funded by the arts college initiative and partly by the LEA and an exciting range of evening classes was now available. Dot Wood reported that all targets for year one had now either been completed or were in the process of completion.

The school received twenty laptops for use by teachers and by September it was anticipated that all teaching staff would have access to one. As a direct result staff were increasingly making use of ICT resources for teaching across the whole curriculum. A third IT room was also being commissioned and it was hoped to have this on line by the end of half term. This new facility would enable the ICT Department to deliver the full ICT curriculum at Key Stage 3 and to improve access for other subject areas. The national strategy at Key Stage 3 had been adopted and this had produced a range of new activities for pupils including control systems and web site design.

By chance, Year 9 Historians, visiting the displays featuring the First World War at the Imperial War Museum, crossed paths with a German school party. The two groups met at the section dealing with the famous Christmas Truce in 1914 which was particularly poignant. During the meeting it was discovered that study of the whole topic in Germany followed very similar lines to that used at Woodroffe.

Fifty six stall holders participated in the PTA Taste of Christmas event which raised just over £2,000. In addition to parental contributions of £20,000 towards the Arts College bid the PTA had contributed an additional £5,000 towards essential equipment and was proposing to donate a further £5,000 shortly. A PTA Auction of Promises later in the year raised a further £3,500.

In March the school music concert featured over 100 pupils. The highlight of the evening had been the orchestral performance of the Lord of the Rings theme which had lasted over twelve minutes and had involved fifty musicians and included a solo by Casper Price-Hafslund. This was repeated at a whole school assembly on the last day of term when 900 pupils had listened entranced as their fellow pupils performed this exciting piece. The Dance Show had been equally entertaining and featured a wide range of dance including street dancing, cheerleading, musicals and jive. The theme was Rock around the Clock and the production had certainly lived up to its title.

Senior Prize-Giving followed a different format to previous years and included interviews of award winners by the Head Boy, Richard Bugler, and the Head Girl, Karolyn Mandy, plus pen portraits delivered with considerable dexterity by the Head of each Year as each individual crossed the stage to receive their prize. Photographs of prizewinners were also displayed as a slide show in the Thornton Pearn Studio immediately after the event. The Head felt that his decision to no longer include the School Song had been more than compensated by the pupils' enjoyment of the evening.

Several staff changes were planned for September. Roy Sleigh was retiring after a teaching career spanning thirty eight years, fifteen of them at Woodroffe. Martin Grier was stepping down as Head of Mathematics but would continue teaching in the Mathematics Department. There would also be two important changes to the Senior Management Team with the creation of two new Assistant Headteacher posts –Sheena Mandy would take up a new role as Inclusion Co-ordinator and James Thomas would take over from her as Head of Sixth Form, in addition to his role as Head of the Geography Department.

As ever the Art Department had a lot of exciting projects to report, the most important being the building of a new two storey extension to the Art and Design Departments. The lower floor would accommodate the new Digital Arts Suite that would further enhance ICT provision across the whole school and the upper floor would provide additional studio space for Art and Design. In September it was intended to introduce a new AS course in Lens-based media and a Vocational Art GCSE. The After-School Art Club for Year 7 was thriving and thirty five members were taking part in a three-day visit to Paris. A colourful banner was now displayed at the main entrance and a number of illuminated glass cases had been purchased for the Reception area to display examples of pupils' ceramic work.

In the English Department pupils had been working on facsimile documents provided by the British Library in a project funded by the Department for Arts, Media and Sport. The aim of the project was to use documents rarely seen outside the British Library to enhance classroom teaching. One group was examining the way Lyme Regis had been presented over time and another was looking at smuggling in the 18th and 19th century. Year 9 had written a multi-voiced fictional narrative based on the real life and death of John Webber, a fifteen year-old apprentice glazier who, it was discovered during research, had been shot on the beach at Weymouth in 1832 whilst carrying tubs for his master. The Project Manager for the British Library had been so impressed by the quality of the work produced that she intended to have it scripted into a play and performed by professional actors.

Thirty new computers were installed in B9, the Business Studies Room, interactive white boards were fitted in three rooms and there were plans to instal data projectors in several locations to accommodate ICT in all subject areas by September. In terms of ICT provision, the school was now well on the way to achieving the Government's targets of one computer for every five pupils and two thirds of staff with laptops. Progress had also been in made in terms of software with the full MS Office XP package available on all computers and a variety of subject specific material installed across the network.

At the end of June eleven pupils and staff from Mountjoy School in Bridport came to Woodroffe to take part in Drama and PE. Each Mountjoy pupil had a Woodroffe pupil assigned to them as a special friend and support for the day. Emily Stones and Anne Cruwys-Finnigan ran drama workshops with the pupils from both schools working together. Everyone had a fantastic time, learning a lot from the experience.

Earlier in the month the Drama Department had also received a party from Gladesmoor Community School in Tottenham, an inner city London school. The group worked with four Year 8 Woodroffe pupils, exploring subjects as diverse as refugees and Mary Anning. The idea of the project was for both sets of young people to widen their social and cultural experiences by meeting and working with children from different backgrounds. The day proved to be a great success with new friends made and old assumptions and possible prejudices forgotten. It was hoped that Woodroffe would make a return visit to Gladesmoor in due course.

The autumn term 2004 started badly with the tragic and sudden death of Matthew Bailey during a rugby match. A shadow was cast over the school but some comfort was drawn from the way in which fellow pupils, staff and governors united in their response to the tragedy. At this sad time the real strength of the Woodroffe community really became apparent.

Jenny Perham took over from Stephen Hallworth as Chairman of Governors. The Head paid tribute to Stephen who had served the school with great dedication for eight years. Irene Benson also took over chairmanship of the PTA from Peter Westoby.

Results had again been encouraging. At Key Stage 3 84% of pupils achieved Level 5 or higher in English, 83% in Maths and 81% in Science and at GCSE 68% had achieved at least 5 A* - C. The Head pointed out that the target for 2005 had now been set at 79%! The Sixth Form had also done well with a pass rate at A level of 98% and an average points score per pupil of 267.5.

By September 2004 the school had just completed its first year as an Arts College and had done so well that it had met all its targets for year one by February. The community plan was particularly impressive with the school involved in numerous activities in the town and beyond. The school's commitment to making its facilities available to the community was confirmed and to this end, in addition to a series of evening classes, a new exercise referral class had been set up together with other fitness classes in conjunction with LymeNet.

The Maths Department, under new Head Jennie Golding, now had two digital projectors and an interactive whiteboard and pupils were already benefiting from the extra dimension to learning that these two pieces of equipment were bringing as they allowed pupils to enjoy interaction and animation this was not possible with a plain white board. There was also the added bonus of access to the internet when the need arose. The Maths curriculum was now a mixture of traditional skills - such as calculation, algebra, geometry and measurement – and applications, including those that involve dealing with graphs and data. It benefited classes to be able to access real data electronically and to deal with it using calculators or computers. However, they also needed to use numbers confidently in everyday situations, to see whether their answers "made sense".

In Year 10 a small number of pupils had opted for the new GCSE Spanish course and good progress was being made. Exchanges with Spain were harder to organise that those with France and Germany but efforts were being made to look into the possibilities.

A Summer School project for children about to enter Year 7 had used as its theme the children's story "Where the Wild Things Are" and some exciting art and drama work had been produced. Another interesting project was about to begin, this time involving Year 10 dramatists who would be working with local artist, Ricky Romain, looking at his paintings and learning more about the fascinating stories that inspired them.

The Young Engineers Club, organised by Nic Wootton, had received an influx of ultra-keen Year 7s, and three new and invaluable members of staff, all brim full of enthusiasm, new ideas and interests. Projects underway included a Royal Navy sponsored marine challenge and the design and construction of a Martian Rover vehicle. In the meantime the Greenpower team, led by Gary Wells had achieved great things with both cars making it into the national finals at Goodwood. "Quicksilver" had won both the Somerset/Dorset heat and the Dorset championship.

Racing for the finish line in the Greenpower car

In Textiles Liz Hankey, Rosie Wiscombe and Charlotte Wild were all winners of a design competition sponsored by New Look with Woodroffe scooping three out of four prizes.. New Look had subsequently had the designs made up to sell within their shops. .

The school embarked on a new venture, joining forces with Beaminster and Colfox as the West Dorset Federation. In this guise the three schools linked up with Weymouth College to offer Year 10 a choice of vocational subjects. As part of this venture four pupils were attending Kingston Maurward on Thursdays to take a course on small animal care and eight were going to Colfox to do hairdressing or construction. All were working towards their NVQ Level 2 qualification.

As part of the school's provision for those that fell into the category "Gifted and Talented" a course had been created in Critical Thinking for pupils in Years 10 and 11. This course, taught by Ian Wood, concentrated on selecting and evaluating evidence, seeing situations from different points of view, and thinking logically – skills required for high grades in A levels as well as for further study.

In order to offer a faster, more direct service for messages home to parents, many of which languished in the bottom of school bags for weeks on end, the school introduced ParentMail, a scheme whereby messages could be sent home via e-mail rather than by "pupil-post".

The School on the Hill

Eight youngsters from Year 10 *(pictured right with Marcus Dixon)* took part in The Lionheart Challenge, a business based exercise where they were given five hours to produce a design for "the school of the future". The task included a 3D design for new buildings, a financial plan and giving a three-minute presentation to an audience of judges. Competing against schools from across the south west, they won the event and, as part of the prize, spent three days the following week, all expenses paid, at the national finals staged within the Palace of Westminster. The highlight was a gala dinner held at a 5-star hotel, during which they gave a presentation of "an innovative media tool for the future". The group also found time during the visit to London to have morning coffee and an informal chat with Oliver Letwin, MP. The Woodroffe team members were Jodie Ryland, Amy Waite-Johnson, Lucy Hunt, Charlotte Sargent, Peter O'Shea, Will Hitchcock, Ross Board and Andrew Styles, all of whom enjoyed a fantastic experience although they were narrowly defeated in the final by a girls' school from London.

As part of their PSE/Citizenship Course Year 8 had been discussing a wide range of issues affecting teenagers culminating in a talk on teenage pregnancy given by school nurse, Maureen Baptist. As part of the course each week two pupils had to take home an "interactive baby" to care for over the weekend. The "baby" had a microchip and was programmed to cry at random intervals. The cry continued until the baby was comforted for a certain length of time. Each tutor group decided who would take the babies home and the agreement of parents was obtained beforehand. Initial enthusiasm waned somewhat as the weekend progressed and the babies woke several times each night! Mrs Baptist returned to school each week with the results of the microchip monitoring which had recorded how well the babies had been cared for. Interestingly the highest score was by a boy, the only one to agree to take baby. However, he did leave his baby crying for a long time one night. Apparently he didn't hear it!

The Science Department welcomed television personality, Johnny Ball, to school in May to talk to Year 9. The Department was also benefiting greatly from interactive whiteboards. This new piece of equipment greatly enhanced the quality of explanation and teaching of the subject. A good example of the use of interactive whiteboards was that pupils had been able to see the first pictures from the Huygens Probe as it descended through the atmosphere of Titan, within an hour or two of the pictures being sent back across the 1.2 billion miles to earth.

Music rehearsals were well underway for the School Concert, which would feature the Wind Band, a group set up by Mary Lowles which included forty musicians. It would be joined by the Senior Choir who would be performing "Zadok the Priest" as a finale with an orchestral accompaniment. Following their success with their performance of the Lord of the Rings, the orchestra were going from strength to strength and would be playing another film score – Jurassic Park – along with the finale from Beethoven's 6th Symphony.

Musicians from Woodroffe play at the Tea Gardens overlooking the Cobb

The Year 12 enterprise group had established its company – Fore Shore Enterprises. It had had several successful sales events for the products it sold which included items made from driftwood collected from Lyme beach. The group were hoping to attend an international Trade Fair in Utrecht.

The school worked closely with the Town Mill on a cross-curricular project entitled "Man and Machines", the culmination of which was an exhibition show-casing the work of Woodroffe pupils. A range of subjects linked to the mill and its role in the community had been studied, including food technology, history, physics, drama and art.

In May 2005 the Head advised that competition for places at Woodroffe had again been fierce with over 370 sets of parents naming the school on their application form. Sadly only 150 places were available so many parents were to be disappointed. The school's popularity had increased to such an extent that in September all year groups would be full.

A School Council was established, which included two representatives from each year group chosen from their own year councils. The School Council was proving to be a very effective way of communicating and listening to views. A recent meeting had discussed the key question "What makes a good lesson at Woodroffe?" and the points raised were published on the school's website. The intention was to involve the School Council in the life of the school at a high level and it was showing that it was more than capable of doing so. It was anticipated that in future the council would be at the heart of school improvement.

The importance of the link between parents and the school was also stressed. Feedback from parents was always most helpful and they were urged to complete and return questionnaires periodically distributed at Parent Teacher consultation evenings. Parents were also invited to attend group discussions on particular issues on which the Governors wished to move forward.

It was announced that the PTA had raised a total of £17,000 throughout the year, including £3,500 generated by the Taste of Christmas event. These funds had been used to install a new sound system in the hall and the next plan was to equip each department with either an interactive whiteboard or a data projector. In addition to providing much needed funds, members of the PTA had turned out to support every school event, thus making another huge contribution to the life of the school.

The Lyme Regis seafront improvements being undertaken over two years were set to provide a most interesting subject for Geographers at Woodroffe. Some Sixth Formers had met Mary Penfold, the Chairman of West Dorset District Council, and staff from the Engineering Department at the new Interpretation Centre on the sand bar to learn about the proposed work.

In March the Year 10 Applied Arts group visited the Aardman Animations Studios in Bristol. The company was busy developing a new film and working on commercials, but they made time to give the party a quick tour and showed live projects being completed in their digital studio. The animators gave advice on how to get into industry, as well as giving technical advice on the animating process, using original models from short films like Wallace and Gromit.

Food Technology students

After eighteen months the school was now at the half way mark in its Arts College designation and the most obvious impact had been the building, equipping and running of the Digital Arts Suite. This had enabled the introduction of two new examination classes, ie GCSE in Applied Arts and an AS in lens-based media, and also the integration of Digital Arts into the whole school curriculum. Groups from History, Physics, Food Technology and Drama used the facility in the successful Town Mill project, the outcome of which was exhibited at the Lyme Medical Centre having previously been shown at the Mill itself.

With Arts College funding the Greenpower car designs had evolved using carbon fibre. The area in the quadrangle had been greatly enhanced by the addition of a steel mural designed by Head Boy, Hugo Bugg. In addition three mosaic panels had been made by Year 10 artists and four large wooden sculptures, designed and made by Tim Sargent, a Sixth Former, had also been erected in the quad area. Evening classes were also continuing in life drawing, ceramics, photography, printmaking and Adobe Photoshop and new additions were Animation and "imovie" editing.

In addition it was announced in June 2005 that the school had been given a prestigious Artsmark Award. This was a national award organised by the Arts Council and available at three levels: Artsmark, Silver and Gold. Given the high standards in all the arts at

The School on the Hill

Woodroffe, the school had been judged to be at Gold standard, and the assessor who had visited earlier in the year was very complimentary about both the quality of the arts provision and the range of activities available.

Excellent exam results were achieved in the summer of 2005. At GCSE a pass rate of 73% achieving 5 A* - C grades was the best ever. Those working at A level had also done well with the pass rate of 96% matching national standards. At Key Stage 3 results were amongst the best in the county with over 90% of those taking English achieving at least Level 5, 86% in Mathematics and 87% in Science.

The summer work programme included the complete refurbishment of the Geography rooms at the top of the school and the replacement of the two temporary huts on the front lawn after over forty years. Four impressive new temporary buildings, of a very high standard, were now sited there, one of which had been adapted to house a suite of 32 Apple Mac computers.

Students at work on the new Apple Mac computers (left)

Also during the summer two sets of toilets had been refurbished, extensive repairs had been made to the central heating system and the school's electrical infrastructure. A new cover for the swimming pool had also been installed, an extension to the finance office had been created, new flooring had been laid in several areas of the building and there had been an extensive redecoration programme.

For the start of the autumn term 2005 changes were made to the curriculum. At A level Psychology and Photography were being offered at A2 and Music Technology was an option running alongside the traditional Music A level. At Key Stage 4 vocational options were in their second year and were proving popular and successful. The school was also building on its relationship with the West Dorset Rural Federation of Schools and Colleges in order to offer a wider range of work-related course at both Key Stage 4 and in the Sixth Form.

A new subject being introduced in Year 10 was Enterprise, with those at Key Stage 4 expected to spend at least five days on it across two years. The school had made a positive start and the first day of term for Year 10 was devoted to an Enterprise Day when pupils were tasked with designing a school for the future, including a full curriculum. There was a real sense of creativity and innovation throughout the day, which was what Enterprise as a subject was all about.

Members of the Sixth Form undertook two days of training with Relate following which they were working with Year 7 as peer mentors and friends providing support and encouragement where needed. The Sixth Form was now the largest in the school's history. Eighty six had returned to embark on AS and GNVQ and a further ten had joined from other schools including two from Germany and one from Japan. In addition sixty three of the previous year's Lower Sixth were studying hard for their A2s.

The Drama Department was extremely busy. The school's production of "Little Shop of Horrors" had been a huge success playing to packed houses; talented Catherine Butler, had got the part of young Mary Anning in a BBC Radio 4 play "The Fossilist" broadcast in September and four Upper Sixth Dramatists had been working with Year 6 pupils from St Michael's School, in Lyme Regis. They were devising a short piece to be performed in front of other children at the primary school.

A party of eighty from Year 7 enjoyed a visit to Paris including a trip up the Eiffel Tower, a cruise on the River Seine and an excursion to Disneyland. The trip brought home to them the need to be able to communicate in French. The exchange visits to Douvres-La-Délivrande in France and Norderstedt in Germany provided other valuable opportunities to build on language skills. In September, as part of the UK European Day of Languages, assemblies had been delivered in French and staff were encouraged to use at least one language other than English during the day.

Excellent examination results were being achieved at GCSE based on just one lesson of RE a week. The start of the new academic year had seen the introduction of the new Dorset Agreed Syllabus for RE, to be phased in over the next two years. This new syllabus was called RE Search: Asking the Big Questions.

The Art Department had received a £12,000 grant from a funding source named NESTA and was using it to work with the Science Department on new projects that mixed digital arts skills with scientific enquiry. With the introduction of the new Art classrooms, complete with thirty two new Apple computers Woodroffe was fast becoming the leading centre of excellence for the digital arts ie film, animation, web design and music technology (new this term), in the South West.

In October all teaching and support staff took part in an unusual training activity. Everyone was asked to organise a day away at another school work-shadowing a colleague doing a similar job to theirs. Many returned to school refreshed and inspired by what they had learned and a few even felt quite grateful to be working in such a nice school as Woodroffe, compared to others!

In February 2006 the Head referred to the inspection which had taken place in November 2005, the outcome of which was that Woodroffe was classified as a good school with outstanding features. He was delighted with this outcome and pointed out that the next challenge would be to ensure that when the inspectors called again, in three years time, the school would be recognised as outstanding.

It was announced that in September a new Art and Digital Technology Department was to be created which would enable the school to adopt a genuinely cross-curricular approach to ICT by sharing the excellent practice already adopted in Digital Art. As part of this initiative a new post of Key Stage 3 ICT Co-ordinator has been established to bring additional expertise into the new Department.

Specialist School status involved Woodroffe in working much more closely with local feeder primary schools and with the community in general – a trend set to continue. The Government's focus on vocational education also meant that schools were now working together much more closely than previously. The next phase of the latter development would see Woodroffe exploring possible links right across West Dorset and East Devon.

In January two members of the pop group "Ricky" visited the school to record Year 7 and Year 8 chanting "easy" for their Football World Cup Anthem. The group was trying to gain an entry in the Guinness Book of Records for the most children singing on a recording and were travelling the length and breadth of Britain to record participating schools.

£1,000 was raised for Children in Need which had been collected throughout the school as part of "Be what you want to be" activities. Sixth Formers who had wanted to collect at Christmas for those less fortunate in other parts of the world had not managed to raise enough to "Send a Cow to Africa" but the £100 which they collected had purchased a flock of chickens and a beehive to help a tribe in Uganda to support itself.

In the Drama Department the Upper Sixth was performing its Unit 4 devised play on two nights to packed and enthusiastic audiences. The piece was called "The Human Animal" and asked the question "What makes a human, human?" It was a fantastic piece of theatre – clever, challenging, sad and at times extremely funny. The Year 8 and 9 Drama Club performed some very funny comic fairytales to their year group, ably supported by two directors from the Upper Sixth. Pupils from the Upper Sixth had finished their community project, working with Year 6 pupils from St Michael's Junior School. All the Year 6 year group had performed for the rest of their school "The Very Mean King", a traditional African story. Everyone involved had worked extremely hard and the Sixth Formers had enjoyed seeing the younger children progress from loud and annoying to hardworking and nice!

Fifty GCSE pupils from Woodroffe studying Food Technology travelled to Birmingham for the BBC Good Food Show. Despite the 5.30 am start the trip was well worth it with the party able to see chefs such as Jamie Oliver and Anthony Worrall-Thompson at work. As usual the group from Woodroffe excelled itself when three of them were invited on stage to take part in a series of activities against another school. Woodroffe was the overall winner with a final score of thirty one against the other school's nineteen.

The Mathematics Department was concentrating on developing basic numeracy for adult life and for employment. Classes were tested for basic numeracy skills, as opposed to the slightly wider mathematical skills, so that particular difficulties could be identified and tracked. A Maths Clinic had been set up during Monday lunchtime, run by Sixth Formers and staff, to provide additional support. Year 7 and Year 9 were benefiting greatly from the "intervention" classes run by the hard-working and extremely patient Teaching Assistants.

A group of Sixth Formers studying Business Studies took part in a "Global Business Challenge" designed to give them a real insight into the world of business beyond the UK. The event was a mixture of practical methods and role play, tackling issues such as fair trade, globalisation and the international economic environment. The group also had the opportunity to develop many important life skills including team work, decision-making and problem-solving. In September a new qualification was to be introduced – the BTEC First Diploma in Public Services. This course was suitable for those interested in a career in any of the main public services in the UK, including the Police, Fire Service, the Armed Forces and the Prison Service.

During the course of 2005 Design Technology at Key Stage 3 underwent dramatic changes to bring it in line with new government strategies. This meant the development of new and exciting courses in Years 7, 8 and 9. The biggest improvement had been in Year 9 where the entire course had been changed to look at developing world issues and the use of sustainable power and building materials. This included building safe water filters, developing housing for the Masai people of Kenya – a tough design challenge – and the construction and testing of a wind generator.

A review of the Year 7 timetable took place during the Spring and Summer Terms with a view to shifting the focus towards Literacy and Thinking Skills. By placing Literacy at the heart of the curriculum, the intention was to ensure that children were better prepared to access all their subjects at Key Stage 3 and thus make better progress at Key Stage 4. With a much greater emphasis on reading, it was hoped to encourage a much more positive approach to studying in general.

In preparation for the introduction of the new Year 7 timetable, teachers were writing schemes of work for the new subjects to be incorporated ie: Literacy and Thinking Skills, Art and Design, People and Places and PE and Health. In this exciting new initiative the school received valuable support from the county's National Strategy team, the Specialist Schools Trust and the National College of School Leadership.

Central government introduced a new system for governors to report annually to parents which meant that the old style governors' report to parents was abandoned, along with the annual parents' meeting, and a new school profile was introduced. The aim of the profile was to give parents a general account of the school and it was particularly useful for new parents when considering applying for a place for their child. The profile followed a set pattern and covered a wide range of topics from examination results to extra-curricular activities.

Year 10 took part in a competitive Design Challenge at Beaminster School. The group had to design a visitor centre for West Bay and construct a model of it out of paper tubing. At the end of the day it presented its ideas to the other groups. Those involved enjoyed the challenge and also working in mixed groups with young people from other schools. There were several innovative ideas for the building and the models were large enough for the teams to sit inside! Those in Year 9 interested in construction also took part in a "hands-on" Build a House Day, and Year 12 enjoyed an engineering/robotics Design Challenge Day organised by the Royal Navy.

The school played a large part in the Lyme Regis Fossil Festival, including the organisation of family workshops for parents and children from the local primary schools, the aim of which was to make large prints based on fossils. Another interesting project revolved around Toyin Solanki, a geologist and writer of rap about rocks, who visited the school for four days. A party of twenty five from Year 8 worked with Toyin for three days, learning the very technical, wordy chants that it then performed in front of an audience of over 300 primary school children and adults at the Marine Theatre. The group had a fantastic time and apparently treated the residents of Lyme to a rendition of their song as they walked back up the hill to school.

During the summer of 2006 many minor alterations were made to buildings which together had made a significant impact on the facilities available within the school. A new PE classroom had been created in the gallery above the sports hall and a science "prep" room had been enlarged to create a new laboratory. One of the most significant changes had been the expansion of the Library which had spread across the corridor and taken out two offices. A new suite of thirty computers had been installed in this extension. Two more of the "temporary" huts had been completely renovated, a glass corridor on D level had been converted into a new teaching space and another set of cloakrooms had been refurbished. In addition a significant amount of much-needed plumbing and electrical work had been completed throughout the school.

The Head was pleased to announce that the school's Key Stage 3 results were among the best in the county: at GCSE 72% achieved 5 A* - Cs and at A level performance continued to rise with 96% achieving grades A – E, and 53% gaining A or B grades. One of the most remarkable set of results came from the fast-track Art group, twelve of whom took GCSE Art in Year 9. All passed and there were some stunning grades including an A*.

The number on roll now reached over 1,000 and every one of them, plus over 100 staff, assembled on the tennis court for a whole school photo at the start of the Autumn Term. This was a major operation as it took over an hour to get everyone in place but the arrangements went without a hitch and the photographic team made a point of remarking on the superb behaviour displayed by the school.

A group of Year 7 children, who joined the school in September 2006, have been asked to jot down their feelings as they made the giant leap from primary to secondary education. The following are extracts from their notes:

Lauren Howard - *"My first day at Woodroffe felt never-ending. Even though it was very scary, moving to a school which was five times bigger, all the teachers and staff were really understanding and helpful..... I really like the fact that we have more responsibility at school – if I have a problem now, instead of going straight to the teacher, I try to sort things out myself..... Overall I have found Woodroffe really fun. It is a lot better than I thought it would be when I left primary school."*

Rachel Tipping - *"....The first thing that struck me when I was finding my way around was the size – it was huge compared to my old school but I wasn't really afraid of that. The thing that I was worried about was the other children; not just from Year 7 but all of them because we were not the big ones in little school anymore, we were the little ones in big school.... So far at Woodroffe I have enjoyed Literacy and English lessons because in Literacy we are learning Latin .... I like the new teachers because they are funny,* helpful and kind but they can be strict at times. I am looking forward to dissecting things in Science and going on the Paris trip later this year. Overall I have found Woodroffe scary, fun and friendly and now I'm loving it!"

Ryan Shilston – *"My first week at Woodroffe was very stressful. All the homework, all the strict teachers. I was also struggling to fit in with everyone else. I guess these are things I should have expected when you become a pupil at a school of over 1,000. When I heard that we would nearly always do three hours of sport a week I was horrified. That was probably the worst piece of news I could have got. The first time we had PE my heart was beating so fast ……. It turned out to be great. We got to run around, jump and go in the Fitness Room with all the weights and gym machines. This turned my week into one of the best weeks I've ever had at school."*

James Dunford – *"At the end of Year 6 I can remember saying to myself "this is it, I'm moving up". This was hard for me as Marshwood was like a family to me (a second family). I was scared of the change to come. But I shouldn't have been. My first day was strange and a mixture of fun and laughter and being scared and shy. My fears were faced when I was lost but it was no worry as a teacher kindly showed me to my class. It changed my perspective of Woodroffe from being big and scary to a bit kind and gentle just like Marshwood…..Lessons are always fun, there is never really a boring lesson. Teachers are always fun and happy. Everything I have been taught this term has helped me understand and helped me to learn more. This has encouraged me to put 100% into everything including sport….This term I don't have a favourite teacher because they are all my favourites and that makes Woodroffe perfect.*

Charlotte Daniels – *"I like the amount of sport that they do in the school. There is a lot more here than there was in primary. I am a lot more sporty now than I was in primary. I am also a lot more healthy and I think more before I do things. I am looking forward to all of the great trips that are going to happen in my time at Woodroffe."*

Peri Trott – *"My first term at Woodroffe school has been great! I enjoy practically everything here, especially Art, French and English. But all of the lessons are fanstastic. I have found my first few Drama lessons fairly challenging because I wasn't very confident in myself but with a little help from the teachers and my friends I love it just as much as any other lessons. I have found many new things I like but I never knew I would like games and going to the fitness room as much as I do. I'm looking forward to lots of things in my future at Woodroffe but especially meeting new people like I have already."*

Hannah Colby – *"I think Woodroffe is, well ….interesting! My first point would have to be the food, there is so much choice. I can't quite believe it. It takes me half my lunchtime to choose…. Secondly, there are so many people! I don't think I have ever seen such a flood like when they are all coming off the courts … Another thing that I really enjoy is all the different subjects – there's so many I can't begin to list them all…. overall I think it's a great school and I am definitely staying until the Sixth Form."*

At the other end of the school, Head Girl, Miriam Hillyard, and Head Boy, Tom Floyd wrote *"Having enjoyed seven years at Woodroffe, we have encountered a comprehensive range of aspects that encompass the essence of the school. The School Council has* been something that we have both particularly enjoyed – the Council provides a voice for the pupils and has now become an integral part of the school. We've participated in activities as diverse as working with the Food Standards Agency and evaluating the new Year 7 Literacy Curriculum.

One of the most notable aspects for visitors to the school is Woodroffe's friendly and warm atmosphere. The friendships formed between pupils in the different years reflects this.

Our favourite memories of Woodroffe include the many and varied school productions, (especially the recent "Little Shop of Horror" where a giant talking plant graced the stage!). The school ski trip was another highlight where we learnt about the limits of some of our teachers' co-ordination and subsisted on watery soup and Austrian chocolate.

The musical opportunities at Woodroffe have been something we've both taken advantage of, bringing together experienced (Tom) and fledgling (Miriam) musicians in concerts, carol services and European tours.

In conclusion, we feel that our time at Woodroffe has been an invaluable experience and we look forward to Higher Education knowing that we have been given a good start in life."

Sketch by ex-pupil, Sarah Kaye

These sentiments from both the youngest and the oldest pupils at the school emphasize the fact that although the school has moved with the times and has kept up with the many changes in education over the years, the qualities that make it so special have endured. It still remains a happy place to grow up and the majority of pupils benefit greatly from being at the school. As it has done for generations, Woodroffe continues to provide a supportive and caring environment that enables each child to feel secure and valued.

CHAPTER 12 - ALBAN JAMES WOODROFFE, MBE, JP (1875 -1964)

Alban Woodroffe was born in 1875. His father was the Honourable James Tisdall Woodroffe, a lawyer of Calcutta, who became Advocate-General of Bengal from 1899 to 1904. The family owned a large estate in Argentina where Alban spent many years rearing cattle.

In 1901 the family came to live at Ware House in Lyme Regis and in 1903 Alban married Annette Laura Talbot of Rhode Hill at the Roman Catholic Church in Lyme Regis. They had one son, Reginald John (Rex), who was born in 1905.

In 1911 he purchased Rhode Hill from his wife's family and during the First World War, when the main house was used as a Red Cross Hospital, Alban and his family lived at the Lodge and he acted as Commandant of the Hospital.

After the war the Woodroffe family moved back into the main house until 1934, when it was sold to provide accommodation for a private Domestic Science College. Alban then moved to White Ley, where he lived until his death aged 89 in 1964. He is buried in the Churchyard at Uplyme Church. Sadly his son, Rex, predeceased him and died in Argentina in 1949. Rex was married to Aileen and had a distinguished career in the Second World War. He also served as a Governor of the school and was an enthusiastic member of the Old Boys' Association.

Alban's commitment to public life was impressive and he worked tirelessly for the community in which he lived. He was the Dorset County Commissioner for Scouts for seven years, Chairman of Lyme Regis Cottage Hospital for twenty three years, a member of Dorset County Council from 1910 to 1963 and a member of Dorset Education Committee from 1910 to 1955, serving on the latter as Chairman for eleven years and Vice Chairman for ten years.

During the period between 1910 and 1914 Alban was elected as Mayor of Lyme Regis on three occasions and he became a County Alderman in 1928. He was also a Magistrate and Sherriff. On 10th October 1932 at a special meeting of the Lyme Regis Borough Council it was proposed that Alban should be awarded the first honorary Freedom of the Borough of Lyme Regis. This honour was conferred on him by the Mayor of Lyme Regis, Mr George Worth, at a special ceremony held at the Guildhall on Friday, 30th June 1933. In a newspaper report that appeared in the News Chronicle the Mayor stated that *"there was no one more deserving of the honour than Mr Woodroffe for the splendid services he had rendered to Lyme Regis over a long period."* Alban replied that he greatly appreciated the honour and that during his term as Mayor he had been proud of the fact that he had been able to come in close contact and mix freely with the working people of Lyme Regis. The illuminated certificate presented to Alban on this occasion is held in the school archive.

Alban was prominent in the foundation of Lyme Regis Grammar School. As Vice Chairman of the Dorset County Education Committee he was fundamental to the establishment of the school in 1923. He was the first Chairman of Governors and held that office from the school's foundation until his retirement from the Board of Governors in 1959. It was largely due to his efforts that the new school building on its present site was erected and opened in 1932. The school was named after him, in the year of his death, when it became a comprehensive school in 1964.

Many ex-pupils have very fond memories of Alban, such as Brian Wood who recalls how he met him when he joined the Uplyme Scouts in 1944. He describes Alban as *"a colossus and did so much for local education but always maintaining the common touch with his scouts."* Other ex-pupils who were also members of Uplyme Scouts remember Mr Woodroffe supervising the scouts swimming in the very cold and dark fresh water lake in the grounds of Rhode Hill House. Apparently Mr Woodroffe, in his capacity as Scout Leader, had to invigilate, ie taste, their practical attempts to gain the Cookery Badge.

Robert McKenzie writes *"From 1939 and the second form onwards I was an evacuee member – I think the only one – of the 1st Uplyme Scout Troop, rising eventually to Patrol Leader of the Wolf Patrol, under the Troop Leadership of Scoutmaster Alban J Woodroffe. Mr Woodroffe was prominent in national Scouting matters and was also the District Commissioner in Devon.*

He was then, I suppose in his early sixties – a distinguished, well-built, fatherly looking white-haired gentleman, owner of the Rhode Hill Estate and resident in Rhode Hill House until he surrendered it for wartime occupation then moving with his wife – a rather frail and infirm lady as I remember her – into the White Ley Cottage. He occasionally spoke about his younger life, practically all spent in the Argentine where he had been a cattle rancher (pre-war most beef eaten in the UK came from the Argentine) and clearly a large scale and pretty successful one…. His son, Rex, was in wartime a Flight Lieutenant and when on leave would occasionally turn up at the Tuesday night Scout meetings.

One wing of the stable block behind Rhode Hill House was given over entirely to scouting. The first floor was a wire mesh enclosed warehouse of scout camping gear and large demountable handcarts and the ground floor was the activity centre for troop activity and gymnastics – it possessed as much equipment as the school itself. Because it was wartime, with quite a lot of enemy air activity over Devon/Dorset day and night, and particularly night time with the Dornier DO 17s pulsating overhead at fairly low altitude en route to the Midlands industrial towns, there was no question of travelling away to camp. Substituted were indoor camps in the stable block with plenty of makeshift cooking. The outdoor aspects included a good deal of tracking, "getting through enemy lines to HQ", etc. and swimming in the quite sizeable lake below the Rookery on the estate.

Mr Woodroffe was often to be seen visiting the school and consulting with the Head, Mr Watton. These consultations certainly included who might be thought suitable prefect material. I had hints from Mr Woodroffe that I might be in the frame but unfortunately one or two pranks, that earned Mr Watton's strap, disqualified me. Mr Woodroffe was consoling….looking back I think he was perhaps particularly considerate toward me as my mother had recently died and the war had split my father, my brother and myself geographically apart. I received one to one fatherly talks and admonitions and interest in my subsequent career seeking fame and future in wartime London. When he came to town I enjoyed evenings at his club when he confessed to loneliness following the death of Mrs Woodroffe. I am sure he was a formative influence for me and I was sorry to learn of his death."

Another ex-pupil with memories of Alban is Neil Adams, an ex-pupil, who later joined the school as an English Master. Neil recalls *"When I came back onto the staff in 1953 I agreed to take on the leadership of the Uplyme Scouts – I had previously led a group in North Devon. Alban Woodroffe had been a close acquaintance of Baden Powell and was involved with the initial work in setting up the Movement – he suggested as much to me personally. The troop he formed at Uplyme must have been one of the earliest in the country. He donated the land on which its HQ stands and contributed considerably towards the cost of its building. Even at that early time it had heating through wall ducts and no obtrusive radiators. He had a swimming pool built near his house, mainly for the use of his scouts and he often took them for trips on his steam yacht that he kept in the Lyme Harbour. For his work for the Movement he was awarded its highest honour, the Silver Wolf, and he was proud of this. After his signature he always appended S.W.*

He devoted much of his retirement to LRGS and his troop of scouts. When I took this over it was in a bad way and leaderless and he was no longer able to cope with its active management. I encouraged its revival by involving boarders from St Andrews where I was House Tutor. Some boys from Lyme even joined. After he left Rhode Hill he lived in a bungalow nearby and I used to visit him there occasionally when he would talk on Baden Powell and the early days of his own involvement."

Jean Bennett nee Austin who was a pupil at Woodroffe from 1939 to 1946 offers another memory of Alban explaining *"I knew Mr Woodroffe. He lived at Rhode Hill House. My uncle, Wilfred Austen, was his butler for many years before the war and he was his Assistant Scoutmaster. He was in the RAF during the war and never failed to visit Rhode Hill when he was home on leave. Mr Woodroffe could not afford to employ him after the war but their friendship continued.*

In a local newspaper report, when he became the first Freeman of Lyme Regis in 1933, Mr Woodroffe stated that he regarded public service as "*the rent one should pay for one's place on earth*". In one simple sentence, this statement must surely sum up this great man to whom the town of Lyme Regis and its inhabitants owe so much.

(Historical information on Mr Woodroffe and his family taken from notes written in 1975 by the late Mr Michael Fairley, a History Master at the School, and from archive material held at the Philpot Museum in Lyme Regis, by kind permission of the Curator, Jo Draper)

CHAPTER 13 – HEADMASTERS

Mr A W M Greenfield, MA, (Oxon) - 1923 to 1927

Sadly not much information is available on Mr Greenfield. No indication can be found of where he came from or whether he had a wife and family. In the governors' minutes he is referred to as "Mr A W M Greenfield, aged thirty three, BA (London) 1911, BA Hons (Oxon) 1922, 2nd Cl. Mod Lang". His BA became an MA after one year as is the tradition at Oxford and Cambridge.

However, we do know that he was selected from a field of no fewer than 217 candidates and that he was very highly thought of by Alban Woodroffe who many years later recorded in notes he made on the history of the school "*The appointment of the Head could not have been a better one. He was just the Head to start a new type of school, with so many innovations to which parents were not accustomed, such as boys and girls being taught in the same classroom, boy and girl prefects, houses, school colours and girls in uniform, an extra year at school, scholarships or free places and then there was organised football and other matters which made this the first secondary school in the county.*"

In a speech that Alban Woodroffe made at Speech Day in 1956 he also publicly paid tribute to the excellent work of Mr Greenfield during the early days of the school, describing him as "*a splendid appointment, as he was the right Head to study the immense amount of detail in the starting of a new kind of school, not only as regards school work but in the corporate side of school life which is so important*".

Ex-pupil Mollie Raison née Wiscombe recalls him as "*a tall, handsome and quite a young man being only in his thirties. He wore his gown all the time, as did the other members of staff, and he wore a mortar board on formal occasions.*" In the governors' minutes there is an interesting reference to a request by the Headmaster to enter the school field via a gate at the bottom of his garden so he obviously lived in a property adjacent to the school. This request was granted at an agreed charge of 1/- per annum!

Mr Greenfield did not restrict his activities merely to the school but was also active in the community. Local newspapers published in April 1925 carried interesting reports on a meeting of the Lyme Regis Debating Society which had met at the Town Hall for its third debate of the season based on the proposition "That the discipline of children in the present generation has been unwisely relaxed". This proposition was moved by Mr Greenfield and opposed by Mr A S Neill, the very progressive educationalist who was Principal of the Summerhill International School in Lyme Regis at that time.

Mr Greenfield had put forward the argument that the two great factors in the training of children were the school and the home, with the latter having the greater influence. He felt that parents should prepare their offspring for the harsh realities of life and equip them with a "good disciplined mind". Children needed guidance and this responsibility lay with parents. Discipline was a necessity but in moderation. Too many rules were counter-productive but a few rules that were never broken were a good thing. Mr Greenfield concluded that discipline was essential in every walk of life and he felt that the country would never have done what it did in the First World War without discipline.

In reply Mr Neill agreed that the army was the best example of discipline but pointed out that in the army the discipline was as a result of fear. He felt that an army was a weapon of destruction whereas education was designed purely of creation. Therefore it was not valid to make comparisons between the army and school. He went on to deplore the fact that children in schools were forced to learn a lot of things which were of no use to them. He felt that if children were not interested in a certain subject they should be allowed to drop that subject. Mr Neill concluded that no-one was good enough to mould a child. Following a fierce debate Mr Greenfield secured thirty five votes and Mr Neill twenty five.

Another example of his keenness to involve the school in the local community was demonstrated in December 1925 when the governors received a request from Mr Greenfield to hold six lectures at the school on English Architecture.

It appears that Mr Greenfield was concerned about the need to provide the pupils at the school with opportunities to participate in physical exercise. He felt that it was essential to develop the school field so that a good game of cricket, hockey and football could be played immediately after school. Road safety was a further area of concern, as he was also anxious to relieve pupils of the need to walk up to the Sidmouth Road ground. Mr Greenfield must therefore have been very pleased to be able to report in 1927 that two hard tennis courts had been prepared on the school playground and arrangements made with the Town Tennis Club for the use of three grass courts on Saturday mornings. When he submitted his resignation to the Governing Body in December 1926, having secured the post of Head of Poole Secondary School, he apologised for the fact that he was leaving so soon and paid tribute to the support he had received from the Governing Body, particularly the Chairman, Mr. Woodroffe.

By the time Mr Greenfield left the school at the end of the Summer Term in 1927, the numbers attending had risen to one hundred and twelve. Upon his departure, in their minutes the governors recorded their *"appreciation of the valuable service rendered to the school"* during his headship and it was agreed that a letter of thanks should be sent to him wishing him good luck in his new appointment. Although there is relatively little information available on record about Mr Greenfield, the man, there is an address that he wrote for the school magazine in 1948 when the school was celebrating its Silver Jubilee and perhaps the words he wrote best reflect his character and personality.

"It was a pleasure to come back to your Speech Day and see the staff and pupils of Lyme Regis Grammar School, of which I was the first Head for the years 1923 – 1927. I spent four very happy years in Lyme. As Mr Woodroffe stated, the school started with very few pupils, in fact many people thought that Lyme was not large enough to support a Grammar School. The fact that the school has been a great success has been due to the vision, foresight and active support of County Alderman A J Woodroffe, MBE, who is still, I am glad to know, the Chairman of Governors, and his fellow governors. It was a happy adventure to start the school. There was nobody to say "we do not do things this way in West Dorset" so that we were able to aim at beginnings on lines which seemed suitable for educational advancement in the very delightful and ancient borough, full of associations of culture and refinement in the past and still flourishing.

Whatever has been achieved by the school has been due to the Head who succeeded me and to the very great interest of the governors, throughout the twenty-five years of its life. Parents and pupils have responded well and made a happy family. The present boys and girls of Lyme now have what I consider to be the most beautiful Grammar School buildings in the South-West of England. I hope the school will continue to flourish and to send out into the world sound citizens, proud to have had the privilege of spending their schooldays in the school and to have the opportunity of making some contribution to the welfare and happiness of others in the careers on which they embark".[1]

Mr S L Watton, MA, BSc - 1927 to 1946

Mr Greenfield must have been a hard act to follow but in Mr Watton the governors found a worthy Head to build on the foundations already laid. This view was reinforced by Mr Woodroffe who, in his historical notes, described how Mr Watton had *"loyally carried on the school on the lines that had been laid down by Mr. Greenfield"*. This time there were one hundred and sixty two applicants for the post, with a shortlist of three candidates invited for interview. At the time of his appointment Mr Watton was forty three years old. He was a linguist who had studied for his professional qualifications in Manchester. We know that he was a family man, with two sons, David and John, and one daughter, Mary, all of whom attended the school and were very popular with their fellow pupils. Mary was Head Girl from 1942/43.

Mr Watton was very highly thought of and his headship covered not only the move from the

---

[1] Extract from the School Magazine dated July 1948

Hill Road site to the new school site but also the period of the Second World War, a very difficult time for everyone. During the latter Mr Watton and his family had more than their fair share of grief as it is recorded that during one tragic week his daughter contracted polio, his wife died, one son was killed and the other captured at Arnhem.

The school magazines perhaps best reflect Mr Watton's style of leadership, the commitment he felt towards the school and its pupils and the warmth with which he was regarded by both the pupils and his colleagues.

At Speech Day in October 1928 he urged pupils to follow principles which were worth treasuring by everyone such as *"What you are is more important than what you possess"* and *"Try to acquire a sense of humour and a sense of proportion"*. To give a different side to his character, at the AGM and Annual Dinner held in October 1938 it is noted that the Head entertained those present by singing "On Ilkley Moor b'aht'at"!!!

By July 1941 the war was casting a huge shadow over the school and with both his sons in the armed forces it must have been a particularly anxious time for Mr Watton. In an open letter in the school magazine to the Old Boys, Mr. Watton advised that over one hundred ex-pupils were now on active service. He assured them that they were not forgotten at school and that Mr Thomas kept the list of names up to date and a copy of that list hung in the corridor for pupils to look through. Mr Watton reminded the old boys that whenever the hymn was sung, and the prayer was said, for *"absent brethren"* they were always in the thoughts of everyone at school. By now the School Magazine was including lists of those who had died in the Service of the Nation, who were reported missing believed dead or were being held as Prisoners of War.

In the school magazine of July 1943 Mr Watton refers to the death of his son, David, who was *"one of the gallant band of parachutists who, fighting as infantry, did such fine work in Tunisia last winter. He fell in German territory somewhere between Beja and Mateur. I wish I could make so fine an end"*. Such a wistful note at the end sums up the grief Mr Watton must have been feeling, as would many parents who had lost sons and daughters in this way.

In the same magazine it was noted that Mr Watton's other son, Lieutenant John Watton, was *"not wasting his time in prison camp: he has made himself a famous artist. In an exhibition of work by war artists held in London recently, John's drawings and paintings were the main feature. By way of a change he, now and again, has a shot at escaping! We offer him our whole-hearted congratulations and admiration"*.

In July 1945 Mr Watton, still obviously grieving for the death of his son, reminded old boys that *"believe it or not, we schoolmasters feel ourselves in a peculiar kind of kinship with our Old Boys, and every time we lose one of them there is a sense of personal bereavement"*.

Upon his retirement in 1946 Mr Watton urged pupils to *"Count your blessings"* pointing out that *"one of the greatest blessings of my life has been the affection so generously given me by 'my young people'"*. Mr Thomas paid tribute to Mr Watton in glowing terms as follows:

"The time has come for us to bid farewell to a very dear friend and Head and it is indeed a hard thing to do. Mr Watton has guided the destinies of this school for the past nineteen years and its record of achievement during that period is one of which he can be very proud. That success is, in no small measure, due to the fact that, not only the staff, but every boy and girl in the school has been so happy under his leadership: their interests have always held first place with him and he has endeared himself to everyone. Mr Watton leaves us assured always of our real affection and esteem and our sincere gratitude for all the he has done for us and for the school. May he live many years to enjoy his well earned retirement, and nowhere will he find a greater welcome than when he visits his old school: those visits, we hope, will be frequent."[2]

Three separate presentations were made to Mr Watton on his retirement, when further warm tributes were paid to him from all quarters. Mr Thomas, Senior Master, presented a cheque on behalf of the teaching staff and kitchen staff. Miss Burcham and Mr Stone *"voiced the affection with which Mr Watton was held by all whose privilege it was to serve under him and reminded the Head that the approaching status of Old Boy carried an obligation to retain an intimate and active link with the school, a link that would give all his friends the pleasure of meeting him often in the years to come."* A H Bevan (Head Boy) and Ann E Thomas (Head Girl) presented Mr Watton with a silver bonbon dish as a token of sincere gratitude and admiration and as a memento of happy days under Mr Watton's Headship. For the school, J Grant, supported by Janet Worth, added the affection of all pupils to that already expressed by others and hoped that the years of retirement would be happy.

It was noted that the first Old Boys and Old Girls Social since the beginning of the war had been held just before the end of the summer term, in honour of Mr Watton. About one hundred old pupils had attended and on behalf of Old Girls and Old Boys Mrs S Chambers and Mr N S Bosence had presented Mr Watton with a gold wrist watch and a substantial cheque in appreciation of his long years of service and devotion to the school and as a token of their affection and gratitude to their old Head on his retirement from active teaching.

In response Mr Watton expressed his gratitude for the splendid presents and for the way the old pupils had fulfilled the promise of earlier days, by their University careers, their earnest endeavour in their jobs of work, and their courage and endurance during the terrible years of war. He felt he had as much, and more, cause for gratitude than they. In a written tribute to Mr Watton contained in the school magazine ex-pupil, Mr Lillington referred to the fact that Mr Watton had come to the school when the first enthusiasm of opening had passed and he had consequently had the difficult job of guiding the school through the early years. It was noted that under his headship the school had grown in size and in prestige.

The above surely sums up a man held in great esteem who was respected by everyone. He seems to have managed to maintain effective leadership of the school, without incurring the element of isolation that sometimes goes hand in hand with responsibility.

---

[2] Extract from the School Magazine dated July 1946

There is one more reference to Mr Watton in school records in 1948, after his retirement, when he was asked to contribute to the school magazine celebrating the school's Silver Jubilee. In his short address Mr Watton referred to the many happy memories he had of the school and the pleasure he got from continued contact with ex-pupils. He reminded the reader that no failure need be permanent and that "*Get up and have another go*" is a motto worth remembering. His final message was "*Good Luck to you all, and may you face life gallantly*".

Mr T B Pearn, OBE, MC, MA – 1946 to 1976

Thornton Pearn came to the school in September 1946, at the age of thirty two and straight from military service. He also was a family man with two daughters, Gillian and Carolyn, both of whom attended the school – Carolyn was Head Girl from 1963/64. Mr Pearn began the first year of his headship as he meant to go on. He immediately highlighted the need for the school to have a flag, a charter of purpose as defined in its motto, and a School Song. The School Song shortly came into existence with words penned by school master, Mr Ellis, and the music written by Mr Pearn himself. He also set the Lord's Prayer to music, and it became a tradition for this to be sung annually at the school's very popular Carol Service held in the local Parish Church.

Right from the outset his message to pupils was firm and direct. He reflected on the fact that although it had been in existence for twenty four years the school was relatively young. He felt that the time was now right "*to claim our inheritance and to fight boldly through the uncertainties of the future*". Mr Pearn pondered on the British characteristic to rise to the occasion when the need arises but suggested that it was preferable to maintain "*the steady flow of quiet, purposeful work towards a worthwhile goal*" which requires "*true courage and real constancy – an unwavering, intelligent and conscious determination to fight for the finer things of life*". He referred to the tremendous sacrifice made by the old boys whose names appeared on the school memorial tablet and he urged pupils to look to the future and to live their lives according to the new motto "Audacia Constantiaque" which meant "by courage and constancy".

In the edition of the school magazine in 1948, which celebrated the school's Silver Jubilee, Mr Pearn impressed upon pupils that their aims should be "*to accept only the highest standards of personal conduct and character and absolutely to reject everything that was shoddy, cheap or mean; to pour out generously all our energies and intelligence in the service of the community and to realise that in the forgetfulness of self lies the deepest happiness.*"

Mr Pearn was always keen to maintain a strong relationship between school and parents and to this end, upon his arrival, he founded the Parents Association. His original intention had been to form a Parent-Teacher Association but by all accounts the staff did not like the idea so he launched the Parents Association with no staff participation.

In 1950 Mr Pearn introduced boarding facilities linked to the school and in this endeavour he had the full support of the Chairman of Governors, Mr Woodroffe. A state-run boarding facility was a new concept and the school was very much a leader in this field. Boarding was originally set up to attract more boys to the school, who were accommodated at St Andrews House which was run by Mr Pearn and his wife. It proved so successful that two years later arrangements were made to accommodate girls at Harcombe House. With boarding numbers continuing to grow, Rhode Hill House was acquired in 1969 to house all girl pupils, with junior boys accommodated at Harcombe House and senior boys at St. Andrews. There is no doubt that the introduction of boarding pupils enriched the school population, giving local pupils the opportunity to mix with fellow pupils from a wide range of family backgrounds very different from their own.

The next hurdle to be overcome was the move from being a grammar school to a comprehensive which occurred in 1963. This was not an easy move to make but Mr Pearn had recognised that the school was still relatively small and would soon have to compete against larger comprehensives further afield. He became even more convinced that action needed to be taken when in the early 1960s plans were being discussed to build a new secondary modern school in the town which would replace the senior section of the local church school. Comprehensive schools were being mooted as the way forward and small grammar schools were falling out of favour. Seeing the writing on the wall Mr Pearn threw his weight behind the transition from grammar school to comprehensive school and thus the Woodroffe School came into being in 1964.

During his time at the school Mr Pearn spearheaded many fund-raising appeals, the most notable being that to provide the school with an outdoor swimming pool. This goal was achieved after a lot of hard work by staff, pupils, parents and the wider community with perhaps the greatest fund-raising event ever being the first fifty mile sponsored walk which took place in 1963. Mr Pearn also presided over the large extension to the school facilities which took place in 1963 when School Hall, Gymnasium, changing rooms, six new laboratories, art and crafts rooms and workshops were created to accommodate the increasing number of pupils, which now topped 600.

The school magazine of 1964 was named "Phoenix '64" to reflect the fact that a new school had arisen from the ashes of the old school. The newly named Woodroffe School would offer *"new possibilities, new problems and a new outlook"*. A poignant time for all concerned but once again Mr Pearn was there to lead the school through this period of transition. In the magazine the view was expressed that the school was *"a continuing community of young, alert and curious minds probing unceasingly towards the future"* and that in school, as in life, it was necessary to give as much as you take. A new ledger was being opened and it was important for names not to appear on the debit side. Reference was made to the school motto which was felt to be particularly appropriate at this juncture in the school's history.

Gaye Raison (now Mrs Baulch), an ex-pupil, was appointed as the Head's Secretary not long after leaving school, taking over from Mrs Jackson who had held the post for twelve years. She recalls *"Major Pearn was greatly respected at County Hall. He was one of the most diplomatic people I have ever encountered and rarely failed to obtain funding for whatever project. He had a real gift of talking out problems with disruptive/rebellious pupils – often reducing them to tears – but in very many cases he turned their lives around, particularly boarders, some of whom came from difficult backgrounds."*

The next big occurrence in the life of the school was the raising of the school leaving age to sixteen, which led to the building of the ROSLA (Raising of School Leaving Age) block in the early 1970's. In 1973 Mr Pearn was awarded an OBE for "Services to Education" and this was largely in recognition of his work at Woodroffe. A further insight into the impact Mr Pearn had on the school during his long Headship is contained in extracts from a tribute to him on his retirement, included in the school magazine:

"Mr Pearn came to the Lyme Regis Grammar School in 1946 at a time when the school had survived the exigencies and austerities of six years of war and was due for expansion. There were 220 pupils of which eight were in the Sixth Form. Mr Pearn set out to enlarge and enrich the curriculum, encourage pupils to stay on to attempt Advanced Level examinations and to integrate the school more closely with the life of the local community. A Parents Association was soon formed to foster local interest."

"Mr Pearn skilfully effected this transition (ie the introduction of boarding) guiding the policy of the school in such a way as to meet the needs of the wider variety of boys and girls who now attended so that by the 1970s it was recognised as an outstanding example of the new, moderate-sized comprehensive school. Numbers grew with the increase in the local population until in the year of his retirement there were nearly nine hundred pupils on roll."

"Mr Pearn contributed largely to the reputation of the school by his personal achievement in becoming a well-known member of a series of BBC radio programmes on education psychology and the problems of young people generally. Towards the end of his career he began to draw attention to the vital importance of the first five years of a child's development. He looks forward to elaborating this theme in his retirement."[3]

Mr Pearn's retirement was marked by a series of festive and ceremonial events. During the last weeks of the Easter Term there were performances of school plays and concerts as a special mark of respect. Presentations were made separately by the Old Pupils' Association, the Parents' Association, and the staff and by the pupils. Glowing tributes were paid on these occasions to a man who, it was felt, had done a great deal to enhance the reputation of the school during his thirty years as Head. Many also expressed the sense of personal loss in that they appreciated the advice and friendship which he had given freely and generously both in the school and in the community.

---

[3] Extract from the School Magazine dated July 1976

The School on the Hill

In retirement Mr Pearn maintained his contact with the school, mainly through Rotary, when he assisted with such activities as adjudicating the Rotary Youth Speaks Competition and in conducting mock interviews for pupils about to leave school. In 1998, many years into his retirement, Mr Pearn received the honour of which he was most proud as it was awarded to him by people who knew him. Like Mr Woodroffe before him, he was made a Freeman of the Town of Lyme Regis which was bestowed upon him "in recognition of his innovative services to education in this community from the time of his demobilisation in 1946 to his retirement in 1976."

Mr Pearn's daughter, Gillian, in conjunction with her sister, Carolyn, pays tribute to her father: *"My aunt once said that Thornton was born to lead. Certainly he was given significant responsibility at a very early age. As the eldest son, from the age of about fifteen, he was put in charge of a large number of younger brothers and cousins on their annual camping holidays. No adults were present – a situation that is quite inconceivable nowadays.*

These qualities of leadership were very much tested during the war. He was in the Royal Artillery and for much of the war was a front-line gunner. Once, the tank he was in went over a landmine. Although injured he survived. He was the only one who did. On another occasion, when all the senior officers present were killed during the early stage of an attack, he took over command and, in the face of extremely heavy enemy gunfire, successfully held a strategically important position. For this act of bravery, he was awarded the Military Cross and the rank of Major. It was no wonder that, as one very "old boy" once confided in me, the pupils were more than a little apprehensive back in 1946 as they sat in the school hall awaiting the arrival of their new headmaster, whose reputation as a soldier had apparently preceded him!

For the next thirty years, Lyme Regis Grammar School and latterly The Woodroffe School, was to be Thornton's life. Being a headmaster was much more than a job for him: it was a vocation. He believed that everyone in the school, staff and pupils alike, was important and was a "part of the same team". If anyone needed his time, he gave of it freely.

I think my sister and I probably saw less of our father than did most children of our generation. He worked very long hours, even by today's standards. Not only did his duties as headmaster take much of his time but as housemaster at St Andrews, he was frequently "on duty" at evenings and weekends as well. "Holidays" were frequently taken up with meetings of governors or with officers at County Hall to discuss and plan for the latest development at school.

Our mother was very supportive of him but if Carolyn or I complained, he would point out that this was his job and, as a result, we were fortunate enough to live in beautiful Lyme Regis in the comfort of St Andrews. He always thought he was "very lucky" – his words – to have the job he loved in the place he loved and he firmly believed that with privileges came responsibilities. I believe he was also very conscious of the many friends and a few of the cousins who did not return with him in 1945. He felt that he owed it to them to build the future for which they had given their lives. For Thornton, this meant giving the children of succeeding generations an education which would enable them to take a successful part in the world.

When Dad was made Freeman of Lyme Regis, he was presented with a breathtakingly beautiful illustrated parchment which now hangs proudly in my study. Part of its text reads 'As a practising educationalist his mind encompassed the global scene but never missed the vital details so necessary for a truly great headmaster and an effective teacher'. He was very moved by this fine accolade and I think it well sums up the contribution he made to the school."

Mr D L Butterworth, MA – 1976 to 1985

If Mr Watton had a difficult task following Mr Greenfield, David Butterworth really had his work cut out following Thornton Pearn, who was held in such affection and esteem by not only the staff, parents and pupils but the wider community served by the school.

Mr Butterworth was a family man with one daughter, Kate, who attended the school. He took up his appointment in April. He came originally from Yorkshire and graduated in History with Honours from Corpus Christi College, Cambridge. He had previously served on the staff of Ashville College in Harrogate, Sale Grammar School for Boys in Cheshire as Second Master, and Head of Upper School of the Hewett School in Norwich. His previous post, prior to coming to Woodroffe, was that of Head of Dayncourt Comprehensive School in Ratcliffe-on-Trent, Nottinghamshire. His interests were history, music, the history of the cinema and athletics, for which he was formerly an AAA coach.

The new Head immediately impressed with the speed with which he took the measure of the school and the community. His obvious awareness of the peculiarities and predilections of the school was much appreciated. He was careful to allay fears about his plans for the future of the school, which included a new structure for the timetable and a broadly-based curriculum for the Sixth Form.

Mr Butterworth felt that every pupil should expect to be given not only every opportunity but also positive encouragement to contribute to the work of the school and, at the same time, to develop his or her own potential. Above all the new Head was determined that in all matters the school should display the virtues of openness and integrity and that it should become more conscious of its own identity.

Mr Butterworth's headship covered a period when funding for education was not generous and very careful management was required of school resources. He worked closely with the Parents Association and was instrumental in founding the Friends of Woodroffe as a means of providing financial and other support for the school.

Also during Mr Butterworth's time at the school a major re-build took place from 1979 to 1982 which caused major disruption to the life of the school although the benefits, when the project was completed, were enormous in terms of new facilities. Despite the huge stress placed on staff by the re-building programme, Mr Butterworth was particularly proud and delighted that pupils took the chaos and disruption in their stride and indeed achieved some of the best results ever.

Mr Butterworth had considerable experience of boarding and was always keen to maintain this facility at Woodroffe. During his time as Head considerable improvements were made to the boarding houses. Aware that Lyme was rather isolated, Mr Butterworth always strove to involve the school in the wider community and he was especially pleased at the school's participation in the first community play, "The Reckoning", in 1978. He also supported the idea of bringing internationally known musicians to Lyme through the medium of the Celebrity Concerts and it pleased him greatly to see Woodroffe pupils benefiting from the subsequent workshops led by these musicians. It was entirely fitting that during his last year at the school Mr Butterworth was made Chairman of the Dorset Association of Secondary Heads.

It is true to say that Mr Butterworth's style of leadership was a lot different to that of his predecessors, particularly Thornton Pearn. He does not appear to have enjoyed his role as Head and this is reflected in a comment made by Deputy Head, Ian Cook, in a tribute to Mr Butterworth published in the school magazine dated July 1985. Ian Cook concluded by saying that in his retirement he hoped that Mr Butterworth *"would be able to take up interests for which recent years have not allowed him time and to live a more normal life than is possible for a Head."*

Best wishes were passed to Mr Butterworth and his family on their move to York where it was hoped they would be very happy. Sadly Mr Butterworth died in 2003 but Mrs Butterworth has provided an insight into her husband's years at Woodroffe which perhaps supports the above comments by Mr Cook.

"For my husband the trouble about Woodroffe School was that Lyme saw the headship as a privilege, while he saw it as a job. An education official came to see him soon after his appointment, looked out of the window at the sea and cliffs, and exclaimed "This must be the best job in Dorset!". "A school isn't run on the view" my husband said coolly.

He came from a very different first headship in Nottinghamshire, where he'd had to convert a secondary modern into a comprehensive with new, energetic and enthusiastic staff. By contrast Woodroffe was long-established under the lengthy headship of Major Pearn, who was rightly much admired. We both liked him a great deal: he never interfered and, indeed, tried unobtrusively to help.

At that stage the school needed a rebuilding programme to bring facilities up to date. My husband was very good at sequencing all the stages, but there was inevitably disruption for the current pupils and staff. He also tried to strengthen the boarding side, which brought in some very good pupils, and enjoyed the weekly visits of "inspection". He was, therefore, angry and disappointed when four girls climbed out of Rhode Hill to join the "French Lieutenant's Woman" film crew party: they were expelled amid a certain amount of controversy.

Throughout his tenure my husband tried to enlarge horizons. With my help with interview practice, a number of pupils applied successfully to Oxbridge. This is not what a comprehensive is for, but, when it happens, it enhances its reputation. I also did a lot of (unpaid) skills teaching in the school, though with what success I can't say! One very important innovation was my husband's insistence that all A level pupils learn to type in case those new-fangled micro-computers took off at work. Was this, or was it not, prescient?!

He enjoyed reasonable relations with the staff, parents and education officials, and cordial ones with the Heads in the area. He was latterly Chairman of Dorset Heads. His happiest relations were with his governors. They were invariably supportive and their criticism constructive. He had two very good Chairmen of Governors and for that he was most grateful. However, I can't pretend his stay in Lyme was a particularly happy experience. Two urban-orientated Cambridge graduates would always have found rural living difficult. The stress eventually made him take early retirement. We gauged reaction wrongly there: we'd thought "Well, at least Lyme will be pleased now?" In fact, it was reported to us that Lyme was furious: "We'll tell him when to go – how dare he do this off his own bat!" He went on to work happily for York Festival, and for York CAB as Deputy Manager. Education he put firmly behind him."

Mr P Vittle, B Phil – 1985 to 1992

Paul Vittle was appointed as Headmaster at the age of 41. He was a family man with one son and two daughters. Formerly he was Deputy Head at West Somerset School in Minehead where he had been on the staff since 1970, for the last term as Acting Head. Originally Mr Vittle came from Bristol where he was educated at Bedminster Down School. He read for his first degree the twin disciplines of Religious Studies and Biology at Exeter and returned to the University there to read for a second, BPhil degree in Curriculum Studies between 1979 and 1981. His first teaching appointment was at Hinkley Grammar School, Leicestershire and then Thornbury Grammar School in Gloucestershire where he moved in 1968 as Head of Religious Education.

Mr Vittle's interests included sport, particularly squash, caravanning, restoring old cars and antiques. He had also been a Marriage Guidance Councillor for some years. When Mr Vittle was appointed a short list of twelve candidates had been drawn up by the Governing Body and two days of interviews had taken place.

Like Mr Butterworth before him, Mr Vittle was a great supporter of boarding, which he saw not only as a means of maintaining the number of pupils on roll particularly in the Sixth Form, but also as a means of enriching the pupil population by bringing pupils from different cultures and countries to mix with children from the largely rural community in Lyme Regis.

His other main passion was a commitment to sharing the school with the community and throughout his headship he went to great lengths to encourage greater use of school facilities out of school time, forging close links with Lyme Regis Town Council and helping to set up Woodroffe Community Association. In this context, with the help of the PTA, the School Shop was created which was to double up as a social area for people attending evening classes. Mr Vittle was also an enthusiastic supporter of the Lyme Regis Run which regularly attracted over six hundred runners of all abilities for the ten mile, five mile and fun run races.

Mr Vittle brought a new energy and sense of purpose to the school and his "child-centred" view of education put greater emphasis on the pastoral side. During his headship there was a move away from vertical tutor groups, which contained pupils of all ages, to horizontal tutor groups which included pupils of the same age. Also as part of the national curriculum the terms 1st, 2nd, 3rd, 4th and 5th forms were replaced by Year 7, 8, 9, 10 and 11.

Another innovation achieved under Mr Vittle's leadership was the formation of the school's Combined Cadet Force, comprising Army, Navy and Air Force Units, which offered pupils an insight into service life and many opportunities to participate in training courses and residential camps. Cadets were able to participate in a range of activities which most would otherwise probably never have had the chance to experience, such as flying, gliding, sailing, boat-handling, navigation, training days in HM ships, outward bound activities such as orienteering and even the opportunity to compete in national and international marksmanship competitions at Bisley.

In 1990 the introduction of Local Management of Schools (LMS) took place. This system offered schools greater control and flexibility in terms of the management of funding. However, although there were opportunities for this, the whole system fell down due to insufficient funds being available to meet the needs of all pupils. The allocation of funds to the school was based on a formula, which provided a certain amount of money for each pupil depending on age. The county wide formula was based not on real or historic costs, but on average costs and the vast majority of Heads began expressing concern to their LEAs about inadequate funding. The dilemma facing Mr Vittle was one of balancing the books and yet keeping the educational needs of pupils central to all decisions.

Against this backdrop, the possibility of schools "opting-out" of LEA control and becoming "Grant Maintained" seemed an enticing prospect, particularly as at this time the LEA was also taking a look at boarding provision across the county, possibly to the detriment of boarding at Woodroffe.

Gradually the idea of applying for Grant Maintained Status gained momentum. Although it was popular with the majority of governors it was not readily accepted by staff, parents and the wider community. A period of consultation was entered into, culminating in a parents' ballot, the result of which was in favour of applying for GM status. An application from the school was accepted by the Secretary of State for Education and the school assumed its new status in September 1991.

This meant an enormous change in role for both the Head and the Governing Body. As the first year as a Grant Maintained School drew to a close, problems began to emerge in terms of balancing the budget. Unfortunately the budget situation and the threat of redundancies led to a vote of no confidence in the Head and the Chairman of Governors at the end of the Summer Term.

Mr Vittle therefore resigned from his post in December 1992 after seven years at the school. Under his leadership a lot was achieved – numbers on roll increased, boarding remained viable, exam results improved and the school's profile within the community was raised considerably and these factors should not be overlooked. Although problematical at the outset, the decision to apply for Grant Maintained Status was one of the most pivotal points in the school's history in terms of the freedom that it gave the school to move forward under its own steam. Mr Vittle has kindly provided his reflections on the time he spent at the school.

"It is not difficult to gather together a collection of words to describe how I felt when I became Head of The Woodroffe School; exhilarated, proud, enthusiastic, creative, and energetic. I recall several years of great achievements for the school at virtually every level.

My incumbency coincided with changes at almost every level. Aspects that we now take for granted, like using the title Headteacher rather than Head; using Years Seven, Eight etc. rather than First, Second Form; the National Curriculum; the introduction of Information Technology; the introduction of a more diverse Special Educational Needs Department and a broader curriculum for post sixteen, all took place during this time. As far as the curriculum was concerned the pendulum swung from content to process and firmly established a pupil centred approach, with the emphasis on fulfilling potential regardless of ability. Other changes that took place during this period included, establishing a Community Association that sought to make the facilities of the school available for general use, and developments in the three Boarding Houses to match the needs of the large number of boarders.

I recall with fond memories the effort put in by staff, pupils, parents and governors in establishing the Fun Runs, the Parents' Association; the school shop; the fund raising Fairs. Indelibly printed on my memory are the outstanding Madrigal Group performances; the Christmas Carol services; BEFRIEND sessions (one of the first mentoring programmes in the country); Ten Tors expeditions and the many other activities that stood alongside the high academic achievement and well deserved outstanding reputation of the school.

As far as my tenure was concerned, when the parents voted for the school to change from local authority control to becoming Grant Maintained, it was for some people, one change too far. So it was hugely disappointing and upsetting that the majority of staff and governors finally framed their parochial needs by criticising the Chair of Governors and me at a time of deep insecurity for them, and I felt saddened and betrayed. Woodroffe has a proud history, but like some other institutions it found 'change – overload' difficult to assimilate.

From how I saw the school develop after I left, it would seem that becoming a GM school did not actually save and help boarding flourish in the way that was expected. Of course local management of schools is now a matter of fact and Foundation or Trust Schools are not the threat they once were. It is good to see that Woodroffe continues to attract higher than average numbers on roll and maintains its good reputation. It was the friendly attitude of the pupils and their achievements in striking a balance between tradition, good behaviour and imaginative learning, plus the dedication of the majority of the staff, that made the vast majority of my time at Woodroffe so enjoyable.

My period as Headteacher ended for me when I was in America attending a very prestigious educational management course, when the staff passed a vote of no confidence in me and Mrs Woodbridge, Chair of Governors, at a time when the governors were rationalising the staff / pupil ratio in order to address a relatively small deficit budget. Sadly what followed was an entrenchment of positions and I remain indebted to the parents, pupils and staff who did remain supportive. Unfortunately after a period of suspension and illness I resigned from my position as Headteacher. Nevertheless this was a period of my life where I am adamant that the positive memories and experiences must far out weigh the negative. "

Following the departure of Paul Vittle, Ian Cook, Deputy Head, took over as Acting Headteacher from 1992 prior to the appointment of Kerrigan Redman.

Mr K J Redman, BA (Hons) - 1993 to 2003

Kerrigan Redman was appointed in September 1993. He was married with two grown up daughters and moved to Woodroffe from Humberside where he had been Head of Bridlington School, since 1988. Bridlington School was an 11 – 18 mixed comprehensive with 1,200 pupils on roll and until 1991 it had been a state boarding school. Mr Redman was an early convert to the concept of Grant Maintained Schools and was keen for Bridlington School to 'opt-out' of Local Authority control. He was frustrated and disappointed that this did not happen and therefore, welcomed the opportunity to take over the Headship of a Grant Maintained School, particularly one that still offered boarding facilities.

Mr Redman gained a BA Honours Degree in Geography at the University College of

Wales, Aberystwyth in 1964 and his teaching qualification at the University of Bristol School of Education a year later. He began his teaching career in 1965 at the Commonweal School, a mixed 14-18 comprehensive, in Swindon, his home town.

In 1975, following two Head of Department posts, firstly at the Ridgeway School, Wroughton and then the Headlands School, Swindon, Mr Redman took up the appointment of Assistant Education Officer Development/Design with Dorset County Council. In this capacity he was involved in the forward planning of school places and the design of new primary and secondary schools in the County.

In 1978 he moved back to school based work, as Deputy Head of Impington Village College in Cambridgeshire. In 1981 he became Warden (Head) of Witchford Village College, also in Cambridgeshire. In both posts he gained valuable experience in Community Education, including youth work and adult education. He moved from Witchford to Bridlington in 1988.

In a newsletter to parents he expressed his feelings on taking over as Head of the school as follows:

"I have thoroughly enjoyed my first half-term at the Woodroffe School. I am most impressed by the excellent relationships that exist within the school, the range and quality of opportunities available to the pupils and the commitment of my colleagues. I have inherited a very good foundation on which to build in partnership with you. I hope you will take every opportunity to become involved in your child's education and the life of the school.

I am particularly pleased to be the Head of a Grant Maintained School with boarding. I believe that both help us to be something special and Grant Maintained status gives us opportunities and organisational flexibility that do not exist within a Local Authority framework."[4]

In the early days of his headship the Mr Redman shared his vision for Woodroffe with parents and pupils. He envisaged a school pursuing excellence that

a. wishes to achieve the best possible academic results;
b. takes account of individual strengths and weaknesses;
c. recognises the value of a range of extra-curricular activities in the development of young people;
d. values its staff and encourages their development
e. is an orderly community where self-discipline rather than imposed discipline is the norm;
f. recognises the importance of the environment in creating an atmosphere conducive to learning and good relationships;
g. emphasizes smartness of personal appearance;
h. is striving to improve the range of facilities available;

---

[4] Extract from Parents' Bulletin dated October 1993

i.	is mindful of its place in the local community and is striving to extend its links;
j.	encourages self-assessment by the pupils through Records of Achievement;
k.	is seeking effective partnership with parents;
l.	recognises the importance of effective links with the world of work;
m.	keeps abreast of developments in Education and modifies its practice accordingly;
n.	values the contribution that boarding makes and is seeking to sustain it;
o.	constantly monitors and reviews its practice;
p.	values its autonomy as a self-Governing School and wishes this to continue;
q.	sees value in Specialist Schools status;
r.	works corporately for the greater good of the institution;
s.	emphasizes quality;
t.	recognises the key role of governors and encourages governor involvement."

Mr Redman made it quite clear that he expected high standards of discipline and strict adherence to the school's dress code. He emphasised the importance of partnership with parents in the education of their children.

Over the period of his headship there were major modifications to the school curriculum both 11-16 and 16-19. The range of opportunities for the pupils expanded both in the formal taught curriculum and in extra curricular activities. New management arrangements were introduced including development planning and performance management for staff.

With the contraction of the Armed Services, the prime source of boarders, Mr. Redman oversaw the inevitable closure of boarding in the late 1990s and ensured that the income from the sale of the three boarding houses was used to create new, much-needed facilities for the school including the Thornton Pearn Drama Studio and the Sports Hall complex. Other areas of the school such as laboratories and workshops were updated and refurbished.

Unfortunately the school encountered financial difficulties when one of the major building projects ran considerably over budget. The Head negotiated an arrangement whereby the LEA stepped in to cover the shortfall which meant the curtailing of capital expenditure for a period of time as these funds were needed to repay the LEA. Court action against the contractors followed but eventually a satisfactory outcome was achieved.

Mr Redman's tenure culminated in the attainment by the school of Specialist School status. He thus ensured that the school was poised, ready to enter a new era as a Visual Arts College, when the new Head took over in September 2003.

The school was inspected twice during Mr Redman's headship and on both occasions the Inspectors' report was positive. In the Inspection Report dated March 2000 it was noted that *"The present Head had been in post for almost seven years. Over this time, his strong and effective management and educational leadership have steered the school forward on many fronts."*

Mr Redman was ably supported throughout his headship at Woodroffe by his wife, Pamela, who sadly died of cancer shortly after his retirement in 2003. Mrs Redman attended many school events with her husband and took a keen interest in the life of the school and its pupils. Mr Redman was active in the local community and as well as being a member of the Lyme Regis Rotary Club, he and his wife served on the Committee of the Lyme Regis Club for Young People, of which Mr Redman was Chairman. He and his wife were also instrumental in establishing a pupil exchange link with the Gymnasium Ludovita Stura in Trencin, Slovakia. Upon his retirement Kerrigan Redman maintained his interest in education by training and acting as an OFSTED inspector. He remained in Lyme Regis for three years before moving back to Bridlington for family reasons.

Dr R P Steward, BA (Hons) MA, PhD - 2003 to date

Richard Steward took over as Principal in September 2003. He is married and at the time of joining the school his young son was just about to enter primary education. His interests outside of school include cycling and, as a talented saxophonist, he plays regularly in local jazz bands.

He studied for his degree at Westfield College, London University where he gained a 2:1 in English and Latin. An MA and PhD followed at Queen Mary College, London University and he studied for his PGCE in English and Drama at St Luke's College in Exeter.

Head with members of the School Council (photo by Brian Neesam)

Dr Steward began his teaching career at Symondsbury College and then Beaminster School before moving to the Cotswold School in Gloucestershire. In 1991 he joined Cheltenham Bournside School and Sixth Form Centre firstly as an English Teacher, then Head of English and finally as Deputy Head. Bournside is an Arts College and Dr Steward was instrumental in helping the school to achieve this status. Although he didn't take up his post at Woodroffe until September 2003, he was appointed in February and his input, together with the efforts of Kerrigan Redman, helped the school to be successful in its own bid for Arts College status.

The School on the Hill

Upon his arrival Dr Steward made arrangements to spend an hour with every member of staff, both teaching and support, in an effort to get to know everyone personally and this gesture was greatly appreciated by all concerned. He has since adopted an "open door" policy making himself freely available for staff, pupils, parents and governors. He set about getting to know the local community by forging links with the schools feeder primary schools, regularly meeting with fellow Heads in Dorset and colleagues at County Hall and becoming a trustee of the Town Mill.

One of the Dr Steward's first tasks was to put together a new prospectus and he was instrumental in setting up a new website for the school. Later on he developed a new uniform for Sixth Forms pupils. His energy and enthusiasm was infectious and he inspired everyone, both staff and pupils, to aim higher and to achieve more. As a Head he leads by example and his hands-on attitude has helped to break down the barriers which sometimes exist between Heads and their staff. At Dr Steward's request, after his first year, his job title was changed from "Principal" to the more familiar "Headteacher".

Dr Steward firmly believes that everything should be child-centred and to this end he set about introducing a new format for speech days. Speeches themselves were dropped and instead parents had the opportunity to hear pupils speaking about themselves before they stepped up to receive their awards. Musical interludes were provided by the school orchestra, jazz band and various soloists and a series of photographs of school activities were projected onto a giant screen. As part of the new approach to Speech Day the School Song, which had been sung on this occasion since 1947, was dropped which caused huge controversy in the local press, particularly amongst ex-pupils. However, Dr Steward was vindicated as by dropping the formality a much more relaxed and enjoyable occasion was created for both pupils and their parents.

As part of his pupil-centred philosophy Dr Steward set up the School Council which now meets with him regularly. This group comprises a girl and a boy from each year group, and provides pupils with a voice in terms of school, national and even international issues. The group set about re-writing the classroom code of practice from a pupils' point of view. It worked very hard to encourage and promote re-cycling and one of its biggest projects was working with the Foods Standards Agency to provide it with input on healthy eating in schools. It also set about forging links with a school in South Africa, with the aim of raising funds for those less fortunate than themselves. The School Council now plays a valuable part in the life of the school and is greatly respected for the work it carries out.

Dr Steward also arranged for focus groups whereby parents are invited to meet with governors to look at particular topics, such as the transition from primary to secondary education, option choices, sixth form courses, etc. This enables parents to have input into the running of the school and provides governors with valuable information on which to base their decision-making.

In October 2004 the school was awarded the Artsmark Gold Award. This is a national award organised by the Arts Council which is available at three levels – Artsmark, Silver and Gold. To be awarded the Gold Standard so soon after becoming an Arts College was a tremendous achievement and the assessor who visited the school was very complimentary about both the quality of the school's arts provision and the range of activities available to pupils. Dr Steward was particularly pleased that in addition to recognising the work of the Art Department the award also valued the work carried out in Drama, Music and Dance.

The Specialist Schools Trust, which oversees the Specialist Schools movement on behalf of the Government, were so impressed with the school's achievements in respect of the arts, not only for its pupils but for the wider community, that they invited Dr Steward to speak at their National Community Conference in Birmingham in July 2005.

As part of his desire to get everyone involved in building the success of the school Dr Steward has ensured that all members of staff, whether teaching or support, share ownership of the School Development Plan which clearly sets out how the school will move forward. In 2005 the school achieved Investors in People status, which is a clear indication that staff at all levels are valued and supported for the work that they do.

Staff worked hard to prepare the school for its next inspection, which was imminent, and which would follow a new more streamlined format. Schools are now required to carry out their own Self Evaluation and inspectors assess a school's performance against this. With just two days notice beforehand OFSTED inspectors advised that they would visit the school on 24th and 25th November 2005. In their report which followed shortly afterwards they declared that the school provided a good education for its pupils and had some outstanding features. The inspectors agreed with the school's view that it was moving from good to outstanding and they noted that leadership and management were good overall with Dr Steward providing excellent leadership.

In 2006 a new literacy-based curriculum for Year 7 was introduced on the basis that all pupils need to fully develop their literacy skills as they begin their secondary education to enable them to achieve more in their studies across all subject areas. This radical new approach to learning is proving to be a great success and should contribute greatly to the school's aim to ensure that every child reaches its full potential.

In recent years exam results have improved steadily year on year and more use is now made of data analysis to monitor the progress of pupils and to identify those that need extra support and encouragement.

Constant changes have always been a feature of education over the years but in recent time schools have had to cope with many more new initiatives all of which place a tremendous burden on Heads who have to implement them. However, Woodroffe is meeting these challenges and continues to be highly regarded. The school now has over one thousand pupils on roll and visitors continue to remark on what a happy, busy and vibrant place it is and they comment particularly on the excellent relationship between staff and pupils.

Times have changed since the school first started in 1923 but the ethos of the school has remained the same largely due to the excellent Heads it has attracted each of whom has brought something special to the school. Richard Steward is carrying on this tradition and in his safe hands the future of the school is assured.

CHAPTER 14 – GRANT MAINTAINED STATUS

Grant Maintained Status was an initiative introduced by the Conservative Government in 1990 that gave schools the freedom to "opt out" of the control of Local Education Authorities (LEAs). This meant that though subject to allocation of their principal funds from the LEA, the money itself came direct from the Department for Education. Some additional funds were provided to "buy-in" whatever services were needed to run the school. Governing Bodies who voted to opt out took over the financial management of their school, they became its admissions authority, they assumed ownership of all assets including buildings and contents and they also became the employer of all staff.

At Junior Speech Day towards the end of the Summer Term 1990 the Head at that time, Paul Vittle, announced that the Governing Body was considering the possibility of Woodroffe opting out. It was ironic that that particular speech day came at the end of a year when the school had been celebrating twenty five years as a comprehensive school and the guest speaker and presenter of prizes on that occasion was Thornton Pearn, a much respected former Head who had steered the school through the difficult transition from Grammar School to Comprehensive School.

One of the principal reasons behind the proposal to consider opting out was mounting concern over the LEA's prolonged negative attitude to boarding at the school and the lack of information and action from the authority over plans to rationalise the three boarding houses at the school. The Chairman of Governors, Mrs Eddie Woodbridge, explained to parents that the ability to offer boarding places played a significant role in ensuring the continuing success of the school, particularly its Sixth Form. With pupil rolls falling nationally she felt it was important to do everything to ensure that new pupils were attracted, particularly those wishing to continue their education up to the age of eighteen. There was also concern over a recent LEA announcement that there would be no building at the school for at least the next four years, even though the existing buildings were extremely over-crowded.

Dorset LEA was reported to be furious at plans by any of the schools under its care to opt out. They were concerned that it would create a two-tier education system, with grant maintained schools better funded and those still under LEA control becoming "dumps" for unwanted pupils; grant maintained schools would become their own admissions authority and could therefore exclude pupils they did not want. The LEA view was that extra funding that would be passed directly to grant maintained schools would mean drastic cuts in the funds available for schools remaining under the care of the authority.

In order to opt out a ballot of parents had to be carried out to ascertain their views. This ballot was initiated by resolutions made at two governors meetings held on 16th July 1990 and 24th August 1990. However, the governors needed to fully consult with parents and staff before the parents made the final decision in the postal ballot.

To this end meetings took place to ensure that parents were fully informed of the benefits, or otherwise, of Grant Maintained Status. At one public meeting, held in a packed school hall, speakers were available to put the case both for and against the proposal, including

Andrew Turner from the advisory body of the Grant Maintained Trust and Martin Rogers from the local government body, Local Schools Information.

Throughout the consultation period Paul Vittle continually emphasized the importance of parents being fully informed before they made the final decision via the parents' ballot. Local MP, Sir James Spicer, pledged his support for the proposal, as did the Chairman of Woodroffe Community Association, Dennis Applebee, and the Chairman of the PTA, Ken Whetlor. The matter was fully debated in the local paper which included letters from parents and members of the community reflecting both sides of the argument.

One parent pointed out that *there was no time limit for opting out and that perhaps then was not the right time.* He explained that the Governing Body and the Head would become wholly responsible for the administration and the finances of the school, a major undertaking, not to be taken lightly. He also questioned whether the necessary commercial expertise and business acumen was available at the school to handle these important areas of responsibility.

Eddie Woodbridge explained that the level of expertise of the Governing Body was more than adequate, since it included an architect, an accountant, a public relations expert, an estate agent, a primary school teacher, a deacon, a police sergeant, successful business people, a retired bursar and people with many other skills.

Another parent, who supported the proposal to change the status of the school, suggested that by opting out the school would give the local community the ability to manage more of its own affairs, enabling the town to hang on to a vital community asset.

However, it was reported that a ballot of teachers had resulted in thirty five voting against the proposal to opt out and twenty five voting for it. Mr Alex Middlemass, county secretary of the NASUWT teaching union, advised that the majority of teachers clearly did not support what he referred to as the "GMS gamble". He felt that a longer period of time was needed to consider all aspects before a final decision was made.

Eventually arrangements were made for the ballot to take place. This was carried out on behalf of the school by the Electoral Reform (Ballot Services) Limited based in London. All parents/guardians were eligible to vote and given the number of divorced parents, some of whom had remarried, it was a major task for the school to establish exactly who should receive a ballot paper. Legally some children had four parents/step parents and each one was eligible to vote. The ballot closed on 16th October 1990.

Notification of the result of the ballot, dated 17th October 1990, was sent to the Chairman of Governors by the Ballot Adviser who advised that of the 1,260 parents eligible to vote 782 had returned a ballot paper which represented a participation rate of 62%. The question put was "Do you wish the Governing Body of your child's school to apply to the Secretary of State for Education and Science for Grant Maintained status in accordance with Chapter IV of the Education Reform Act 1988?"

527 of those that voted (67%) were in favour and 255 (33%) were against. There was a suggestion in the local press that the voting process had been flawed but (although there

The School on the Hill

were one or two minor slip-ups in the mailing system) the ballot, which was administered by the Electoral Reform Society, was pronounced valid.

And so the Governing Body had the go ahead to submit a proposal to the Secretary of State for the acquisition of Grant Maintained Status. The result was announced in the press by the following statement:

"The Head and the governors of the Woodroffe School are, naturally, very pleased that 67% of parents voted in favour of opting out. Having informed the appropriate authorities, we now have to wait for the Secretary of State for Education to make his final decision. If he approves, the proposed date for the implementation of Grant Maintained status is 1st September 1991….. We now have a great deal of work to do in order to submit a detailed statement of our intentions and a bid for capital expenditure"

The proposal to the Secretary of State for Education was published by the Governing Body on 15th November 1990 and confirmed the suggested date for implementation as 1st September 1991.

Early in 1991 the governors received the news that they had been waiting for, that the school had successfully achieved Grant Maintained status. The Secretary of State for Education had given his approval which meant that from 1st September 1991 the school would no longer come under LEA control. It would also receive a capital grant of £180,000 and a transitional grant of £65,000.

Paul Vittle re-iterated his belief that grant maintained status was in the best interests of the school. Preparation for implementation included the appointment of a Bursar and a consultatnt architect to assist with the submission of a capital expenditure bid to be submitted to the DfES. However, just as important was the on-going process of demonstrating to parents, staff, and the community that Woodroffe would benefit and develop as a result of its new status, and would not change its nature as a comprehensive school.

The school then began preparations for September and it was announced that with effect from April 1991, Peter Rickard would be taking over as Bursar. Mr Rickard had a distinguished naval career having commanded the Leander class frigate "HMS Penelope" during the 1982 Falklands campaign. Upon leaving the Navy in 1988 he became Senior Assistant Bursar at Bristol University. It was explained that the post of Bursar would involve close links with the Woodroffe's senior management team and the board of governors.

It was also announced that the school had appointed The Jonathon Ball Partnership of Bude, as its consultant architect. Described as a well-known company that had worked with schools in Cornwall, the partnership would help the governors to submit a capital expenditure bid to the DfES.

During the preparation period for opting out there was a lot of speculation about what the future would hold for the school when it assumed its new status and there were rumours that it might change back to being a Grammar School. However, Eddie Woodbridge firmly ruled out this idea, stating in the local press that Woodroffe would not seek to reintroduce selection and that the Governing Body did not wish to alter the nature of school. She stressed Woodroffe was a comprehensive school where admission for both day and boarding pupils was not linked to ability and it would continue to cater for pupils of all abilities.

Eddie Woodbridge advised that she had recently attended the London Conference at which the Secretary of State for Education, Kenneth Clarke, had revealed that schools which had opted out did not have to wait five years to apply to change their status. However, having just celebrated twenty five years of comprehensive education, the Governing Body, under grant maintained status, intended to build on the success of the past and provide even greater opportunities for all children in the area.

In June 1991 the school ran a successful one day conference at Rhode Hill entitled "Options for Change" which was set up to give guidance to other schools considering applying for Grant Maintained Status. Seventy two delegates attended, representing thirty six schools from the south and south west. Speakers included Adrian Pritchard (National Director of the Grant Maintained Centre), Andrew Turner (Director of Choice in Education), Pam Bailey and Stephen Hillier (Department of Education and Science) and Roy Ludlow (Head of Beechen Cliff School, Bath).

At Senior Speech Day in July 1991 Paul Vittle advised parents and guests that grant maintained status meant that the school was at an important cross-roads in its development with many big decisions to be taken if it was to capitalise on the opportunities now available to it.

On the same occasion the future of the school over the next five to six years, as she saw it, was sketched out by the Chairman of Governors. The expectation was that there would be an appreciable improvement in conditions for pupils and staff with over-crowding significantly reduced, more books, smaller classes and hopefully own school transport. To achieve these aims the school would have to submit bids to the DfES for funding.

And so on 1st September 1991 Woodroffe assumed the mantle of a grant maintained school and there is no doubt whatsoever that this was a pivotal moment in the history of the school. The brave decision to opt out gave the school the flexibility it so badly needed to develop into the forward thinking and progressive school it is today but unfortunately the transition period was not without difficulties and these soon began to emerge.

Due to a decline in the demand for boarding places, in October 1991 the governors decided to close the boarding facility at Harcombe House, which had been established in 1952. Junior boy boarders were moved to their own wing at Rhode Hill, where girl boarders of all ages were housed. Senior boys remained at their boarding house at St Andrews.

Also building work at the school, designed to create additional offices for administrative purposes, proved to be extremely contentious. The new offices were sited in the former school hall where a mezzanine floor was installed to make the best use of the space available. Many of the original features were retained including the oak beams and the mullioned windows but unfortunately the wood panelling was painted a rather unfortunate shade of pink to match the pink and green colour scheme chosen by the architects and this caused much consternation within the school community. It was at this point, during the renovation work, that the school Honours Boards were removed, never to be seen again, an oversight bitterly regretted to this day by many an ex-pupil. The facility did however, provide a good use of the space and brought the Head's offices and Reception together at the front of the school.

View from the top of the stairs

Stairs leading up to the mezzanine floor

Reception desk & door to the Terrace

During the Summer Term it began to emerge that for a variety of reasons the school needed to make savings and therefore faced possible redundancies. Mr Vittle pointed out that many Heads, not only in Dorset, but nationwide, were having to face up to the fact that educational institutions were no longer protected or immune from the harsh realities facing the business world. He felt that at Woodroffe it would be possible to overcome these difficulties, due to the fact that all the staff remained hard working, committed and, above all, enthusiastic about the school.

As the first academic year as a grant maintained school drew to a close it was announced that the governors were now looking at ways of reducing spending by £100,000, which was equivalent to 5% of the school's overall budget. With staffing costs representing the largest proportion of the school budget, it became obvious that this was the area where cuts would need to be made and the possibility of voluntary redundancies was explored. Paul Vittle pointed out that when the school achieved grant maintained status it had made a conscious effort to sustain a high level of staffing and there was no doubt that if it had remained under LEA control, up to four members of staff might by then have been made redundant.

Having increased staffing levels the governors now realised that at 95%, the percentage of the school budget required to meet staffing costs was too high, leaving insufficient monies available to administer and service the school. They therefore had to implement cuts, hopefully with minimum damage to the curriculum, in the sure knowledge that the following year the budget would increase due to the growing number of pupils returning to the Sixth Form and starting in Year 7.

Unfortunately the need to cut staffing costs coincided with the attendance of Paul Vittle at a prestigious international management course in the USA, partly funded by the school. He was aware of the unease among the staff regarding his attendance on this course and discussed the matter with the Chairman of Governors. She consulted with fellow governors who generally felt that he should attend this course as the school would benefit from what he learned. However, despite the support of the Chairman and the Governing Body, when Mr Vittle attended the course he was subsequently condemned by the Dorset Branch of the National Union of Teachers for not being at the helm when his school was "foundering on the rocks".

The situation escalated even further when the local press announced that the school was facing a deficit of approximately £120,000 although this was refuted. The Bursar pointed out that the accounts to be published in August would show a much lower figure and he explained that the deficit had been incurred as a result of the carry forward from before September 1992, when the school was administered by the LEA.

The budget situation and the threat of redundancies led to a vote of no confidence in the Head and the Chairman of Governors at the end of the Summer Term, a thoroughly unpleasant and painful experience for everyone involved, no matter what their views. However it was announced that the school would be re-opening as normal after the summer holidays and efforts continued to be made to find a way forward. It is believed that originally the vote of no confidence had been in respect of the Head and *all* the governors but it was amended to the Head and Chairman of Governors before a vote was taken, possibly to prevent the imposition of a board of governors from outside the school.

The start of the Autumn Term proved to be extremely difficult with many hours spent trying to resolve the problems that faced the school and the breakdown in relationships which had occurred between staff, the governors and the Head. However, no compromise could be found and after a very difficult period for all concerned, Mr Vittle was suspended from his post at the end of September and the Chairman of Governors resigned from the Board of Governors.

The community was greatly shocked and understanding of what had transpired was greatly hampered by the fact that very little information was available as the matter subsequently went to court. Within the local area there was a lot of support for Paul Vittle who during his time at the school had worked hard to unite the school and the community. Also, under his leadership, the school had prospered with the numbers on roll steadily increasing and excellent examination results achieved.

Despite everyone's best efforts, the difficulties between the Head and the Governing Body could not be overcome, and in December it was announced that by mutual agreement Paul Vittle would not be returning to the school. The whole sorry saga placed a tremendous strain on both Paul Vittle and his family, who had supported him throughout, and he subsequently suffered a period of ill health, an outcome no-one would have wished for.

Upon the departure of Paul Vittle, Ian Cook, Deputy Head, stood in as Acting Head for the academic year 1992/1993 and the Vice Chairman of Governors, Tony Terrett, took over leadership of the Governing Body. Eventually stability at the school was restored and the school, greatly chastened by the experience, entered a new phase in its development upon the appointment of new Head, Mr Kerrigan Redman, who joined the school in 1993. One of the first priorities of his Headship was to consider the future of boarding, as the second boarding house at St Andrews had closed in July immediately prior to his appointment.

Eddie Woodbridge, who was a governor from 1987 until 1992 and was Chairman of Governors from 1989, recalls her time on the Governing Body as follows: *"Wanting to give something back to the school that had contributed so much to our five children's progression on to higher education, in July 1987 I became an LEA governor.*

Two factors always thwarted the implementation of any major progress being made by the governors – lack of money and lack of vision by various officials in the Education Department at County Hall. However, thanks to the vision and energy of the Head the children benefited from improvements that cost time rather than money. They thrived and grew as individuals, gained a sense of self-worth, took pride in their achievements and gained the confidence to seek further challenges, of which some, like 'Beating Concorde' encouraged team-work between staff and pupils. As a former Outward Bound Instructor I was very aware of the importance of these wider aspects of education. Academic standards remained high, but school was no longer seen as 'just an exam factory.'

By 1989 four sub-committees had evolved, covering finance, curriculum, boarding and PR. These committees met on a regular monthly basis, and made recommendations to the full board at its half-termly meetings. My work as a Counsellor for the National Association for Gifted Children led to discussions with the Head to see if facilities could be created for children with a high IQ – after all, we were a comprehensive school with a brief to meet the needs of all children. There was insufficient money to do anything then, but note was made to look at the situation again in the future.

I was Chairman when the school entered Local Management of Schools and somewhat cynically wondered if the whole scheme had been dreamt up because County Hall couldn't make the meagre resources stretch to meet costs, so the impossible task was being given to the governors to deal with instead. Similarly, due to a lack of positive marketing by County Hall, we were concerned by the decline in the number of new boarders; and there was also a worrying drop in the number of pupils staying on into the Sixth Form - both factors were important to the long-term success of Woodroffe. Several years earlier the LEA had recommended that the three secondary schools in West Dorset should become schools for eleven to sixteen year olds, and a Sixth Form college built to cater for the needs of older pupils, but this was strongly resisted at the time, and the idea dropped. But there was always the feeling that it could and would be resurrected at a later date.

As early as 1987 one governor was asking if Woodroffe would be 'opting out', but the rest of the Board felt that the Grant Maintained concept was very experimental, and we should wait and see how things developed in the schools which had already opted out. With the introduction of LMS we had to balance a budget which was not adequate to cover the staff costs, so had to accept a 3% overspend due largely to meeting curriculum needs. It was against this background that the decision to consider the implications of going Grant Maintained was finally made.

Several governors, the Head and I included, were dubious, but we sent for all available literature both for and against opting out. The Head and I made a fact-finding visit to an already existing GM boarding school, Old Swinford Hospital, in Stourbridge, and further long discussions took place at governors meetings, before the first vote to decide whether or not to put the idea of pursuing GM status to the parents. Up until the time of the first vote, all deliberations had to be absolutely confidential as there was a definite possibility that the LEA, which was strongly opposed to opting out, would take over some, if not all of the boarding houses. Once that first vote was taken however, all assets were frozen. This very necessary secrecy caused a degree of ill-will among the staff, the PTA and the Heads of the feeder schools, but following explanations most of them understood and totally accepted the predicament with which we had been faced.

In an attempt to improve communication within the school the Head had introduced Wednesday Notes, a weekly staff bulletin, and realising the importance of good communication, I asked for copies of the notes too, and also re-introduced the custom once carried out by a former Chairman of Governors, to be available to staff after school on Thursday afternoons. At the same time I agreed with the three Deputies that if ever they felt the need to discuss anything with me, this could be arranged on an ad hoc basis.

We held a public meeting with speakers from the DES, LEA and the Unions, followed by a detailed question and answer session on the pros and cons of opting out. Other meetings were organised between staff of already existing GM schools, the Woodroffe staff, and members of the various teaching unions. When the parental ballot eventually took place, 67% approved of GM status, and in February 1991 we heard that we had gained DES approval to become Grant Maintained as from September of that year.

An even busier time followed while we carried out all the necessary preparations required for going GM; the appointment of grounds maintenance personnel, architects to provide a feasible long-term building programme, a bursar, auditors, caterers and insurance and banking facilities. One governor who was a professional accountant was given responsibility to over-see the work of the Bursar.

The day of incorporation, 1st September 1991, was a Sunday; term hadn't started, and everything was peaceful and quiet. The following morning, the editor of one of the local papers rang to ask 'What was I going to do about the radon problem now that Woodroffe had become GM?' It transpired that a parliamentary candidate whose party was opposed to GM was trying to make political mileage about the unexpectedly high readings just received back from the measurements on sensors that had been placed in and around the school a few weeks earlier. We suspected there had been a mix-up in the labelling of the sensors, and arranged for further readings to be taken, where our suspicions were proved correct. But it was interesting to note the level of political feeling against GM status in Dorset, and the amount of confusion and public interest a newspaper could stir up among its readers.

We were fortunate to have a varied group of individuals serving as governors. We had a good mix of people who fell into the categories of original thinkers, resource investigators, shapers, monitor evaluators, organisers, team workers and completer-finishers so necessary for a balanced committee A vast amount of issues was dealt with:- capital bids to improve the library and the science and technology facilities were submitted; the Educational Assets Board was repeatedly contacted with regard to boarding issues; the restructuring of the SEN department was set into motion; and a bid made to the Foundation for Sport and Arts made for the provision of a dual-use Sports Hall, as well as the usual run-of-the-mill activities

Balancing the various aspects of governors' responsibilities continued – with many meetings both in and out of school. My deteriorating sight problems affecting night vision meant that I could no longer drive at night, but most meetings were in the daytime, and I could always manage to get a lift if they weren't. Financial problems still persisted, and among other things was the possibility that we would have to make two or three members of staff redundant. The Bursar and I visited the DES in London, where we explained financial difficulties in great detail, and we left feeling that we really were making progress at last.

However, there was still a degree of unrest among some of the staff who felt that for political reasons Woodroffe should not have become Grant Maintained, and originally a vote of no confidence in the Head or the governors was taken; this was later amended to Head and Chairman of Governors. Along with many others, I feel that over the ensuing weeks things were not dealt with in a professional or correct manner, and on 21st September I resigned in protest, but here is not the place to elaborate or dwell on these deficiencies.

With hindsight I find it ironic that the political party that was so opposed to the whole GM philosophy when it was in opposition embraced it with open arms once it got into power (albeit changing the name to 'Foundation') and the leader of that party ensured that his own children attended one such school.

It was an exceptionally busy five years, but I am convinced that the parents' decision to become Grant Maintained was the right one; it set Woodroffe on the path that allows it to continue to thrive and succeed today."

CHAPTER 15 - LYME REGIS GRAMMAR SCHOOL WAR MEMORIAL

BILL ASHMORE

DAVID WATTON

ERIC BRITTON

ROY STAPLEFORTH

CYRIL CADDY

KEN BLACKMORE

JOHN HUSSEY

'JERRY' SEARLE

BRYAN TEAGUE

JOHN SMALL

JOHN GOODFELLOW

KEN HALLIDAY

SYDNEY HENDERSON

FRANK MOORE

HORACE HOLMAN

JIM VAN ALLEN

The memorial plaque was originally sited in the old school hall and remained there when the space was eventually put to use as a library and then as a drama studio. In 1992 this area was converted into offices for administrative staff and a mezzanine floor was installed to provide additional office space. At this time the memorial plaque was removed and re-sited along the top corridor of the old school.

The school magazine of July 1946 included a photograph of the memorial. Mr Thomas pointed out that the beauty of the tablet lay in the simplicity of its design. He advised that the response of everyone to the memorial fund had been more than generous and he remarked upon *"the nobility of sentiment"* expressed by donors which he felt represented *"a beautiful tribute to our comrades"*. The prayer read by the Rev Carew Cox when the memorial was unveiled was as follows: *"O Thou Who art heroic love, keep alive in our hearts that adventurous spirit which makes men scorn the way of safety, so that Thy will be done; and make us, O Lord, by Thy Grace, to be worthy of those courageous souls who in every age have ventured all in obedience to Thy Will, and for whom the trumpets have sounded on the other side: through Jesus Christ our Lord"*[1].

Subscriptions for the memorial amounted to £71 and the cost of the stone was estimated to be £50. The surplus was used to buy a suitably engraved lectern and a large, leather-bound bible for the school. These items were dedicated by the Vicar, the Rev C Carew-Cox, at a special service held in the School Hall on 28th June 1949. In asking the former Head, Mr Watton, to unveil them Mr Thomas said *"In a very special way the Old Boys of the school who are in our thoughts at this moment were Mr Watton's boys"*.[2] Major Pearn read the 23rd Psalm, Pamela Taylor, Head Girl, recited Lawrence Bunyan's well known lines *"They shall grow not old…."* and the Old Boys' President, Mr Hodges, read a passage from the Book of Wisdom.

Background Information on ex-pupils who died in the service of their country, whose names are carved on the school memorial plaque.

William Frederick Caldwell Ashmore was born on 21st March 1920 in Gorakhpur, United Provinces of India. William lived in Chideock and was the son of Major E J C Ashmore, DSO, MC, 10th Gurka Rifles. He enlisted in the Royal Sussex Regiment as a regular solider on 26th September 1938 serving with them in Chichester and with 2nd Battalion Royal Sussex Regiment in Devonport and Belfast. He completed Officer Cadet Training in February 1940 when he was commissioned into the Kings Own Yorkshire Light Infantry (KOYLI). He joined 1st Battalion KOYLI on 2nd March 1940 at Galashiels and remained with them until 21st March 1941, when he embarked at Liverpool for transit to India and an attachment to the Indian Army. On arrival in India William was posted to 1st Battalion 10th Ghurkha Rifles at Razmak on the North West Frontier. He was a Company Commander with them until 15th January 1943 (he was wounded in Wariristan on 6th July 1941). William was then transferred to the 1st Battalion 8th Ghurkha Rifles with

---

[1] Extract from the School Magazine dated July 1946
[2] Extract from the School Magazine dated July 1949

whom he continued to serve in Burma until he was killed in action on 20th February 1944 aged twenty three.[3]

William wrote to the school on one occasion *"… I am allowed to say that I am a proud member of HM's 14th Army and that Lord Louis is our Army Commander …. I now speak a pretty fluent line in Gurkhali, Urdu to quite an extent as well, and have picked up a smattering of Assami – quite a linguist in fact!*

We are not so cut off from things that we don't get the odd copy of "Illustrated London News". Grand work by John and a consolation for him. Heaven preserve me from being a POW….. I'm sure David was an excellent paratrooper, and I don't need to be told that he went out like the gallant fellow he was. One day, DV, I shall come back to Dorset, and I'll climb Golden Cap once again, and Golden Cap to me will be his memorial.

This is my sixth year of soldiering and yet the LRGS days are extremely vivid. As a pupil (forgive the term!) I must have been some problems – I find the Gurkha and myself are temperamentally suited. I like and admire the little men enormously and am very happy indeed amongst them. They are the finest poachers on earth. God help Farmer Marsh if I were to bring my Company to Seatown. There would be no sign of fur or feather in a week!"[4]

Sadly William did not make it home to climb Golden Cap as a memorial to his school friend, David Watton, as he must have been killed shortly after writing this letter.

Kenneth Blackmore - In 1942 it was reported that Kenneth, who was a Sergeant in the Royal Army Ordnance Corps, had died in the service of the nation. Ken was a local man and he had two brothers, Frank and Maurice Blackmore. He was married but he had no children.

Eric Britton was a Pilot and served as a Flight Lieutenant in the RAF. He lived at the Cobb, Lyme Regis and his father, Fred, was a local postman. Eric lost his life over Germany in 1944. After the war his mother donated a school prize in his memory. It is believed that his family moved away from Lyme Regis many years ago.

Cyril Caddy was the son of Mr and Mrs Caddy who were builders in pre-war Lyme Regis. His father, Burt, had a brother who was a plumber. The family was not related to other families in Lyme Regis who bear the same surname. Cyril is remembered as a keen sportsman. He was married to Betty (Madge) who was also a former pupil of the school. Cyril was in the Royal Army Ordnance Corps and served in France and the Belgium Campaign. He lost his life in the evacuation after the fall of France on the SS Lancastria and died on 17th June 1940, aged twenty six. In the school magazine of 1941 it was

---

[3] Information provided by Lt Col C N. Fraser 2 GR, Liaison Officer Brigade of Ghurkhas, Ministry of Defence (Army), on 4th March 1991 in response to a request by Mr Ronald Baker.

[4] Extract from the School Magazine dated July 1944

noted that Cyril had been one of the first to respond to the nation's call. Cyril is remembered with honour on the Dunkirk Memorial.

John Goodfellow was the son of John and Ada Goodfellow of Charmouth. He was twenty five years old when he died on 12th June 1941. Prior to the war he had qualified as a teacher of music at the Royal School of Music and was the organist at Charmouth Parish Church. John was a member of the Royal Marine Band attached to HMS Ajax. He is buried at the Khayat Beach War Cemetery.

In a school magazine it was stated that *"John saw a great deal of action in the Mediterranean, including the Battle of Matapan and the Greece evacuation. After recovering from wounds received in one engagement he had an attack of appendicitis from which he died. In a letter to his parents, his comrades spoke very highly of his courage, cheerfulness and devotion to duty."*[5]

Ken Halliday was the only son of Mr and Mrs G Halliday of the old Cloverdale Garage. He was born in Lyme Regis and served in the RAF as trainee Air Crew. Ken lost his life in a flying accident on 11th May 1945 at Colehill and is buried in Lyme Regis Cemetery. He had been home on leave less than a fortnight before his death. Hundreds of people attended the funeral of this popular young man. Pulman's Weekly News dated 22nd May 1945 carried an article entitled "Lyme Regis Mourning – Death of a Young Airman" as follows:

"Rarely has there been such a striking demonstration of sorrow in Lyme Regis as that at the funeral on Wednesday of Aircraftsman Kenneth William Halliday, RAF, only son of Mr and Mrs George Halliday, Cloverdale Garage, Charmouth Road and only grandson of the Mayor and Mayoress (Alderman and Mrs W J Emmett). Aged twenty he had been serving in the RAF for about eighteen months and lost his life in a flying accident, two 'planes colliding. Deceased was being trained in flying. "He was making excellent progress" writes his Commanding Officer "and we looked forward to seeing him develop into a fully qualified Service pilot".

After leaving Lyme Regis Grammar School, he worked in his father's business. He was a member of Lyme Regis Flight of the ATC and also a member of the ARP. He was a keen sportsman and at Association football showed promise of making a first-class goalkeeper. He was very popular. The funeral took place at the Cemetery where the large attendance was representative of all phases of life in the town. The Rev W H Cook (curate) officiated and members of the RAF acted as a bearer party."[6]

Thanks to Mrs Carol Robson, niece of Ken, who kindly provided press cuttings and information about her late Uncle.

Sidney Henderson lived in Uplyme and is remembered as a keen sportsman and a "bright lad". It is believed that his father was a local postman. Sidney joined the RAF straight from school. He lost his life at Middle Wallop due to a hit and run traffic accident on 19th March 1941 which was believed to involve a military vehicle. At the time of his

---

[5] Extract from School Magazine dated July 1941
[6] Extract by kind permission of Pulman's Weekly News

death he was a Corporal. The school magazine of 1941 recorded that *"his death means the cutting short of a most promising career."*

Horace Holman was the son of Charles and Lucy Holman and he lived in Uplyme off Tappers Knapp. His father was a gardener at the big house close by. The family was not related to the local Holman family. Horace was a Pilot Officer (Navigator - Bomber Command) RAF. Horace lost his life over Hamburg on 28th July 1943, aged twenty one. He is buried in Hamburg Cemetery.

John Hussey – not much is known about John although in the Commonwealth War Graves archive there is a reference to a John Fitzroy Hussey who was a Leading Aircraftsman in the RAF Volunteer Reserve. It states that he was killed on 4th September 1942 at the age of twenty nine. Also that he was married and that his parents lived in Yeovil. It has been impossible to ascertain if this was the John Hussey who was a pupil at LRGS but a reference in the school magazine of July 1943 states that John had the sad misfortune to be killed in an air-raid.

Frederick Marsh – Frederick is another ex-pupil on the memorial plaque who has been difficult to trace. However, local resident Peter Loveridge has advised that Frederick was in fact known as Peter and his parents were Mr and Mrs James who used to run an electrical shop at the top of Hill Road. Frederick was the son of Mrs James from her first marriage. It is believed that he served in the RAF and died during an air raid.

Frank Moore was the son of James Crispin Moore and Elizabeth Sandoe Moore who lived in Church Street in Lyme Regis. The family originally came from Cornwall. Frank's father was the Chief Coastguard in Lyme Regis for many years. Upon leaving school Frank worked in a bank before joining the RAF (Marine Section). For a while he served with the Air Sea Rescue Unit at Lyme Regis before he was posted overseas. He was captured when Singapore fell to the Japanese and spent time in a prisoner of war camp. Frank made three attempts to escape and it is believed that punishment for this led to his death. Consequently, he was always listed as missing presumed dead rather than killed in action.

Frank married a colleague in the bank and had one son, Peter. He had two brothers, Philip Moore, a Cobb resident for many years, and Henry (Jim) Moore who was Clerk to the Governors at LRGS from 1928 to 1935.

Information on Frank, and his photograph, has been kindly provided by his niece, Mrs Mary Delves née Moore, daughter of Jim, who attended LRGS with her elder sister, Sybil, and her younger brother, David.

Tom Reakes - it was recorded in the Governors' Minutes of December 1945 that *"LAC Tom Reakes was listed as missing, believed drowned, in an attempt to save the life of a fellow airman"*. In the school magazine of July 1946 Mr Thomas also reported on the death of Tom, a former Shaftesbury House Captain, stating that he *"had lost his life in attempting the rescue of two of his brother airmen"*. Mr Thomas went on to add that *"I have seen letters from his CO in which he expressed a very high opinion of Tom, who, he wrote, was very popular with his colleagues"*.

The School on the Hill

Tom wrote to the school from India as follows: *"I am still fit and well out here in this "gem" of the East: at least, some people call it a gem. Since arriving I've had some leave at Darjeeling. It was really grand and almost like returning to "Blighty" for a few days. It was very cold and we had to take blankets in addition to our greatcoats when we went to a cinema show. Some contrast – the present temperature is over the hundred degree mark. Working dress is as follows – shoes, socks, shorts and bush hat. .The other day I found, in an old "Illustrated London News" some of John Watton's sketches. I've been looking for some for ages: they're grand."*[7]

A letter from Tom was also received from South East Asia - *"Out here it seems almost unbelievable that the war in Europe is at last over. I only wish that I could be with you in "Blighty" to celebrate the event……We shall be having our own celebrations, of course, but it's not the same as being with your own folk. Our official celebration day is at the end of the week…..I'm very much looking forward to an Old Pupils' Reunion when we all get back – I even think we'll have to get some cricket and football matches arranged – it would be good to be walking out to the wicket again with Wilf Potter…."*[8]

Unfortunately Tom did not live to see the reunion he was so looking forward to attending. After the war his mother continued the practice established by her son from the time he left school to the time of his death, to present an annual prize for Special Improvement at Speech Day in his memory.

Ex-pupil, **Graham Brown** remembers *"I was a friend of Tom Reakes and knew him well even before we were at the Grammar School together. His home was in Rocombe and he attended Uplyme School before going to the Grammar School where he excelled at all sports. He worked for an electrical business in Lyme Regis for a few months until he joined the Royal Air Force. He served in the Far East doing radio work and I understand his death was due to a drowning accident and was at the very end of the war. He is buried in the Kranji War Cemetery in Singapore and his name is on the Uplyme War Memorial. When I did my National Service I spent eighteen months in the Far East and was able to visit his grave in Singapore in 1948."*[9]

Tom had been Head Boy from 1938 to 1939 and in his memory his parents, Mr and Mrs W F Reakes, donated a Challenge Cup for Cricket - School V Old Boys Association.

Henry Searle was the son of James and Minnie Searle and the husband of Phyllis Searle. He was a member of one of Lyme's oldest families. Henry served in the Royal Air Force Volunteer Reserve as a Warrant Officer and a Navigator. He lost his life in a flying accident on 27th January 1944 at the age of thirty five. The school magazine dated July 1944 states that *"'Gerry' Searle was killed while carrying out the perilous duties of air-crew instructor."*

John Small was the son of Charles and Elizabeth Small and was a Coder in the Royal Navy serving on HMS Neptune. In the school magazine of 1942 it was noted that John

---

[7] Extract from School Magazine dated July 1944
[8] Extract from School Magazine dated July 1945
[9] Information from correspondence between Graham Brown and author dated September 2006

The School on the Hill

was reported missing, believed killed. In actual fact he died on Friday, 19th December 1941 aged twenty six. John's name is on the Plymouth Naval Memorial which is situated centrally on The Hoe, looking directly towards Plymouth Sound. John left a widow, named Christine. She and another war widow at that time were described in the school magazine as *"bravely carrying on and presenting a cheerful front to the world. Their courage is an inspiration"*.

Roy Stapleforth was the eldest son of Mr and Mrs George Stapleforth of Uplyme. His father ran a garage at the top of Haye Lane and his uncle, Stan Stapleforth ran Station Garage next door. He served in the Royal Air Force Volunteer Reserve as a pilot and held the rank of Flying Officer. His role was in Coastal Command. Roy was the Skipper of a Catelena Flying Boat which was lost in the Mediterranean. He died on 18th August 1944 aged twenty three.

Bryan Teague was a Captain in the Royal Marines. He lived at Lyme Regis and later at Weymouth and was affectionately known as "Bonny". Bryan was the youngest son of Mr and Mrs V Teague. His father was the Bank Manager at Lloyds Bank in Lyme Regis. Bryan lost his life shortly after D Day, in June 1944. Mr Watton reported that he had *"met a glorious death in battle in Normandy"*. The same magazine included a message from Mr. Thomas as follows: *"I have persuaded Mr. Teague to allow me to insert the following extract from a letter received from Bryan's CO – '…. it may be some consolation to you to know that he suffered no pain – he was shot through the heart. As an officer I miss him I think more than any other casualty; he was proving such a good troop leader. As a messmate he is irreplaceable'."*[10]

Jim Van Allen was the son of Mr and Mrs Van Allen, Estate Agents in Broad Street, Lyme Regis. He was a Sergeant in the Royal Army Ordnance Corps. Jim lost his life at Matrak, North Africa on 29th June 1942. **Pat Lomax** née Wilkins is the niece of Jim Van Allen and she has kindly provided the following background information on Jim.

"Vandelow Henry James Allen (Jim) - He was born on 7th October 1916 at Hog's Hill in Beaminster. His parents moved to Lyme Regis in 1918/1919 – living at 34A Coombe Street. They moved to Pyne House, 10 Broad Street, in the mid 1920s. He had one sister, Marjorie (she later married Les Wilkins). Jim did not marry – he enlisted in 1939/1940 – at the age of twenty three. When Jim left school he joined his father Van H. Allen in his estate agency of that name, working from Pyne House. At the outbreak of war he enlisted in the RAOC – Bren Carriers, 5th Battalion, East Yorks Regiment, Service No 7623839. Jim was eventually posted to North Africa as part of the Middle East Forces. He was there from late 1940 until his death.

We still have many of the letters he sent from there – all telling of his longing to be home and of his thoughts of Lyme, the countryside and the sea. Jim was killed on 29th June 1942 during the battle for Mersa Matruh – the same day the Germans captured Mersa Matruh. At the time of his death he held the rank of Sergeant. My grandparents were notified that he was missing but had to suffer two years of waiting before receiving final confirmation of his death from the War Office in 1944. Jim is buried in the military cemetery at El Alamein."

---

[10] Extracts from School Magazine dated July 1944

David Watton was the second son of Mr Sidney L Watton, Headmaster of Lyme Regis Grammar School. He served in the Ist Battalion Parachute Regiment. David lost his life in the North Africa landing in November 1942. Mr Watton reported that *"David was one of the gallant band of parachutists who, fighting as infantry, did such fine work in Tunisia last winter. He fell in German territory somewhere between Beja and Mateur. I wish I could make so fine an end."*[11]

Michael Gearing - Michael served in the RAF and it is understood that he lost his life in the service of his country on 19th February 1947. In the Governors' Minutes of March 1947 it was reported that Mrs Gearing had asked whether his name could be added to the Roll of Honour. Regrettably it was not possible to grant this request as by this time the tablet was full. However, his family donated to the school "The Marcus Cup" for House Cricket in memory of Michael. Inscriptions on this trophy indicate that it was awarded to Woodroffe house in 1958, Shaftesbury in 1959, Woodroffe in 1960 and Shaftesbury in 1961. It was resurrected in later years as it re-appeared in 1972 and 1973 when it was awarded to Blake House.

Grateful thanks to Mr Cecil Quick of the Lyme Regis British Legion who helped to piece together some of the above information. Many of the war dead were his contemporaries and his memories were invaluable. The names of ex-pupils who fought during the Second World War, as shown in the School Magazine of July 1945, are listed at Appendix 4. Chapter 4 which covers the period 1939 to 1945 includes extracts from correspondence between the school and ex-pupils serving overseas.

Bravery Awards

The following Bravery Awards were reported in various editions of the School Magazine throughout the period of the Second World War.

Flight Sergeant Harold Freeman, RAF - Commended by the King for bravery and devotion to duty during the blitz while in the Metropolitan Police Force (reported in the School Magazine of July 1944. Harold's father, Charlie Freeman, was the schoolmaster at Uplyme School.

Captain J F Dawson, RA, Military Cross (1942 -1943). It was reported in the School Magazine of July 1943 that *"He went to Tunisia with the Anglo-American expedition last Autumn and took part in the recent battles there"*.

Captain D J Owen, Royal Corps of Signals, GHQ, Liaison Regiment was awarded an MBE.

Lieut C B Cook, RN, Captain C Hodges, Dorset Regiment, Sergeant W F Kenney, DSM, RAF, Flight Sergeant S J Philbrick, RAF, Sergeant Frank Stretch and Flight Sergeant S Venton, RAF were all mentioned in Despatches.

In the School Magazine dated 1945 Mr Thomas advised that *"particulars of them all are not available but here is an extract from a Dorset paper about **Frank Stretch**: '....*

---

[11] Extract from School Magazine dated July 1943

Sergeant F. Stretch saved the life of one of his section and almost alone captured twenty seven Germans in a cellar. The first man of his section to enter a large house, in the dark, was attacked at the point of the bayonet by a German hidden behind the cellar door. Sergeant Stretch shot the German before he could do any more harm and then routed no less that twenty seven reluctant enemy out of the cellar below."' It is known that Frank lived in Whalley Lane and that his father was the station master at Lyme Regis. In the same magazine Mr Thomas reported that **Flight Lieutenant R J Woodroffe** had also been mentioned in Despatches *"for his splendid work as adjutant of a famous squadron".*[12]

The bravery and the sacrifice of the young men from Lyme Regis Grammar School who gave their life in the service of their country is not forgotten by present day pupils at Woodroffe School. Each year a wreath of poppies is placed on the school memorial plaque and special assemblies on the theme of Remembrance are held. The Head Boy and the Head Girl attend the Remembrance Parade and Service held at St Michael's Parish Church and a large contingent of cadets from the Woodroffe School Combined Cadet Force, in full uniform, also take part. The tree planted on the front lawn by the family of the late Lieutenant Simon Rodwell, who died in 1984 in the South Atlantic, also reminds pupils that young people in the armed forces have, in more recent times, also given their lives in the service of their country.

It is hoped that by recording in this book the courageous acts of these brave men, their memory will be kept alive for many more years to come. Also, for pupils at the school today, these will become more than just names engraved on a plaque but real people, not unlike themselves, who were called upon and were not found wanting.

The School Memorial Tablet, formerly located in the old school hall - can now be found on the top corridor in the old part of the school

---

[12] Extracts from School Magazine dated July 1945

CHAPTER 16 – HISTORY OF BOARDING

The creation of boarding places at the school was very much the brain child of Thornton Pearn and he was ably supported in his endeavours by the Chairman of Governors, Alban Woodroffe. Virtually from the moment he arrived in 1946 Major Pearn's long term aim was to provide a boarding facility at the school. He was very much aware that there were many pupils across the county who qualified for a place at a grammar school education but had difficulty getting to one due to the fact that they lived in remote, rural locations. The Head also felt that boarding would attract more boys to the school. At this time, a state-run boarding facility was quite unusual and the school was very much a leader in this field.

SAINT ANDREWS

In 1948 the Local Authority was persuaded by Major Pearn and Mr Woodroffe to purchase St Andrews, which opened on 13th September 1950, providing accommodation for a maximum of thirty five boys. In his report to Governors the Head advised that the house had opened with only <u>seventeen minutes</u> to spare! Apparently ten days beforehand it was clear that to open on time would be impossible without additional manpower. Assistance was therefore requested from staff and pupils. Offers of help came in from all quarters and work went on from 8.00 am until 10.00 pm, including the weekend, with as many as forty volunteers, including ex-pupils, travelling from as far afield as Thorncombe and Chideock to lend a hand. The Head was proud of the assistance that was given, concluding that the whole effort was in the best tradition of the school.

By December the new house had settled down, overheads were being kept within estimated costs and there were no problems in terms of health or discipline. However, there were concerns that it might be difficult to retain the services of the cook due to a serious discrepancy between wages at the boarding house and in hotel service. The cook was obviously a very important person at St Andrews; the average gain in weight per boy over the first eight weeks was four pounds!!

Immediately prior to the opening of St Andrews in June 1950, a special meeting of the Governing Body was called to consider a proposal by the local authority to purchase the Springfield Hotel, at the top of Woodmead Road, to provide boarding accommodation for girls, a suggestion firmly opposed by the Chairman of Governors. He was dismayed that the Local Authority was considering the purchase of the property, not as an annex for further boys, but to provide accommodation for girls.

The Chairman felt very strongly that the governors should not proceed with the purchase of the property but several fellow governors were interested in pursuing the matter and a lengthy debate ensued. The local authority suggested that Springfield could be used to accommodate girl boarders as there were sufficient boarding places for boys already available within the county. It was felt that the provision of boarding places for girls at Lyme Regis would not only strengthen the academic quality of the school, more so than by the admission of more boys, but it would also meet the need of the county for more boarding places for girls as at this time there were three hundred boarding places available in the county for boys and only sixty for girls. This discrepancy meant that the number of boarding places available at St Andrews was to be restricted to thirty and would not expand as had originally been envisaged.

The Chairman remained adamant in his objection to the purchase of the Springfield Hotel as he was convinced that LRGS should concentrate on providing boarding accommodation for boys only, consolidating its operation at St Andrews where he felt additional places should be provided. A vote was taken and the Chairman's proposal that the scheme for purchasing Springfield should be rejected was carried.

The idea of providing boarding accommodation for girls was still being pursued, however, and shortly afterwards the governors considered a proposal by Miss Williams of St Mary's, Uplyme to provide boarding accommodation for up to twenty girls. St Mary's was currently run as a children's holiday home, principally for children whose parents were abroad. Subsequently this proposal was not pursued, as the Local Authority indicated that they preferred to offer boarding places which were under the direct control of the school, with children accommodated in school boarding houses.

Shortly afterwards, having rejected the proposal to board girls with Miss Williams at St Marys, the LEA agreed to rent Harcombe House, fully furnished, from Mrs Francillon (a member of the governing body and a friend of Alban Woodroffe). Harcombe could accommodate up to forty eight girl boarders and allowing for some minor capital expenditure, it was estimated that the cost of maintaining the house could be achieved at approximately £5,184, which gave an average cost per boarder per annum in the region of £108. Harcombe took in its first group of girl boarders in September 1952.

Major Pearn and the Chairman of Governors may have got their way in terms of providing boarding accommodation at the school, but there was concern within the local community about the amount of ratepayers' money being spent providing boarding facilities at the school and this is reflected in an article which appeared in the Lyme Regis News on Friday, 3rd October 1952 (Price at that time 3d).

Virtually the whole front page was dedicated to the article, which featured several black and white photos of both Harcombe and St Andrews. The article was headed "The price of a notable Lyme Regis Education Venture". It explained that anxiety about the cost to the local ratepayer of the two boarding houses at St Andrews and Harcombe had led to a request for figures by a meeting of Lyme Regis Town Council. The Editor had subsequently spent a day with the Chairman of Governors and the Head, visiting both the boarding houses and having his many questions answered. He felt sure that the responses he had received would allay fears that had been expressed about costs.

He went on to explain that there was no denying that a lot of money had been spent at St Andrews. The house and grounds had cost £10,000, adaptations, re-wiring, central

The School on the Hill

heating and other essentials a further £8,000 and the cost of building of additional dormitories, which were under construction, would add a further £4,500, making a grand total of £23,400. The cost per pupil was quoted as £132 per annum. About 60% of this cost was a charge on public funds, both county and national, with the remainder being met by boarders' parents and other authorities who boarded children at the school. Of the 60% from public funds, the County ratepayers found about 40%. The Editor suggested that it was up to the reader to decide if he or she felt that £23,400 for a boarding house for thirty boys was extravagant and he felt that their opinion would be very much based on the value they placed upon a boarding education.

It was pointed out that Harcombe was an even better bet from the point of view of the ratepayer and taxpayer. It was leased to the Local Authority, furnished and fitted, at a net cost of just £500 a year, for fourteen years with an option to renew. It was suggested that the leasing of Harcombe was a shrewd investment, as the property could accommodate at least fifty girls.[1]

By 1959 St Andrews was home to thirty four boys and Harcombe accommodated fifty girls so both houses had more than exceeded the expectations placed upon them. The set-up in each establishment was very different. Life at Harcombe was run under a benevolent dictatorship but at St Andrews there was a House Committee representing each year group, with great authority given to the House Captain. The day to day routine in each house was as follows:

Routine from Monday to Friday	Harcombe (Girls)	St. Andrews (Boys)
Rising Bell	7.00 am	7.30 am
Breakfast	7.40 am	8.05 am
Leave	8.15 am	8.45 am
Return	4.50 pm	4.30 pm
Tea	5.10 pm	5.10 pm
Shoe Cleaning	5.50 pm	5.50 pm
Preparation	6.00 pm	6.00 pm
Supper	8.00 pm	8.00 pm
Prayers	8.10 pm	8.10 pm
Lights Out	According to age	According to age

Baths and washes for groups, according to age, under the supervision of Matron.

Weekend Routine

Harcombe - Girls clean own rooms during Saturday morning and are free Saturday afternoon. Household jobs done by girls:

4 girls lay breakfast	2 girls cut bread and butter
6 girls clear tables	6 girls wait at table

---

[1] Information taken from an article in Lyme Regis News dated 3rd October 1952

6 girls wait at table with tea   2 4th formers make supper drink
4 wash up supper mugs   Seniors serve meals
Saturdays extra to above:
All clean their own rooms and do jobs round the house
4 girls do second vegetables but not potatoes
4 girls wash breakfast dishes and tea dishes but not lunch (different girls from those doing the supper dishes)

Sundays – as above but do all vegetables (4 girls)
On Sunday Church is compulsory in the morning and girls are free in the afternoon. "Free" may mean organised activities as arranged by Housemistress.
6.00 pm Sunday – Guide Meeting.

St, Andrews - Boys are divided by House Captain into teams, whose duties include:

Peeling potatoes (by machine) Friday and Saturday evenings only
Laying and clearing tables
Evening stoking of boilers (one boy, exempt from all other duties)
Tidying dormitories after breakfast (NOT cleaning)
Tidying washrooms after breakfast (NOT cleaning)
Washing supper crockery nightly and Sunday tea
Washing (by machine) football kit by 2 boys (exempt all other duties)
One Senior by rotation – responsibility for supervision of Junior and Middle School prep – checked by Housemaster on duty nightly after supper

Sunday morning Church compulsory but many boys go voluntarily in the evenings.
Saturday mornings – games or gardening. Saturday afternoon free.
Sunday afternoon organised outing or ramble, or free.
NB Boarders write home when they wish (privately) but all write on Sundays (officially).

By 1959 the Governing Body agreed that efforts should be made to provide transport for the two mile walk home to Harcombe House at the end of the school day and a vehicle was subsequently acquired, to be kept at Harcombe, with the handyman nominated as driver.

In 1966 the lease on Harcombe House was renewed for a further seven years. Although the girls' boarding house was running at full capacity with fifty girls and further applications on-going, numbers at St Andrews had dropped slightly which reflected a national trend. It was subsequently decided to produce a boarding brochure to promote the advantages of a state boarding education to parents. An order for one thousand brochures was placed at a cost of £6.

RHODE HILL

In 1969 the demand for boarding places, particularly for girls, was such that the Local Authority decided to purchase Rhode Hill. All girl boarders were transferred to this establishment, with junior boys accommodated at Harcombe House and senior boys at St Andrews. By this time Harcombe had been purchased. Boarding continued to thrive for many years but gradually throughout the 1980s the demand for boarding places diminished, largely due to a reduction in funding by the armed forces for service families.

As the decade drew to a close the Local Authority reduced the number of boarding places at the school as part of its reorganisation of boarding provision across the county. This meant that of the 179 boarding places available at Woodroffe, fifty nine were to go by September 1991 when the authority proposed to provide 120 boarding places for both boys and girls at a purpose built facility within the school grounds. However, following a request from school governors, the authority agreed to increase this number to 140 boarders.

In 1991 the school achieved Grant Maintained status and the governors had full control over the school's finances, acquiring full title of the three boarding houses and the school site and buildings. The governors subsequently announced that they were considering building a new boarding complex for 140 pupils on land adjacent to the school site for which they were negotiating with the developer for the site. The intention was to finance the purchase of the land by using the proceeds from the sale of one of the existing boarding houses.

Sadly, nothing came of this initiative which fell apart as the developer in question wanted all the land at St Andrews but unfortunately the governors, much to the dismay of the Bursar, Peter Rickard, had given half of it back to the Local Authority some eight years previously, as at that time they felt that they did not need it! Although every effort continued to be made to market boarding, sadly, with numbers dwindling, in 1991 Harcombe House closed with the junior boy boarders transferring to Rhode Hill which became a mixed boarding facility for the first time in its history. In 1993, with numbers further reduced, St Andrews was closed and senior boys joined the junior boys at Rhode Hill. By 1996 it became apparent that the boarding operation was no longer viable and the decision was made to close Rhode Hill with the remaining thirty two boarders moving to boarding accommodation at Allhallows College. Sadly Allhallows began to experience its own difficulties and in 1998 it also ceased to operate. The handful of Woodroffe boarders that remained were accommodated locally until they had finished their exams.

It was a sad end to what had been a glorious period in the history of the school. In its heyday the school had almost 200 boarding pupils and there is no doubt that the introduction of boarders to the school greatly enriched the learning experience for local children who had the opportunity to study alongside those from such far flung places as Hong Kong, the United Arab Emirates, the Falkland Islands, Turkey, France, Germany, Switzerland, Japan, Libya, Ghana, Singapore and Cyprus - even Tripolitania, Damascus and Nyasaland at one point - to name but a few. There were concerns that numbers at the school would drop without the influx of boarders but in fact the demand for day places grew steadily with the popularity of the school and at the time of writing the school roll is at its highest ever.

There are separate chapters dedicated to each of the three boarding houses.

The School on the Hill

BOARDING HOUSEPARENTS					
HARCOMBE	Dates	**ST ANDREWS**	Dates	**RHODE HILL**	Dates
Mr & Mrs Jowett	1952/1964	Major & Mrs Pearn	1950/1973	Mr & Mrs Deasey	1969/1971
Dr & Mrs Morrish	1964/1968	Mr Middleton	1973/1987	Mr & Mrs Boyce	1971/1974
Mr & Mrs Badman	1968/1977	Mr & Mrs Hibberd	1987/1993	Mr & Mrs Hayday	1974/1975
Mr & Mrs Pengelly	1977/1987			Mr & Mrs Draper	1975/1982
Mr & Mrs Ennals	1987/1991			Mr & Mrs Ayers	1982/1986
				Mr & Mrs Pemberton	1986/1988
				Mr Chambers & Miss Kabia	1988/1989
				Mr & Mrs Sleigh	1989/1993
				Mr & Mrs Ennals	1993/1996
Closed	**1991**	**Closed**	**1993**	**Closed**	**1996**
	Boarders transferred to Allhallows in 1996 Allhallows closed two years later in 1998				

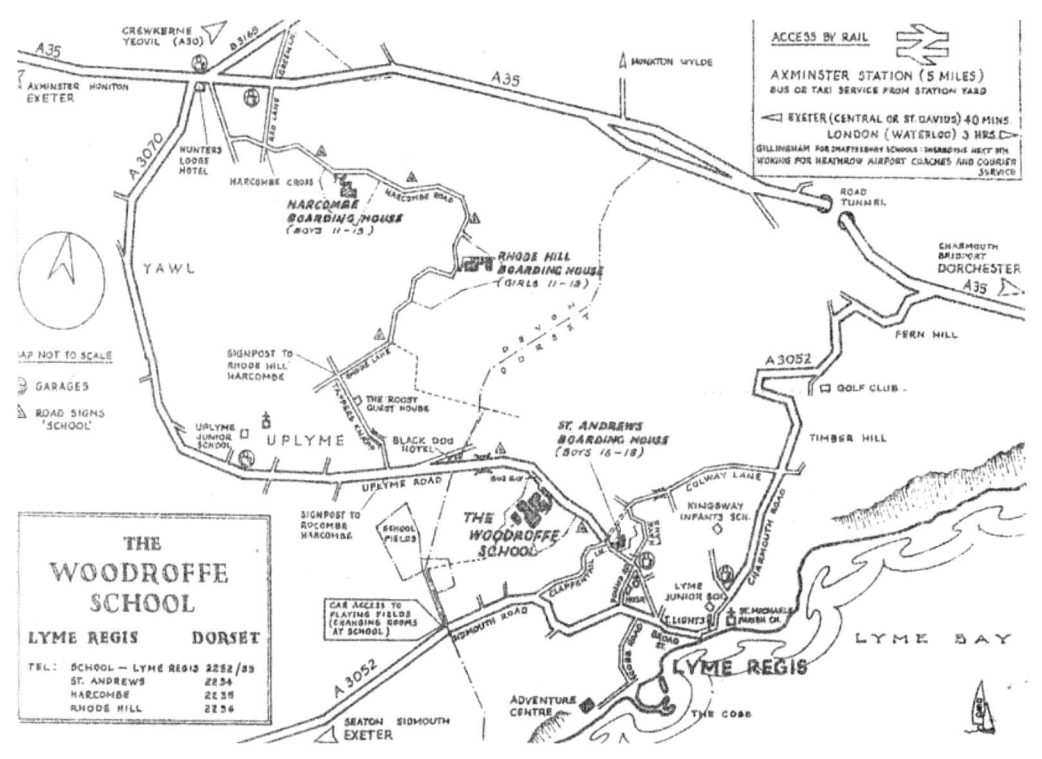

CHAPTER 17 – ST ANDREWS

(Photograph courtesy of Keith Wiscombe)

St. Andrews ceased to be a boarding house for senior boys at the Woodroffe School in July 1993. At that time the house stood in 1.12 acres comprising mainly lawned garden. Adjacent to the main plot was a further 1.84 acres, previously used as playing fields, but this was sold separately by the school to developers and is now occupied by a small estate of private houses. The property itself was converted into holiday flats and bed and breakfast accommodation.

The house dates back to the Georgian period, and has an interesting history. It is believed that it was once a chapel dedicated to St Andrew. There is also a suggestion that it was regarded as a medieval shrine due to its connection with St Andrew's Well, one of the earliest and best sources of Lyme's water supply. In 1905 it was converted to a private hotel and an extension was added. 1938 saw extensive alterations when the property was divided into flats and in 1950 it was purchased by the local authority for boarding accommodation for LRGS.

The opening of St. Andrews is referred to in the school magazine of July 1950 as follows: *"After nearly two years' planning (and plotting!) St. Andrews is nearly ready to receive the first entry of boarders to LRGS. The difficulties in the way have been immense and a debt of gratitude is owed to many "officials" for their help and, particularly, of course, to the Chairman, Mr. Woodroffe, who in this venture has been an untiring, driving force. Few County Councillors, we hear, will forget his magnificent reply to a wild accusation that the place was falling down. "Nonsense, ladies and gentlemen! One side only!".*[1]

---

[1] Extract from School Magazine dated July 1950

The first boarders admitted to St Andrews were A B Trecher, J Rodda, D Leicester, B J Hillier, D O'Neil East, R Long, M Clinch, M Myers, P Fisher, R M Kilburn, B Lewis, P Sanders, H Symonds, J McGinley, D Poore, H Fisher. A pupil describes in great detail his first year at St. Andrews as follows:

"When we heard that we were coming to St. Andrews, memories of school stories went through out minds, of huge granite buildings, looking cold, bare and desolate from outside and with bare walls, uncomfortable furniture and beds inside. We found when we came that the house was very different from this. Indeed when we arrived on 13th September 1950 – the day it was opened – it was difficult to find, for it had no similarity whatever to any boarding house we had ever seen or heard of.

On entering the house we were surprised to find the Common Room very comfortably furnished with easy chairs, settee, a polished table with a bowl of flowers on it, a carpet on the floor, a wireless and an electric clock. The panelled walls were, we thought, a very light colour for a boys' boarding house. The Common Room was not only heated by a lovely stone-coloured stove but also by the central heating system. The Dining Room is furnished with highly polished Australian oak tables and polished chairs and linoleum – there is also a stove of the same type as in the Common Room…. The food was also of good quality. Again this room is painted a light colour – yellow…….

Looking back over the year, most of us have had an enjoyable time…… We St. Andrews boarders are very lucky when you consider the amount of times we are allowed out…..In October Mr. Pearn went to a great deal of trouble to get us some extra special fireworks for a firework display…..A recent event was the arrival of a mechanical plough to break up some rough ground, so that we could get some cabbages planted. It was quite amusing to see us learning the way to use it. During the last few weeks of term, boys could be seen sitting on blankets in baths covered in foam, looking like film stars in a Cecil B. de Mille epic. The great blanket wash was most successful – a fitting end to our first year at St. Andrews."[2]

Not long after the boarding house opened, the local authority was asked if the grounds could be put in good order following which the boys would take over responsibility for their upkeep. Shortly afterwards a lot of boys took up gardening as a hobby and eventually sufficient vegetables were grown to enable the boarding house to dispense with buying them. Fruit was also in abundance and in one year a staggering 800 lbs of home grown fruit was bottled in the boarding houses.

Neil Adams, a former pupil of the school, and a Housemaster at St Andrews from 1953 to 1955 writes *"The boarding house for boys, called St. Andrews, was near the main school and housed some thirty boys……The age range of the boys was from eleven to eighteen and many were from service families overseas or from broken homes. Talking to them on an informal basis gave me quite an insight into domestic backgrounds and problems which, in those days, rarely surfaced in schools. There was a boy whose parents had been killed in a car crash and whose only relative was an older brother. Then there was*

---

[2] Extract from School Magazine dated July 1951

the boy whose mother had died and, after re-marriage, his father had died – he never received a letter during his stay and his only pocket money came from cleaning my shoes at an inflated rate and the matron and myself were the only persons who sent him birthday cards.

Dorset had an arrangement with the Falkland Islands whereby one or two of their pupils could be placed in Dorset boarding grammar schools and one boy came to us. On the first night of his arrival I asked him what had struck him most about England. "The trees, the trees", he said, having come through the New Forest and never having seen a tree before, since the Falklands don't have any.

I shall never forget my first evening at St. Andrews. After prayers and a short interval I toured the main dormitories to ensure that all lights were out – the Sixth Formers were allowed to stay up late – and then settled down in my study to prepare some lessons. After a short while I began to hear rustling noises and the sounds of movement. I soon discovered that there were boys in their pyjamas moving from room to room throughout the building. Firm action was needed to establish my authority I thought and walked round with a cane under my arm and a loud voice raised declaring that anyone out of his dormitory after Lights Out without permission would be caned. No more movement but after an hour or so a hesitant knock on my door. A very small boy shivering in his pyjamas – "Please, sir, can I got to go to the toilet?"

Enquiries discovered that my predecessor had been known to depart to the nearby pub shortly after Lights Out and not return until closing time. Meanwhile the boys were enjoying their freedom with smoking and other activities. I discovered another reason why my predecessor had left! Apparently one night he had returned drunk from the pub, lost his way and ended up in the office of the Headmaster's wife, who dealt with the House accounts. He then relieved himself in her wastepaper basket!! He had to go!

In May 1955, due to a shortage of accommodation at school, the games room at St Andrews was converted to a needlework room for use by female pupils. By 1957 Commerce was also being taught at the boarding house.

A further insight into life at St Andrews comes from a short article which appeared in the school magazine of 1955, entitled "Christmas Show at St. Andrews" in which it was explained that the boys had been troubled by the fact that they had been unable in recent years to entertain the Harcombe girls due to lack of space. This year a show had been staged, depicting life in two imaginary boarding houses "Heartbreak House" and "St. Agnes". Readers were asked to imagine the largest and heaviest boy in the house dressed as the Fairy Queen and wearing hob-nailed boots, a chorus of toughs armed to the eyebrows with daggers and pistols and a burlesque based on a staff meeting. Music and lyrics were written especially for the occasion. The Matron's Song, entitled "Minnie the Matron", included such memorable lines as "With my most repellent liquor I will make you sicker quicker". When an influenza epidemic hit the boarding house some time later, hopefully "Minnie the Matron" had the opportunity to give them their comeuppance!

One summer a dramatic fire gutted "Spindles" the home of Mr Awford, which was adjacent to St Andrews. However all was not lost as an eager army of St Andrew's boys saved literally all of the furnishings. To mark his gratitude Mr Awford presented £20 to the House Welfare Fund which was used to purchase camping equipment.

*View of St Andrews from the garden
(Photograph courtesy of Peter Rickard)*

The Head and his wife left St Andrews in 1973 to take up residence nearby. Their daughters, Gillian and Carolyn, grew up in the boarding house and recall life there as follows: *"Life was not always a bed of roses for the headmaster's daughters. We were never going to be the most popular girls in the school, although I have to say we were treated very fairly by staff and fellow-pupils alike and there were some advantages. Not least of these was having the run of the huge house and grounds of St Andrews during the school holidays.*

The boys' boarding house was just that to the many pupils who passed through it but for Carolyn and me, it was our home from the time we were toddlers until we left to get married. Dad was right: we were lucky to live there. It was a magical and sometimes mysterious place. I remember the veranda, its glass supported by wrought-iron columns through which roses grew. It afforded a magnificent view of Lyme Bay and gave the old house a gracious charm. It was here we learned to roller-skate and very quickly too, for the sloping site meant that one end was over a metre off the ground. To lose balance there and plunge off was bound to end in tears! Then there was the huge azalea bush on the front lawn which made a wonderfully perfumed, if rather sticky tent in early summer. And through the orchard and behind the compost heaps were the ruined foundations of a small cottage. We spent hours digging for treasure here but only ever found broken shards of rather uninteresting pottery.

There were also two wells, one in the field behind St Andrews and one in the old vegetable garden. They were both very small, yet never ran dry even in the hottest summer. I once found a book of local history which claimed that for centuries, pilgrims and travellers had used the well at St Andrews as a watering place. Unfortunately, the book didn't say where this historic well was located. We never did find out if it was one or neither of "ours".

Wet days indoors could also be enjoyable. We became very passable table-tennis players, tried our hands at darts and took advantage of the many exciting boys' adventure tales in both the Junior and Senior libraries – although on gloomy winter afternoons, the gaping empty rooms and long, lonely corridors, not to mention the strange wheezes from the sinister boiler room, could suddenly become all very spooky and unnerving.

I remember the Autumn half terms when Carolyn and I would sit with Mum in the huge bay-windows of the "big" dormitory chewing sweet toffee-apples while Dad braved the elements to treat us to a fantastic firework display form the lawn below. Catherine wheels whizzed, rockets flew into the night sky and golden rains and silver fountains spilled out their brilliant stars. Those were indeed magical times."

Mr Fred Middleton took over as Housemaster from the Head. Boys from St. Andrews played hockey against "eleven raving girls with hockey sticks from Rhode Hill". Eventually the hockey matches were abandoned and instead the boys from St Andrews played football and rugby against the Harcombe boys. Several boarders also enjoyed a potholing expedition in the Mendips with Mr Thomas. Despite getting soaked to the skin and frozen to the core, all the party enjoyed themselves and returned home safely.

The boarders also did their bit for the local community. The Mayor arranged for the boys to assist with painting the railings on the sea front ready for the summer visitors and he subsequently presented them with a certificate in appreciation of their efforts. They also joined forces with girls from Rhode Hill to help out at an Old Time Music Evening for pensioners held at the Marine Theatre by waiting and serving drinks. Help was again provided by boarders, when they assisted with refreshments and showing guests to their seats at the town's Jubilee Concert. On another occasion the boys helped the Lyme Regis Society in their bid to clear the River Lym of all litter. When heavy snow fell in March 1978 St Andrews became a mixed boarding house for one week whilst the road to Harcombe and Rhode Hill was impassable. An operation "worthy of the Swiss Alps", involving the Adventure Centre and their radio controlled Land Rover, had been needed to rescue some pupils from Axminster Station.

The boys enjoyed a wide range of activities including camping expeditions to Dartmoor, shopping trips to Exeter, fossiling, football matches and house basketball, table tennis and darts tournaments. For the latter the house handyman, Fred Derrick, donated a cup known as "Fred's Cup". There were also strenuous walks, one of which covered a forty five miles route and involved fourteen and a half hours of walking. Once their exams were over, the boys also turned their hand to decorating work at the boarding house.

Mr Alan Brown was an Assistant Houseparent at St Andrews from 1983 until its closure and has many happy memories of the boarding house: *"I joined the teaching staff at Woodroffe in September 1983 and at the same time became Assistant Housemaster to Fred Middleton at St Andrews. I have nothing other than fond memories of my years at St Andrews both living in and as a midweek houseparent. Fred (Middleton) was a legendary housemaster to work for and there was never a dull moment. Routine was extremely important in the house – ten seconds late for breakfast meant an apology to top table and clearing away all the tables at the end of the meal, whilst a one minute delay in returning from a weekend evening out resulted in spending the next night in the house. Twenty five minutes late was a complete disaster – one week of incarceration! Sunday night was always room and house inspection. There was usually some hilarity to be gained by planting something forbidden in or around your bedroom.*

We awaited with trepidation the arrival home of the Sixth Formers on a Friday and Saturday night. The housemaster sat in his chair twiddling his thumbs and eyeing up each boy as he returned at 10.00 pm to check for signs of intoxication…. For birthdays, it was customary for each boy to join the staff for a sherry before tea and a ceremonial cutting of a cake with a sword. The cake was shared amongst the boys with the largest piece always going to Fred's dog, Snoopy. The hospitality at St Andrews was second to none, especially at Christmas when the housemaster hosted guests and Upper Sixth Formers to a pre-dinner drinks party. Christmas was very special at all three boarding houses and, as a young housemaster attending the Junior Boys, Girls and Senior Boys festivities all in one weekend usually meant gaining a few pounds in weight.

I remember one of my first weekends in charge when Fred was away. I was awakened at about 1.00 am by some of the Year 11 boys complaining of noise from next door. Sure enough there was a raucous party going on. I called politely over the wall for them to keep the noise down but to no avail. The boys suggested that by using a length of hose attached to an inside tap we could dampen the spirit next door. This I did to the initial amusement of the boys and some of the guests next door. However, the water was swiftly followed by a piece of loose stone from the wall thrown by one of the boys. It was decided that that was enough but too late – the party goers were upset and came knocking at the door. Making sure all the boys were in bed I was checking the house when there was a tap on the door. I politely asked the reveller to go away only to discover it was Matron who we had inadvertently locked out. She was not amused!!

Thankfully the police were rare visitors to the house but on one memorable occasion they came to retrieve a barrel of beer removed from the Nag's Head by a group of pupils. Fortunately it was still full! On another occasion they knocked on the door to enquire why my bicycle was hanging from the top of the St Andrews' flagpole and why my car was wrapped entirely in pink toilet paper. I couldn't explain until someone reminded me that it was April Fool's Day. Despite all this, in my eight years in boarding, I never saw or had to deal with, the bullying that is so often associated with some boarding regimes. St Andrews was always a very happy house. As well as all the fun we had, boarding produced some superb all round pupils who have gone on to great success in adult life. I am proud to call many of these pupils good friends now."[3]

In 1987 Mr Middleton resigned from his post as Houseparent after seventeen years in charge of the boarding house. He was replaced by Mr and Mrs David Hibberd, supported by Mr Brown and Mr Wood. St Andrews closed as a boarding house in July 1993 when all the boys were transferred to Harcombe to join the junior boys under the care of Mr and Mrs Ennals.

---

[3] Information provided by Alan Brown dated November 2006

CHAPTER 18 - HARCOMBE HOUSE

Harcombe House was originally a finishing school for young ladies, who were taught skills such as needlework, cookery and home-craft. The girls had small single or shared bedrooms and the larger rooms were classrooms for sewing and dressmaking.

In 1952 Harcombe House was leased by Dorset County Council from Mrs Francillon, a member of the Governing Body, on a fourteen year lease. It offered accommodation for a maximum of forty eight girls but when it opened initially it housed just thirteen. The houseparents in charge were Mr and Mrs Jowett. Mrs Jowett was a popular member of the teaching staff and she and her husband quickly established a family atmosphere at the house which was to endure until they left the boarding house twelve years later in 1964 to set up home in Lyme Regis.

A Lower Sixth pupil reflects on her time at Harcombe as follows: *"For two terms now I have been a boarder at Harcombe. When Harcombe first opened I thought how awful it would be to be a girl boarder, but now I realise how extremely fortunate I am. What has impressed me most is the cheerful and friendly spirit of everyone and the way in which everything runs so smoothly. There is never a dull moment at Harcombe. How could there be with three pianos, a radiogram and thirty-four girls? One never finds time to be bored.*

The School on the Hill

We are very lucky in having such a spacious garden, although we do not always think so when we have to do weeding on Saturday mornings in the summer! We have two tennis courts and also table tennis, and one of the joys, I think, of living with so many people is that one can always find a partner somewhere. There is always someone who can make a joke, wash and set hair or take up a hem. The food is excellent – I consider myself a walking advertisement as I have put on nearly two stones in weight since I have been here!

Harcombe girls in their panama hats

Each girl has a certain job to do for one week. These jobs follow a rota and the way in which they are carried out without any fuss is really amazing. As we all belong to School House there is, on the whole, a good sense of sportsmanship and a willingness to work for the House. On Saturday mornings, after our rooms have been cleaned, we all aim to do something for the House itself. In the summer we do gardening and perhaps in the winter we clean windows. This term has been an extremely busy one for the girls and the staff. We have even had the Fire Brigade here for a practice. When they had finished they gave a showerbath to the girls, who had changed into their bathing costumes. "[1]

Mrs Jowett presides over the stirring of the Christmas Cake

The Summer Term of 1959 was the last for the original founder-members of Harcombe House who would be leaving after seven happy years and one describes her time at Harcombe as follows: *"Harcombe is a low, white rangy building rearing like a lazy arm among the green of the fertile valley to which it belongs. It is a summer house in the sense that it seems to flourish and come alive only in the late spring and summer, smooth*

---

[1] Extract from the School Magazine dated July 1956

green lawns stretching down to a blaze of opulent rhododendrons, and on a clear day a small triangle of blue sea to be seen beyond them. Beds of lupins and giant poppies flanking the central path, the screen of fir trees facing the house making their still dark watch over the sunken garden, the weeping birch tree and the swing – so much to be admired and remembered. There were thirteen of us originally and these were the happiest of days. My memories of that first year are hazy but Matron Rawlings figures in a lot of them. Tall and trim with iron grey hair and long bony fingers, she was an unbending disciplinarian and a fanatical stickler for table manners and cleanliness. For me goodbye to Harcombe is goodbye to school life and to seven years of my life well spent."

Another pupil describes one of the many Harcombe Jives which were very popular not only with boarders but with day pupils as well: *"The room was masked with flowers, single blooms on the window sills and massive ferns entwined round the boiler. From the record player on a table near the door boomed forth the deep voice of Elvis; small parties of nervous teenagers drifted into the room, boys and girls uneasily splitting into two groups. Girls were the first to dance, but in a relatively short time nearly everyone was on the floor. The company was mixed, from boisterous to more sedate seniors. Few of the males knew how to jive, so the first half of the evening was taken up by lessons.*

In the dining room Victor Sylvester was available and those seeking a rest from the loud rhythm of rock and roll at any time during the evening could relax to the soothing strains of his orchestra. On the whole though, the popular music had the largest following. Dresses were extremely picturesque, short and balloon like with hoops and stiff petticoats. The boys, not to be beaten, came in tight jeans of various colours, and spectacular shirts – Farrant's black and white cowboy one and Fortnam's black one, certainly the most startling.[2]"

Mrs Jowett established the Harcombe Girl Guide troop, and in May 1961 it was invited to provide the Guard of Honour and Standard Bearers for a service to commemorate the centenary of the Girl Guides at Exeter Cathedral, attended by Lady Baden Powell.

---

[2] Extract from the School Magazine dated July 1959

The School on the Hill

A bus was purchased for Harcombe in 1959 for the two mile trip to school and back. Eventually a larger vehicle was acquired which meant that the bus could transport all boarders in one journey rather than two.

When Mr and Mrs Jowett left Harcombe in 1964 their successors were Dr and Mrs Morris who remained in charge until 1966 when Mr and Mrs Roy Deasey took over. The latter subsequently moved to the new larger girls' boarding house at Rhode Hill in 1969 and Mr and Mrs David Badman took over at Harcombe. Mr Badman recalls those days as follows: "*Dorset had just bought Rhode Hill and the forty eight girls from Harcombe were moving there and the first four years of boys from St. Andrew's were taking their place. We were told that we would start with about thirty boys for the first year so we could set up the new establishment – we opened in September with forty eight! So there we were, thirty old hands, eighteen new boarders, many of whom had never boarded before, one tutor from St Andrews and the rest of the staff still wet behind the ears. We also had two sons under the age of three. It was an interesting time to put it mildly*

The house itself, still at that time rented furnished, did not lend itself easily to use by boys. The largest room on the ground floor was used as a laundry and it took a year or so before machinery could be moved to make an indoor playroom.

Mrs Francillon, the owner, made a state visit once a year to see how her property was being looked after and to see where her husband's ashes were buried. She was never quite easy about big rough boys being in the house she had built up from a small cottage in 1918. She was probably right – when Dorset bought Harcombe the County Valuer nearly had a fit when he saw the many valuable pieces of antique furniture that were in daily use. We had to arrange replacements rapidly. One item the boys were not allowed to touch was a redcoat uniform that had belonged to General Gordon of Khartoum, who was a relative of Mrs. Francillon. It was stored in a locked cupboard and we were greatly relieved when it was removed. My last duty for Mrs Francillon was when her ashes were buried in the garden with her husband.

Every Sunday morning we walked the boys to Matins in Uplyme Parish Church. There was a hornets' nest in a tree in a field near the road, which a bright spark chose to throw stones at on the return walk – it rapidly became a rout. Everyone managed to beat the insects but it was a close run thing.

Locked lofts, cupboards and rooms were always a challenge to the boys. Being an old house we often had leaks in the roof but there was one that the builders could not trace. Much later at a reunion I was told that a plastic bag of home brew had been hidden in the loft but then burst, staining the ceiling. Another place we eventually found was being used for contraband was the cellar under the toilet block – perhaps too many prison escape stories? Then there was the time when we lost the plastic bucket we used to soak the nappies of our baby son. A little later it was found in the hobbies caravan with a mix of home brew in it; from the look of it the original contents might have been more appetising."[3]

Under the care of Mr and Mrs Badman, the boarders enjoyed bonfire parties, mackerel fishing, trips to Yeovilton Air Base, discos, bonfire parties and model making competitions. A model railway was constructed in one of the lofts, inter-year and inter-house football games were organised and camping trips to Dartmoor. The boys also visited the Devon and Somerset Gliding Club where they were able to experience gliding. On one memorable occasion a party visited the Silver Jubilee International Air Tattoo at RAF Greenham near Newbury where they enjoyed eight solid hours of flying displays, including an appearance by the Red Arrows.

As Mr and Mrs Badman left Harcombe in Christmas 1977, to be replaced by Mr and Mrs Pengelly, they reflected on their eight and a half years at the boarding house. Reference was made to ghosts; days when the Agas were used for cooking and anthracite boilers for hot water and heating; the blast of the whistle to herald a fire drill; the winter morning when breakfast was served by the light of a fire engine's searchlight after a small fire put out the electrical system. Fire played a part in the life of the house, as during particularly dry seasons forest fires sometimes reached the property boundaries. Reference was also made to the many happy social occasions – the discos and the parties, particularly the most recent to celebrate the Silver Jubilee of Harcombe when Mrs Jowett had returned to the house to cut the cake.

In 1978 heavy snow disrupted the normal routine of the house and on one occasion members of the teaching staff travelled to Harcombe to deliver lessons. Upon their arrival in September of that year, Mr Ennals and Mr Roberts valiantly took on the re-painting of the top dormitory. Fourth year pupils also took up the challenge and re-painted their common room – in a delightful combination of black and fluorescent green! This colour scheme was described by Mr Pengelly as "daunting to the eye" but it proved to be an "agreeable combination".

One aspect of life at Harcombe after the arrival of Mr Ennals was "Ennals Tours" which involved parties of boarders setting off for visits to a variety of places including

---

[3] Information provided by Mr Badman November 2006

Southampton, Yeovilton, Bridport and Exeter with Mr Ennals at the wheel of the Harcombe bus. The trips invariably ended, like all school trips, with a stop-over somewhere on the way home for fish and chips. The "Harcombe Holidaymakers" got a bit carried away on one visit to Exeter and arrived home with a variety of pets purchased from Exeter Pet Club. Eventually the mice and gerbils were donated to the school's Pets Club run by Mr Rice while the rest were found good homes.

Mr Ennals also organised swimming and canoeing groups and a Harcombe football and handball competition which featured such teams as the "Wilson Wanderers", "Trickey's Trotters", the "Harcombe Globetrotters" and the "Funkey First Years". The Harcombe Discos continued to thrive and there was one with a "Captain Beaky" theme.

During 1980 considerable improvements took place at the house including a large amount of internal redecoration work undertaken by Miss Fray and Mr Furzey. Miss Fray had also been busy in the garden and, in an effort to encourage the growth of new trees, to replenish the large number lost up and down the country through Dutch Elm disease, she suggested starting a Tree Club. The idea was to involve the boys in growing their own tree from seed or seedling and then caring for it until it was big enough to plant and grow unaided. Miss Fray pointed out that it could take up to five or six years but suggested that it might be nice to for pupils to find a tree to grow up with.

In early 1982 the extreme weather led to new activities - toboggan making and more importantly toboggan testing. The occupants of the house endured heavy snow, storm force winds, power failures and then a seemingly endless period of rain. The Railway Loft and the Modelling Room were well used by the boys who also undertook to decorate parts of the house.

In 1983 Mr Ennals married and in 1984 he and his wife, Clare, left Harcombe to take up an appointment at St Mary's on the Isles of Scilly. They were greatly missed but when Mr and Mrs Pengelly left Harcombe in 1987 Mr and Mrs Ennals returned to take over.

As the demand for boarding places diminished, the governors made the decision to close Harcombe in 1991, with junior boys transferring to Rhode Hill.

John Ennals writes: *"September 1978 saw my arrival at Harcombe. Also starting at this time was Steve Roberts and we were under the leadership of John Pengelly. One of our first jobs to do before the boarders returned was to paint the top dormitory an awful orange colour. Harcombe housed sixty boys (1st to 4th years in those days) and the total number of boarders was approximately 180 – twenty per cent of the school population. The boarders were mainly from the forces, privately paid for and a few social care cases.*

My role was to organise and supervise the out of school time for the boarders – meal times, duty teams, prep and evening activities which included indoor football and table tennis competitions; the grounds and woods surrounding the house made great areas for "French and English", a favourite game enjoyed by the boys. When the boarders were at school I was free so I used to help at the Lyme Regis Adventure Centre and in return we were able to use the equipment for canoeing, mackerel fishing trips, etc at the weekends and evenings in the summer.

One asset which was not being used at weekends and in the evenings was the Harcombe bus. I asked if it could be – enquiries were made and I went to Dorchester to take my county test and this gave rise to "Ennals Tours" which included trips to Southampton for shopping, swimming, cinemas, ice skating and football (nothing to do with the fact that Southampton is my team!). My mother used to be an emergency contact and each boarder had her number. There were also boarders/weekend trips to Cornwall loaded with tents and canoes, and swimming at the school pool after prep in the summer.

In 1983 I married and in January 1984 Clare and I moved to the Isles of Scilly to run a mixed boarding house of eleven to sixteen year olds who came from the off-islands to St Marys, Monday to Friday, for their secondary education. Clare and I returned in February 1987 with our daughter, Kimberley.

We created a car track in the field behind the house where the boys learned the basics of driving. Fortunately there was a line of fir trees at the bottom of the track which formed a natural crash barrier – staff kindly donated old cars from which the boys removed the glass and welded in roll bars – luckily not required! During the autumn term we kept a couple of pigs and for those interested there was a rota for looking after them – feeding (selected waste from the kitchen), cleaning out and watering. The meat we always had back, which was superb for Sunday lunches and summer barbecues.

One weekend, a "house day out", walking on Dartmoor was planned. The previous night three boys had run away. I decided to do the trip and Clare stayed back with our two year old son, Daniel, to liaise with the Head and police. On our return there were three police cars, police dogs and a police helicopter circling the area. The boys had stolen a car from Lyme, driven to Weymouth and Salisbury and back where they had got the car stuck in a ditch in a lane near the house. I was cross with myself for teaching them to drive but, as the police said, at least no-one was killed or injured.

A 5.00 am start, four hundred mile round trip to Alton Towers (a real test for the bus and driver) became the regular end of year trip, stopping for fish and chips in Chard on the return journey.

The end of the Cold War had an effect on the need for boarding by the forces and boarding also became less fashionable, with people becoming more mobile. Numbers had gradually been falling during the 1980's. When the school opted out in September 1991 it was decided that one of the houses must close. In October 1991 Harcombe closed and it was a sad day for everyone. I had enjoyed my ten years at the House. Years 7 to 9, plus myself and the cars and the bike transferred to Rhode Hill and the Year 10 boys moved down to St Andrews. At this point Clare finished with boarding and she and the children went to live in our house in Axminster.

In September 1993 Clare and I took over the running of Rhode Hill. Over sixty boys and girls from Year 7 to the Sixth Form in one house, plus the new Head in the grounds in his caravan. The size of Rhode Hill enabled the boarders to have common rooms for the boys, girls and Years 10/11. Meal times have always been an important part of house routine – tables were mixed eleven to eighteen boys and girls; punctuality and standards *were expected and I was able to address the whole house – weekend breakfasts were quite a leveller. After a few weeks life began to settle down and for the first time we had the same rules for all and everybody knew what was expected.*

Christmas was always a special time in boarding – a long term, for some the first time away from home and flying half way around the world to see parents. Armed with a chainsaw, ten pupils and the mini-bus we used to go and cut down a twenty foot tree, drag it out of the woods and load it on top of the bus. The top of the tree was dressed on the floor before being erected in the corner of the hall. On Sunday there was the cake competition followed by Christmas cake and mince pies. The following weekend was the Christmas dinner where staff and guests were invited – the cooks did a fantastic job catering for 120. Everybody made a real effort and I was always very proud of how the boarders would rise to the occasion. The evening would finish with carols around the tree and then the unofficial drinks for staff and Sixth Form.

We had regular trips to the theatre. One of my first trips with Year 10 boys from Harcombe to the Brewhouse in Taunton saw a play where Dawn (beginning of a new day) came on – young, blonde and naked – no problems filling the next trip! Activities such as "Pumping Stations" (teams of four attacking and defending) became mixed affairs where we would drive to St Mary's wood, walk for ten minutes up to the old pumping station – it would be dark, cold, wet and muddy but thoroughly enjoyable – and then back for showers and hot chocolate.

Despite having a very good OFSTED report the numbers continued to decline and a decision was made in the Spring of 1996 to close Rhode Hill in July, and the pupils were transferred to Allhallows to board. The money we had made from the tuck shop and cream tea afternoons was spent on a final house trip to Jersey for the day on the Condor. The assets from the sale of the three boarding houses were used by the school for the building of the Sports Hall and the Drama Studio.

I haven't mentioned names on purpose but would like to pay tribute to all the care staff, teaching and support staff, cooks, cleaners, laundry staff, handymen and gardeners, who have given such loyal service over the years. There is one person I will mention. He was at Harcombe when I started in 1978 and is at school at the time of writing. He was handyman at first and then became handyman, gardener, bus driver, mini-bus driver at Rhode Hill. If it snowed he would walk two and a half miles from his house in Uplyme to Harcombe. The most loyal and reliable member of staff – thank you Peter Furzey."[4]

(All photographs taken from the photo albums of the late Mrs Ernestine Jowett by kind permission of her family)

---

[4] Information provided by John Ennals in May 2006

CHAPTER 19 – RHODE HILL

Rhode Hill House from the front lawn

Rhode Hill is a Georgian house, formerly set in twelve hundred acres which was built by Admiral Talbot with prize money from his naval career. He and his family settled there in 1830. At that time the perimeter of the estate ran from Colway Lane along the Lyme Regis/Charmouth Road, then to Penn, Raymonds Hill, Whitty Down, back down Springhead Road, into Uplyme and thence down to the old railway station and back along Colway Lane. The Talbot Arms was named after the Admiral and he and his wife are buried under the nave at the Roman Catholic Church in Lyme Regis. It was his son and daughter-in-law, a wealthy French lady, who in about 1890 transformed Rhode Hill from a square, stuccoed Georgian house into the brick "Queen Anne" house of today.

In 1910 the Talbots fell on hard times financially, perhaps because of the cost of renovations to Rhode Hill, and decided to sell the estate. In the meantime one of the Talbot girls, Laura, married Alban Woodroffe, who lived at Ware House and was Mayor of Lyme Regis. Laura persuaded her husband to buy Rhode Hill, to keep it in the family. He did so but he also retained Ware House.

In 1914, when the First World War broke out, Rhode Hill was turned into a convalescent hospital for wounded soldiers. Mr Woodroffe was Commandant at the Hospital and moved into the lodge on the estate. After the war he moved back into the main house, but it is believed that he never really enjoyed living there. In 1934 the house was sold to Mrs Francillon, who ran a Ladies Finishing School at Harcombe, and it became a school for Domestic Science. Mr Woodroffe moved to White Ley where he lived until his death in 1964. Aileen, his daughter-in-law lived in Colway Lane.

Rhode Hill came into the ownership of the Local Authority in 1968 and it was opened as a boarding facility for girls on 10th September 1969. At that time senior boys were accommodated at St Andrews and junior boys at Harcombe. When Rhode Hill first opened its doors to girl boarders the Head, then Thornton Pearn, told them that they had a new house and that they would, in time, create their own traditions. The house was a lot bigger than Harcombe and accommodated an extra twenty girls. Junior girls were housed in the main building with accommodation for sixth formers provided in the adjacent stable block. Many of the ex-Harcombe girls missed the family atmosphere they had enjoyed at Harcombe and were dubious as to whether that atmosphere could be re-created in the much larger house with a bigger population.

The Houseparents from 1969 to 1971 were Mr and Mrs Deasey. Mr Deasey taught English at the school and was a popular member of staff. He and his wife were succeeded by Mr and Mrs Boyce. Members of the teaching staff who were assistant houseparents and tutors at Rhode Hill around this period included Miss Bareham, Mrs George and Mrs Bland. Mr Boyce was also a teacher at the school, and he and his wife remained at Rhode Hill until 1974.

The Entrance Hall at Rhode Hill

Mr Boyce recalls that Mr Deasey had lifted the requirement that girls wore white gloves to church and he went one step further and made church on Sunday voluntary, as was the case for boys at St Andrews. The result was that very few girls chose to go to church! Mr and Mrs Boyce were in charge of Rhode Hill when boarding was at its zenith and at one time the house accommodated ninety-one girl boarders, who in many respects were the academic cream of the school, as all the older girls had to have passed the 11+ exam, even after the Grammar School went comprehensive. In 1974 Mr and Mrs Draper took over from Mr and Mr Boyce.

As at St Andrews and Harcombe, the girls at Rhode Hill enjoyed a wide range of activities including horse riding, hockey, modern dancing, swimming and rounders plus annual social events such as discos, Easter Egg hunts, a Pancake Race and Christmas festivities.

The house Activities Fund purchased camping equipment for the Ten Tors team and this was also used by the girls for weekend camping expeditions in the house grounds. The

The School on the Hill

latter involved a meal around the campfire, a sing song and then a night under canvas, before the campers were awoken at 5.00 am by the dawn chorus. Other girls worked for the Duke of Edinburgh's Award and part of their community service involved tree felling and clearing the wood at the nature reserve at Newland's Wood. This project was supervised by Mr Chambers and the highlight of the day was the cooking of baked potatoes in the bonfire lit to burn debris.

Girls at Rhode Hill had to endure a long daily trudge to school on foot. In the summer they had to swat their way through armies of flies and pick their way through the fallen silage left in the lane by Taylor's farm. In winter they had to battle against arctic winds that blew down Rhode Lane. Various strategies were employed to beat the cold including shoes inside gumboots, three pairs of leg warmers, even concealed hot water bottles. The final straw was always the steep hill at Tappers Knapp but the girls struggled and staggered on, true to the tradition of the boarding house. Another cross they had to bear was the need to wear armbands, which was particularly galling when they were dressed up for an exeat.

Girl boarders making their way to school (Photograph from school archive)

In August 1980 Mr and Mrs Hutchings retired as Head Gardener and Matron at Rhode Hill. Frank Hutchings had an amazing record of service at Rhode Hill having begun his career fifty one years previously when he was employed by Alban Woodroffe as a gardener's boy. He was one of a team of six gardeners, whose first job on autumn mornings was to remove every fallen leaf from the grass by 10.00 am!

Karen Smith (nee Mace) a boarder at Rhode Hill from 1981 to 1988 has written the following:

The A – Z of life as a boarder at Rhode Hill

April Fools Day, a licence to cause havoc; cling film on the toilet seats, blue food colouring in the milk jugs …
Bumpy, the forbidden short-cut from school (whose footprints were those in the wet concrete?!)
Christmas – a magical time; skits, dorm and cake competitions.
Day bugs (our name for non-boarders).
Easter egg hunt; searching for the cream egg with your name on it.

Forfeits and dares after lights out. My favourite memory was asking someone to go to the top of the house and roll the toilet paper all the way to the bottom. When caught the culprit offered "my friend has a cold!".
Gated for a whole term in the Fifth Form for going to a party uninvited. (We WERE invited!).
Harcombe Discos, the highlight of EVERY term.
Illness – anyone remember the banana custard bug?!
Jobs, jobs, jobs.
Kajagoogoo, Duran Duran; the heart throbs of the day.
Loading bay, the place to go for a lift back from school (buried under 80+ bags!).
Midnight feasts (yes they really happened!).
Night-time games; stations, hurdling over the towel racks …
Over 80 teenage girls living together in harmony!!!!!! Not a hormone in sight ….
Piling into the TV room on a Thursday night to watch Top of the Pops.
Quiet for prep, overseen by power crazy Sixth Formers.
Report at 4.30 (4.15 if you had been really naughty, or so I heard!)
Shoe check by power crazy fourth formers!
Toast, dripping with butter, for supper.
Up rookery (another forbidden place!).
Visits to town on a Saturday afternoon to buy the latest single from Woolworths and a quarter of pear drops.
Woodman (Matron) and her magic cold-zapping potion lemon and gees (linctus)
Xmas shopping trips to Exeter.
Years have passed but there are …
Zo many fond memories!!

In July 1982 Mr and Mrs Draper and their three children left Rhode Hill to move to Bridport, after seven happy years as houseparents. Great sadness was expressed at their departure. During their time at Rhode Hill they established many deep-rooted traditions and would be remembered for their kindness and concern for the many girls that had been under their care. Mr and Mrs Ayers took over in September 1982. Mr Ayres was an SEN teacher who had been teaching at the school since January 1980.

The Dining Hall at Rhode Hill

The School on the Hill

In March 1985 it was announced that Mr Tom Woodman, the indefatigable mini-bus driver and "the very handyman" at Rhode Hill planned to retire in the summer, after twenty years at the boarding house. With Tom's retirement the last link with the well-known Lyme Regis/Axminster railway line, known as the "Bluebell Line", was to be severed as Woodroffe "inherited" some of the staff when the line closed in 1965. Tom was the engine driver of "Lyme Billy", one of the Venerable Adams 4-4-2 tank engines, beloved of railway photographers. He was at the controls for the last journey of the train through the picturesque countryside between Lyme Regis and Axminster.

In 1986 Mr and Mrs Ayers left the boarding house and this marked a period of change with Mr and Mrs Colin Pemberton taking over until 1988 and Miss Kabia and Mr Chambers standing in until the appointment of Mr and Mrs Roy Sleigh in 1989.

Mr and Mrs Sleigh remained in charge until 1993 when Mr and Mrs John Ennals took over as Resident Houseparents. This was the year that Harcombe House closed and for the first time in its history Rhode Hill was accommodating both girl and boy boarders. Two Sixth Form girl boarders reflected on this change.

The Old Stable Block

"*Since the beginning of this school year Rhode Hill has changed dramatically. Mr and Mrs Ennals became our Houseparents and the senior boys from St Andrews moved up to Rhode Hill to join the rest of the boarders. As well as new Houseparents and the addition of senior boys, Rhode Hill also had to adapt to the new Head, Mr Redman, and his family taking up residence in a caravan in the grounds for a short period!*

The Sixth Form have managed to mix together well. The social life has been enjoyed by everyone with parties and Lyme night life! We were also lucky enough to become domesticated with our own washing machine, tumble drier and microwave which have been put to good use. Part-time jobs are always encouraged in the Sixth Form and many of us take up this opportunity......At the weekend we all enjoy riding the motor bike and driving the car in the grounds... Relationships between the staff and pupils have strengthened over the year, making Rhode Hill a closer place to live. Year 11 and the Upper Sixth have now reached the end of their life at Rhode Hill and to mark this sad occasion Year 11 went out skittling in Uplyme and the Upper Sixth went for an Italian meal in Seaton. We sometimes complain about Rhode Hill but we will miss it really!"[1]

During the Autumn Term 1994 boarding was inspected by Mr Brian FitzGerald, a Government advisor and former HMI, who was now a Registered Inspector. In his report he stated: *"This is a good boarding house with a pleasant, welcoming and friendly ambience. The standards of care and welfare of boarders are good. The staff give freely of their time and effort to the best interests of the children and young people in their charge. It is clear that this is appreciated by the boys and girls in boarding. Boarders are welcoming, friendly and well behaved. They clearly grow in self-confidence in the time they are in the house and they impressed with their willingness to talk openly and share their thoughts and feelings about life at Woodroffe".*

Mr and Mrs Ennals took over responsibility for the management of catering at the house in June 1995 and during the Easter holidays a German Band, with connections with the Town Band, stayed at the house for five days. The fifty three German musicians gave a joint concert at school with the Town Band and the Madrigal Group. In the summer holidays a German summer school also made use of the boarding facilities.

In February 1996 a presentation was made to Mr Peter Furzey, the house driver, handyman and gardener, to mark thirty years loyal service.

Unfortunately, after long and careful deliberation, the Governing Body decided that due to the national decline in demand for boarding places, the facility at Rhode Hill was no longer viable and the decision was made to close the house in July 1996. Arrangements were made to transfer the remaining thirty two boarders to Allhallows where they were to be accommodated in a wing, newly named Rhode House, under the care of Housemaster, Mr Griffith, and Matron, Mrs Philbrick.

The School Prospectus in 1998/1999 outlined the arrangements for boarding pupils who had transferred to Rhode House at Allhallows College.

"Allhallows College is an Independent co-educational boarding and day school for pupils aged from 11 – 18. It occupies a 140 hectare site combining playing fields, agricultural land, nature reserve, cliffs and beach set in an important geographical area of the south coast. The College has a sports complex incorporating a magnificent sports hall, all weather playing area, a heated swimming pool, a rifle range and facilities for climbing, abseiling, riding, fishing and canoeing. Older pupils are able to join the College's Coastguard Unit and Fire Service.

Rhode House is a wing of the main school building with its own entrance. There are clearly defined dormitory areas for boys and girls alongside mixed social accommodation. The Head of House is an Allhallows Master, resident on the school site, and he is assisted by a Matron who is resident in Rhode House. Other Care Staff are employed on a part-time basis, including teaching staff from Woodroffe.

---

[1] Extract from the Governors' Report to Parents dated 1993/1994

Self-discipline is encouraged throughout the house. A basic framework of house rules exists, gradually relaxing as the pupils get older leading to a fairly independent, though still supervised environment in the Sixth Form. Older pupils are encouraged to set an example and lead the younger ones in the team, in house duties and routines. Boarders are bussed to and from school. After-school activities are encouraged and most boarders get involved in groups such as CCF, Duke of Edinburgh Award Scheme, drama, music and sport. Meals are taken with other College boarders in the well appointed dining room. Visits to larger towns for shopping, ice rinks, cinemas or sight-seeing are arranged at weekends according to demands. Other activities are arranged from time to time and Woodroffe pupils are eligible to join in the College's musical, dramatic and sporting activities, including team games. "[2]

An Upper Sixth boarder at Rhode House, Allhallows gave an insight into the new boarding arrangements from a pupil's perspective: "*This has to be one of the strangest arrangements brought to boarding in the South West. A state boarding house was to close and join with a private boarding school and I was to be part of it! First impressions – large imposing building in which we would live. No sign of life, except for the one or two teachers left wandering the courtyard. (The Allhallows pupils returned later than us.) We were shown to our house, where we were greeted by the familiar smiling face of Mr Williams, and two smiling strangers who were named "Houseparents".*

As the weeks sped by Allhallows started to show signs of life. Socialising took place and friends were made. I think that the unusual mix of boarding has developed fast and worked well. I am sure that visitors would find it hard to distinguish Woodroffe boarders from their Allhallows counterparts. The move would have been particularly hard if it were not for the support of Mr Williams, who stood by us throughout the year, and the kindness of our Houseparents, Mrs Philbrick and Mr Griffith, who whilst building Rhode House up to strength, made sure we were accepted and classed as part of Allhallows College by staff and pupils."[3]

Sadly the boarding arrangement with Allhallows came to an abrupt end when in Easter 1998 the College also closed its doors. By this time there were only a handful of Woodroffe boarders remaining at Rhode House and these were accommodated locally until they had completed their examination studies. Shortly after its closure in 1996 Rhode Hill was sold. The new owners converted the property and apportioned the grounds to provide a total of seven dwellings, three in the main house, three in the stable block and the Lodge Cottage. The three properties in the main house are now referred to as Talbot House (the central wing), The Park House (the west wing) and The Red House (the east wing).

(*Historical information taken from two sources - notes held at the Philpot Museum in Lyme Regis courtesy of David Mostyn and notes published by Mike Fairley in the school's newsletter dated December 1976. Photographs courtesy of Peter Rickard*)

---

[2] Extract from the School Prospectus dated 1998/1999
[3] Extract from the Parents' Bulletin dated November 1997

CHAPTER 20 – THE MADRIGAL GROUP

The Madrigal Group was founded in the Autumn of 1961 by Brian Manners. The idea of forming such a group came about when Mr Manners was talking to some Sixth Form pupils about a Madrigal Group he had started at his previous school. Initially there were fifteen members in the group who were volunteers, but it wasn't long before entry was by audition and a pre-requisite was the ability to read music. At this time the Senior Choir was very strong but it had over one hundred members, which made it difficult in terms of transport when it came to attending festivals. Brian Manners decided to start a smaller group, hopefully singing to the same standard, which could travel easily. The minimum age requirement was fifteen years, as this was the stipulation for competitions.

Denise Hayes, one of the founder members wrote in the school magazine:

"When Mr Manners first announced his intention of starting a Madrigal Group everyone was a little dubious. Mainly, I think, because most people were not very sure what a Madrigal is, let alone how to sing one. In spite of people's doubt and the alarming prospect of an audition to get in, the Madrigal Group prospered. Everyone was delighted when Mr Manners broke the happy news that we were to going to sing at the Bath Music Festival. But when it actually came time to sing, I do not think you could find fifteen more nervous people anywhere. It was in an adult class so we felt quite proud of ourselves when we came first with our own choice, but unfortunately the set piece pulled us down so that we ended up third with 85%. We travelled back from Bath in pitch darkness as the lights on the school bus had fused; no-one seemed to mind. We sang all the way back except for a brief stop at Crewkerne to buy the usual chips.

We sang next at the West Dorset Music Festival at Bridport which is not competitive. From there we went to the Paignton Music Festival, where we faced the handicap of only eight people being allowed to participate. As Mr Manners could not decide who should compete he drew names out of a hat with the exception of Sally, who had to sing as she was the main support of the tenors. (No, this is not a mis-print, they rely on her for their high notes). We came second this time to a highly efficient adult group. I think we would have done better if everyone could have sung, as the eight felt more nervous than usual because they were so isolated. The Madrigal Group had now increased its numbers to nineteen. We made our debut at Speech Day when Brian Davies excelled himself singing the solo part of the "Turtle Dove".[1]

Within two or three years the group had grown in size. There were seven people to each of the five voices plus two reserves which made a total of forty five. It was necessary to have such a large number as the group could be depleted from time to time by illness, exams and other unforeseen circumstances and there needed to be a ready supply of fully trained substitutes, particularly for competitions and the BBC. Over the lifetime of the Madrigal Group it is estimated that some 450 singers were amongst its ranks. Soloists were rarely featured, it was strictly a group activity.

---

[1] Extract from the School Magazine dated 1962

The Madrigal Group in the mid-Sixties

The group worked hard to reach a very high standard and to maintain it. Boys and girls rehearsed once a week separately and the whole group met twice a week to rehearse together, mainly during the lunch break. In time the Madrigal Group sang a short piece at the start of morning assembly and these were often written by pupils in the group.

In the late 1970s/early 1980s a self-management system was put in place for the Madrigal Group, whereby a representative for each of the five voices attended regular meetings with staff. In this way there was a pupil input into all decisions made relating to the group and members were also able to offer their views when any problems arose. It was always Brian Manners' intention that the group should be run democratically and on a self-regulatory basis and over the years this arrangement worked very well.

Initially uniform was worn for all public appearances but this was frowned upon in competitions, particularly when competing against adult choirs, so for a time school uniform was scrapped. Later pupils reverted to wearing uniform which featured a special tie which was presented to each member after one year's service. These ties were designed by George Lloyd-Jones and the first batch was presented to Madrigal Group members by Lyme Regis Town Council, the Mayor at that time being Councillor Alec Richards. As the group began competing against continental and American choirs the girls started to wear long, navy blue, wrap around skirts.

The School on the Hill

At one of the Eisteddfods the group was befriended by Brian Kaye of the King Singers. He noted that the singers did not have T-shirts to identify them and he eventually performed at the school to help them raise funds to have a specially embroidered T-shirt made, to wear at competitions. Adult helpers who escorted the group to the various competitions and festivals were each presented with one of the Madrigal Group ties and in time a red embroidered headscarf was designed for lady helpers.

When travelling, especially abroad, there needed to be a high ratio of adults to pupils and initially the group was escorted by Brian and Dorothy Manners and Ernest Wellings. By 1980, due to the number of singers, a support group was formed comprising Ron and Margaret Hercock and Bob and Elaine Kendrick. Ron Hercock looked after finances, Margaret Hercock was a qualified nurse, Bob Kendrick was in charge of transport and Elaine Kendrick looked after the girls, took their rehearsals and was Brian Manners' deputy in an emergency. No pianist was required for performances as the group sang unaccompanied.

The Madrigal Group sang madrigals, anthems, part songs and spirituals and they even tried their hand at singing in the style of the Swingle Singers. In latter years Mr Manners also bought licences and arranged pop songs, including the work of the Beatles, which the group performed to much acclaim. For the visit to Germany in 1969 the group had to learn to sing "Oh No John!" in German – no mean feat!

It was the proud boast of the Madrigal Group that they had sung in every parish church within a fifteen mile radius of Lyme Regis, including the now defunct Congregational Church in Church Street. They performed at the Guildhall, the Assembly Rooms and the Pump Room in Bath, the Palace Theatre in Paignton and the Fairfield Hall in Croydon. Locally they appeared at Pilsdon Manor, Catheston Manor, Sadborow, Colfox School in Bridport, Broadwey School in Weymouth, The Priory School in Exeter, the local Golf Club, the Marine Theatre, the Regent Cinema, the Buena Vista Hotel, the Royal Lion Hotel, on the Cobb for RNLI Week, at various pubs and even on street corners!!

The group also broadcast with the BBC virtually every year from 1980 to 1990. They appeared with Brian Johnston in "Down Your Way" and with Harry Secombe in "Highways"; they sang at a BBC Songs of Praise at Exeter Cathedral and they took part in the radio programme "Let the People Sing", which was recorded at Exeter Cathedral Chapter House. It is worth noting that when a television or radio appearance took place, the group had to travel to the studio and performed live. However, on one memorable occasion the BBC came to the Madrigal Group, when Sue Lawley visited the school to hear the group sing. In 1969 they also broadcast for the American Forces Network, and Italian and German TV during the trip to Berlin.

Invitations were accepted to sing in Holland, Germany, Belgium, Luxembourg, Austria and Yugoslavia, and the group performed at Konzertsall in Berlin, Kippenbergschule in Bremen, The Castle and the British Embassy in Belgrade, the Rektors Palace in Dubrovnik, St Michael's Church in Luxembourg and St George's Church in Berlin.

They were even invited to sing in America in 1983. However, this trip never took place as air fares rocketed due to the oil crisis and the high cost of travel meant that the proposed visit had to be called off. Many years later, when Malcolm Matthews had taken over leadership of the group following the retirement of Brian Manners, a visit to America was arranged to Lyme, Connecticut in conjunction with the Lyme Regis Junior Band. The American band they visited then returned to Lyme Regis on an exchange visit and a highly successful joint concert was held in the school hall.

The group also regularly travelled to Llangollen to take part in the Eisteddfods. They never won a trophy there as the standard was extremely high. The best they ever achieved was to come sixth out of an international field of thirty. However, their Trophy list was impressive and included the Ilchester Cup won in Weymouth on three occasions, the Kingsbridge Cup won in Paignton, also three times, the Will Channing Shield won in Exeter and the Town Trophy won in Paignton in 1968 when the group achieved the highest mark in the whole festival.

Llangollen International Eisteddfod 1983

Travel, particularly foreign travel, was expensive so the group held fund-raising events to cover costs with any shortfall covered by the school's Hope Wright Fund. The Rotary Club of Lyme Regis were extremely generous in their support and often contact was made with Rotary Clubs in the countries to which the group travelled. It is estimated that altogether the Madrigal Group travelled over ten thousand miles.

In 1969, from 31st August to 14th September, twenty nine singers, escorted by Brian and Dorothy Manners and Ernest Wellings, set off for Berlin to attend a Music Festival, travelling via Dover and Ostend and on to Amsterdam where the party enjoyed some sight-seeing including a boat trip on the canals. Following a stop at Arnhem, where a visit was made to the museum and the war cemetery, the party moved on to Munster where overnight accommodation was provided at the HQ of the Royal Greenjackets.

The next stop was Bremen where the group put on a concert at a school, with pupils staying overnight with German families. The final leg of the journey to Berlin involved crossing the East German frontier. On the Sunday morning several songs were sung at a local Forces church. These were recorded and later broadcast on the Forces Network in Cologne. The following evening the group made its contribution to the Festival by appearing at Konzertsall Bundesalle, where sixteen songs were performed. The groups' final appearance took place the next evening when it took part in a concert which also featured a Scottish Dance Group and The Johannischer Choir, a large choir from Germany.

Prior to their departure from Berlin the party was entertained to lunch at the British Consulate. On its final evening the group attended the Opera to see a magnificent performance of Puccini's "Tosca". The journey home via Brussels included a six hour delay at the East German frontier but eventually everyone arrived safely back at Lyme Regis, exhausted but happy.

In 1971 the group travelled to Dubrovnik via Dover, Calais, Brussels, Koblenz, Rudesheim, Bonn, Klagenfurt, Salzburg, Beograd and Sarajevo. The return journey took the party through Split, Ljubjana, Venice, Milan, Basel, Luxembourg, Brussels, Calais and then back to Dover. The group left the UK on 19th August returning on 11th September. The group comprised nineteen girls and fourteen boys and was led once again by Brian and Dorothy Manners and Ernest Wellings.

After spending five days on the coach, with a bit of sight-seeing in between, the group reached Yugoslavia on 24th August and was immediately struck by the poverty they witnessed. Yugoslavia's only motorway was described as being the width of the Crewkerne Road at home with a farm track surface of rough concrete.

On the evening of 25th August the Madrigal Group performed at an open air concert at a Youth Camp in Belgrade. Many of the group were appalled at the conditions in the camp which was occupied by boys who volunteered three weeks of their holidays to help their country by building roads. These boys formed the audience for the open air concert and needless to say, did not fully appreciate the entertainment that was laid on for them. However, the evening was rounded off with a visit to the most modern hotel in New Belgrade which enabled the group to see another side of life in Yugoslavia. Sight-seeing the next day took in a visit to a mosque and an orthodox church, following which the group performed at the British Embassy for staff and their families. In the evening there was another open-air performance, this time at a flood-lit park where the group sang ten songs, all of which were well received.

The next day the journey to Sarajevo took nine hours. Heading for Dubrovnik the weather turned hot and sunny and as they descended the mountain the party got its first view of the Adriatic coastline. After a couple of days sight-seeing the group went for an audition at the Rektor's Palace which led to an offer to perform at a concert there on 4th September.

The journey home included short stops in Venice and Milan, before crossing into Switzerland and travelling up the St Gothard Pass where the party enjoyed the most spectacular sights of the trip. A stop in Luxembourg included a performance at a church with acoustics as good as those at the Rektor's Palace in Dubrovnik. The journey home continued into Belgium, on to Brussels and then to Calais where the party caught the ferry to Dover before heading back to Lyme Regis. All who took part in the trip described it as truly memorable and the experience of a lifetime.

The trip to the 10th Youth and Music Festival in Vienna, which took place from 9th to 18th July 1981 involved a year of hard fund-raising in which many parents were involved. In particular John and Pat Richards organised and catered for the annual "Wine and Cheese". Many local organisations also helped the group to accumulate over £4,300, including a donation of £1,000 from the Rotary Club of Lyme Regis.

The party of forty two singers, escorted this time by Brian Manners, Ron and Margaret Hercock and Bob and Elaine Kendrick, flew from Gatwick and arrived in Austria to temperatures touching 91°F. A long coach journey to Krems followed where accommodation was provided in a hostel. Various sight-seeing excursions took place before the party moved to Vienna. Day three of the visit saw the festival opening ceremony with gruelling rehearsals beforehand held outside in the baking heat. This was the first time that the various orchestras and choirs had sung together and initially was rather chaotic. Performers came from America and Hungary to take part.

After the concert, which was followed by a reception at the Rathaus, a disco was held for all festival participants. The next day the group sang at a church service held in a church in which Schubert once performed. The acoustics were fantastic and the congregation was very appreciative. During the afternoon and evening, rehearsals took place for the performance of Glück's Orfeo. The conductor expected professional standards and had no sympathy for those suffering from tiredness and the intense heat.

On day five the group took part in a competition at the Haus der Begegnuny followed by more Glück rehearsals. However, the group managed a bit of sightseeing when it squeezed in a visit to the Belvedere Palace, the summer residence of a family of the Viennese nobility, which was built in the style of Versailles. By now although it was still warm, heavy rain had arrived and this meant that open air rehearsals were no longer possible. The concert in the evening, attended by nearly eight hundred people, was spectacular, with the soloists receiving three curtain calls. Even the very exacting conductor was pleased! By the end of the evening many of the performers were suffering from heat exhaustion.

The group gave its last performance at an old people's home the next day where it was given a very warm welcome. The day was rounded off with a visit to the fair with many enjoying a ride on the giant big wheel, which provided a spectacular view of the whole of Vienna, the dodgems and the roller coaster.

The following day the group went to a matinee performance given by the competition winners at which it was clear that the standard of the other choirs was extremely high. Choirs from Poland and Switzerland tied for first place, the Canadians were second and the choir from Witchitah Falls (from Texas) tied with the Norwegians for third place. It was eventually announced that the Madrigal Group had come sixth, with an overall rating of excellent. A choir from Sherborne beat them by just one point. Sightseeing and shopping followed with some of the boys playing a football match against members of a Cardiff Choir and the day was rounded off with a celebration of the excellent competition results.

The final day was spent shopping and sightseeing before the long trip home began with a train journey. Choirs from Newcastle and Sherborne were also on the train which took the party through Bavaria, up the Rhine Valley, through Brussels and on to Ostend where the party caught the ferry. The final leg passed off without mishap and the party arrived back in Lyme Regis at 1.30 pm on 18th July. Tributes were paid to Brian Manners, Ron and Margaret Hercock and Bob and Elaine Kendrick who had led their party and coped with all the problems and tensions. The group's final trip with Brian Manners was to Gronau in West Germany in 1990.

When Brian Manners retired later that year the new Head of Music, Malcolm Matthews took over leadership of the group, which continued to prosper. When he in turn retired in 1998 the group disbanded. However music still plays a very important part in the life of the school and the annual concerts and cabaret performances showcase the many musical talents of the school, which now features a very popular Jazz Band, an excellent Orchestra, a Wind Band, the renowned Early Music Group (under the direction of John Seabrook – Head of History) and many other ensembles. Although the emphasis now is more on instrumental music rather than choral, the school has an enthusiastic and well supported Senior Choir which includes staff members as well as pupils.

The Madrigal Group will always have a special place in the history of the school and all those lucky enough to have been a member have many treasured memories of being part of such an illustrious group. Many former members travelled huge distances to attend a reunion several years ago and at the end of the evening enjoyed singing together once again for old times' sake. Surprisingly enough most could still remember their parts and the dynamics!

It is worthy of note that the reputation of the Madrigal Group was such that even to this day Mr Manners still receives requests for the group to perform.

(*Information and photographs provided by Brian Manners*).

CHAPTER 21 – NINE DECADES OR DRAMA[1]

Drama has always played a huge part in the life of the school, ranging from light sketches to Shakespeare to full scale musical productions. Over the years hundreds of pupils and staff have enjoyed working together to provide first class entertainment for parents and friends.

In addition to school productions, pupils have taken part in high profile community plays such as "The Reckoning", written and directed by Ann Jellicoe in 1978, "The Western Women", also written by Ann Jellicoe, and performed in 1984 and during the Autumn Term of 1999 the school staged "Torchbearers" in conjunction with the National Youth Music Theatre.

Originally, drama productions were produced and directed by members of the English Department but a separate Drama Department was created in September 1997 when the subject was established in its own right and Ellen Howard (now Mrs Kumar) was appointed as Head of Drama. The Department has since grown in strength and has benefited greatly from the state of the art facilities provided in the Thornton Pearn Studio, built in 1999, and the appointment of a second Drama specialist, Anne Cruwys-Finnigan. She and Ellen Kumar are now joint Heads of the Drama Department and together they work hard to ensure that the high standard of performance, that has always been a tradition at the school, is maintained.

Today Drama remains a popular subject with pupils across the school. Key Stage 3 pupils (Years 7 to 9) greatly enjoy their weekly Drama lessons, relishing the chance to explore themes/issues, playtexts and theatrical genres and creating their own drama which reflects their own experiences. GCSE and A level uptake has grown significantly and it is now seen as a subject for boys as well as girls. As ever, participation in Junior Drama Club, school productions and theatre visits remains high.

Unfortunately there is no central record of every production staged at the school over the years. Information has been gleaned from a variety of sources and is very patchy. In some cases there is just an indication of the work performed and the date, in others there is a cast list, and for some performances there is a critique written either by a member of staff, a pupil or the local press.

Whilst acknowledging that the list of productions is not complete, it is hoped that this chapter will give a fleeting glimpse of the huge range of performances that have been staged at the school across the decades, and that it will help ex-pupils to recall their enjoyment in taking part in school productions.

---

[1] Grateful thanks are expressed to Mr David Coates for his many contributions to this Chapter including photographs

List of Plays	
1928	The Grand Cham's Diamond
1929	The Thread of Scarlet/Between the Soup and the Savoury
1931	X = O A Night of The Trojan War
1933	Scenes from St Joan
1938	Alice in Wonderland/Mr Sampson/The House with the Twisty Windows
1945	1066 and All That/Dick Whittington
1946	The Stolen Prince/The Old Lady Shows Her Medals/Country Dances
1948	Androcles and the Lion
1950	The Princess and The Woodcutter/Down on the Farm
1952	The Idea
1954	Toad of Toad Hall/The Dear Departed/Piper's Pool
1955	Jonah and the Whale
1956	The Stolen Prince/The Coventry Nativity Play/It's Great to be Young
1960	Widdershins/The Poetasters of Ispahan/King Melon
1961	Separate Tables/The Merchant of Venice
1962	The Rape of the Belt
1963	Turandot/The Pied Piper of Hamelin
1964	The Pied Piper/Widdershins/Turandot
1964	Grand Spectacular
1966	The Magic Flute
1967	Hansel and Gretel
1968	Amahl and the Night Visitors/Noah's Flood
1969	As You Like It
1970	The Merchant of Venice
1973	Che Guevara
1975	Pygmalion
1976	The Thwarting of Baron Bolligrew
1976	An Elizabethan Evening
1977	The Importance of Being Ernie/Festival of One-Act Plays/A Christmas Carol
1978	The Ghost Train
1978	The Reckoning
1979	Oliver
1979	Romeo and Juliet
1980	A Midsummer Night's Dream/The Chimney Sweeps/Black Comedy
1982	The Real Inspector Hound/The Birds
1983	Twelfth Night
1985	The Crucible
1987	Holy Moses/Under Milk Wood
1988	The Caucasian Chalk Circle
1989	Black Comedy/The Real Inspector Hound

1992	Dr Faustus
1993	Oh! What a Lovely War
1995	In Holland Stands a House
2003	Oliver
2004	Yeh-Shen
2004	Where the Wild Things Are
2005	Little Shop of Horrors

Drama in the 1920s

End of the Autumn Term 1928: The Drama Society read "**The Grand Cham's Diamond**".

End of the Spring Term 1929: "**The Thread of Scarlet**" (Boys) and "**Between the Soup and the Savoury**" (Girls)

Drama in the 1930s

Thursday, 29th October 1931 (Speech Day): X = O A Night of the Trojan War (a poetic play by John Drinkwater)

Pronax:)	Greek Soldiers	E D Lillington
Salvius:)		H F Phillips
Ilus:)	Trojan Soldiers	J W Small
Capys:)		J Dawson
A Greek Sentinel:		J Hoskins
A Greek Servant:		J F Watton

Friday, 21st July 1933 (Speech Day): Scenes from "**Saint Joan**" (George Bernard Shaw)

Captain Robert de Baudricourt:	J F Dawson
Steward:	R C Nute
Joan d'Arc:	N M Collins
Squire Bertrand de Poulengey:	D Mawdsley
The Lord Chamberlain (de la Tremouille):	R C Nute
The Archbishop:	D J Owen
Page:	W Prescott
Gilles de Rais (Bluebeard):	D A Phillips
Captain la Hire:	J Goodfellow
The Duchess de la Tremouille:	G M Forster
Lady in Waiting:	M E Jefford
Man at Arms:	H A Dickenson
Dunois:	D Large
Page:	D Watton

1938 - The school's Dramatic Society presented three short plays at the end of the Autumn Term in 1938. The first was **"Alice in Wonderland" in five acts**, the cast being drawn mainly from the junior forms and the production was directed by Miss Gordon.

Alice:	Mary Watton
The Duchess:	M Stark
The Cook:	B Aldridge
The Hatter:	V Batten
The March Hare:	W Rutherford
The Dormouse:	E Street
The Cheshire Cat:	W Ball and B Gage
The White Rabbit:	E Hodder (the White Rabbit),
The King of Hearts:	E Camplin
Gardeners:	P Perry, C Lancashire, W Stapleforth
Executioner:	B Snell
Gryphon:	R Prescott
Mock Turtle:	D Sellars

The second play was **"Mr. Sampson" by Charles Lee**, a story of a farm labourer who cannot decide which of two elderly sisters he wishes to marry. The play was produced by Miss Carson.

Mr Sampson:	W Potter
Catherine Stevens:	D Shave
Caroline Stevens:	P Hunt

The final play was **"The House with the Twisty Windows"** by Mary Packington, a tragedy which dealt with a number of English people who find themselves in a cellar-prison in Petrograd during the Bolshevik Revolution in 1918. All parts were taken by members of staff who it is stated "certainly reproduced the desired tension and "creepy" atmosphere". Mr Watton, as James Roper "delighted his audience by the way in which he kept up his legal air even in the midst of adversity".

Derrick Moore:	Mr Kemp	Anne Sorrell:	Miss Gordon
Heather Sorrell:	Miss Hoare	Teresa, Lady Ponting:	Miss Carson
James Roper, KC:	Mr Watton	Stephan:	Mr G A Taylor
Charles Clive:	Mr W E Taylor		

Drama in the 1940s

1945: "1066 and all that" – a musical comedy staged by the School Dramatic Society, after a lapse of five years.

Troubadour:	Brock
Henry VII (and several other parts):	Camplin
The Crusader and Colonel Bygadsby	Bevan
The Crusader's Wife:	Ann Thomas
Katherine Parr and wife of Common Man:	Joan Enticott

Queen Elizabeth:	Jillian Ramage
Julius Caesar and Henry V :	Kemp
Mrs Bygadsby:	Kathleen Smith
Sergeant and Christopher Columbus:	Crate
The Common Man:	Neil Adams

The play took the audience through the realms of history in short humorous scenes, each depicting a different period. The Common Man in the first scene fell asleep in the Hall of Fame and was transported in his dreams through history. In turn he found himself among the Romans, Crusaders, Plantagenets, Elizabethans, Georgians and the Victorians and his adventures among them were extremely amusing.

The part of the Common Man was played by Neil Adams and he was congratulated for his skilful acting which required him to sustain his part right through the play which he managed most successfully. The acting of the whole cast was also excellent as was the singing of the chorus. By all accounts this production was a resounding success and all involved were congratulated on a high quality performance which had involved many changes of scenery and a large cast.

Christmas 1945 - For the first time in its history the School Dramatic Society staged a pantomime **"Dick Whittington"** written and produced by Dennis Ellis. The story was told in traditional pantomime style and three performances were given to well attended, appreciative audiences.

The School on the Hill

Chorus:	Janet Worth	Idle Jack:	Leonard Tuner
Cook:	June Bass	Alice Fitzwarren:	Jillian Ramage
Dick Whittington:	Rita Turner	His Cat:	Pamela Morton
Captain Breeze:	Harold Lanfear	Sultan of Morocco:	David Hallet
Spick:	Derek Gaitch	Span:	Jack Helm
1st Passer By:	John Richards	2nd Passer By:	Barbara O'Kell
Grand Vizier:	Michael Kemp	Chief Justice:	Harold Lanfear
Lord Treasurer:	Philip Parkhurst	Keeper of Palace	Tony Broom
Guards:	Nona Shaw and	Yvonne Dawes	
Captain of the Guards:	Barbara O'Kell	Scribe :	Elizabeth Powell
Messenger:	Jill Taylor	Dancer:	Zena Furnis
Mrs. Fitzwarren:	Ann Thomas	Ald. Fitzwarren:	Michael Kemp
Broker's Men:	Derek Gaitch and Jack Helm		
Maid:	Jill Taylor	Soloist:	June Bass
Dancing Girls:	Joy Smith, Joan Gollop, Jean Wheller, Dorothy Turner, Margaret Smith, Margaret McNeil, Maribel Hastead and Barbara Larcombe		

July 1946: Three productions – Critique as follows: "*Dan Totheroh's* **"Stolen Prince"** *brought eleven pupils to the boards for the first time and none disappointed. B Boalch appealed as the young prince and June Upjohn made a confident and promising beginning. We shall see more of her. T Prince, L Turner and M Rugg all made interesting and capable debuts. The Matthews brothers played soldiers solidly and convincingly. J Helm governed the properties on the stage with an attractive air of bewilderment tempered with his characteristic humour. He is building a reputation. From H M Beaven as the Chorus we got all the polish we expect from him. P Parkhurst dealt faithfully with the small part of the Executioner. The most interesting part was Cynthia Rattenbury's "Nurse". She played with a steadiness worthy of a more experienced performer and sang beautifully. Having so soon learned the lesson of "stillness" on the stage, she can look forward to a highly successful career in school drama.*"

Delightful Picture – "*The setting, although it depended on costume in the absence of orthodox scenery, made a truly delightful picture. The peach blossom against the black, the warm breeze of the autumn leaves against the delicate greens of gown and shawl were typical glimpses of the blend. Employing, as it did, so many novices a certain raggedness of pace could have been forgiven. It is high praise to say there was none of this. Only a little slowness at the climax marred the tempo. Miss Male's music was ably rendered and supported by the orchestra, B Chubb, R Keeley and B Wheaton. It was a refreshing piece of unsophistication. Miss Gordon is to be congratulated.*"

"*Barrie's* **"The Old Lady Shows her Medals"** *was the very stuff of theatre. It called for characterisation first, last and all the time. Again we were not disappointed. M J Kemp, as the soldier, put up a performance that was in the best class of schoolboy acting. He was all that he was supposed to be. Nona Shaw played excellently as the Old Lady, a part that has everything to tax the most accomplished actress. It would, of course, have been too much to expect complete representation of such a role by a girl of fourteen. The trio of charladies, R Turner, M McNeil and B O'Kell, found easier characters and settled in them well. A H Beaven appeared again, gave a convincing clergyman with one* *particularly delightful exhibition of flexibility. It is to the credit of the six performers and Miss Carson that the production was so enjoyable and satisfying."*

Country Dances – *"The country dances were delightfully executed and set. The physical training display, excellent in itself, might have seemed a little out of place amidst the dramatic activities. Yet the quality of both PT and dancing, the grace and rhythm, leads one to suggest that Miss Stote Blandy and the girls would find a fertile field in mime and simple ballet."* [2]

January 1948: "Androcles and the Lion" by Shaw – *"In this play comedy and tragedy fused. K Symes, as Androcles, struck just the right note of timid, self-deprecatory humour, while Nona Shaw, as his wife Megaera, produced a gem of characterisation. M J Kemp, as the Captain, gave his usual polished performance and Patricia Gladding, making a first appearance in a "star" part, as Lavinia, scored a personal triumph. F Foxwell was, of course, ideally suited by his physique to the part of Ferrovius, but his innate kindliness prevented him giving full reign to the ferocity for which his part called. On the other hand J W Grant, as the Centurion, produced a formidable gruffness of manner and toughness of action which, on at least one night, literally "shook" another member of the cast. Compton James' interpretation of Caesar was a clearly envisaged one, and crisp in its attack, while mention must be made of C.S. Wilson's competent Lion – a most difficult and well-played part. One most creditable thing was that for most of the large cast it was a "first performance" and the result not only speaks well for the very hard work put in by the producer, Dennis Ellis, and the players themselves, but is a happy augury for the future."* [3]

Drama in the 1950s

3rd & 4th March 1950: March Medley - This was a light entertainment performed by the school and staff and consisted of a Concert and two plays. The Concert was described as a great success with Miss Green joining the ranks of the choir and the Headmaster conducting the music. In addition to the choir there two vocal solos by Cynthia Rattenbury and three clarinet solos by David Hall.

The first play was entitled **"The Princess and the Woodcutter"** by A A Milne, *"a fanciful humorous little comedy"* it was performed by the lower school and produced by Miss Gordon, Miss Stainton was responsible for the dancing and Miss Male was at the piano. The play was introduced by Hazel Hopkins. The cast included Ann Stapleforth as the Queen, Buik as the Woodcutter, Judith Williams the Princess, Ramage was *"the pompous little King"* and three Princes (Red, Blue and Yellow) were played by Bosence, R D Wright and Storer. A little Minuet which closed the play was performed by G Payne, D Rugg, A Stapleforth, J Williams, Gay, Ramage, Buik and Bosence.

The second play, entitled **"Down on the Farm"** by Ivor Brown, was described as a farcical, satirical sketch and was performed by members of the staff supplemented by

---

[2] Extracts from School Magazine dated July 1946
[3] Extract from School Magazine dated July 1948

pupils. The play revolved around an outsize turnip, about the size of a football, which the Ministry of Agriculture had condemned for its girth. Mr Eldridge took the part of Meadows who had moved to the country to find peace and quiet but was reduced to the verge of insanity by red tape and forms. Miss Dane was his niece, *"a charming land-girl"* and Miss Partridge, whose performance was described as *"riotously funny"* took the part of the lady sent by the Ministry to investigate the conditions of land-girls on Meadows' farm. Mr Leigh played the part of Weasel, B Telfer the City Physician, and Ernestine Jowett as Mrs Mopper *"made a delightful happy-go-lucky slap dash housekeeper"*.

Special mention was made of Miss Dane's herculean efforts, against all odds, in making and hanging the new stage curtains in about three hours, as the material had only arrived on the afternoon of the performance.[4]

July 1952: The Idea: A humorous operetta in two acts with music by Gustav Holst performed at the Summer Fete – As a conclusion to the school's first ever Fete, the school presented "The Idea". This operetta was written by Holst for the girls to perform at the school where he was teaching and was thus ideally suited to children's voices. The storyline concerns the Prime Minister who had become possessed of a wonderful idea through which he hoped to bring happiness to the people of his country. But when this idea is applied it results in discontent and wildest confusion. The populace rise up in revolt, but they are pacified by the promise to revert to the old state of things, and the assurance that the Prime Minister will NEVER have another idea.

Leading roles were taken by Robert Wheadon, delightful as the half-witted King, Ann Stapleforth, a charming comedy Queen, Brian Tunnicliffe, admirably cast as the comic Prime Minister, Rachel Perry, pure-voiced as the Prime Minister's wife, Judith Williams, appealing as Mona, the Knitting Woman and Norman Cork, the youngest in the cast and a very efficient page. The chorus was sparkling and tidy and the Musical Director, Mr Thackray, was heartily congratulated on the performance, as were Don Cameron, Stage Manager and Ernestine Jowett and Miss Satterley, who were responsible for the delightful Tyrolean costumes. Mr Edridge excelled both as Producer and replacement for the injured George Lloyd-Jones in the role of Max, shining as a singer, comedian and dancer![5]

King:	Robert Wheadon	Queen:	Ann Stapleforth
Prime Minister:	Brian Tunnicliffe	Caroline (his wife):	Rachel Perry
Max (a sentry):	Everard Lloyd-Jones	Page:	Norman Cork
Mona (knitting woman)	Judith Williams		

Members of the Chorus: Daphne Keeley, Sheila Brewer, Elizabeth Todd, Janet Long, Barbara Morris, Margaret Bennett, Ruby Hodder, Avril Thackray, Rosemary Matcham, Barbara Rattenbury, June Evans, Rachel Keeley, Roger Keeley, John Paul, Jack McGinley, Brian Wiscombe, Michael Thomas, Gwyn Llewellyn

---

[4] Extract from School Magazine dated July 1950
[5] From a report by Miss Carson in the School Magazine dated July 1952

March 1954: Toad of Toad Hall - A play from Kenneth Grahame's Book based on **"The Wind in the Willows"** by A A Milne. Music by H Fraser-Simpson. Produced by Neil Adams

"Ruby Hodder sustained the long and arduous title-role with vigour and confidence and received maximum support throughout from Badger (Jack McGinley), Water Rat (Norman Cork) and Mole (Pamela Weaver). The attractive personality of the Water Rat was vividly portrayed by Norman Cork, whose acting showed great promise. A first former, Pamela Weaver, was quite at ease on the stage as the naïve Mole, whose zest for adventure had been sharpened by the contrast between his new, crowded experiences and his hitherto obscure life at Mole End.

The numerous other characters had also responded to their training and their acting reached a high standard. Roger Keeley made the Policeman suitably indignant and bucolic, the Judge (James Cross) directed the Court proceedings with due solemnity and in this was guided by the Usher, Philip Logan who played the part (in the absence, owing to the illness of Graham Watkins) with just the necessary amount of droll inconsequence. The Gaoler (Michael Dawling) looked satisfactorily menacing, and in the Dungeon, when Toad's fortunes had reached their nadir, Mary MacDonald and Hazel Worcester convincingly represented the venal washerwoman, who for a consideration allowed Toad to impersonate her and her niece Phoebe, originator of the plan.   Ann Stapleforth brought out the earthy shrewdness of the Barge-woman whose perspicacity nearly ruined Toad's escape.   The play was introduced and rounded-off with the correct note of quietness by Sheila Enticott and Carol Bowditch, who acted the Nurse and the little girl, Marigold, in the Prologue and Epilogue.

From Alfred the horse, down to the tiniest of the field-mice, the others in the cast proved themselves good troupers one and all. The music composed by H Fraser-Simpson formed a most attractive feature of the play and this, under the direction of Reg Pocock, assisted by Judith Williams as pianist, was warmly and deservedly applauded"[6]

---

[6] Extract from School Magazine dated July 1954

The School on the Hill

Marigold:	Carol Bowditch	Nurse:	Sheila Enticott
Mole:	Pamela Weaver	Water Rat:	Norman Cork
Badger:	Jack McGinley	Toad:	Ruby Hodder
Alfred:	Micheal Green, John Warren		
Policeman:	Roger Keeley	Goaler:	Michael Dawling
Usher:	Graham Watkins	Judge:	James Cross
Turkey:	Margaret Gill	Duck:	Paul Apanasewicz
Washer-woman:	Mary Macdonald	Phoebe:	Hazel Worcester
Fox:	David Backhouse	Barge Woman:	Ann Stapleforth

Ferrets: Elizabeth Tapper, Janet Jackman, Janet Richards, Philip Logan, John Watson
Weasels: Gillian Case, Jennifer Shaw, Patricia Jerrard, Hilary Bowditch
Stoats: Barbara Whiles, Sally Rees, Joan Jeffries, Elizabeth Eades
Field Mice: Jenifer Gould, Michael Bowrah, Sheila Davison, Judith Bishop
Mama Rabbit: Rosemary Keeley   Lucy Rabbit: Hazel Cowling
Harold Rabbit: Angela Shaw   Other Rabbits: Susan Wells, Patricia O'Mahoney
The song "Wind in the Willows" was sung by Ann Stapleforth

The following two plays were performed at the summer fete in **July 1954**.

"The Dear Departed" by Stanley Houghton - This play dealt with the squabbles of a suburban family over the possessions of the dead grandfather lying upstairs. The exaggerated seriousness was amusing and the effect of the entrance of the grandfather, who was not dead at all, can easily be imagined.

Mrs Slater:	Ann Stapleforth	Victoria:	Pamela Weaver
Henry Slater:	Roger Keeley	Mrs Jordan:	Ruby Hodder
Abel Merryweather:	Jack McGinley	Ben Jordan:	Paul Sanders
Producer	Neil Adams	Asst Producer:	Hazel Hopkins
Stage Manager	R.F. Pocock, Esq.	Scenery	Art Department
Costumes	Ernestine Jowett		

"Piper's Pool" by Helen Hope - This second, more serious play also dealt with death, and it showed an old man dying and the thoughts that ran through his head. His dreams of a better world to come were brought by the Piper of Dreams who lived in a nearby pool. The play was notable for fine characterisation and the use of poetic language.

An Old Man	Paul Apanasewicz	The Piper of Dreams:	Pat Turner
A Business man	Michael Dawling	An Old Rascal:	Norman Cook*
Spirits of the Pool	Hazel Cowling, Judith Bishop, Susan Wells,		
	Angela Shaw, Jenifer Gould, Carol Bowditch		

* On the afternoon before the performance Norman Cook was hit on the head by a cricket ball and was taken off to hospital. Neil Adams borrowed his father's gardening clothes and played the part himself for which he received a good reception.

31st March to 1st April 1955: "Jonah and the Whale" by James Bridie. Produced by Neil Adams - the author, James Bridie, *"believes that human nature does not change a great deal through the ages, which is perhaps why in this production he shows a* commercial traveller in a fancy costume who might well have stepped out of a dusty Austin with a glib smile and a curly moustache. Perhaps this is why the characters in his play are people who might be found in any city or village today. Only the costumes are different. The play is a kind of morality and is thus a far cry from the school's last production "Toad of Toad Hall". It was suggested that "such a play is not easy to stage or to understand" and that perhaps "the pith of the play is to be found in the character of Jonah. It was noted that the cast "worked hard at their tasks" but the lead part of Jonah, played by Norman Cork, carried the production. The production of "Jonah and the Whale" was staged at the Church Hall but it was hoped that next year a new stage at the school would be ready for use.[7]

Jonah:	Norman Cook	Voice of the Whale:	The Producer
Miss Hupplefeather:	Ann Stapleforth	Josibiah:	Paul Apanasewicz
Euodias:	Hazel Hopkins	Hashmonah:	Peter Evans
Naaran:	Judith Williams	Shual:	Peter Laycock
Bilshan:	Gerald Lavers	Sentry:	William Stork
Captain:	David Cozens	Purser:	Michael Dawling
Sailor:	Peter Gollop		
Sophereth:	Cynthia Budden	Eshtemoa:	Rosemary Campbell
Zuph:	Helen Moore	Ziz:	Sylvia Luckert
Shiphrah:	Josephine Alexander	Stachys:	Diana Emmett
Tolad:	Judith Bishop	Hadadezer:	Ruby Hodder
Tola:	Jenifer Gould	Zamirah:	Pamela Weaver
Two Girls:	Margaret Gill, Joanna Foster		
Villagers:	Patricia Attfield, Penelope Tunnicliffe, Michael Clinch, Michael Green, Edgar Mays, Janet Richards		
Passengers:	Patricia O'Mahoney, Mary MacDonald, Elizabeth Tapper, Rex Edwards, Patricia Turner, Michael Bowrah, Paul Latham, Christopher Leaver, Andrew Henderson		

In 1956 the school entered two plays in the Dorset Drama League Festival. Although no cups were won the experience was interesting and stimulating for the forty pupils who took part.

The first play was **"The Stolen Prince"** by Dan Totheroh. This was acted in the Chinese fashion, with no scenery and featured a Property Man, played by Paul Latham, who remained on stage throughout indicating essential facts to the audience by various means. A garden was represented by a little peach blossom on a stick, a river by a roll of blue cloth and Autumn by a few leaves blown from the fingers of the Property Man. Penny Shaw took the part of Joy, the little prince, and Pat Turner was Li Mo. Other pupils in the cast were M Gill, P Atfield, D Emmett, A Hobbs-Briggs, A Shaw, P O'Mahoney, Apanasewics, Watson, McKenzie, Bowrah, Leaver and Mays.

---

[7] Extract from School Magazine dated July 1955

The second play was the **Coventry Nativity Play** which included outstanding performances by Jean McKenzie as Mary, W Smith as Herod, Josephine Alexander as Gabriel with other parts played by P Blanchard, J Bishop, C Budden, S Walker, J Eades, E Morgan, J Bosence, P Tunnicliffe, J Sansom, Lukats, P Evans, Paul, A Henderson, Howard, Knight, Crabbe and P Smith.

"It's Great to be Young" was also staged in **1956**. This was a revue rather than a play and the cast numbered 106. By all accounts this production took a great deal of organisation and a flavour of the chaotic nature of this revue is best described by a line from the report that appeared in the school magazine, ie *"how the boys and girls were pushed and harried off the stage, dragged in and out of the costumes and ended up in the right place at the right time was a constantly recurring miracle but somehow item followed item"*.[8]

Reference was made to the Junior House Drama Competition which was a new innovation. Three plays had been produced by the three houses, which were cast, dressed and produced entirely by people form the three lower forms of the school. They produced their own reports on their efforts, which are very vivid and capture the fun that was had by all

Drama in the 1960s

The first three major productions of the 1960s were under the direction of Tim Cock, ably supported by the Head of Department, Brian Earnshaw.

17th to 19th March 1960 – "Murder at the Vicarage" by Agatha Christie

According to the Head's Report to Governors dated May 1960 "a highly successful school play – "Murder at the Vicarage" (Agatha Christie) played to three full houses and I am grateful to the members of staff, particularly Timothy Cock, producer, for the work which was put in".

In 1961 each of the three houses performed a play and wrote a report on their efforts.

"Widdershins" School House: Report by David Arnold – "*We practised this Rattigan play in the Laundry Room at Harcombe under the firm control of Jane Eades and although there were times when tempers were frayed a little, it was jolly good fun. Mr Sheepshanks, played expertly by Tim Arnold, was a cynical Witch Hunter who went around England with a doddering old vicar called Parson Longshaw. He was played by Michael Ramscar. We were a bit worried about Ramscar, until he stepped on the stage, then he was an immense success. These two villains came upon Bradby one summer morning in 1645. They thought they could get "Old Mother Thorpe" (Sandra Parker) as a witch but the villagers thought differently.*

---

[8] Extracts from School Magazine dated July 1956

The villagers were played by Kim Silburn, Tom Stones, Howard Stones, and Tony Dix. Zoë Dean, the village idiot, fitted her part like a glove. Susan Garvin played very well indeed and so did Lesley Clarke. Patricia Kenny, Susan Creed, Linda Milnthorpe and Alun Stevens made up the crowd, getting in their "rhubarbs" just in the right place! Alan Bealing fell ill at just the last moment. This could have been the end of the play but Kim Silburn took over the part of the village idiot's brother with only one day left. He had everyone horrified and hysterical at the same time with his loud screams, trying to better his sister, Zoë. I played the village gaffer. Of course a lot depended on our two neurotic producers, Priscilla Ryall and Paul Hewlett. Anyway the play was a tonic all round."

"The Poetasters of Ispahan" Shaftesbury House: Report by Ruth Smith – *"Inefficient from the very beginning, the junior children from Shaftesbury House started rehearsing for their play in the Christmas Term of 1960. In the Easter Term, months later, it was just presentable. The play had an eastern flavour to it. Christopher Powell, whom we all called "Cuthbert", was the producer. After many auditions or readings, Cuthbert chose people for the various parts. Within a week at least three of the children had dropped out and others took their parts. Cuthbert, from the beginning, was more concerned about the props and clothing than the acting. When the cast started to act it was almost time to perform the play.*

On the night, the cast appeared dressed in wonderful garments, thanks to Cuthbert; and the play, which was supposed to be a comedy, produced some rather faint murmurs of laughter from the audience. I was the Princess Silvermoon and my father, Kennaugh, a very rich jeweller, wanted to marry me to Virginia Homyer, or Judith Hallet, or Peter May or John Broom or Albert Vickery. In the end, in spite of the chaos of rehearsals, the play was quite good."

"King Melon" Woodroffe House: Report by Hugh Hallett – *"From the start of the rehearsing an excellent job was done by the producers – Gillian Wiscombe and Carolyn Pearn. They had a struggle to get people for the play, but in the end they won. After many rehearsals, the night of the play came. We watched the other plays and they were very good, which disheartened us. The play commenced. It went off with a bang. Looking back afterwards, perhaps it would have been better if we had gone off the stage with a bang and kept going out of the door.*

Fairy Mumbo and Fairy Gurgle were very well played by Barbara Hopkins and Mary White. Then on came the king, played by Hugh Hallett, who wasn't bad, but could have learned his lines more thoroughly. Susan James's performance as Princess Caraway shone right through the play. King Melon's army was richly portrayed by Trevor Hodder, Beryl Barden, Sylvia Roe and Jennifer Carter. Their singing would have aroused a dead cat if there had been one in the audience. Cheryl Turner played the part of Melon's mother. She was just right for the part, all jolly and roguish, and she acted splendidly. Philip Bowditch's highwayman was completely baffled by the deaf old lady, Ella Ritter, and the very small child, Barbara Smith. The drunken sailors raised the roof and Massey Holland, Pauline Sartan and Dorothy Sparks had good hic-cups.

In the last scene, not to be outdone, the tiring women, played by Jocelyn Marsh, Anthea Gregory Smith, Isobel Preece and Angela White, sang lustily while they stuffed Princess

Caraway into her dress. But there was one disaster. Susan James had to give me a purple handkerchief and, of course, she forgot and took it on stage with her so Melon had to use a white one and the audience laughed unkindly. We finished with a grand dance that was more like a funeral process and one bright spark fell over. But I think we gave the audience their laughs for the evening."[9]

1961: Separate Tables – Produced by Tim Cock. *"It is always a little difficult to talk objectively about a play one had produced although, as you know, I have never been reluctant to blow my own trumpet. I am in fact going to be subtle and let somebody else blow if for me. We were very fortunate and stand indebted to Mr Earnshaw's publicity, in having a charming lady from The Times Educational Supplement witness one of our performances. This journal has of course national coverage and it blazed our efforts, as did TV throughout the country. I quote:*

'The production was completely absorbing and well thought out. The long difficult part of Mrs Railton-Bell was played with an assurance far beyond the actress' years, and great depth was given to the interpretation of the suppressed daughter. However, the bouquet must be handed to the girl who played Mrs Shankland. She has good stage presence and a remarkable quality of stillness which many a great actress would envy. There were several excellent characterizations and moving performances.'

A fear shared by many people before the production was that school children could never portray the "adult" emotions of the characters in "Separate Tables" because of their immaturity. There always does seem to be a tendency, presumably an adult defence mechanism, to deny that adolescents can feel deeply or intensely. Personally I felt no qualms concerning this; I knew my cast to be both sensitive and perceptive. One of their greatest assets technically was the ability to grasp the idea of dramatic pace – usually a bane of amateur theatricals".[10]

Addendum: This production caused a major stir in the town with many protests regarding its "unsuitable" sexual content. It even aroused a debate in none other than the national paper "The Times Educational Supplement" with letters hotly in support or, equally hotly, in opposition. Needless to say, the school weathered the storm and Tim Cock produced again before departing for other shores.

Mabel & Doreen (Waitresses):		Susan Cradduck and Judith Bosence	
Lady Matheson:	Yvonne Unwin	Mrs Railton-Bell:	Jean McKenzie
Miss Meacham:	Margaret Roy	Mr Fowler:	John Harrison
Mrs Shanklin:	Josephine Alexander	Miss Cooper:	Caroline Whistler
Mr Malcolm:	John Paul	Mr Stratton:	Graeme Thompson
Miss Tanner:	Elizabeth Doy	Miss Railton-Bell:	Rosemary Knight
Major Pollock:	Roger Harris		

---

[9] Extracts from School Magazine dated 1961
[10] Extract from School Magazine dated 1961

July 1961: The Merchant of Venice – Producer: Tim Cock
Main Players: Brian Earnshaw, R J Harris, R Bateman, R Knight, C Pender, G Thompson, C Whistler, J McKenzie, J Mount, R Bishop and R Harrison

"The Dramatic Society presented an extract from the Merchant of Venice. It was an open-air production "in the round". The performance took place in the evening but the hoped for full moon did not appear although the odd star was visible. Modern dress was worn, owing to a lack of funds and time.

Mr Earnshaw played the part of Shylock and his performance was described as "splendid as it was unconventional". There was concern as to whether the supply of hydrangeas on the terrace would hold out as Lorenzo (Christopher Pender) would pick one for his adored Jessica (Rosemary Knight) at each rehearsal. Apparently one rather mangy, bedraggled specimen remained for the actual performance.

With great difficulty a pony was obtained for the performance, accompanied by his doting owner, Judith Biscoe complete in riding rigout. With Nerissa (Jean Mckenzie) Judith led the pony with Portia (Caroline Whistler) perched precariously on its back. Unfortunately the pony refused to carry Caroline any further than the back row of seats and she had to dismount, leaving the audience rather bemused when a riderless pony was led through their midst.

A spectacular touch was the "crowd" – a vast collection of 4th, 5th and 6th formers disguised as drunkards, flower sellers, soldiers, young ladies of dubious repute and road sweepers. Margaret Roy had practised to perfection a "magnificent spit" at Shylock but unfortunately had had to leave for Wales the day before the performance. Reference was made to the magnificent efforts of Mr Manners with a tape recorder hidden in the bushes which had emitted blasting trumpets or romantic violins at just the right moment.

1962: Drama Society Production of "The Rape of the Belt" - The Director, Tim Cock, expressed his gratitude to the cast which "was able to recognise the intricacies of timing, pace and innuendo and at the same time apply an enthusiastic, full-blooded approach".

This colourful and spectacular play was based on one of the myths of Hercules and his struggles with the Amazons. Costumes, of course, were a feast for the eye and the destruction of the on-stage tower was memorably achieved. The experienced and highly talented actors included Jean McKenzie, Caroline Whistler, Roger Harris, "Mini" Mount, Elizabeth Doy, Bonny Unwin, Glenys Parry, Rosemary Knight and Margaret Roy.

Mount revelled in the part of Heracles and Harris rather stole the show with his romping Theseus. Jean Mackenzie and Caroline Whistler were commended for their portrayals of Antiope and Hippolyte respectively. It was noted that all the other characters had their moments – Bishop as a beery Zeus, Bonny Unwin as a catty Hera, Glenys Parry an awesome Hippobomene and Margaret Roy a matronly Thalestris. Last but not least Elizabeth Doy and Rosemary Knight were described as *"fluttering delicately in the background as attendant women"*.

Hera:	Bonny Unwin	Zeus:	Roger Bishop
Hippobomene:	Glenys Parry	Theseus:	Roger Harris
Heracles:	John Mount	Antiope:	Jean Mackenzie
Diasta:	Rosemary Knight	Anthea:	Elizabeth Doy
Hippolyte:	Caroline Whistler	Thalestris:	Margaret Roy

1963: Prize-winning Dorset Drama League Productions at Weymouth

Some five one-act plays were entered, with Sixth Formers assisting new English Master, David Coates, in three of these. The major works were Mr Coates' dramatisation of the story of Puccini's Opera "Turandot" and of the famous poem "The Pied Piper of Hamelin" (in which Jennifer Searle, known as 'Titch' made her mark as a delightful Irish cook – not in the original poem!). "Turandot" boasted a cast containing some of the school's best and most experienced actors, with Rosemary Knight, an imperious ice-cold Princess. Austin Wilkes, a boy of premature sophistication, suitably senile as her father, the Emperor, and Mike Yates as the traditional handsome Prince. Comedy came in the trio of Court Officials, Ping, Pang and Pong (David Fayle, Christopher 'Cuthbert' Powell and Adrian Pearson).

1964: "The Pied Piper", "Widdershins" (with Anthony Walkey in the leading role) and "Turandot".

This was an outdoor presentation, for public consumption, played on the Terrace and steps. Mike Yates was less the traditional fairy-tale Prince this time, having broken an ankle shortly before the one-off performance. "Gingerly" could perhaps best describe his ascent and descent of the steps as he attempted to win the ice-cold Princess – whom he had little difficulty in thawing with a kiss, once he had answered her three riddles.

In 1964 the Lyme Regis Grammar School became The Woodroffe School, an event which was marked with a "Grand Spectacular" in the new school hall.

Devised by the new Head of English, David Coates, it was based on the idea contained in the Jules Verne novel and film "Around the World in 80 Days". The format was to have two leading characters, played by Michael Ramscar and Janis Lemon, embark on a world-tour for their honeymoon. Countries visited included North America, where a large cast of (mainly Junior) Indians danced and sang around their totem pole, suitably attired; Central America for a rousing chorus from "Oklahoma" and the Mid-West for a cowboy skit, written by David Coates in rhyming verse, starring Michael Parnham, at that time as a 2nd former rather small for his age, and called "The Ballad of Little Titch" (no doubt subsequently banned as politically incorrect!). The Producer found himself shortly being reprimanded by Joan Green on account of the garter clearly visible on Miss Lulubelle Lewcock's thigh. (Those were innocent days!). Spain was visited and Michael and Janis found themselves caught up in the drama of Bizet's Opera "Carmen". Drama was evident even before the production, when Kim Silburn, scheduled to play Don José, the romantic lead, left school, to be replaced at late notice by the Producer – much to the discomfort of Carmen (the luxuriously locked Annie Greenshields) whose hair managed to thwart all of Mr Coates' attempted kisses.

The spectacular entry of the Toreador (Hugh Hallett) was marked by an eruption of red roses – where they came from the Producer was advised not to ask! Russia followed with a parade of peasants (Year 1 Remove) past the Kremlin, a violin solo of "The Dying Swan" and a comic version of the ballet "Swan Lake": the girls of 3C objected to the 'indecency' of wearing tutus in public, so the boys gleefully stepped in, wore the tutus over their football shorts and were one of the highlights of the evening. Finally, the two wanderers returned to Britain, where they enjoyed the Highland Games (courtesy of the PE Department) before ending back among the buskers of London.

The whole presentation was a triumph of organisation, with contributions from all areas of the school, pupils and staff, particularly Brian Manners and the Music Department. The dress rehearsal was abandoned uncompleted at 11.00 pm but in true theatrical tradition, everything turned out to be 'all right on the night'.

1966: A bold new venture marked the next three years of Drama at Woodroffe – Opera – beginning with a work often produced at Glyndbourne and Covent Garden, Mozart's **"The Magic Flute"**. This obviously required major collaboration between the Music and Drama Departments – the latter really only an extra dimension to the English Department. David Coates and Brian Manners were both key members of the Lyme Regis Operatic Society and approached the task with dedicated enthusiasm – as did the large cast: the whole of the Senior Choir and Madrigal Group plus juniors to sing the roles of the three boys (doubled to six, as were the three ladies, to give added weight and confidence to the three-part singing).

The work was cut and music transposed down somewhat where required and the singing was of an excellent quality throughout. Particularly outstanding were Ruth Smith as Pamina, Jocelyn Marsh as Papagena, Jennifer Beecroft (in the originally stratospheric role of the Queen of the Night), Alistair Eggleston as Papageno (his aria "'Tis love they say" being frequently hummed along the corridors) and Tom Stone in the challenging low bass role of Sarastro, the High Priest. The youthful Billy Gooderham was an appealing Tamino, the hero, and George Rendle, a suitably malevolent Blackamoor, Monostatos. Great chorus numbers and the Egyptian costumes and scenery were spectacular. Scenery constructor, 'Ricky' Richards swore his sets were bomb-proof but one night a great pillar lurched towards the audience, only to be held by the proscenium curtains. Tragedy of a different nature was narrowly avoided on a different occasion when Tom Stones, blissfully relaxing in the boys' changing room, failed to arrive on cue to rescue Ruth Smith from a fate worse than death at the hands of George Rendle. Luckily he was rousted onto the stage just as Ruth and George were about to collapse with fatigue and embarrassment! The 'orchestra' was Brian Manners at the school organ at the back of the hall. Pages were efficiently (occasionally) turned by David Coates. The cast performed without conductor or prompt – evidence of their thorough preparation and dedication.

1967: Another Opera, to follow on from the success of "The Magic Flute". This was Humperdinck's charming fairy-story work, **"Hansel and Gretel"**. Again there was great collaboration between Departments, with Ernest Wellings' Junior Choir playing a major role. The construction team presented a splendid witch's cottage and major roles were again allotted to Billy Gooderham (Hansel), Jocelyn Marsh (a delightful Gretel), Alistair

Eggleston (their Father) and Jennifer Beecroft (the Witch) zooming around the stage on her sparkler-lit broomstick and singing with joyful malevolence.

1968: the final Opera of the trio, a more modern work, Giancarlo Menotti's biblical fable **"Amahl and the Night Visitors"**, a one-act Opera combined on this occasion with the medieval mystery play **"Noah's Flood"** produced by the newly-arrived boarding house master, Fred Middleton, assisted by pupil teacher, Joanna Stirling. David Coates, Brian Manners and Ernest Wellings were again to the fore in the production of "Amahl and the Night Visitors".

"Amahl and the Night Visitors" was described in the press as "*a sparkling performance of an exceptionally difficult production which called for plenty of stamina, and the cast was not found lacking*". Certain roles were doubled and the three Kings were each allotted a page, to bolster their musical lines: their "*harmonious singing*" was described as "*a feature of the evening's entertainment*". Both Amahls were outstanding, making light of their difficult music. Julian Bolt was particularly appealing as the poor lame boy, whilst the only blot on Stephen Lloyd-Jones' performance was the occasional glimpse of blue and white striped swimming trunks beneath his short, brown Middle Eastern tunic!

The Mother – Alison Emmett and Amanda Huxter, who both "*made a very difficult task look comparatively easy*".
The Three Kings – David Shilling ('Humorous'), Chris Fisher, Adrian Pearson
The Three Pages – David Fayle, Michael Denver, Nicholas Clarke (all six of whom "*gave performances which could scarcely be faulted*").
Shepherds and Shepherdesses: Sarah Bowyer, William Pedley, William Price, Colin Rowsell, John Evans, Michael Groves, Jenny Jones, Claire Perry, Kirstine Davis, Julia Tomes, Judith Manners, Belinda Taylor, Cynthia Dare, Judith Pedley, Verity Stiff, Andrew Parnham, Edward Rowe, John Denham (eventually a Government Minister!), Jenny Rowe, Robert White, Richard Hale, Stephen Pembroke, Alex Gear.

(From left to right:

Main characters:

Amanda Hunter
Stephen Lloyd-
Jones
Alison Emmett)

"Noah's Flood" was described as *"sparkling and most entertaining"*.

God:	Rory Jonzen	Noah:	Allan Lawson
Noah's Wife:	Rachel Douglas	Japhet:	Nicholas Stapleton
Ham:	Jonathan Hillier	Shem:	Robert White
Japhet's Wife:	Lynn Andrews	Ham's Wife:	Alison Blake
Shem's Wife:	Amanda Foreman		

Animals: E Jackson, A Dawson-Taylor, S Cox, S Collier, C Kidson, N Williams, C Saunders, J Wilkins, F Richardson, D Massey, K Climo, P Ede, A Newstead, S Appleby, J Whitaker, V Wicks, C Livings, J Foreman, S Blake, K Newman, P Bell, N Douglas, C Austin, G Hitchcock

Gossips: Y Marsh, J Brown, A Corbyn, C Johnson, J Gittins
Costumes: Sally Morse, Belinda Richards, Jill Ibrahim

July 1969: **"As You Like It" by William Shakespeare** - This was an open air production, directed by David Coates. The play was cut to the bare essentials and the parts were connected together by means of the two presenters who gave an added touch of humour. Period costume was worn and the play took place on the Terrace making good use of the Library door and the side doors for entrances and exits.

Notable performances were made by Anthony Walkey, who handled the part of the melancholy Jaques excellently – his rendering of "All the world's a stage" was magnificent. David Fayle and Janet Corbin made the most suitable twosome as Touchstone, the fool, and Audrey, the Country Wench, accompanied by two baby goats on loan from a nearby farm. Steven Evemy – the Duke in exile –played the part of the fatherly Duke very well and the rest of the cast were just as praise-worthy and deserved congratulation for bringing to life, for one hour, a snatch of the Elizabethan era.

Thanks were extended to Mrs Giles, in particular, for lending her sewing machines, helping to make the costumes and her direction of the dance routine. The production raised the sum of £16 4s 0d.[11]

Drama in the 1970s

1970: **The Merchant of Venice** was described in the press as *"an outstanding production by Mr D E Coates, with remarkable attention to detail throughout. The young players handled difficult parts with the ease and confidence of seasoned actors and prompting just wasn't necessary"*. The stage set was based on that at the Globe, with an inner stage and a gallery above used both by musicians and actors. Costumes, medieval in style, were the responsibility of Myra Wood, who also played Jessica. "Court Musicians" on recorders, were B Hayball, C Bromfield and V Barnes.

---

[11] Extract from "Lyme Juice" dated November 1969

Anthony Walkey as Shylock closely watched by David Fayle.

Trudy Richards performed a song she had composed herself.

Antonio:	Christopher Fisher	Bassanio:	Michael Denver
Portia:	Shelagh Patterson	Nerissa:	Virgina Matthews
Lorenzo:	Phillip Wrigley	Shylock:	Anthony Walkey
Prince of Arragon:	Jane Richards		

Other players:
D. Austin,
S Austin, S Raffo,
T Richards, J Seamark,
A Harrison, D Braine,
J Corbyn, D Fayle,
A Pearson, T Apps,
S Evemy, K Rand,
T Greenhalgh,
B Richards,
E Sandon-Humphries,
A Parsons, S Hobson,
M Groves, J Hodgson.

(Front left: Michael Denver as Bassanio, Front right: Phillip Wrigley as Lorenzo and Myra Wood as Jessica)

1973: "Che Guevara" produced by Walter Poole, with Stephen Evemy in the leading role, proved to be yet another of the school's controversial productions, this time on account of its "language" and political rather than sexual content.

1975: reverted to a more conventional play, **George Bernard Shaw's delightful comedy "Pygmalion"** (re-titled "My Fair Lady" when presented on stage and screen as a highly successful musical). The play was presented on two nights of the ambitious four night "Woodroffe Festival" which brought to the public gaze practically every activity promoted by the school: Art, Gymnastics, Science, Careers, Music, Metalwork.

"Pygmalion" presented great acting opportunities to David Murray (Henry Higgins) and Claire Pole (Eliza Doolittle) a role she was to have shared with Julia Harris, who unfortunately succumbed to the flu epidemic). Packed audiences applauded the play on both nights.

Henry Higgins:	David Murray
Eliza Doolittle:	Claire Poole
Alfred Doolittle:	David Hercock
Mrs Higgins:	Jane Collier and Joy Raymond
Mrs Pearce:	Katy Price and Sally Collier
Freddy Eynsford-Hill:	Jonathan Baker
Colonel Pickering:	Richard Edwards
Set and Décor:	Mrs M George and Frances Whistler
Set Construction:	Mr R H Johnson
Costumes:	Miss Y Robertson, Joy Gittens
Make-up:	Miss J Green and Assistants

April 1976: A Drama Evening to mark the retirement of Thornton Pearn featuring "The Thwarting of Baron Bolligrew" – *"This boisterous "pantomime" entertainment featured an extensive cast and was enjoyed by a large and enthusiastic audience, so large in fact that at one point it seemed as though people would have to be turned away due to overcrowding. The cast included the Brainless Blackheart, Bolligrew's henchman, who was portrayed in a masterly fashion by Andy Rattenbury, and the scheming Sir Percival Smoothley-Smoothe played by Simon Williams. Bolligrew – loudmouthed, heartless and opinionated – was ideally suited to Mark Fowler and Jon Baker was excellently cast as the "hair-brained" Dr. Moloch, Regius Professor of Wickedness at the University of Oxford. Finally, Ann Woodman, making her acting debut, made an excellent Oblong. The elusive Dragon who lived in the "eternally void" depths of his lair was realistically simulated by members of the "Dynamite Disco" run by ex-pupils. Credit was given to them for the complicated technical effects achieved with the help of two 135 watt amplifiers and stroboscopic lighting.*

Supporting the main programme were an extract from "Toad of Toad Hall" by the Juniors, a reading from Dickens by David Sutherland Graeme and Diane Jones, a short play by the French Department and a short recital by the Junior Girls Madrigal Group."[12]

---

[12] Extract from Newsletter dated July 1976

July 1976: An Elizabethan Evening - Organised by David Coates, Mr Eames and John Hollis this consisted of excerpts from Shakespeare's **"A Midsummer Night's Dream"** and **"The Merchant of Venice"**, poetry recitations, music and dancing and a rhyming extravaganza. The performances took place on the open air verandah in front of the school and also included music for the lute, songs by the Madrigal Group, poetry reading and dancing.

Easter 1977 - "The Importance of Being Ernie" – *"The dramatic talent of the Woodroffe School was exploited to the full in the Easter production of "The Importance of Being Ernie". Over 100 aspiring thespians took part in a production that ran for three nights in front of packed houses. The play was an expanded version of "Ernie's Incredible Illucinations" by Alan Ayckbourn and was drafted into its final form by John Hollis in a few effortless bursts of creativity. By Christmas everything was going smoothly. The third act was considerably strengthened by the combined intellects of Andy Rattenbury and Jon Baker who added the "This is Your Life" scene to the play – a triumph of wit and inspiration!*

The performances themselves were well received. Mike Stead in the title role gave three excellent performances. An unfortunate chance meeting between his motor bike and a lorry resulted in an extremely brave last night performance when he was deprived of the use of 79% of his bodily functions (no discernible difference in quality was apparent!). Julia Harris and Andy Rattenbury proved excellent choices for Ernie's long suffering parents… Mark Fowler made a brief but typically authoritative guest appearance as Humpty Dumpty and Alison Potter, in the third year, excelled herself as Alice. Bob Nantes making his much acclaimed acting debut, proved conclusively that he had missed his vocation as a 1950's style rock n'roll idol. His performance was notable for the many off-the-cuff lines which he injected felicitously into the script. One, in particular, lingers stubbornly in the memory: "You may touch me if you like - £1 a go – ladies only please – I have my reputation to think of!". Philip Ede and Frank White delighted "the pit" with an absurdly eccentric boxing bout (from which neither of them have yet recovered) and Lloyd Dormer, as a German Officer, was so convincing that he has received several anonymous letters of congratulation from obscure addresses in South America. The whole cast ought to be praised for its dedication, particularly the juniors. The sets, painted with consummate skill by the indefatigable co-producer, Paul Pickard, incorporating many ultra-modern design techniques, appeared to float on air as if by magic. The lighting and special effects were, as usual, in the capable hands of David Newman and Nigel Glover.[13]

In July 1977 - a **"Festival of One-Act Plays"** was held in the school hall. Four plays were produced by Years 1 to 4. The 1st year play was **"The Princess and the Pirate"**, the 2nd year play was **"Chez Boguskovsky"** by A.J. Talbot and the 3rd year play was **"There's an End of May"** by Kenneth Lillington. These three plays had a common theme of crime and detection. The 4th year performed **"St Joan"** by George Bernard Shaw. The 5th and 6th forms contribution to the Festival were two one-act plays by Tom Stoppard – **"After Magritte"** and **"The Real Inspector Hound"** both directed by John

---

[13] Extract from Newsletter No.5 dated December 1977 penned by Jon Baker

Hollis. In "After Magritte" there was a surprise performance by Mr Eames. Pupils participating included Vicky Sindall, John Baker, Nicky Murdoch and Justin Cozens.

A report on "The Real Inspector Hound" described the play as *"an intellectual farce which lampoons pseudo dramatic critics, the golden age of the detective-story complete with Baskerville hounds and the "who's for tennis" comedies of the thirties"*. Of particular note was the performance of Chris Williams, complete with long cigarette holder. Andrew Rattenbury (subsequently to gain nation-wide acclaim as an actor, playwright and TV script writer for such successes as "The Bill" and "Teachers") held the audience's attention completely with supporting roles taken by Mark Fowler, Simon Williams, Anne Woodman, Patrick Baker, Robert Nantes, Mea Webb and finally David Newman as a *"prodigiously handsome corpse".*

December 1977: "A Christmas Carol" - A large number of 4th formers presented an adaptation by the Dorset Drama Adviser, Leslie Williams, of Charles Dickens' famous story. The production was dominated by the character of Ebeneezer Scrooge, played by Billy Geraghty, who gave a remarkable performance, managing most effectively the transition from miser to merry old man, despite being on stage almost non-stop. Nicola McCrae and Debbie Herbert were ghastly old gossips, Alison Potter and Wendy Van der Plank took leading roles and smaller parts were taken by Paul Farrant, Tracey Jones, Gareth Jones and Helen Broom. Kevin Irish made a very natural, cheerful, cheeky boy and Kevin Lowther, from the 1st form, was an appealing Tiny Tim. Mr Barber's group of dancers contributed greatly to the Christmas party spirit and the costumes were produced under the experienced direction of Miss Nicola Hill.

1978: "The Ghost Train" by Arnold Ridley – Produced by John Hollis and presented as his swan-song, this play boasted among its participants (mainly Sixth Form pupils) a real live Station Master from Axminster in the crucial Station Master's role. This play was a comedy with creepy overtones.

End of the Autumn Term 1978: "The Reckoning" by Ann Jellicoe - 1978 was a remarkable year in the history of Drama at the school. Ann Jellicoe, professional actress, playwright (eg "The Knack", subsequently a successful film) and producer at London's Royal Court Theatre, moved to Lyme in 1974 and in 1978 she approached the school to suggest the staging of a Community Play. This was to be a play on a very large scale based on the Monmouth Rebellion which began in Lyme in 1686. The play was to involve parents and other adults and subsequently the Vicar of Lyme, the Town Clerk and the Town Crier, all played themselves. The school spent the major part of the Autumn Term in 1978 preparing and as the term drew to a close, activity reached fever pitch with over fifty members of the staff and pupils taking part in rehearsals. Students from Exeter University were involved, as were members of the local amateur dramatic society and Medium Fair, a professional theatre company, who also taught Sixth Formers how to use the technical equipment. There were public meetings, and community sewing groups and pupils had the opportunity to work with a professional writer/director in a series of workshop sessions. Overall 200 people were involved in this exciting production.

Westward Television filmed and screened a preview and a small article appeared in the Times Educational Supplement. The production was fully funded by grants and sponsorship and was a complete sell-out. It was noted that on the Saturday night the audience had been almost as interesting as the play, as it had featured an international theatrical impresario, a National Theatre Director, two other professional directors and four nationally known actresses! Reviews were published in the national press including the Times Educational Supplement and The Guardian and, in the latter, pupil Helen Broom and teacher, David Coates, were picked out for special mention. An extended review of the production was also printed in the monthly theatre magazine "Plays and Players".

"The Reckoning" began with a gigantic happening, the Cobb Ale Fair, held in the school hall, featuring craft displays and stalls among which the promenading audience could wander quaffing their Cobb Ale. Into this scenario the play erupted with the audience able to move from one centre of action to the next as there were three stages for important scenes. The production was described as a splendid piece of theatre; dramatic, exciting, bloodthirsty, totally absorbing and above all, maintaining an air of spontaneity.

Participants from Woodroffe also included teachers Ian Cook, Paul Pickard and John O'Connor and pupils Wendy Van Der Plank, Rory Anderson, Jeremy Patten, Sarah Hibbert, Simon Pipe, Karen Woodbridge, Patrick Baker, Lindsey Gannon, Justin Cozens, Angharad Thomas and finally, Billy Geraghty who got the action under way.

From left to right: Ian Cook, David Coates, Simon Pipe, Tony Arlidge and David Hibberd (Photograph provided by David Coates)

Final comment from "The Guardian": "*Scores of children had an experience to remember*". Ann Jellicoe went on from this first community venture to produce further community plays in Seaton, Bridport, Dorchester and abroad, all to great acclaim: but the Woodroffe Community Play at Lyme Regis was the first!

From left to right: Wendy van der Plank, Nikki McCae, Helen Broom and Margaret Thomas *(Photograph from school archive)*

22nd to 24th May 1979: "Oliver" by Lionel Bart - This production was aimed at younger pupils, too young to have taken part in "The Reckoning". It involved a large number of pupils, acting alongside members of staff. The producer was John O'Connor and Mark Riddington was the Musical Director. Both were excellent. The local press described the production as a highly entertaining show featuring a well-balanced blend of pupils and staff. The show was well-dressed, rarely lacked pace and the chorus work was enthusiastic with songs such as "Food, Glorious Food" rendered particularly well.

Timothy Dunn gave a sincere performance as Oliver and the role of the Artful Dodger was taken by Tom Everett, who breezed along with infectious confidence, dropping and adding "aitches" all over the place. Jeremy Patton was an excellent Noah Claypole and Hugh Everett and Billee Sellman were an ideal pair as Mr and Mrs Sowerby. Only a few senior pupils were permitted roles in the show, including Karen Woodbridge as Widow Corney, Charles Purser as Bill Sykes and Jenny Alford as Mrs Bedwin. Staff members also took part in this production with Miss Shanni Nutt, an SEN teacher, playing Nancy, Walter Poole as Fagin and George Lloyd-Jones, a former Senior Master, came out of retirement to play Bumble. Jill Chase undertook the choreography, Marilyn Fox helped with costumes and Judith Cook, wife of the Deputy Head, took charge of the make-up department. Richard Hudson was responsible for front of house, Paul Pickard was in charge of set design and David Badman was Stage Manager.

1979/1980: The mammoth effort of "The Reckoning" was followed by a somewhat abbreviated presentation of Shakespeare's **"Romeo and Juliet"** produced by Walter Poole, and with 'Basil' Broom and Jenny Ibrahim in the two title roles.

As we arrive at the end of the 1970s, tribute must be paid to David Sutherland-Graeme whose dramatic offerings enlivened many a morning assembly during the 1960s and 1970s. Most notable among these was the excerpt from T S Eliot's "Murder in the Cathedral" with himself as Thomas a'Becket and Andrew Rattenbury heading the four murderous knights.

Drama in the 1980s

July 1980: "A Midsummer Night's Dream – *"This Shakespearian comedy was produced by John O'Connor who was congratulated for drawing every ounce of humour from the script. He also showed great wisdom in teaming up with fellow staff members Walter Poole and Paul Skelton to form the comedy trio of Bottom, Quince and Snug. The cast was almost word perfect and it was obvious that there had been thorough preparation by all connected with the production. Much care was taken with sets, costumes, and lighting and, if there was a limited budget, it certainly did not show. Countless hours must have gone into the making of the exquisite costumes for the fairy characters. Set design was by Sue Davies and Mark Riddington built a special apron stage which projected into the auditorium. Nicholas Brown composed music especially for the production and choreography was by Jill Chase."*

Titania:	Alison Potter	Oberon:	Sarah Stead
Puck:	Wendy van der Plank*	Helena:	Lindsey Gannon
Hermia:	Helen Broom	Lysander:	Tom Everett

Demetrius:	Tim Doyle	Duke of Athens:	Hugh Everett
Queen of Amazons:	Anna Rust	Cobweb:	Joanna Crouch
Peaseblossom:	Siobhan Porter	Moth:	Debbie Lucas
Mustardseed:	Sadie Hennessey		

Other cast members: Jeremy Patton, Mark Williams, David Hughes, Suzi Johnson, Alison Higgins, Harriet Pinney, Robyn Sellman, Stephen Oatham, Philippa Hall, Tina Hughes, Karen Moyland-Jones, Luci Payne, Rory Anderson, Kevin Irish

* Wendy Van der Plank continued her acting career after leaving school, taking the leading role in the BBC Children's television series "Forever Green".

December 1980: "The Chimney Sweeps" - This play was written by Anthony Delves and was performed by the lower school. Paul Skelton was the producer and John Haylock was in charge backstage. It was set in the early 19th century before the reforms of Lord Shaftesbury. Philip Moseley was commended in particular for his role as the greedy master sweeper and Toby Pennington for the emotions he aroused in his portrayal of Ned, the doomed apprentice. Stephen White and Alistair Goodchild also played their parts well and the whole cast was praised for its enthusiastic performance.

William Blake	Petrina Oxenbury	Ned:	Toby Pennington
His mother:	Katkin Mayne	His father:	Bruce Evans
Jacob Sharp:	Philip Moseley	Rosie:	Helena Smee
Ruff:	James Telfer	Priest:	Sarah Hibberd
1st pauper:	Steven White	2nd pauper:	Nick Pridden
Shiner	Alistair Goodchild		

Apprentices: Christopher Howe, Vanessa Johnson, Poppy Williams, Trudy Robson, Derek McCullough, Miranda Smith, Philip Everett, Helen Wood, Kate Butterworth

December 1980: "Black Comedy" – *"This play was written by Peter Shaffer and performed by Sixth Formers. The plot was complex, very funny and demanded a high degree of technical accomplishment. Hugh Everett played the central role of the young sculptor, anxious to impress his fiancée, her father and a potential foreign patron. Tim Doyle carried the difficult role of the outrageously camp Harold Gorriage and his limp-wristed caricature earned well-deserved laughter. Anna Rust as the debutante fiancée provided competent support as did Helen Broom and David Hughes and the latter was praised for his portrayal of a much older character. Lindsey Gannon, playing the prim and proper spinster with the unexpected taste for a tipple, delighted the audience with her mannerisms. The sight of her clutching her handbag and whisky bottle was particularly memorable as was Hugh's hideous braying laughter."*

Brindsley Miller:	Hugh Everett	Carol Melkett:	Anna Rust
Miss Furnival:	Lindsey Gannon	Col Melkett:	David Hughes
Harold Gorringe:	Tim Doyle	Clea:	Helen Broom
Schuffanzigh:	Jeremy Patten	George Bamberger:	Christopher Warne

July 1982: the Real Inspector Hound – *"Nine senior pupils took part in this play which was a big hit for Ronnie Barker and Richard Briers. The two theatre critics, Moon and Birdboot, were played by Tom Everett and Julien Cozens, Mark Williams took the part of*

the fierce Major Magnus, Jeremy Holmes portrayed the playboy, Simon Gascoyne, Paul Witcher was Inspector Hound and Wayne Loveridge took the part of the corpse, who had to play dead throughout the whole play. Gail Turner took the upper crust role of Lady Cynthia, Debbie Lucas was the sporty and trim Felicity Cunningham and the home help, Mrs Drudge, was played by Helen Oatham. The latter gave an excellent performance. As essentially the narrator and scene-setter, she had a lot of lines to learn which she mastered well and her diction was excellent.

However, the stars of the show were not the performers on stage but the two theatre critics, Moon and Birdboot, as contrasting in their outlook on life, morals and work as in their dress. Moon, who was properly dressed in evening suit and bow tie and the slovenly Birdboot grated on each other's nerves and much of the entertainment was provided by them conducting their own quite separate dialogue (often irrelevant to the stage play but important to their own abrasive relationship). The unexpected twist at the end is the sudden realisation that the two critics are suddenly part of the action as all hell breaks loose on stage and murders abound. John Haylock, as Producer, was congratulated for doing a good job in developing a close-knit team who drew the best from each other.

A second feature of the programme was another comedy performed by junior pupils and produced by Julia Lamb entitled **"The Crimson Coconut"** by Ian Hay. This play, set in a London restaurant in the 1930s concerned a bomb plot and involved the waiter and a female foreign spy. Pupils who took part were Chris Howe, Geraint Evans, Mark Kolya, Louise Franklin, Poppy Williams, Philip Moseley, Vanessa Johnson, Justin O'Kelly and Sarah Hibberd as Prompt."

9th to 11th December 1982: Paul Skelton, Head of English directed a Junior School Drama production of **"Birds"** (a modern adaptation by Caroline Bennitt of the comedy by Aristophanes). This gave nearly fifty second and third formers a chance to act and sing wearing ingenious costumes designed and made by Susan Davies, Julia Lamb and Sharon Wallin. Musical direction was by Nicholas Brown. A number of other staff and senior pupils were involved behind the scenes.

March 1983: "Orpheus in the Underworld" – Jacques Offenbach. This operetta was produced by Ian Cook with Brian Manners as the Musical Director. In an article written by David Sutherland-Graeme he stated that *"having watched Woodroffe performances for thirteen years, and reviewed most of them, I consider Orpheus in the Underworld the most professional that I have yet seen"*.

He praised both Ian Cook and Brian Manners for instilling in the cast sheer enjoyment in performing to a high standard. He praised Jo Bartle for her performance as Eurydice and he suggested that John Haylock's Jupiter *"had a jovial coarseness which at times was nearer to music hall than comic operetta"*. However his diction and that of Paul Skelton as Styx, servant to Pluto, was excellent. Tom Everett took the part of Orpheus and Steve Richardson played Hermes, the messenger of the Gods. The performance of the Can-

Can was particularly worthy of note but the most memorable aspect of the production had been the obvious enjoyment of all the participants.[14]

Addendum: In the opinion of at least one member of the audience, the undoubted scene-stealer in this production was the magnificent pair of legs attributed to young PE Master, Steve Richardson, fully displayed in a costume of more (or less) than authentic brevity.

End of Spring Term 1984: "The Western Women" - This community play, staged at the school, was written by Ann Jellicoe, based on a short story by Faye Weldon. The inspiration for the play came from a poem by a local Vicar, written in 1644, which local author John Fowles brought to the attention of Ann Jellicoe. The poem was entitled Joaneridos or The Western Women, which is how the play got its title.

The production opened a season of special events held in Lyme Regis to mark the 700th anniversary of the Town's first Charter. Over forty senior pupils and staff attended the workshops and were trained and directed by Ann Jellicoe, Roddy Maude-Roxby and William Gaskell of the National Theatre. Like "The Reckoning", staged at the school in 1978, "The Western Women", based on the Siege of Lyme by the Royalists in 1644, had a strong and dramatic story line. There were ten performances in total and the production featured promenade performances whereby actors and audience mingled together.

---

[14] Extract from Newsletter No. 21 dated June 1983 written by Mr Sutherland-Graeme

20th to 23rd March 1985: "Twelfth Night" by William Shakespeare - *This year's school play was Shakespeare with a difference; "Twelfth Night" in (roughly!) 1920's costumes. "Twelfth Night" is a comedy, as funny today as 400 years ago, and the play was produced by John Haylock, to bring out all the humour possible. Many of the laughs were derived from the costumes worn: Nick Pridden playing the Jester, Feste, dressed as a punk with two-tone hair; Ian Morris playing the Steward Malvolio, in bright yellow stockings; Toby Pennington, playing the "rather nice" Sir Andrew Aguecheek, looking very naff in purple silk trousers; Miranda Armstrong playing the heroine Viola dressed as a man. There was some excellent type-casting – Jeremy White as the drunk, sex-mad Sir Toby Belch, Philip Everett as the lovesick Duke Orsino and Duncan Shaw as the cool, romantic Sebastian. The audience (and John Haylock) seemed very taken with Vicki Morely's dress, and Vicki Shaw's cavorting (as Maria) with Sir Toby went down very well with the audience.*

Most of the credit for all the laughs and fun must go to John Haylock and his assistant, Louise Franklin. Many thanks go to all those who helped to construct the excellent set, to Mary Badman and her make-up team, to Chris Badman for the lighting, to the musicians and to all those who sold tickets, ushered or were car park attendants. Finally spare a thought for John Haylock's beard, badly torn and ravaged after about four months of pulling at rehearsals.[15]

6th, 7th and 8th March 1986: "The Crucible" by Arthur Miller, produced by Walter Poole. *"All participants were 4th and 6th formers and members of the school's senior Drama Club. A report in the local paper stated that "Mr Poole guided his young players expertly, bringing out the full emotional content of the play and this, coupled with the high drama of the four acts, made for an intense and enjoyable production. Not only was it successful as a whole, but it contained outstanding performances by a relatively inexperienced cast."*[16]

Abigail Williams:	Anna Roberts	Elizabeth Proctor:	Sally Newman
Mary Warren:	Katheryn Strong	Giles Corey:	Toby Pennington
John Proctor:	Martin Bartle	Danforth:	Michael Cugley

Other cast members included Julian O'Kelly, Duncan Gray, Jonathon White, Samantha Colins, Jerome Shapland, Samira MacKenzie, Ellen Toms, Sam Perlo, Stella Elvin, Jo Carter, Matthew Smith, Aaron Driver, Heather Mace, Penny Holloway, Sarah Farley, Richard Hobbs, Rebecca Percival, Jackie Ball, Lucy Lindsay, Marie-Phillipe Bew, Fiona Bradley, Sheila Snell, Lorna Blackmore and Katie Govier.

1987: "Holy Moses" by Chris Hazel and "Under Milk Wood" by Dylan Thomas - "Holy Moses" is a jazz arrangement of the Moses story in song and Bible readings. The readings were narrated with expression and clarity by Jackie Ball. The singing was rendered with obvious enjoyment by the pupils of the junior choir, conducted by David Manners, with accompaniment by Brian Manners.

---

[15] Extract from Newsletter No. 27 dated June 1985 written by Toby Pennington
[16] Extract from Lyme Regis News dated March 1986

"Under Milk Wood" was written by Thomas in the 1950s as a radio play. Walter Poole and his team of 4th, 5th and 6th formers were brave to undertake this production but they did it well. The cast took several parts each showing great versatility and commendable effort in capturing the lilting inflections of the Welsh accent.

The imaginative set constructed by Timothy Saville consisted of a set of windows through which the audience could view the various characters in their private worlds of joy and sadness, lust, laughter and loneliness. The play bore witness to the endless hours of toil put in by Walter Poole and his team. It was hilarious in places, moving in others and extremely entertaining throughout.

The cast included Fiona Bradley as Polly Garter, Nicholas Everett playing Blind Captain Cat and Mr Pugh, Georgina Burke as both Mrs Cherry Owen and Mrs Ogmore-Pritchard, Glynn Cameron-Watkins as Beynon and Cherry Owen, Rebecca Percival as Mrs Pugh and Rosie Probert, Tim Leatham as Sinbad Sailors and Organ Morgan, Maria Davis as Mary-Ann Sailors and Myfanwy Price. The narrative "first" and "second" voices were pre-recorded extremely clearly by Paul Rochester, Peter Wild, Lorna Morrison and Suzanna Smith and other voices on the tape belonged to Caroline Davine, Moby Hill, Lisa Holmes, Daniel Saphorgan, Richard Spalding and Keith Williams.

1988: "The Caucasian Chalk Circle" - This play by Bertholt Brecht was focussed on the basic dramatic theme of the vulnerability of goodness in a world of evil. The story is of Caucasian peasants acting out two plays, their revised version of the old legend of "The Chalk Circle". The first story was of Grusha, the servant girl, who saved the noble child abandoned by his family as they fled for their lives. The second story concerns Azdac, a lawyer's clerk, who finds himself in a judge's position. The two stories were brought together when Azdac judged Grusha by the test of the Chalk Circle and the motherhood of the child was given to the servant girl. The play was expertly produced by Walter Poole, and Tim Saville was in charge of set design.

Grusha was played convincingly by Maisie Hill and also by her understudy, Mary MacDonagh, who performed on the second evening of the three performances. Matthew Smith played the part of Grusha's lover and showed a good understanding of the part. Minor parts were played by Annabelle Oldfield, Dougal Bird, Michael Munday, Glyn Cameron-Watkins, James Poupard, Michael Moylen Jones and Esme West. Other actors were Sarah Brown, Polly Crine, Jackie Ball, Phillip Young, Marie-Phillipe Bew, Penny Holloway, Stella Elvin, Kylie Beck, Ian Robinson, Andrew Quin, Helen Driver, Crystal Price, Rachel Duncan Anderson, Diana Panduro, Tracey Rosser, Ross Jenkins, Kieron Harris, Darron Upchurch and Garyth Cameron-Watkins.

1989: "Black Comedy" and "The Real Inspector Hound" - This was a double bill of comedy. The plot of the first play, **"Black Comedy",** was built around a house plunged into darkness by a blown fuse. The main characters were played by Carla Pole as the gin-sodden Miss Furnival, Anita Cross as Carol Melkett, Lisa Holmes as Clea, Matthew Lohnes as Colonel Melkett, Daniel Price as Harold Gorringe and Glyn Cameron-Watkins as Brindsley. Keith Williams as Schuppanzigh and Robert Applin as Bamberger both added extra laughs with their put-on foreign accents.

"**The Real Inspector Hound**" featured Emma Stephenson, who was given short notice to perform her role as Moon and carried it off very well. Nichola Bryne, who was to have played Mrs Drudge, became ill several days before the performance and the part was shared between Natalie Price and Rachael Duncan-Anderson who performed on different nights. Phillip Young took the part of Magnus, Jo Calame was Lady Cynthia Muldoon, Kim Turpin played Felicity Cunningham and Moby Hill was Inspector Hound himself. The cast was completed by Luke Owen as Simon Gascoyne and Simon Jaques as Birdboot.

Drama in the 1990s

1992: "Dr Faustus" by Christopher Marlowe – "*The production was directed by Ian Wood and fellow members of staff joined the cast, including John Haylock, Walter Poole and Julia Lamb-Wilson. The voice of Mick Jagger singing "Sympathy for the Devil" and the casting of Mephistophilis as a corrupt and beautiful woman made a refreshing departure from the traditional images expected in productions of this 17th century drama.*

In an atmospheric set, created by Dot Page, Faustus, frustrated by science turns to magic. He calls on Mephistophilis, with whom he strikes a fatal bargain, to sell his soul in return for twenty four years of life and power. The play followed Faustus during that time, in scenes where characters are conjured up such as the Seven Deadly Sins and, notably, Helen of Troy, of whom Marlowe wrote the immortal line "Is this the face that launched a thousand ships?"

Faustus as a young man was played with youthful earnestness by Darren Evans, a sixth form pupil with convincing stage presence. The older Faustus, played by another sixth former, Oliver McDonagh, produced an excellent performance in which the doomed necromancer's gradual descent into despair was poignantly portrayed. Becky Jones, as the malevolently beautiful Mephistolphilis, created a tangible sense of evil and doom in a powerful and professional performance. Deputy Head, John Haylock, was truly satanic as Lucifer, while the Good and the Bad Angels, played by Harriet Marsh and Maya Ray, contrasted the sweetness of salvation with the decadent powers of evil. English teacher, Walter Poole, portrayed the Pope as an acid and malicious fool to excellent comic effect. Moments of black comedy were provided by teachers Alan Brown and Julia Lamb-Wilson and by pupil, Nicola Sweetland. A group of five Year 9 pupils – Jamie Middleton, Julie Hancock, Ginnie Norris, Lucy Gorfin and Fiona Bird, provided a diabolical retinue for Lucifer and were frightening reminders of the nature of Faustus' ultimate fate.

The technical crew, headed by Mr Badman, created light and sound to chilling effect and the backstage crew of pupils and staff enabled competent scene changes and colourful makeup and costumes to support the performers. This production was Woodroffe at its best – uniting pupils and teachers in creative team work."

25th to 26th November 1993: "Oh What a Lovely War" - Year 9 were studying the Great War as part of the national curriculum in History. The topic was large enough to involve a lot of other departments including English, Art and Design and RE. It seemed appropriate to end the project with a production that would involve the whole year group and extracts from the popular stage musical "Oh What a Lovely War" was an excellent choice.

It was reported in the local paper that *"Woodroffe School pupils played to capacity audiences last week in a superb production, laced with nostalgia, humour and pathos, reflecting life in this country up to and including the Great War. The show, produced and directed by Ian Wood and John Seabrook, featured 150 Year 9 pupils and was presented as a celebration to mark the 75th Anniversary of the end of the 1914 – 1918 War. The first half, entitled The World that was Lost, spotlighted Britain on the eve of the great conflict through the skilful and enlightened use of drama, poetry and music. It was a thought-provoking platform from which the youngsters launched into extracts from the show and the film "Oh What a Lovely War".*

The all-round success of the evening was due in no small measure to the very imaginative use of special, often, very simple, effects. News flashes onto the stage and symbols, rather than conventional props, were cleverly used, while the sounds and smells of war were evoked with explosions and smoke. Particularly evocative was the flashback to the days of the silent cinema and the directors are to be congratulated too on the amount and pace achieved with so many pupils in a limited amount of space. There can be no denying, however, that the greatest assets at the disposal of the production team were the innocence and sincerity of youth which captured the mood and tenor of a class-ridden society before and during the "war to end all wars".[17]

30th/31st March 1995: "In Holland Stands a House" - a play about the life and times of Anne Frank presented by the pupils of The Woodroffe School.

March 1998: "My Fair Lady" - The lead part of Eliza Doolittle was taken by two pupils, Katie Moore and Lizzie Sweetland, performing on alternate nights, and John Haylock took the part of Eliza's father, Alfred. Many pupils were involved on stage and others worked hard off stage constructing scenery, collecting props, and assisted with marketing, etc.

July 1998: "A Midsummer Night's Dream"

July 1999: "Summer Loving"

---

[17] Extract from the Lyme Regis News dated November 1993 – article written by Mr David Cozens

A cast of over 100 played to packed houses in an exciting production of "Summer Loving". *The photograph below features the Pink Ladies with Danny.*

Helen Warner, Helen Bennett, Toby Michael, Melanie Easton and Louise Pearson

October 1999: "Torchbearers" - The world premiere of this musical "Torchbearers" was staged at Woodroffe. It was a great honour that the highly acclaimed National Youth Music Theatre had chosen the school as the setting for this very exciting project. "Torchbearers" was a full length, two-act musical, which told the story of a group of women who battled to overcome many difficulties to achieve liberation. It contained both comic and touching dramatic moments and had an impressive musical score composed by the Musical Director, Lin March. The production provided pupils with a wonderful opportunity to work with talented theatre professionals and participate either as performers or as members of the production team.

Drama in the 21st Century

July 2001: "Bugsy Malone" directed and produced by Ellen Kumar.

8th to 11th July 2003: "Oliver" by Lionel Bart produced by Anne Cruwys-Finnigan and Ellen Kumar - the local press described this modern version of Oliver as *"a vibrant production bursting with innovation and flair"*. The article went on to say that *"The youngsters do justice to one of the greatest British musicals of all time in a presentation featuring a refreshing cocktail of evocative choreography, confident singing and a slick mix of the traditional with the trappings of twenty first century technology. The settings are simple, but effective, the costumes interesting and the pace good, while there is commendable utilisation of space on stage and above. It is all brought together and spiced by a superb eight-piece orchestra."*[18]

There was particular praise for the chorus work which provided an excellent launching pad for a praiseworthy team effort. Tom Bevan-Jones in the title role, and Tom Livingstone as Mr Bumble were described as *"superb"* and other performers worthy of particular note were Kat Tucker as Widow Corney, Richard Bugler as Fagin, Jo Cooke as Nancy, Will Livingstone as Bill Sykes, Rob Cheeseman as Dodger and last but not least, Clemmi Sheppard in the cameo role of Charlotte.

October 2004: Year 7 Drama Club production of Yeh-Shen – a Cinderalla Story from China - The tale of Yeh-Shen, although set in China and differing in some detail, is basically the same as the familiar European fairytale of Cinderella. The story is at least one thousand years older than the earliest known western version. One of the ancient Chinese manuscripts on which the story was based was written during the T'ang Dynasty (618 – 907 AD) and sets the events of the story happening "before the time of Chin (222 – 206 BC).

The story was used as the basis for the performance developed by the pupils using a physical theatre style. This meant that they became everything that was needed, making the shapes out of their bodies and working very much as a team. For example they became a river bank, a fish, trees and a road – amongst other things.

Taking part in this unusual production were Alex Smith, Chloe Fairchild, Arianna Derrett, Sammy Guppy, Emily Hollway, Luke Steet, Stephanie Hallam, Katie Brown, Shannon Dunn, Ashleigh Rice, Robyn Taylor, Emma Bowditch, Bethany Chick, Jennifer Wooderspoon, Jenny Watts, Jessica Harrington, Olivia Gray, Rachel Chew, Julia Johnson, Jessica Chalkley, Catherine Butler, Jasmine Maidens, Jamie Perkins, Alex Munro, Harriet Secrett, Frankie Heffernan, Angelica Hart, Reza Shields and Laura Addy. Celia Cruwys-Finnigan provided musical assistance.

---

[18] Extract from the Lyme Regis News dated July 2003 – article written by Mr David Cozens

Summer School 2004: "Where the Wild Things are" by Maurice Sendak - The show featured youngsters from local primary schools and was devised and directed by Anne Cruwys-Finnigan, and Tom Livingstone. Community Art Teacher, Alison Bowskill, assisted by Scott Robson, was responsible for technical support. The performance was the climax of two weeks of hard work and dedication, with the pupils contributing artistic ideas and solving problems throughout.

Acting company: Corrine Amos, Elena Brake, Catherine Butler, Jazmine Colley, Celia Cruwys-Finnigan, Chloe Fairchild, Jasmine Harding, Julia Johnson, Beth Jones, Benjamin Kapur, Helena Loughton, Hannah Mackenzie, Magenta Down, Abby Perratt, Megan Rorstad and Alexander Smith.

The art crew designed and created masks, costumes and scenery using the story as a starting point before coming up with their own ideas. Crew members included Hazel Barnes, Jonathan Caddy, Heather Grant, Elysia Jennings, Jake Sawyer, Carey Shurey, Robyn Taylor, Joanne Turner, Nathan Wren and Dean Skinner.

July 2005: "Little Shop of Horrors" - The play was set in London in the 1950s and was directed by Ms Cruwys-Finnigan and Ms Emily Stones, produced by Ellen Kumar. Once again the local press was effusive about the production, which featured over sixty pupils, describing it as "an energetic and vibrant show with first class singing, dancing, music and acting". There were accolades for the beautiful singing voice of Jayne Burdett, who played Audrey, and Jake Dove, who did a wonderful job as Seymour, his first singing role. Reference was also made to the fine performance of Tom Bevan-Jones as Mr Mushnik and the excellent Gutter Girls.

However, the highest praise was reserved for Mark Fowkes as Orin the dentist, who was described as "mad, eccentric, enthusiastic and funny". The spectacular plant, which was animated by several Year 7 pupils actually inside it, also received a special mention as did its creators – Angus Johnson and Alicia Sievering.[19]

Seymour:	Jake Dove	Audrey:	Jayne Burdett
Mr Mushnik:	Tom Bevan-Jones	Orin (Dentist):	Mark Fowkes
Ronnette:	Laura Davenport	Chiffon	Fern Jellyman
Crystal	Abby Newman	Ms Bernstein:	Verity Rudge
Mrs Luce:	Ellen Love	Miss Snip:	Tamsin Cook
Mr Martin	George Penman	Interviewer:	Tom Baptist

---

[19] Extracts from Lyme Regis News dated July 2005

CHAPTER 22: THE SCHOOL SONG AND THE LORD'S PRAYER

An article in the School Magazine dated 1947 (Major Pearn's first year as Headmaster) described the origins of the School Song.

"Some twenty four years ago, the Chairman of the Governors said that he thought there should be a School Song. Since then several attempts have been made either to write the words or compose a tune but at last in the early months of this year Mr Ellis produced a draft of the words and the Headmaster wrote a musical setting. From then on the history of the song is interesting. It was discussed and criticised by both juniors and seniors. Suggested amendments were argued over and either accepted or rejected. Next, the music was considered in music lessons and involved discussions took place – especially among the seniors – as to the value of repetition, whether a succession of octaves over emphasized the climax, and among the learned few, a bitter argument concerning the relative merits of a "straight" accompaniment as opposed to one which contained, as one critic put it, "all the fanfares of a brass band without any wind to blow it along!

However, the song finally took shape and had its first public performance at Speech Day in July 1947. Since then it has been recorded. As a matter of interest and record, we print the words below:

> *What high endeavour shall our voice proclaim?*
> *What of our purpose; what alway our aim?*
> *What dedication as today we stand,*
> *Sons and daughters of this ancient land,*
> *Sharing together in work and play,*
> *Singing as one in pride of school today,*
> *O School! May we be worthy yet of thee!*
>
> *May we upon ourselves in Life rely;*
> *May every gentleness our strength belie;*
> *And with humility our valour bind,*
> *Cherishing honour in heart and mind*
> *So that, in our labours here,*
> *Forged and disciplined, our purpose clear*
> *O School! May we be worthy yet of thee!*
>
> *Sing both of triumphs that have gone before,*
> *And of the hope that when we sing no more,*
> *It shall be said of us, in ev'ry way,*
> *'Twas our endeavour to be worthy yet of thee!"*

The magazine also included an article entitled "OK for Sound" which described the first recording of the School Song as follows:

"Visitors to the Grammar School on Thursday, 24th July 1947 saw the terrace transformed by massive switchboards and multifarious wires. Inside the hall near the main door stood

a large electric loud speaker and a business-like microphone on a telescopic tripod, whilst a short distance away was a pedestal on which was fixed a red bulb. Massed around was the choir backed by the remainder of the school – all slightly excited at the thought of recording two songs.

First we sang the School Song for purposes of timing and balance, and then, when the engineers were satisfied, we sang it again, this time for a preliminary recording. At its conclusion came the first thrill of the afternoon – we hear the record played back to us! Now came the real recording. "Silence please!" came through the loud speaker, and then through the quiet, "Stand by for the red light – you can begin when it lights up!". A pause, the light glows, Mr. Ellis, conducting, raises his arm, and once more we plunge into the opening words. At the end comes a definite feeling of relaxation and then we are asked to do it all again! "Just in case ….." And so for the fourth time that afternoon the School Song echoed around the building.

Next came Vaughan Williams' "Let us now praise famous men". After singing it once we waited, old hands at this game – and then were surprised by the engineer arriving to say that he had taken an excellent "pull" on the first rendering. So ended a most interesting – and exhausting – afternoon, and now we await the arrival of the records, which can be bought through the school by anyone interested."[1]

From 1947 onwards the School Song was performed at every Speech Day until 2004 when the new Head, Richard Steward, felt it was time for a change. His feeling was that the song and the sentiments that it expressed were outdated and that it no longer had a place in the school. There were mixed feelings about this decision both at school and in the wider community and articles appeared in the local press expressing both support for and disagreement with the Head's decision. The ex-pupils' association were particularly opposed to the end of a tradition that had endured for almost sixty years. However, although the School Song is now lost to future generations it is being kept alive as it is performed with great enthusiasm at the reunions organised by ex-pupils every four years. On these occasions it can be heard blasting out from the pubs in Broad Street well into the early hours of the morning.

An early recording of the School Song can be heard on the School website at www.woodroffe.dorset.sch.uk.

Major Pearn also composed a musical setting for The Lord's Prayer which was still performed at the annual Carol Service up until 2005. Initially the tradition was for the Head Girl to sing the first line but in time she was joined by other sopranos.

Copies of the score for both the School Song (in Brian Manners' hand) and the Lord's Prayer are reproduced in this book by kind permission of Major Pearn's daughters, Gillian and Carolyn, who own the copyright.

---

[1] Extract from the School Magazine dated July 1947

The Lord's Prayer

For The Woodroffe School, Lyme Regis

© Copyright 1983 T.B. PEARN

The School on the Hill

CHAPTER 23 - COMBINED CADET FORCE

The Woodroffe Combined Cadet Force (CCF) was commissioned in April 1992. All three services were represented which was particularly important as a combined cadet force received more support than a one service detachment. It offered training for life and all sorts of exciting adventures were on offer for cadets, from flying to shooting.

Initially the Unit was under the command of Squadron Leader Richard Farrant, who worked at the school as a laboratory technician. Richard, who was educated at Woodroffe, was the leader of the 420 ATC Unit at Bridport for some years and had been an RAF reservist since 1969. The CCF was open to boys and girls from the age of thirteen years and over and was over-subscribed from the outset. The Unit was fully funded by the Ministry of Defence with all uniform, equipment and training provided free of charge.

The Head and the school's Contingent Commander, Squadron Leader Richard Farrant RAF(VR) welcome Lieutenant Paul Farrant RN to the school (Photo provided by Mr Vittle)

The inauguration was a colourful occasion, with the star attraction being the arrival of former pupil Lieutenant Paul Farrant, son of Richard Farrant, who landed his Sea King helicopter at the school. In addition to the visit of the Sea King helicopter, the school was also visited by a Lynx helicopter from 815 Naval Air Squadron, Portland and an RAF Wessex Search and Rescue helicopter.

A planned search and rescue demonstration had to be abandoned due to poor weather on the day but just after the opening ceremony a Nimrod aircraft performed a low level fly-past. On the ground The Devon and Dorset Regiment's Army Youth Training Team ran a mobile assault course and small-bore rifle range while the Cadet Training Team from Bovington gave abseiling demonstrations from the school building. Service personnel from as far afield as Shropshire, Portland and Culdrose were also in attendance

West Dorset MP, Sir James Spicer, attended the opening ceremony which was performed by the Chairman of the Joint Cadet Executive from the Ministry of Defence in London, Col H G Willmore. He referred to the reduction in the size of the services nationally but gave reassurances that there were no plans for a reduction or change to the Combined Cadet Force movement. Col Willmore advised that there were also no plans to diminish support for the Combined Cadet Force which was an excellent organisation that had been in existence for over forty years. He explained that it was unusual to see the formation of a full contingent and the school was therefore to be congratulated on its enthusiasm and energy.

Throughout the day it was stressed that membership of the CCF would not be compulsory. What was on offer was an opportunity for character building and many former CCF cadets had indicated that membership of a combined cadet force had been the best part of their school life.

The school tennis courts provide a landing site for several helicopters on CCF Inauguration Day – April 1992 (Photograph courtesy of Peter Rickard)

The President of the Lyme Regis Branch of the Royal British Legion, Mr Cecil Quick, welcomed the formation of the Woodroffe CCF unit, which he hoped would attend the Armistice Parade in the town, swelling the already well supported parade and making it even more special.

In time the Royal Navy Section established an official link with the Trafalgar Class submarine HMS Trenchant of the Second Submarine Squadron, based at Portsmouth. However, the Navy Section ceased to operate in 2000 when the officer in charge, David Manners, had to withdraw for family reasons.

Since its inception the CCF has been well served by two School Staff Instructors (SSIs). The first was Mr Colin Cockram, who was employed by the school as a Design Technology Technician, and latterly Mr Mike Goodrick who is the school's ICT Systems Manager. Both had previously served in the armed forces. Initially the commissioned officers of the Woodroffe CCF were all members of the school staff, trained by the services to which they were attached. However, non-school staff, with service backgrounds have assisted the unit from time to time.

The CCF Unit is subject to Biennial Inspections and it continues to thrive offering the cadets a huge range of exciting new experiences including shooting, gliding, parachuting, field craft, patrolling and orienteering.

Extracts from Parents' Bulletin give a flavour of the types of activities enjoyed by the cadets.

The Royal Naval Section of the CCF visited their Parent Establishment at HMS Osprey at Portland during the summer of 1992. The cadets enjoyed a thirty minute flight in a Sea-King helicopter and landed on the deck of the RFA Blue Rover. There was also a tour of the air traffic control centre, a diesel electric submarine and a frigate, a fire fighting display and a twenty minute voyage around Portland harbour in one of the Navy's new patrol vessels, HMS Blazer. The day concluded with "Beating Retreat" accompanied by the band of the Royal Marines.

In May 1993 Cadets from the CCF Unit were in training for the Royal Military Police Chichester March. This was a twenty five mile speed march, due to take place in August. Army and Air Force cadets attended annual camps in July at Penhale in Cornwall and RAF Coltishall respectively. The RN Section took possession of a 6m motor vessel for training purposes, to be kept in the harbour at Lyme Regis during the summer months. In addition the RN provided the cadets with two "Topper" sailing dinghies to provide them with greater opportunities to get out on the water and put their seamanship training into effect. More good news was that the Lyme Regis Sailing Club had offered the naval cadets associate group membership, thus allowing them to make use of their facilities including the rescue boat!

After the initial excitement of the inauguration numbers were maintained and in addition the MOD increased the size of the establishment to fifty Army cadets, thirty six Royal Navy cadets and thirty six Royal Air Force cadets. By July 1993 most cadets had completed the bulk of their basic training and were thus able to move on to more exciting and challenging duties.

In October 1993 the cadets raised £422 for the British Institute for Brain Injured Children through a sponsored march. Air Cadet Sgt Sally Ford was chosen for special duties at an international air tattoo at Fairford and was highly recommended on her conduct. Sally had been on duty in the Information Centre and had coped admirably when two Russian Mig 29s crashed. When she finished her duties Sally was taken to RAF Brize Norton to catch a flight on a VC10 to Cyprus, where she spent three hours before returning to the UK.

Naval cadets made an exciting visit to Devonport where they were given a guided tour of HMS Lancaster, a look around the Private Naval Museum and a slap-up meal in the Junior Ratings Mess in HMS Drake, followed by thirty minutes of high speed manoeuvres in Plymouth Sound in dory type assault craft. At thirty five knots the ride was extremely bumpy but one cadet described it as the most thrilling time of his life so a good time was had by all.

In late February 1994 the Royal Navy Section took part in one of the largest search and rescue exercises ever seen in the Lyme Regis area. The exercise involved some seventy people including Coastguard Auxiliaries from Lyme Regis and Allhallows, Lyme Regis Lifeboat, Naval Helicopters from RNAS Portland, the Police and thirty Woodroffe cadets. It was organised in order to practise a large scale casualty evacuation. By now the unit's boat was back in the water after a £2,500 overhaul by the Royal Navy but bad weather was preventing full use of this facility.

In October 1994 the unit had a total of ninety eight cadets across all three services. Cadets from the RAF Section visited Exeter Airport for flying experience in Bulldogs, a two-seater aircraft used exclusively by the RAF. Each cadet had the opportunity to fly for about forty minutes.

Cadets in the Navy Section enjoyed a day flying in a helicopter from the school pitch during half term in October 1996 and attended a field day in Portland. The RAF section also took to the air, gliding at RAF Chivenor and they too gained some air experience flying at Exeter. The Army cadets were concentrating on map reading and attended a field day at RAC Bovington where they examined and rode in tanks.

During the Summer holidays in 1999 the Army Section had a very successful camp in Germany when a party of twenty cadets went to Paderborn to stay with the Queen's Royal Hussars. The journey by coach travelling across France, Belgium, Holland and Germany was gruelling but the trip was worth it. New CCF accommodation built adjacent to the Sports Hall was making a significant difference to the running of the CCF at this time.

From October 2002 cadets in Year 10 were able to study at school for a BTEC First Diploma in Public Services. The award is accredited through EdExcel and can be used for entry to higher level courses.

The School on the Hill

By February 2006 there were sufficient cadets to form squads within the Army and RAF sections (by now the Navy section was no more). With points awarded and deducted for various activities, termly awards and an overall annual prize, this allowed for some healthy competition to develop.

Personnel who have served with the Woodroffe Combined Cadet Force since its inception include:

Name	Service
AKRAM Zahid	RAF
COCKRAM Colin	SSI
COPE Alistair	Army
EDWARDS Alison	Army
FARRANT Richard	RAF (Contingent Commander)
GOODRICK Mike	SSI
HUMBLE-SMITH Emily	RAF
HUTCHINGS Chris	RAF
JONES Martin	RAF
MANNERS David	Navy
MOUNTJOY Rebecca	RAF
RUFFLE Stuart	Army
SANSOM Darren	Army
UNWIN Phillipa	Army
WHATLEY Sarah	Army
WHATMORE Mike	Navy
WILLIAMS Jan	Army (Contingent Commander)
WOOTTON Nic	RAF (Contingent Commander)

Inspecting Officers for the Biennial Inspections:

1994	Brigadier R C Wolverson
1996	Lt Col W M McDermott OBE
1998	Group Capt Cross OBE
2000	Brigadier A J Fait OBE
2002	Air Vice Marshall J D L Fessey RAF (Rtd)
2004	Col O J H Chamberlain TD FRCIS
2006	Wing Commander G S Clayton Jones

CHAPTER 24 – THE DUKE OF EDINBURGH'S AWARD SCHEME

The award scheme began in 1956. It provides young people between the ages of fourteen and twenty five, whether able-bodied or with special needs, with an opportunity to experience challenge and adventure, to acquire new skills and to make new friends. It fosters self-discipline, enterprise and perseverance but above all it is fun. There are three levels of Award – Bronze, Silver and Gold, and each has an increasing degree of commitment. To gain any one of these levels each individual has to complete four sections – expeditions, skills, personal recreation and service. For Gold, participants must also complete a residential project, away from home for at least five days.

Approximately 5,000 young people achieve a Gold Award each year and around 225,000 are taking part at any one time. Around 3 million have taken up the challenge of the Award since its inception and around two million hours of voluntary community work have been undertaken. Across the world eighty countries operate the Award Programme in one form of another. HRH The Duke of Edinburgh is the Award's Patron and HRH Prince Edward is a Gold Award holder and a Trustee.

In gaining Awards young people learn by experience the importance of commitment, enterprise and effort. They discover a great deal about themselves and come to know the enjoyment of working with and for other people.

Gold Award Holders from Woodroffe

1965 - William Turner
1975 - Michael Newman
1976 - Andrew McPherson and Tim Maunder
1979 - Caroline Rattenbury, Alison Clegg, Anne Woodman
1981 - Joanne Pratt
1982 - Matthew Payne, Tom Brown
1983 - Nigel Dallas-Conte, Patrick Smith, Simon Gray, Jeremy Higgins,
  Joanna Crouch
1985 - Diana Maxwell
1986 - Sarah Woodbridge, Sarah Hibberd, Katkin Mayne, Amanda Maxwell,
  Derek McCullough, Toby Pennington, S. Wellman
1987 - Christopher Smith, Katherine Steels, Giffard Harrison
1988 - Eleanor Umbers, Karen Frost, Katy Roche
1990 - J Frost, L Morrison, Ruth Saphorgan, J Townsend
1992 - Georgina Burke
1993 - Nicholas Bell
1994 - Matthew Moore
1995 - Thomas Morgan
1996 - Jackie Sadler

The School in the Hill

March 1973 – this group of pupils was the first to receive Bronze Award certificates in Assembly.

They also won the Awford Shield for their contribution to the social life of the school.

Gary Larcombe   Liz Rice   Jamie Adsley   Hilton Jackson   Janice Sweetland   Mike Newman   Carolyn Rattenbury

Top Left: Learning to use a primus stove at the Lyme Regis Adventure Centre in preparation for a Duke of Edinburgh Award expedition.

Above: Head of PE, Mick Mawer, with the first Bronze Duke of Edinburgh Award group camping out in Marshwood Vale – March 1972

Left: Another group of stalwarts about to set off on an expedition.

(Photographs provided by Mick Mawer)

CHAPTER 25 - TEN TORS

Dartmoor National Park covers some 368 square miles of terrain with hills topped by granite outcrops called Tors. At its lowest point it is 325 feet above sea level and the highest hill reaches 2018 feet. Only two major roads cross the moor. The prison is situated in the middle of Dartmoor. Approximately 156 square miles of the moor is owned by the Ministry of Defence and is used by the British Army as a training and firing range.

Ten Tors was conceived in 1959 when three Army officers felt that the moor would provide a challenge for civilians as well as soldiers. During the first year 203 boys and girls took up this challenge but now entry is limited to 400 teams of six teenagers. The teams, depending on age and ability, face hikes of thirty five, forty five or fifty five miles between ten nominated Tors over two days in May.

Conditions on the moor vary greatly from year to year. In 1998 temperatures were in the eighties ($26^{o}C$) throughout the event and dehydration was a major risk. On the other hand in 1996 Dartmoor was struck by a snow and sleet storm over the Ten Tors weekend and 2,100 of the 2,400 participants had to be evacuated from the moor due to poor visibility and numbing cold.

Woodroffe first entered teams in the Ten Tors event in 1969 and participation by pupils has continued ever since with both boys and girls taking part. The only year when teams were not entered was in 2001 when the event was cancelled due to the outbreak of foot and mouth disease.

Training for the event is rigorous with teams required to spend three weekends on the moor prior to the event. Each team member has to carry all items of kit including a rucksack, sleeping bag, waterproof jacket with hood, waterproof trousers, warm headgear, footwear, gloves, a water bottle, a whistle, survival bag, water sterilisation tablets and a complete change of clothes. In addition the team has to carry maps, route cards, two tents, torches, compasses, first aid packs and food packs, etc.

The expedition begins at 7.00 am on the Saturday and in order to qualify for an award, teams must cross the finish line by 5.00 pm on the Sunday. Each team has to navigate and hike around a course allocated to it and has to check-in at Army observation points on each of the Tens Tors on its course. One night must be spent on the moor. Those teams completing the expedition receive a certificate recording the achievement and each team member is awarded a Ten Tors Medal.

In 1999 the Ten Tors Expedition celebrated its 40th Year. The Duke of Edinburgh summed up what Ten Tors is about when he wrote in the 1999 programme "The Ten Tors Challenge continues to attract young people with initiative and a sense of adventure. It requires careful planning, physical fitness, endurance and team work to achieve success and I am sure that everyone who has taken part in the Challenge has come to appreciate that these qualities are essential for any enterprise to succeed".

Appendix 1: Teaching Staff List (incomplete)

There is no central record of teaching staff. The following has been compiled from a variety of sources and is incomplete in terms of dates and subjects taught. Every avenue has been explored but regrettably some staff may be missing. Maiden names are included if staff married whilst at the school.

1953 - 1957	Adams	Mr	Neil	English	
1976 - 1977	Aimé	Mlle	Nelly	French Assistant	
2002 to date	Akram	Mr	Zahid	Science	
1978 - 1979	Albaredes	Miss	Dany	French Assistant	
1980 - 2004	Albert	Mrs	Claire	Physics	
1972 - 1976	Allen	Mr	R J	Modern Languages	Head of Dept
1947 - 1947	Andrew	Mr		Mathematics	
1992 - 1993	Armes	Mr	Anthony		
1959 - 1967	Arrowsmith	Mr	John	Physical Education	
1961 - 1967	Arrowsmith	Mrs	Edwina	Commerce	
1957 - 1958	Atkin	Miss	Lilian	Domestic Science	
1975 -1976	Austin	Mr	D	Mathematics	
1980 - 1995	Ayers	Mr	David	SEN	Boarding Housemaster
1967 - 1993	Badman	Mr	David	Head of Chemistry	Senior HOY/Housemaster
1978 - 1993	Badman	Mrs	Mary	Careers/Parentcraft	
1960 -1960	Baker	Mrs	D	French	
2005 to date	Banfield	Mr	Martin	Business Studies	Head of Dept
1973 -1980	Barber	Mr	Steve	Physics & Mathematics	
1966 - 2002	Bareham	Miss	Joan	Science/Exams Officer	Head of Lower/Middle School
1926 - 1930	Barnes	Mr			
1988 to date	Barnes	Miss	Rebecca	Textiles	
1992 - 1998	Barron	Mrs	Jane	Mathematics	Head of 6th
1954 - 1957	Bartlett	Miss	Irus	Domestic Science	
1972 - 1990	Bax	Mr	Alex		
1970 - 1971	Baxter	Miss	J	Physical Education	
1964 - 1966	Bearden	Miss	Di	Physical Education	
1980 - 2006	Bennett	Mr	Paul	English & Media	
1990 - 1990	Bennett	Mrs	Sue	Music/PE/Maths	
1970 -	Bennett	Mr	Wilfred	Mathematics & Chemistry	
1953 - 1953	Berry	Mr		English (temporary)	
1998 - 2000	Bevan	Miss	Rachel	Music	
1941- 1941	Blake	Miss	C		
1969 - 2003	Bland	Mr	Richard	General Science - ICT	Head of Dept
1971 - 1977	Bland nee Maggs	Mrs	Sheila	History	
1998 to date	Bland nee Maggs	Mrs	Sheila	History	
1965 - 1968	Blount	Miss	V	Mathematics	
1930 - 1938	Blunt	Mr		Science	
1956 - 1959	Boucher	Mrs	V A	Commerce/Domestic Sci	
2003 to date	Bowskill	Mrs	Alison	Art	
1967 - 1969	Boyce	Mr	R L C	Economics	Boarding Housemaster
1970 - 1992	Boyce	Mr	R L C	Economics	Head of Sixth Form
1923 - 1926	Bridgeman	Mr	J W		
1955 - 1957	Briggs	Miss	H M	English	Senior Mistress

1967 -	Brooke	Mr	Richard		
1978 - 1990	Brown	Mr	Nicholas	Music & Mathematics	
1983 to date	Brown	Mr	Alan	Geography	Head of Year
2005 to date	Bruford	Mrs	Ann	Design Technology	
1972 -	Buckingham	Miss	S	Geography	
2000 to date	Bugg	Mrs	Anna	Physical Education	
1973 -	Bullock	Mr	J	Woodwork	
1939 - 1945	Burcham	Miss	D C	Preparatory	
1973 - 1975	Burnett	Miss	Gail	Mathematics	
1958 - 1987	Burton	Mr	Kenneth	Mathematics	Senior Teacher/Head Dept
1976 - 1985	Butterworth	Mr	David	Headteacher	
1973 - 1992	Caffrey	Mr	Tony	Science	Head of Biology
1948 - 1954	Cameron	Mr	W	Boys Physical Education	
1953 - 1953	Cameron	Mrs	W	PE (temporary)	
1976 - 1978	Canning	Miss	J A	Mathematics	
1923 - 1955	Carson	Miss	J G	Senior Mistress	
1975 to date	Chambers	Mr	David	PE	Boarding Housemaster
1935 - 1937	Cheales	Miss		Domestic Science	
1924 - 1926	Chilvers	Miss			
1959 -	Chivers	Mr	A C	Physics & Mathematics	
1980 - 1984	Chourot	Mr	Henri	Modern Languages	
2005 to date	Clarke	Mr	Edward	PE	
1975 - 1978	Clements	Mr	Adrian	Mathematics	
2005 to date	Clulee	Mr	Jeremy	Science	
1963 - 1979	Coates	Mr	David	English	Head of Dept
1986 - 1987	Coates	Mr	Peter	History and RE	Head of Dept
1958 -1962	Cock	Mr	T J	English	
1968 - 1986	Cook	Mr	John	Science	Head of Dept
1978 - 1993	Cook	Mr	Ian	English	Deputy Head
1989 to date	Corbett	Mrs	Liz	Science & Geography	Careers Co-ord
2002 to date	Coudert	Miss	Sophie	Modern Languages	Head of Dept
1997 - 1998	Coughlan	Mr	P J	Business Studies	
1986 to date	Cowling	Mrs	Jenny	Environmental Science	
-1971	Coxon	Miss	A	History and Geography	
1997 - 2000	Craig	Mr	Andrew	Modern Languages	
1929	Croker	Mr	W.G.		
1991 to date	Cropp	Mrs	Vanessa	Psychology & Library	
1953 -1956	Cross	Mrs	D	Commerce	
1998 - 2000	Crossley	Mrs	Judith	Modern Languages	
1972 - 1972	Crowther	Mr	G L	Geography	
2002 to date	Cruwys-Finnigan	Mrs	Anne	Drama	
1978 - 2000	Culham	Mr	Keith	Mathematics	
1978 to date	Culham nee Hoyne	Mrs	Jo	PE/Geography	Deputy Head

1998 to date	Cullimore	Mr	Jon	Music	Head of Dept
1970 - 1985	Currah	Rev.	Michael	Religious Education	
2003 to date	Curtis	Miss	Tracey	Art	
1947 - 1951	Dane	Miss		Domestic Science	
1979 to date	Dart nee Davies	Mrs	Sue	Art	
1997 to date	David	Miss	Natalie	Modern Languages	
1986 - 1987	Davies	Miss	Elizabeth	Home Economics	
1964 - 1973	Davies	Mr	H W	Maths & Rural Science	Transfer from Senior School *
1981 - 1992	Davies	Mrs	Marianne	Modern Languages	
1996 - 2005	Dawson	Mr	Peter	Modern Languages	Head of Dept
2002 - 2005	Day	Miss	Julia	Geography	
1998 - 2000	Dean	Miss	Teresa	Design Technology	
1964 - 1972	Deasey	Mr	Roy	English	Head of Boarding House
1976 - 1978	Deasey	Miss	L R	Girls PE/Classics	
1978 - 1979	Deepen	Herr	Heio	German Assistant	
1995 - 1996	Dell	Miss	Karen	Modern Languages	
1979 - 1980	Demont	Mrs	Doris	French Assistant	
1925	Dibden	Mr			
1975 -1978	Dickinson	Miss	J A	SEN	
1978 - 1988	Dillon	Mr	Peter	Science	
1984 - 1985	Dillon nee Dubourg	Mrs	Pascale	Modern Languages	
1976 - 1977	Donovan	Miss	Susan	English	
1974 - 1996	Dowle	Mr	Roger	Design Technology	Head of Dept
1967 - 1984	Draper	Mr	Roger	Science	Director of Studies/Hd Biol
1967 -	Draper	Mrs	Valerie	Shorthand & Typing	
1967 - 1968	Drinkwater	Mrs	O	Art	
1976 - 1976	Driver	Mrs	D	Resources Unit	
1989 - 2000	Driver	Mr	Les	Art	
1980 - 1981	Dubourg	Mlle	Pascale	French Assistant	
1962 - 1963	Duckham	Miss	G P	Physical Education	
1961 - 1962	Dupuy	Mlle	C	French Assistant	
1972 - 1977	Eames	Mr	J D	English	
1957 - 1963	Earnshaw	Mr	Brian	English	Head of Dept
1996 - 1998	Edington	Mr	Stephen	Design Technology	
1949 - 1953	Edridge	Mr			
2003 to date	Edwards	Miss	Alison	Design Technology	
1988 to date	Elliott	Miss	Kathy	Modern Languages	
1925	Ellis	Miss			
1945 - 1951	Ellis	Mr	Dennis		
2003 - 2004	Elsworth	Mrs	Susan	Special Educational Needs	
2003 - 2004	Emery	Mr	Michael	Design Technology	
1938 - 1947	Evans	Mr	D W	Science	
1963 - 1966	Evans	Miss	Gillian	Domestic Science	
1995 to date	Everidge	Mrs	Christine	Special Educational Needs	Co-ord of SEN

1965 - 1985	Fairley	Mr	Michael	History	Head of Dept	
1966 - 1967	Fargue	Mdms	P	French Assistante		
1961- 1967	Finey	Miss	Rose	Biology		
1995 to date	FitzGerald	Mrs	Diana	Religious Education		
1990 to date	FitzGerald	Mr	Hugh	Religious Education	Head of Year	
1987 - 1981	Fleming	Mrs	Abbi	RE/Careers		
2002 to date	Fletcher	Mrs	Jacqueline	Modern Languages		
2000 - 2000	Foulsham	Mrs	Liz	Science		
1959 - 1959	Fox	Miss		Physical Education		
1968	Franks	Mr	Ian	Mathematics		
1967- 1968	Frency	Mlle	E	French Assistante		
2005 - 2005	French	Mr	Benjamin	English		
1981 - 1982	Frontier	Mdms	Katherine	French Assistante		
1996 - 1997	Frost	Miss	Rebecca	Modern Languages		
1982 - 1983	Gaskin	Mrs	S	Mathematics		
1964 - 1965	Gauthrot	Mdms	M	French Assistante		
1975 - 1984	Geary	Mr	Dennis	Technical Studies	Head of Dept	
1969 - 1986	George nee Lane	Mrs	Mary	Art	Head of Dept	
1984 - 1985	Gilbert	Mlle	Mireille	French Assistante		
1964 - 1974	Giles	Mrs	A C	Needlework	Transfer from Senior School *	
2001 - 2001	Glare	Miss	Elizabeth	English		
2004 to date	Golding	Mrs	Jenefer	Mathematics	Head of Dept	
1967 - 1975	Goldsmith	Dr	H	Nursing Course		
1935 - 1967	Gordon	Miss	J C	Classics		
1989 - 1992	Graham	Miss	Helen	Languages		
1948 - 1979	Green	Miss	Joan	Mathematics	Deputy Head	
-1982	Green	Mrs	Margaret	Needlework		
1984 -	Green	Mrs	Margaret	Needlework		
1923 - 1927	Greenfield	Mr	A	Headmaster		
1979 - 1979	Greenhalgh	Miss	L			
2005 to date	Greenhough	Mr	Michael	Art and ICT		
1963 -	Gregory	Mr	D			
1973 - 2006	Grier	Mr	Martin	Mathematics	Head of Dept	
1966 - 1977	Groves	Mrs	B	Domestic Science	Head of Dept	
2002 - 2005	Grundy	Miss	Michelle	Science		
1979 - 1980	Gurmin	Mr	Ian	Modern Languages		
1993 - 1993	Gurmin	Mr	Ian	Modern Languages		
1987 - 1990	Haggerty	Mr	Steve	PE/Geography		
1988 - 1990	Haggerty nee Robb	Mrs	Gill	PE/Maths		
1940 - 1943	Hall	Miss	E	Preparatory		
1944 - 1945	Hamilton	Mrs		Girls Physical Education		
1979 - 1979	Hare	Miss	Caroline	Modern Languages		
1959 - 1963	Harris	Miss	Margaret	Domestic Science		
1973 - 1976	Hayday	Mr	C	Environmental Science		

1980 to date	Haylock	Mr	John	English	Deputy Head	
1956 - 1958	Hayter	Miss		PE/French		
1956 - 1957	Head	Mr	H G	Engineering & Geog		
1959 - 1961	Hey	Miss		Commerce		
1996 - 1996	Higgins	Mr	Jonathan	Science		
1970 - 1982	Hills	Mrs	Vera	Commerce		
1959 - 1960	Hinton	Miss	J	French		
1937	Hoare	Miss	F L	Domestic Subjects		
1967 - 1970	Hobson	Mr	John	Physical Education		
1995 - 1998	Holland	Miss	Sally	Music		
1973 - 1978	Hollis	Mr	John	English		
1984 - 1986	Holmes	Mr	Stephen	Physical Education		
1975 - 1976	Horder	Miss	Jill	English		
1953 - 1953	Howe	Mr		English		
1959 - 1962	Hudson	Miss	R	Physical Education		
1976 - 1996	Hudson	Mr	Richard	Environmental Science	Head of Year	
2006 - 2007	Humphries	Miss	Stephanie	Music		
1977 - 1992	Hunt	Mr	Michael	Special Educational Needs	Head of Dept	
1978 - 1994	Hunt	Mrs	Margaret	Special Educational Needs		
1991 to date	Hutchings	Miss	Sharron	Physical Education	Head of Year	
1985 to date	Hyde	Mrs	Carol	Hyde		
1973 - 1974	Ibanes	Mlle	H	French Assistante		
1989 - 2005	Inskip	Mr	Bob	ICT	Head of Dept	
1988 - 2005	Jaques	Mrs	Jan	Business Studies	Head of Dept	
1998 - 1998	Jerrett	Mr	Nicholas	Design Technology		
1923 -	Joels	Miss				
1947	Johnson	Mr		Handicraft		
1974 - 1990	Johnson	Mr	Howard	Woodwork		
1985 to date	Johnson	Mr	David	Modern Languages		
2003 - 2003	Johnstone	Mrs	Alex	Modern Languages		
1956 - 1960	Jones	Mr	R	Science/Biology		
1977 - 1978	Jones	Mr	Trevor	English		
1979 -	Jones	Miss	Sylvia	Geography	Senior Mistress	
1986 - 1996	Jones	Mrs	Clare	Modern Languages	Head of Dept	
1948 - 1980	Jowett	Mrs	Ernestine	Domestic Science	Careers/Boarding Mistress	
1986 - 2006	Joyner	Mr	Chris	Physics	Head of Department	
1978 to date	Kabia	Miss	Julie	Home Economics		
1939	Kemp	Mr	J			
1962 -	Knapman	Mrs		Physical Education		
1979 - 1980	Kudla	Miss	Claudia	German Assistant		
1998 - to date	Kumar	Mrs	Ellen	Drama	Head of Dept	
1947 - 1950	Lake	Mr		French & Music		
2001 to date	Lake	Ms	Lynn	English	Head of Dept	
1962 - 1963	Laloux	Miss	Lucille	French Assistante		

1980 to date	Lamb-Wilson	Mrs	Julia	English	
1975 -1978	Lammas	Miss	Sue	Physical Education	
1973 -1986	Lee	Mrs	O M T	Modern Languages	Head of Dept
1972 - 1973	Lelong	Mlle	M	French Assistant	
1934 - 1935	Lewis	Miss		Domestic Science	
1964	Lloyd-Evans	Miss	T	English	
1951- 1978	Lloyd-Jones	Mr	George	Art	Head of Dept/Sen Master
1977 - 1979	Lord	Miss	H M	Modern Languages	
2003 to date	Loveland	Mr	Justin	Geography	Head of Dept
1940 - 1954	Lovering	Mr	E L	Physics	
1994 - 1995	Mackie	Miss	Helen		
1961- 1967	Maconochie	Mr	Ian	Chemistry	Head of Dept
1942 - 1956	Male	Miss	G M	History	
1941	Man	Miss	Gladys		
1991 to date	Mandy	Mrs	Sheena	Physical Education	Assistant Head/Inclusion
1961 - 1990	Manners	Mr	Brian	Music	Head of Dept
1986 to date	Manners	Mr	David	Mathematics	
1996 - 1996	Martin	Mr	Peter	Modern Languages	
1975 - 1976	Martin	Mlle	M	French Assistant	
2003 - 2003	Martine	Miss	Brigitte	Modern Languages	
1990 - 1998	Matthews	Mr	Malcolm	Music	Head of Dept
1971 - 1974	Mawer	Mr	M A	Physical Education	Head of Dept
1971 - 1973	Mawer	Mrs	M	Mathematics & Science	
1945 - 1949	McDowell	Mrs		Preparatory	
-1975	McInnes	Mr	A	Physical Education	
1943	McPherson	Miss		Physical Education	
2005 to date	Medd	Miss	Sophie	Physical Education	
1976 -1980	Medlock	Miss	Lynn	English	
1988 to date	Melvin	Mrs	Jan	Food Technology	Head of Year
1996 - 1996	Mermagon	Mr	Nigel		
1976 - 1976	Mevel	Mrs	J P	French	
1969 - 1986	Middleton	Mr	Fred	English & Careers	Head of Boarding House
1970 -	Millar	Miss	P	English	
1966 -	Miller	Mr	Gregory	English	
1959 - 1959	Moll	Mr		Physical Education	
1953 - 1955	Money	Miss	Jean	PE & French	
1983 - 1984	Montagne	Mlle	Brigitte	French Assistante	
1977 - 1978	Moreau	Miss	Francoise	Modern Languages	
1979 - 1979	Mowlem	Mrs	M	Modern Languages	
1943 - 1949	Munt	Miss	E	Preparatory	
-1928	Murray	Mr			
1988 - 1990	Musselwhite	Mr	Lee	Religious Education	Head of Dept
1991 - 1994	Nel	Mr	Chris	Mathematics	
1969 -1969	Nicholls	Miss	Elizabeth	Art	

1964 -	North	Mrs	M	French	
1957 - 1957	Nutman	Mrs	N J	Domestic Science	
1978 - 1980	Nutt	Miss	Shani	Special Educational Needs	
1977 - 1980	O'Connor	Mr	John	English	
-1982	Page	Mrs	Yvonne	Needlework	
1942 - 1943	Parsons	Mrs	L	Domestic Science	
1995 to date	Patterson	Mrs	Pam	Special Educational Needs	
1963 - 1964	Payman	Mr	G B	English	Head of Dept
1946 - 1976	Pearn	Mr	T B	Headmaster	Boarding Housemaster
1963 -	Pearn	Mrs	E		
1992 - 2003	Pearson	Mrs	Jenny	English	
1974	Pengelly	Mr	J	Physical Education	Head of Dept/Boarding
1970 - 1976	Perigal	Mrs	S B	Resources Unit	
2006 - 2006	Petty	Mr	Simeon	Art	
1968	Philby	Miss	P	English	
1973 -1980	Pickard	Mr	Paul	Art & Crafts	
1984 - 1985	Pike	Mrs	T	Art & Design	
1952 -1961	Pocock	Mr	R M	Music	Head of Dept
1964 - 1969	Pocock	Mrs	M	Art	Transfer from Senior School *
1971 -	Poole	Mr	Walter	English	
1954 - 1970	Porter	Mr	N C	Physics	Head of Department
1967 - 1976	Preston	Mrs	H	Classics	
1962 - 1981	Price	Mr	Ron	Geography	
1970 - 1974	Pugh	Mr	Malcolm	Woodwork & Handicrafts	
2000 - 2001	Purchall	Mr	John	Design Technology	
1969 - 1970	Pyle	Mr	J A	English	
1989 - 1995	Randle	Miss	J	Special Educational Needs	
2003 - 2005	Rankin	Miss	Louise	English	
2007 to date	Ransome-Williams	Mr	Simon	Science	
1967 - 1967	Raynes	Mrs	Dorothy	Art	
1972 - 1974	Read-Wilson	Mr	Crispin	English	
1987 - 1991	Reaney nee Bown	Mrs	J E	Physical Education	Head of Dept
1993 - 2003	Redman	Mr	Kerrigan	Geography	Headteacher
1964 -	Reeks	Mr	D M	English	
1964 - 1974	Richards	Mr	W	Head of Technical Studies	Transfer from Senior School *
1981 - 1983	Richardson	Mr	Steven	Environmental Science	
1973 -1983	Riddington	Mr	Mark	Mathematics	
1965 - 1965	Rigby	Miss		Domestic Science	
1978 - 1980	Roberts	Mr	Steve	English	
1944 - 1947	Romans	Miss	H A C	Domestic Science	
1972 -	Roskell	Mr	E C	Remedial Department	
2001 - 2002	Rosser	Miss	Susan	Drama	
2005 to date	Ruffle	Dr	Stuart	Science	
2000 to date	Ryerson	Mrs	Sarah	Music	

Dates	Surname	Title	First Name	Subject	Role
1947 - 1949	Sanders	Miss	M R	Physical Education	
1961	Sanders	Mr		Music	
1951 - 1956	Satterley	Miss		Domestic Science	
2003 - 2005	Savage	Miss	Chantal	Physical Education	
1986 - 1988	Saville	Mr	Timothy	Art	
1986 - 1986	Scott	Mr	Colin	Modern Languages	
1987 to date	Seabrook	Mr	John	History	Head of Dept
1964	Seale	Rev.	R L		
1946 - 1972	Shaw	Mr	G B	Modern Languages	Head of Dept/Sen Master
1966 - 1981	Shaw	Mrs	Doris	Modern Languages	
1989 to date	Shaw	Mrs	Jean	Science	
1976 - 1978	Sherman	Mrs	R	Music	
1974 - 1975	Shorten	Mr	P	English	
1974 - 1976	Shorten	Mrs	J P	Geography	
1997 - 2001	Sims	Ms	Juliana	English	Head of Dept
1991 & 1994	Sinclair	Mrs	Carolyn	Textiles	
1979 - 1997	Skelton	Mr	Paul	English	Head of Dept
1981 - 1983	Sykes	Mr	John	Computer Studies	
1928 - 1965	Slaney	Miss	M M		
1989 - 2004	Sleigh	Mr	Roy	PE & Physics	Head of Boarding House
2006 to date	Sloan	Mr	Richard	English	
-1927	Smith	Miss			
1993 - 1993	Smith	Mrs	Marie-Christine	Modern Languages	
1967 - 1968	Smith	Mr	P J	English	
1993 - 1994	Smyth	Miss	Anna	Science	
1996 to date	Snowling	Mr	Ian	Physical Education	Head of Dept
1993 - 1994	Soleilhet	Mlle	Florence	French Assistant	
1982 - 1997	Spence-Thomas	Mrs	Deirdre	Business Studies	
1983 - 1984	Spitaleri	Ms	Ellen	English	
1949 - 1953	Stainton	Miss	Olive	Physical Education	
1985 - 1988	Steed	Miss	Lesley	Textiles	
2003 to date	Steward	Dr	Richard	English	Headteacher
1973 - 1973	Stock	Miss	Glendon	Science	
1941	Stone	Mr	F H	Metalwork	
1954 - 1958	Stones	Mr	T	Boys PE	
2004 - 2005	Stones	Miss	Emily	Drama	
1944 - 1947	Stote-Blandy	Miss		Physical Education	
2001 - 2002	Summers	Miss	Melanie	Mathematics	
1970 - 1981	Sutherland Graeme	Mr	David	English	
1974 - 1996	Swainston (Kelsall)	Mrs	Mary	Modern Languages	Head of Year
1971 to date	Sweetland	Mr	Chris	Science	Head of Dept
1971 -	Sykes	Mr	J	Mathematics	
1966 - 1968	Tarr	Miss	Janet	Physical Education	
1968 -	Tarr	Miss	Elizabeth	Physical Education	

1929 - 1961	Taylor	Mr	W E	Science	Deputy Head and HOD
1947 - 1947	Taylor	Mrs	W E		
1934 - 1965	Taylor	Mr	G A	Workshop Instruction	
2002 - 2003	Taylor	Mr	Chris	Design Technology	
1971 - 1972	Taylor	Miss	A	Physical Education	
1950 - 1951	Thackray	Mr	R M	Music	
1984	Theobald	Mr	John	Design Technology	
1926 - 1958	Thomas	Mr	W H	Senior Master	
1975 to date	Thomas	Mr	James	Geography	Asst Head/Head of 6th
1977 - 1979	Thorne	Miss	Margaret	Domestic Science	Head of Dept
2005 to date	Thornett	Miss	Claire	English	
1947 - 1947	Thornhill	Mr		Junior Handicraft	
1972 - 1975	Tidy	Miss	C A	Physical Education	
1988 - 1990	Tingle	Mrs	Paula	Science	
2000 - 2002	Trueman	Miss	Elizabeth	Modern Languages	
1989 - 1994	Varndell	Mrs	Susy	SEN/Music	
1977 - 1978	Veile	Miss	Christa	Modern Languages	
2006 to date	Vincent	Mr	Neil	Mathematics	
2006 to date	Vincent	Mrs	Sarah	Design Technology	
2000 to date	Vine	Mr	Richard	Art	Head of Dept
1985 - 1993	Vittle	Mr	Paul	RE	Headteacher
1991 - 1991	Walcott	Mr	Michael	English	
1988 to date	Walker	Mrs	Karen	Science	Head of Year
1982 - 1984	Wallin	Miss	Sharon	Needlework	
1979 to date	Warne	Mrs	Hilary	Food & Childcare	
-1973	Warren	Miss	C	English	
1927 - 1946	Watton	Mr	S L	Headmaster	
1964	Way	Mr	D	Science	Transfer from Senior School *
1963 - 1977	Wellings	Mr.	Ernest	SEN	Transfer from Senior School *
1988 to date	Wells	Mr	Gary	DT/Mathematics	
1994 - 1995	Whatley	Miss	Sarah	Modern Languages	
1984 - 1995	White	Mr	Andrew	Science	
1969 -	Whittle	Mr	Donald	French and German	
1977 -	Wickens	Mr	David	History	
1983 - 2005	Williams	Mr	Jan	Mathematics	CCF Contingent Cmdr
2000 - 2000	Williams	Mr	Simon	Mathematics	
1970 - 1974	Williams	Mr	Brian	Mathematics	
1944 - 1945	Williamson	Miss	G	Prep/Domestic Science	
1963	Wilsdon	Mr.	David	Religious Education	
1957 - 1971	Wiscombe	Mr	John	Geography & Workshop	
1981 - 1988	Wong	Miss	Yin	Env. Science & History	
1988 to date	Wood	Mrs	Dot	Art	Director of Arts
1988 to date	Wood	Mr	Ian	History	
2005 to date	Wooderson	Ms	Gina	Mathematics	
2000 to date	Wootton	Mr	Nic	Design Technology	Head of Dept
1980 -	Yeo	Miss	Lorna	History	
1976 - 1976	Youds	Mr			
1998 - 2000	Young	Mrs	Elaine		Head of Sixth

* Denotes staff from the Lyme Regis Senior School in Church Street who transferred to Woodroffe in 1964

Appendix 2: Support Staff

Office/Admin	Head's Secretary	Bursar	SEN	Midday Supervisors
BONNER Pauline	(In date order)	RICKARD Peter	BARRATT-PEARCE Janet	ALLEN Carolann
BURROWS Rachel	HAMPSON Mrs	SLEIGH Gill	BREACH Sonya	BARTLETT Paula
CHADNEY Sue	PARTRIDGE Miss	**Finance**	BRITCHFORD Heather	BIZLEY Ruth
CREEDON Cindy	JACKSON Mrs	PERRY Margaret	BUSH Caroline	CASE Helen
CROSTON Gill	RAISON Gaye	SUMMERS Kathy	CHESTERTON Susie	CASTLE Mrs
DAWSON Peter	BAX Sylvia	TOWNSEND Kath	COOPER Sarah	CROSS Hayley
DIXON Diana	WARR Gilly	**Site Staff**	DAVENPORT Gemma	ELLIOTT Jan
FARDON Vanessa	**Technicians**	BAKER Derek	EDWARDS Wendy	FORSE Mrs
FAIRLEY Barabara	BADMAN David	DAVEY Mal	ENRIGHT Kate	GAIT Mrs
GODDARD Alan	BALL Mary	DRING Graham	FORTNAM Barrie	GALE Dennis
HEWSON Rosemary	BRETT Derek	EMMETT H	GOLDING Geoff	GIBBS Alicia
HILL Caroline	BURT Jason	FISHER C	GREEN Marion	HITCHCOCK Betty
KEW-DONNELLY Ruth	CLARKE Laurence	FURZEY Peter	HALDEN Carol	KNIGHT Jenny
LARCOMBE Sheila	COCKRAM Colin	GRIFFITHS Kevin	HALL Jill	LARCOMBE Suzanne
LOWE Carys	FAIRLEY Maureen	GUPPY Terry	HEFFERNAN Kim	LATCHAM Joanne
MATTHEWS Jill	FARRANT Richard	LAVEROCK John	JOHNSON Linda	MILLER Christine
MOWBRAY Sally-Ann	GOODE Mike	LEE Mr A A	McCLINTOCK Susan	MORRISON Mrs
NEWMAN Sarah	GOODRICK Mike	MARSH Harry	MOORE Ros	PEMBERTON Nichola
PAYNE Julie	HUMPHREYS Tracey	MACANLEY Mr	NEWMAN Rebecca	POWER Josephine
PEDDER Elizabeth	INGREMS Claire	PRICE David	OLLIS Sarah	PYLE Mrs
PIERCE Sarah	KINGSHOTT Mrs L	ROWE Brian	PERRY Rodney	REED Mrs
PIERCE Vicky	MORRIS Trefor	ROWSELL Mr	PETTIFER Sue	TAYLOR Tracey
PITTARD Rachel	NEESAM Brian	STOCKER T	PHILLIPS Jeff	WASON Lynette
SAWBRIDGE Caroline	NICHOLSON Andrew	SWEETLAND Claire	PITT Joan	WASON Ruth
STEVENS Jackie	POLDING David	WATTS Ewart	RUSSELL Zandra	WILKINS Julie
STRUTHERS-FROST Barbara	RICE Ron	WHITE Nigel	SECRETT Trish	WISCOMBE May
TOWNSEND Michael	ROBSON Chrissie	**Kitchen Supervisors**	SIMPSON Tracey	WOOD Mrs
WALSH Elizabeth	ROBSON Scott	BARLOW Marion	SKILTON Kate	WRIGHT Mrs
WARE Cherrill	STRUTT Alan	CRABB Margaret	SNADDON Doris	YATES Diane
WELLS Sue	SUMMERS Mark	DEVEY Terry	TWEDDLE Denise	
WILSON Alex	TAYLOR Paul	JUDD Jackie	VINE Sue	
	TERRY Nichola	NASH Mrs	WILLEY David	
	WATTS Linda	SOLWAY Mrs	WINWARD Simon	
	WILSON C S	WADHAM Miss		

Appendix 3 – Head Boy & Head Girl (List incomplete as no central record kept)

Date	Head Boy	Head Girl	Date	Head Boy	Head Girl
1923 - 1924			1967 - 1968	Alistair Egglestone	Maureen Hills
1924 - 1925			1968 - 1969	Ken Everett	Sheena Cockburn
1925 - 1926			1969 - 1970	Martin Hills	Victoria Besley
1926 - 1927	J Mence		1970 - 1971	William Pedley	Virginia Matthews
1928 - 1929			1971 - 1972	Sherren Hobson	Rosemary Bowditch
1930 - 1931			1972 - 1973	Anthony Buke	Belinda Taylor
1931 - 1932			1973 - 1974	Mark Prince	Nicola Dare
1932 - 1933			1974 - 1975	Colin Lowther	Sally Collier
1934 - 1935			1975 - 1976	Andrew Rattenbury	Sheila Bax
1935 - 1936			1976 - 1977	Clive Lathey	Kathleen Thomas
1936 - 1937			1977 - 1978	Stephen Scholar	Nicola Murdoch
1937 - 1938			1978 - 1979	Mark Parris	Karen Woodbridge
1938 - 1939	T B Reakes	M J Lane	1979 - 1980	Ewan Kelbie	Nikki McCrae
1939 - 1940	Cecil Hodges		1980 - 1981	Myles Harrison	Susan Cotton
1940 - 1941	W E Potter	M E Stark	1981 - 1982		
1941 - 1942	V A Nutland	M E Stark	1982 - 1983	Nigel Dallas-Conte	Karen Moylan-Jones
1942 - 1943	E R Camplin	M L Watton	1983 - 1984	Robert Farrant	Amanda Maxwell
1943 - 1944	G G Baker	P A Underhill	1984 - 1985	Robin Tarling	Katkin Mayne
1944 - 1945	A H Beaven		1985 - 1986	Jeremy White	Miranda Smith
1945 - 1946	A H Beaven		1986 - 1987	Duncan Gray	Sally Newman
1946 - 1947	H W Gladding	Patricia Gladding	1987 - 1988	Peter Wild	Rebecca Percival
1947 - 1948	J Grant	Jillian Ramage	1988 - 1989	Matthew Smith	Maisie Hill
1948 - 1949	C W Wilson	Pat Gladding	1989 - 1990	Tristan Harris	Natalie Price
1949 - 1950	M J B Kemp	J Taylor	1990 - 1991	Timothy Davis	Claire-Louisa Smith
1950 - 1951	E J Harniman	J Taylor	1991 - 1992	Gavin Lewis	Angela Spalding
1951 - 1952	D Kirkland	Daphne Keeley	1992 - 1993	David Bentley	Rebecca Jones
1952 - 1953	R Keeley	Rachel Keeley	1993 - 1994	Simon Holt	Carla Mansbridge
1953 - 1954	Roger Keeley	Jennifer Lawrence	1994 - 1995	Dominic Holland	Harriet Marsh
1954 - 1955	P Sanders	Ann Stapleforth	1995 - 1996	Harold FitzGerald	Kelly Avis
1955 - 1956	R St J Cross	Judith Williams	1996 - 1997	Toby Guiducci	Isabel Rawlins
1956 - 1957	H C Hoare (Jim)	J Shaw	1997 - 1998	Adam Clark	Victoria Smyth
1957 - 1958	W H F Lang	Katharine Hulburd	1998 - 1999	Robert Hankey	Anna Case
1958 - 1959	N N Newall	Betty Ody	1999 - 2000	Benjamin Davenport	Elizabeth Richards
1959 - 1960	John Watson	Margaret Mackie	2000 - 2001	Benjamin Coombs	Beth Atyeo
1960 - 1961	Paul Apanasewicz	Patricia Attfield	2001 - 2002	Jonathon Warren	Louisa Pearson
1961 - 1962	Richard Bateman	Barbara Jemphrey	2002 - 2003	Murray Saunders	Katherine Whiteman
1962 - 1963	Roger Bishop	Susan Cradduck	2003 - 2004	Richard Bugler	Karolyn Mandy
1963 - 1964	Paul Hewett	Carolyn Pearn	2004 - 2005	Hugo Bugg	Emily Baigent
1964 - 1965		Rosemary Knight	2005 - 2006	Fraser Wallace	Faye Cable
1965 - 1966	Pat Roper	Roberta Dare	2006 - 2007	Tom Floyd	Miriam Hillyard
1966 - 1967	John Calder	Sonia Love	2007 - 2008	Jake Dove	Hazel Hathway

Appendix 4: List of Ex-Pupils who served in World War II

The school magazine published in July 1945 included the following list:

Died in the Service of the Nation:

J Goodfellow	Mus.	Royal Marine Band
C Caddy		Royal Army Ordnance Corps
J Small	Coder	Royal Navy
K. Blackmore	Sergt.	Royal Army Ordnance Corps
S Henderson		Royal Air Force
D A Watton		1st Battalion Parachute Regiment
J Hussey		Royal Air Force
H F Searle	Warrant Officer	Royal Air Force
B J Teague	Captain	Royal Marines
K Halliday		Royal Air Force
E Britton	Pilot Officer	Royal Air Force
W F C Ashmore	Capt.	1/8th Gurkha Rifles (14th Army)
R Stapleforth	Flying Officer	Royal Air Force

Reported Missing, Believed Killed:

J Van Allen	Sergt.	Royal Army Ordnance Corps
H Holman	Sergt. Pilot	Royal Air Force

Reported Missing, Believed Prisoner of War:

F Moore		Royal Air Force (Marine Section)

Prisoners of War:

D Rowe	Lce/Cpl	Corps of Military Police
E D Lillington	Sgt Conductor	Royal Army Ordnance Corps WO Class 1

With the Colours:

J Alner	LAC	Royal Air Force
W Allen		Fleet Air Arm
P Baker	Flt. Mechanic	Royal Air Force
B T R Baker	LAC	Royal Air Force
R Baker	Air Cadet	Royal Air Force
G Baker		Intelligence Corps
W Butt	Sergt.	Royal Air Force
D Boutland	Sergt.	Royal Air Force
L W Baker	Cpl.	Royal Air Force
G J Bussell	P/Officer	Royal Navy

E J Bridle	LAC	Royal Air Force
S H Bosence	Sergt.	Royal Air Force
M Bamford	S/Sergt.	Royal Engineers
L W Bull	LAC	Royal Air Force
N Bowditch	LAC	Royal Air Force
G Cheyne	LAC	Royal Air Force
R E Copp	S/Sergt.	Royal Army Ordnance Corps
J Case	Cpl.	Royal Air Force
R N V Canney	LAC	Royal Air Force
C B Cook	Lieut.	Royal Navy
F C Chappell		Royal Air Force
H Chappell		Army Technical School (Boys)
I H Clarke	LAC	Royal Air Force (Radio Location)
J Culley		General Service Corps
L Chaffey		Royal Marines
P Childs	Lieut.	The Buffs
G Chandler		Fleet Air Arm
D Copp	Cadet	Royal Air Force
J F Dawson, MC	Capt & Adjt	Royal Artillery
P Davies		South African Air Force
D Dampier	Cpl	4th Dorsets
J Dunning		Royal Army Ordnance Corps
G Diment	Cpl	Royal Engineers
A C Dickenson	Cpl	Royal Air Force
P Downing		Royal Air Force (Operations Research)
C J Eglon	Section Cmdr.	British Red Cross, MEF
C Fewins	Lieut.	Royal Artillery (Educational Section)
W Farmer		8th Devons
W. French	Sgt.	Air Borne Troops
H Freeman	LAC	Royal Air Force
D.Good	LAC	Royal Air Force
N D Gollop		6th Dorset Regiment
S Gollop		Royal Army Pay Corps
P Gordon		Royal Air Force
G Glyde		Royal Armoured Corps
J Genge		Royal Engineers
R Gage	Signaller	Royal Navy
A Henderson	Pilot Officer	Royal Air Force
V Homyer	Chief P/Officer	Royal Navy
C W H Hall	Flt./Sergt.	Royal Air Force
E Healey		Royal Artillery
W E Hodges	Cpl	Royal Army Ordnance Corps.

Name	Rank	Unit
C Hodges	Captain	Dorset Regiment
J Holman		Royal Army Ordnance Corps.
J R Hider	LAC	Royal Air Force
G Hider		Royal Air Force
J Hoare		Royal Air Force
J Hoskins	Capt.	Royal Tank Corps
J Hall	3rd Officer	Merchant Service
J Hambidge	Sergt.	Royal Artillery
J E Harvey	Radio Officer	Merchant Navy
F Hiscock	P/Officer	Royal Navy (Dispensing Pharmacist)
H Hiscock	Cpl	Royal Air Force
A Halliday		Royal Navy (Radar)
W Jelley	Flt. Sergt.	Royal Air Force
D Jefford	P/Officer	Royal Navy
W F Kenny	Sergt.	Royal Air Force
W Loosemore		Fleet Air Arm
H Lugg	Cpl.	Royal Artillery
A W Love	Cpl.	Royal Air Force
A E Love	LAC	Royal Air Force
C Lancashire		Royal Signals (Wireless Operator)
W Matthews	Sergt. Major	4th Dorsets Regiment
H R N Marker	Lieut.	Royal Engineers
K Marker	Cpl	Royal Artillery
R Moore	Lieut.	4th (Brit) Div. Provost Coy.
J Mothersole	CSM	Royal Engineers
H Medley	Flt/Serg.	Royal Air Force
J McDonnell	Lieut.	Royal Artillery
D Mawdsley	Captain	Royal Army service Corps
J Manfield		Royal Navy
C MacGillivray	Pilot Officer	Royal Air Force
D Mence		Royal Air Force
K Northcott	1/C Stoker	Royal Navy
R C Nute	Chief P/Officer	Royal Navy
E Nute	P/Officer	Royal Navy
V A Nutland		Royal Air Force
D J Owen	Capt.	Royal Corps of Signals, GHQ Liaison
S Philbrick	Flt. Sergt.	Royal Air Force
H Philbrick	Sergt.	Royal Air Force
C W Powell		REME
R J Parsons	Cpl	Royal Air Force
W S Prescott	Capt.	Intelligence Corps.
V R Pitfield	Sergt.	2nd Dorset Regiment

Name	Rank	Service
W E Potter		Royal Armoured Corps.
R J Prescott	Sub. Lieut.	Fleet Air Arm
A Pincott	Sub. Lieut.	Royal Navy
J Ridgewell	Sgt. Obsr/Nav.	Royal Air Force
J Rattenbury	Lieut.	Royal Naval Volunteer Reserve
S Rowe		Royal Air Force
T Reakes	LAC	Royal Air Force
F Rowe		Royal Air Force
R J Sharpe	P/Officer	Fleet Air Arm
A Stocker	Sergt.	Royal Army Pay Corps
F Stretch, MM	Sergt.	1st Dorset Regiment
D Saunders		Royal Electrical & Mechanical Engineers
W E Sweetland		Royal Army Service Corps
V P Smith	L/Cpl	Royal Army Service Corps
S C Stapleforth		Royal Army Service Corps
D J Stapleforth	Cpl	Royal Air Force
C W Searle	L/Cpl	4th Dorset Regiment
W Southcombe		Royal Air Force (Wireless)
M Saunders		Army Technical School (Boys)
C Sansom		Royal Sussex Regt. 9th Armoured Division
J Scott	P/Off. Instructor	Royal Air Force
B Snell		Royal Armoured Corps
B Stretch		Mechanical Transport
L Thresher	Sergt.	Royal Electrical & Mechanical Engineers
M V Tucker	Chief PO	Fleet Air Arm
R J Tucker	Petty Officer	Fleet Air Arm
F Turner	Lce/Sergt	Royal Artillery
G Towner	P/Officer	Royal Navy
P M Teague	Lieut.	Att. 30th Devons
E. Turner	Cpl.	Army Dental Corps
R Tinkler		Royal Navy
S Venton	Flt/Sergt.	Royal Air Force
J F Watton	Lieut.	The Border Regiment
J Watson	Cpl.	Royal Armoured Corps
K Wallbutton	LAC	Royal Air Force
D Williams	Mus.	Band, Grenadier Guards
C G Warren	LAC	Royal Air Force
G Wiscombe	Warrant Officer	Royal Air Force

Appendix 5: Trophy List

Name of Trophy	Date and Name of Recipient	
House Championship Lyme Regis County Secondary School – Presented by the Rt Hon The Earl of Shaftesbury KP, GCVO, GBF	1923 – 1926 Woodroffe 1927 – 1929 Shaftesbury 1930 – 1932 Woodroffe 1933 – 1934 Shaftesbury 1935 Woodroffe 1936 – 1942 Shaftesbury 1943 Woodroffe	1944 – 1945 Shaftesbury 1946 Woodroffe 1948 Woodroffe 1949 – 1953 Shaftesbury 1957 Woodroffe 1958 School House 1959 & 1960 Woodroffe
Interhouse Football Cup Presented by A J Woodroffe, JP, CC Chairman of Governors and County Education Committee - 1924	1923 Woodroffe 1924 Shaftesbury 1925 & 1926 Woodroffe 1927 - 1929 Shaftesbury 1930 – 1932 Woodroffe 1933 – 1946 Shaftesbury 1947 – 1952 Woodroffe	1953 Shaftesbury 1954 & 1955 Woodroffe 1956 & 1957 School Hse 1958 Woodroffe 1959 – 1962 Shaftesbury 1972 Blake 1973 Blake
Dorset Choral Association	1925 - 1927 Sturminster Marshall Band of Hope Boys 1928 1st Colehill Boy Scouts	
Lyme Regis Grammar School Inter-House Boxing Cup Presented by R J Woodroffe, Esq	1930 Woodroffe 1931 – 1936 Shaftesbury 1937 & 1938 Woodroffe	
Tennis Singles Championship (Cup)	1932 E M Small 1933 M Jefford 1934, 1935 & 1936 B Dampier 1937 M E McDonnell 1938 M J Lane 1940 M L Watton 1941 M C C MacGillivray 1942 & 1943 M L Watton 1944 A M Hunt 1945 & 1946 A E Thomas 1947 & 1948 R M Turner 1949 to1952 J Long 1953 S Woollard	1954 & 1955 J Williams 1956 J Frampton 1957 & 1958 R Toye 1959 J Richards 1960 J Williams 1961 P G Shaw 1962 C Pearn 1963 M Matcham 1964 C Pearn 1965 & 1966 J Biscoe 1972 & 1973 A Foreman 1976 N Murdoch 1982 M D Williams
Junior Cross Country Cup	1933 Stratton	
Lyme Regis Grammar School Hockey Shield 1938 Presented by Mr & Mrs Staples	1938 & 1939 Shaftesbury 1940 – 1942 Woodroffe 1943 Shaftesbury 1944 Woodroffe 1945 & 1946 Shaftesbury 1947 Woodroffe 1948 & 1950 Shaftesbury	1951 Woodroffe 1952 Shaftesbury 1953 Woodroffe 1954 Shaftesbury 1957 – 1960 School House 1961 & 1962 Shaftesbury
Challenge Cup – Cricket School V Old Boys Assoc Presented by Mr & Mrs W F Reakes In memory of their son T B Reakes	No recipients named	
West Dorset Schools Athletics Association Shield	1949 to 1953 LRGS 1954 Bridport Grammar School	

Senior Girls	1955 & 1956 LRGS	
West Dorset Schools Athletics Association Shield Senior Boys	1949 to 1952 LRGS 1953 LRGS/Bridport Grammar 1955 Beaminster Grammar	1956 Bridport Grammar 1957 Colfox School
West Dorset Schools Athletics Association The Abbott Shield – Secondary Grammar	1950 & 1951 Lyme Regis 1952 Bridport 1953 – 1957 Lyme Regis 1958 Barnes (Colfox) 1959 Hardys (Colfox)	Intermediate 1963 Beaminster 1964 Colfox 1965 Beaminster
Old Girls' Association Hockey Shield	1952 – 1954 School House 1963 School House	1971 Blake 1972 Blake
West Dorset Schools Athletics Association The Abbott Shield – Secondary Modern	1954 Bridport General 1955 – 1957 St Francis School 1958 Beaminster School 1959 – 1961 St Francis School	1962 Beaminster Boys 1963 Eggarton & Lewesdon (Beaminster) 1964 Woodroffe
Lyme Regis Grammar School Physical Education Girls	1955 J Williams 1956 – 1958 H Bowditch 1959 P Attfield 1961 S Hulburd & C Wiscombe 1962 M Matcham 1965 P Curtis 1968 & 1969 H Legg	1971 C Guinn 1972 A Foreman 1973 A Blake 1974 J Fairley 1975 J Fairley & L Smith 1976 S Rodwell 1977 A Jones
Lyme Regis Grammar School – Physical Education Boys	1956 – 1958 R Jones 1959 R Hutchinson 1960 & 1961 R Budden 1962 F C Pile 1963 A V Fasolino 1966 A R Stephens	1969 & 1970 M H Hills 1972 – 1975 S Perry 1976 M Perry 1978 S Angus and M Parrish 1979 M Parrish
Lyme Regis Grammar School Inter-house Tennis Competition Presented by Ruth Toye November 1957	1957 Woodroffe 1958 School House 1959 Woodroffe 1960 School House	1961 Woodroffe 1962 Woodroffe 1963 Woodroffe 1973 Blake
House Cricket The "Marcus" Cup – In Memory of AC2 Michael Gearing RAF – 19.02.47	1958 Woodroffe 1959 Shaftesbury 1960 Woodroffe 1961 Shaftesbury	1972 Blake 1973 Blake
Girls' Athletics Standards Trophy (Cup)	1958 – 1961 School House 1962 Shaftesbury	1972 A Bearpark 1973 J Foreman
Lyme Regis Grammar School Netball	1962 School House 1963 Woodroffe	1973 Blake 1974 Blake
The Warne Cup for Rugby	1971 Somers 1972 Blake/Lister 1973 Blake	
First Year Cross Country Cup	1972 N Legg 1973 S Rattenbury 1974 R Harris	1981 R Retter 1986 M Wiscombe 1987 J Romain
Shield Presented by Mr J Awford	1972 J Hellier & C Guinn 1975 D Skinner 1977 T Foote	1980 T Herbertson 1984 Allan Dampier 1985 Katie Butterworth

1st Year Boys' Physical Education	1972 N Legg 1973 S Rattenbury 1974 R Harris	1986 E Burke 1987 Mark Hill
The Woodroffe School House Swimming Cup	1972 & 1973 Blake	
Junior Girls Double Tennis Trophy	1972 J Foreman & L Jordan 1973 J Foreman & E Jordan	

Junior Girls PE Cup	1972 & 1973 J Foreman
	1974 C Murphy
	1975 A L Bown
	1976 L E Gannon
	1977 S E Bown
	1978 J D Pratt
	1979 A A Halsey
	1980 M N Payne
		1981 S F Peach and
		    K D Cross
		1982 Cheryl Askew and
		    Diane Maxwell
		1983 and 1984
		    Vicky Woodbridge
		1985 S Eyres and
		    L Craddock

Athletics Standards Cup	1972 C Spurway 1973 K Walburn & D Burkhalter 1974 P Hardy	
Junior Swimming Cup Presented by Blue Lagoon Swimming Pools Limited	1972 & 1973 K Wiseman 1974 G Bell & B Jones 1975 R Chittenden & S Hurrell	1976 S Bown & K Pembroke 1983 D Duke
First Year Girls' PE	1972 S Andrews 1977 T Samways 1980 R Miller 1981 V L King 1982 V Woodbridge 1983 S Eyres	1984 Lisa Craddock & Ruth Saphorgan 1985 J Woodbridge 1986 Anita Smith 1987 Myfanwy Griffith
The Endeavour Cup for Girls' Physical Education Presented by Mrs P M Browne	1973 S Blake 1974 S Andrews 1977 L Smith 1978 & 1979 K J Wood	1980 J Pratt 1985 & 1986 S Huey 1987 D Maxwell
The Endeavour Cup for Boys' Physical Education Presented by Mrs P M Browne	1973 P Bell 1974 R Bilson 1975 G Barton	1976 H J S Williams 1978 J K Hawkes
The Woodroffe School Cup Modern Languages - French	1974 E Warne 1976 A Dunne, C Bennet 1977 H Everett 1978 T Everett 1979 T Chard 1980 K Healey 1981 K Butterworth	1982 T Pennington 1983 S Townsend 1984 N Everett 1985 S Elvin & R Thom 1986 J Shepherd 1987 D Jones and R Duncombe-Anderson
The Woodroffe School Modern Languages German Cup	1974 P Vaughan 1975 D Peach 1976 C Goddard 1977 H Jordan 1978 H Everett	1979 R Keeley 1982 T Pennington 1983 Kate Butterworth 1985 A Roberts 1986 K Tucker
The Woodroffe School Senior French Cup	1974 Elizabeth Warne 1975 Rachel Bown 1976 Linda Johnson 1977 Cindy Dare	1980 Ghislaine Silvers 1983 Nichola Meadley 1984 Nicola Harding & Sally Newman

		1978 Helen Jordan	1986 Sally Newman
		1979 Susan Tristam	1987 Stella Elvin
The Woodroffe School The Spoken Word		1975 Sally Collier 1976 & 1977 Jonathan Baker	1981 Helen Broom 1987 Glyn Watkins & Georgina Burke
The Woodroffe School Chess Trophy (Cup)		1975 Lister	
VIth Form Chess Championship		1976 M Newman 1977 S Poole	
Senior Debating Society Brain of Woodroffe		1977 – 1978 J Cozens 1978 – 1979 S Pipe	

The Hart Shield for
  Junior Music
		1981 Jason Brooks
		1982 Jeanne Lee
		1983 Sally Newman
		1984 Simon Brooks
			1985 Amy Tukcker
			1986 Simon Brooks
			1987 Rachel D-A and
			    P Duplock

The Woodroffe School Junior German Cup		1983 T Shepherd 1984 S Snell 1985 Glyn Watkins	
The Woodroffe School The Eli Emmett Trophy for Art and Craft		1983 A Nuttall	

The Woodroffe School Award for
Drama presented by Lindley and
Daphne Baker (Cup)
		1983 Josephine Bartle
		1984 Josephine Bartle
		1985 Nick Pridden
			1986 Martin Bartle &
			    Anna Roberts
			1987 Fiona Bradley &
			    Peter Wild

The Kidson Cup Girls' Cross Country		1985 V Woodbridge 1986 S Burke	
GTi Electronics Group Ltd Special Award for Excellence in Information Technology (Cup)		March 1991 Aubrey Kingsbury April 1992 Louise Nash	
The Woodroffe School Victrix Ludorum Cup		No recipients named	
Victor Ludorum		No named recipients	
The Malcolm Pugh Sports Cup - School V Staff Presented by Mrs G Pugh		No recipients named	
Rotary Club of Axminster Lecturette Winner		No recipients named	
Woodroffe School Enterprise Award (Shield)		No recipients named	
Staples Cup		No named recipients	
The Endeavour Cup for Senior Boys – Presented by Mrs N Browne		No named recipients	
Hoyne Challenge Plate		No named recipients	
West Dorset Rugby Sevens Junior Cup		No named recipients	
Tutor Group Quiz Cup		No named recipients	

Appendix 6: List of Governors

(Incomplete information as no central record of Governors who have served is held)

Dates	Surname	Name	Role
1931 - 1964	Allhusen	Major O	Devon LEA
1935 - 1953	Atterbury	Mr	Clerk to the Governors
1976 -	Atyeo	Mrs B M	Dorset LEA
2003 to date	Auckland	Mr Keith	Parent Governor
1964 - 1974	Awford	Mr J A	Dorset LEA/PTA
1975 - 1976	Awford	Mr J A	Dorset LEA
1978 - 1983	Badman	Mr D	Staff Governor
1971 - 1975	Bailey	Capt P I E	
1940 - 1955	Baker	Mr R W	Lyme Regis Borough Council
1969 - 1979	Baker	Mr R W	Dorset LEA
1996 - 2006	Baker	Mr Colin	Parent Govenor
1985 to 1989	Bax	Mrs Sylvia	Clerk to the Governors
1998 to date	Beck	Mrs Jane	Dorset LEA Governor
1985	Beckett	Mrs L I	Clerk to the Governors (LEA)
1992 - 1996	Beddows	Mr David	Parent Governor
1996 - 2000	Bennett	Mr Paul	Teacher Governor
1992	Birks	Mr Michael	First Governor
1945 - 1947	Blanchard	Mr H (Mayor)	Lyme Regis Borough Council
1989	Bolton	Mr Jim	Co-opted Governor
1954 - 1955 1957 - 1966	Bonning	Mrs L S	Lyme Regis Borough Council Dorset Representative
1953 - 1955	Bosence	Mr N	Parents Representative
1923 - 1930	Bowden Smith	Mr	Devon
1955 -	Bowditch	Mr J C	Lyme Regis Borough Council
1983 - 1985	Boyce	Mr Rod	Teacher Governor
1949 ? - 1958	Bragg	Capt OC	Dorset LEA
1965 - 1968	Bredin	Brig A E C	Devon LEA
2003 to date	Broad	Mr Jeremy	Parent Governor
1979 - 1981	Broom	Mr H J	WDDC
	Brown	Rev Doreen	First Governor
	Brown	Mr Peter	First Governor
1971 - 1974	Browne	Mrs B P A	Parents' Representative
1952 -	Buck	Mrs M	Bridport District Council
2003 -	Burleigh	Mrs Sophy	Parent Governor
1995 - 2000	Burton	Mr Peter	Co-opted Governor
1978 - 1983	Caffrey	Mr A	Staff Governor
1994	Carlé	Mr Peter	First Governor
2007 to date	Calow	Mrs Janet	Partnership Governor
1928	Cartwright	Mrs	Dorset LEA
1992 - 1996	Case	Mr Michael	Parent Governor
1977 - 1980	Chappell	Mr R F	Devon LEA
1962 - 1974	Charles	Rev J H A	Dorset LEA
1976 -	Chase	Mr J G	Dorset LEA

1996 - 2000	Chessell	Mrs Gwen	First Governor
1985	Clements	Mr Adrian	Mathematics
1996 - 2000	Coleman	Mrs Nicola	Parent Governor
1976 - 1979	Cook	Mr John	Staff Governor
2000 - 2004	Cook	Mr Robin	Parent Governor
1998 to 2007	Coussens	Mrs Audrey	Clerk to the Governors
1928 - 1954	Cox	Rev Canon Carew	LR Primary Schools Rep
1996 to date	Cozens	Mr David	Partnership Governor
1923 - 1937 1958 - 1967	Crawford	Lt Col	Devon Representative Devon Representative
2004 to date	Cruwys-Finnigan	Mrs Anne	Teacher Governor
2003 to date	Cumming	Dr Ian	Parent Governor
2006 to date	Daly	Mr Mat	Staff Governor
1989	Davey	Mrs Maureen	LEA
2003 to date	Davies	Mrs Susan	Parent Governor
1992 - 1996	Dixon	Mr Patrick	Parent Governor
1983	Dowle	Mr Roger	Teacher Governor
1974 -1976	Edwards	Mrs P J	Dorset LEA
2006 to date	Elliott	Mrs Lyn	Partnership Governor
1923 - 1927	Ellis	Mr	
1940 - 1945	Emmett	W J (Mayor)	Lyme Regis Borough Council
1955 - 1958	Emerson	Mrs G A	Parents' Representative
2000 - to date	Etherington	Mrs Maureen	Community Governor
1983 -1987	Everett	Mr M	Parent Governor
1959 - 1975	Eyre	Cdr W J	Beaminster District Council
1999 - 2003	Faverty	Mr Jim	Parent Governor
1959 - 1984	Fortnam	Mr F D	Lyme Regis Borough Council/LEA
1995 to date	Fortnam	Mr Peter	Partnership Governor
1970 - 1976	Foulger	Col R E A	Bridport Rural District Council/WDDC
1976 - 1979	Fowell	Mr W G	WDDC
1976 -	Fradgley	Mrs P J	Dorset LEA
1942	Francillon	Mrs Angela F	Dorset LEA
1923 - 1925	Freeman Roper	Mr	
1980 - 1987	Gardner	Mr F	Devon LEA
1985 -	Gibson	Lt Col Hugh	First Governor/Chairman
2001 - 2005	Golds	Mr Trevor	Partnership Governor
1999 - 2003	Goodrick	Mr Mike	Staff Governor
1958 - 1969	Gould	Mr B	Parents' Representative
1937 - 1958	Greenshields	Lt Col	Devon LEA
1969	Gunnell	Miss R	
1996	Hallworth	Mr Stephen	Parent Governor/Chairman
1977 - 1980	Hart	Mrs J B	Parent Governor
1990	Heath-Coleman	Mr Graeme	Parent Governor
1974 -	Hercock	Mr R W	PTA/Dorset LEA

1989	Hicks	Mrs Julie	Parent Governor
1964 -	Hills	Mrs V	Parents' Representative
2006 to date	Hillyard	Mrs Caroline	Parent Governor
1962 - 1972	Homyer	Mr V J	Lyme Regis Borough Council
1974 -	Homyer	Mr V J	WDDC
1990 - 1998	Hoskins	Mrs Marilyn	Parent Governor/First Governor
1988 - 2000	Howe	Mr John	First Governor
1977 -	Howlett	Mr W D	Devon LEA
	Hudson	Mr Richard	Teacher Governor
1995 - 1999	Johnson	Mr David	Parent Governor
2000 - 2004	Joyner	Mr Chris	Staff Governor
1985 - 1986	Kabia	Miss Julia	Staff
1991 -	Kaye	Mr Andrew	First Governor
1977 - 1979	Keattch	Mr C J	
1924 - 1966	Kennedy	Mrs E M	Dorset LEA
1966 - 1974	Kennedy	Mr J	Dorset LEA
2006 to date	Kew	Mr T	Partnership Governor
1976 - 1978	Kidson	Mrs B P	PTA
1947 - 1957	King	Mr A F (Mayor)	Lyme Regis Town Council
1979 - 1986	Kolya	Mr Karl	Chairman
1966 - 1974	Lillington	Mr E D	Dorset LEA
1972 -	Lumsden	Mrs C L	Dorset LEA
1992 - 1996	Mandy	Mrs Sheena	Teacher Governor
1991 - 1995	Manners	Mr David	Teacher Governor
1983 - 1987	Manfield	Mrs Sylvia	Devon LEA
1923 - 1924	Markby	Mrs	Co-opted Lady member
1974 - 1978	May	Mr M J	Devon LEA
1974 - 1982	McLellan	Mr W	WDDC
1980 - 1987	Mead	Mr G T	Dorset LEA
1946 - 1956	Milward	Mr W E	Dorset LEA
1950 -	Milroy	Mr	
1994 - 1997	Monson	Mr Peter	First Governor
1928 - 1935	Moore	Mr	Clerk to the Governors LEA
2002 to date	Mowbray	Mr Adrian	Parent Governor
	Neil	Mr Stuart	First Governor
1976 -	Nuttall	Major J E	WDDC
1983 -1986	O'Kelly	Mrs Julia	Parent Governor/Devon LEA
1968 - 1974	Oliver	Mr R	Devon LEA
1969 - 1978	Olof	Mr M V	Devon LEA
1931	Owen	Mr	Lyme Regis Borough Council
	Parker	Mr David	Parent Governor
1950 - 1950	Partridge	Miss	Acting Clerk to the Governors
1983	Partridge	Miss A	Clerk to the Governors LEA
1923 - 1967	Pass	Lt Col A D	Dorset LEA
1949 - 1964	Pass	Mrs K O	Dorset LEA

2000 - 2003	Paxman	Mr Anthony	Partnership Governor
1964 - 1974	Peacock	Mrs M D	Beaminster Rural Council
1968 -	Pedley	Professor R	Dorset LEA
1988 to date	Perham	Mrs Jenny	Dorset LEA Governor
1926 - 1943	Pinney	Maj Gen Sir R	
1949 -	Pinney	Mr M A	Beaminster RDC
2002 - 2005	Pomeroy	Mr David	Parent Governor
1996 -	Poupard	Mrs Sheila	First Governor
1976	Powell	Mr W G	WDDC
1984 - 1999	Pratt	Mr Barrie	First Governor/Chairman
1968 - 1969	Preece	Mrs M E	
2006 to date	Pullinger	Mr Neil	Community Governor
1979 - 1980	Raikes	Rev Robert	Dorset LEA
1934 - 1940	Ramage	Mr	
1985	Rattenbury	Mrs C E	
1992 - 1997	Rawlins	Mrs Cora	Parent Governor
1991 - 1998	Rickard	Mr Peter	Clerk to the Governors
2000 - 2006	Robinson	Dr Barry	Co-opted Governor
1956 - 1964	Rowcroft	Maj Gen Sir Bertram	Dorset
1949 - 1952	Russell	Capt S C	Bridport RDC
1989	Sadler	Mrs Jo	Parent Governor
1923 - 1928	Sharley	Mr	Clerk to the Governors
1958 -	Shields	Capt C St B	Beaminster District Counci
1985	Slater	Dr B C	Clerk to the Governors
2003 - 2004	Sleigh	Mr Roy	Teacher Governor
1958 - 1964	Smith	Mrs N E	Parent Teachers Association
1923 - 1928	Spurr	Mrs	Co-opted Lady member
1951 – 1954 1955 - 1972	Staples	Mrs B M	Lyme Regis Borough Council
1981	Stevens	Mr A	Dorset LEA
2003 to date	Steward	Dr R P	Headteacher/Staff Governor
1983 - 1987	Stickland	Mr J	Dorset LEA
1979 - 1983	Swainston	Mrs M	Staff Governor
	Sweetland	Mr Chris	Teacher Governor
1985	Tarling	Mr T	
1949 - 1955	Taylor	Mrs W E	Parents' Representative
1981 - 1984	Taylor	Mr Mark	Clerk to the Governors
2000 to 2006	Taylor	Mrs Caroline	Co-opted Governor
1988 - 1999	Terrett	Mr Tony	First Governor/Chairman
1985	Thomas	Mr James	Staff Governor
2000 to 2004	Thomas	Mr Howard	Parent Governor
1989	Thorne	Mr Charles	Co-opted Governor
1954 - 1961	Tiarks	Rev G A	Dorset Representative
1969 - 1974	Tidswell	Mr S	
1983	Toogood	Mr P J	Clerk to the Governors LEA

1985	Toohey	Miss Pauline	Clerk to the Governors LEA
1969	Turner	Mr R	Parents Representative
1998	Vivian	Mr Keith	First Governor
2003 - 2006	Warr	Mrs Gilly	Staff Governor
1928 - 1931	Washer	Mr	Lyme Regis Borough Council
1955 - 1958	Webster	Rev S	
1991	Whitfield	Mr Richard	First Governor
1992	Wicks	Mrs Jean	First Governor
1996 - 2000	Wicks	Mr John	Parent Governor
1971 - 1974	Wicks	Mr F D	
1955 - 1958	Williams	Mr W H	Parents' Representative
1972 - 1978	Williams	Mr S B	Lyme Regis Borough Council
1985 -	Williams	Mr S	Dorset LEA
1923 - 1928	Willson	Rev	
1980 - 1987	Wilsdon	Mrs Sylvia	Parent Governor
1966 -	Wood	Mrs J	Devon LEA
1989 - 1992	Woodbridge	Mrs Eddi	First Governor/Chairman
1923 - 1961	Woodroffe	Mr A J	Chairman of Governors
1929	Woodroffe	Mr R J	
1964 -	Woodroffe	Mrs R J	Dorset LEA
2004 to date	Wootton	Mr Nic	Teacher Governor
1933 - 1940	Worth	Mr	

Appendix 7: Chairman of Governors

1923 - 1960	Woodroffe	Mr Alban
1959 - 1964	Rowcroft	Maj Gen Sir Bertram, KBE, CB
1964 - 1975	Eyre	Cmdr W J, RN
1975 - 1984	Fortnam	Mr Douglas
1984 - 1987	Kolya	Mr Karl
1987- 1989	Gibson	Lt Col Hugh
1989 - 1992	Woodbridge	Mrs Eddi
1992 - 1997	Terrett	Mr Tony
1997 - 1999	Pratt	Mr Barrie
1999 - 2001	Chessell	Mrs Gwen
2001 - 2004	Hallworth	Mr Stephen
2004 to date	Perham	Mrs Jenny

Appendix 8 – Ten Tors Teams

Listed below are the names of some of the pupils past and present who have taken part in this gruelling event:

1976
David Hart, Paul Bell, Nigel Glover, Michael Burgess and Mark Stephenson (Captain)

1979
Jane Thompson, Nicky Clift, Fiona Brookbanks, Jane Olof, Catherine Edwardes, Claire Williams (Team Leader), Jackie Lathey and Andea Dunn (reserves)
Simon Pipe, John Buttfield, Leigh Geary, Andrew Murray, Laurie Wrigler, Simon Fowler (Team Leader), Hugh Bennet, Richard Edmonds and John Maunder (reserves)

1980
Jane Ronan, Susan Philips, Jo Crouch, Siobhan Porter, Joanne Pratt and Wendy van der Plank (Team Leader) Louise Woodman and Sarah Stead (reserves)
David Hughes, Michael Payne, Nigel Dallas-Conte, John Higgins, Charles Evans, Jonathan Maunder (Team Leader), Sean Jones, Iain Watters, Simon Telfer (reserves)

1981
Maria Brown, Jo Bartle, Lauraine Shaw, Mandy Maxwell (withdrew due to an injury), Maria Staples, Siobhan Porter (Team Leader) Cathy Herbert and Sue Jefferies (reserves)
Guy Smith, William Smee, Simon Gray, William Smee, Miles Harrison, Charles Evans (Team Leader), Reserves – Ian Watters and Ian Turner

1982
Maria Brown, Jane Van der Plank, Sue Woollard, Sarah Woodbridge, Katkin Mayne, Shiv Porter (Team Leader), Debbie Johnson (reserve)
Matthew Payne, Kirk Flanagan, Tim Clarke, John Chubb, Terry Prince, Adrian Wood, Miles Lowther, Jeremy Higgins (Team Leader)

1984
Adam Rigler (Team Leader)

1985
45 mile team - James Dillon, Derek McCullough, Guy Horsfall, Kevin Hunt, Graham Prebble, Simon Redfearn (Team Leader) David Hunkin and Jeremy White (reserves)
35 mile team - Katie Bentley, Sue Jenkin, Alison Herbertson, Vicky Woodbridge, Sally Peach (Navigator), Heather Crawford (Team Leader)

1986
45 mile team - Owen Dillon, David Hunkin, Jason Blackmore, Peter Blackmore, Philip Vittle, Jeremy White (Team Leader)
35 mile team - Kerry Joyce, Karen Warner, Amanda Hiett, Vicky Shaw, Sue Huey and Vicky Woodbridge (Team Leader)

1987
45 mile team - David Hibberd, Darcy Muncer, Iain Logan, Robert Radley, Stephen Broadhurst, Andrew Calame (Team Leader)
35 mile team - Kerry Joyce, Jackie Poulton, Eleanor Umbers, Katie Roche, Lorraine Jenkins, Fiona Bradley (reserve), Vicky Woodbridge (Team Leader)

1988
45 mile team - Stephen Broadhurst, Simon Walters, Robert Radley, Michael Moylon-Jones, Jason Fernie, Paul Beavis (reserve), Simon Smith (Team Leader)
35 mile team - Sam Eyres, Kathy Downey, Stella Elvin, Maisie Hill, Sinead Burker, Kylie Beck (reserve), Jackie Poulton (Team Leader)

1989
45 mile team - Ian Hunter, Daniel Saphorgan, Luke Naven, Tony Broadhurst, Steven Davey, Gareth Sweetland (reserve), Mark Pemberton (reserve), Richard Spalding (Team Leader)
35 mile team - Anita Cross, Georgina Burke, Ruth Saphorgan, Jo Calame, Jo Frost, Nicky Bradley (reserve), Chelsea Davine (reserve), Natalie Price (Team Leader)

1990
45 mile teams (both girls and boys) - Peter Edmonds, David Pratt, Nicholas Gray, Phil Hutchinson, Tim Davies, Ross Jenkins (Team Leader)
Kate Fleming, Jackie Sadler, Polly Duplock, Mandy MacDonagh, Natalie Shepherd, Tasmin Lovelace, Jess Woodbridge (Team Leader)

1991 (first time a mixed team was entered in the event)
Emma Sweetland sprained her ankle and was not able to compete.
Tom Eaton, Aubrey Kingsbury, Hannah Sadler, Claire Knight, Alistair Robbins, Angela Spalding (Team Leader)

1995
Natalie de Pinho, Volker Lamp, Nina Bergius, Paul Wallis and Harry FitzGerald (Team Leader). Heulwen Powell walked with the Bournemouth Youth Walkers Association

1996

CCF team – Sgt Nick Ollive, Cpl Gaeton Beresford, Cpl Robert Smith, L/Cpl Dan Buckley, Cadet Jessica Williams and Cadet Guy Holloway

1998

35 mile route - CCF - Guy Davis, Helen Crossley, Patrick Rattenbury, Warren Jones, Adrian Phillips and Taku Sato (Team Captain)

45 mile route - Daniel Salde, Chris Cozens, Ben Helsby, Matthew Bujniewics, James Drew, James Chesterton and Chris Pierce (Team Captain)

1999 (40th anniversary of Ten Tors)

35 mile course - CCF - Oliver Bailhache, Mat Davies, Chris Jenkins, Aaron Ray, Pat Rattenbury, Guy Davies and Darren Sansom (Team Captain)

45 mile route - Michael Salt, Simon Williams, Lee Aplin, John Bird, Edward Davis, Paul Gosling and Joe Joyner (Team Captain)

2000

45 mile route – Beth Ateyo, George Chesterton, Henry Guest, Mark Bailey, Spencer Davis and Taku Sato (Leader).

35 mile route – CCF – Sean Budden, Mitch Christopher, Humphrey Guest, Daniel Humble-Smith, Patrick Rattenbury and James Cope (Leader)

2001

Foot and mouth

2002

45 mile route – Michael Tappin, Stuart Doble, Harry Rabbetts, Seb Unwin, Rachel Cope and Judith Westoby (Team Captain)

2003

Rachel Cope, Theo Wilmot, Pippa Wyatt, Oliver Dixon, Matthew Trice, Laura Morley. James Everidge and Luke Taylor had also participated in training but were not selected for the squad

2004 and 2005 – no information available

2006

55 mile route – Rachel Cope, Pippa Wyatt, Shane How, Hamish Findlay, Jake Kondon, and Hugo Bugg (returning from last year)

45 mile route – Hamish Martin, Robert Cheeseman, Harry de Greff, Adam Packman, Phil Spencer and Kit Connell.

Teams are trained on a voluntary basis by members of staff, both teaching and non-teaching. Staff who have been involved in the training of Ten Tors included Mr Fred Middleton, Mr Michael Newman, Mr Andrew McPherson, Mr David Chambers, Mrs Karen Walker, Mrs Jo Culham, Mr Mark Riddington, Mr Richard Hudson, Mr Alan Brown, Mr Alistair Cope and Mrs Kath Townsend.

Appendix 9:

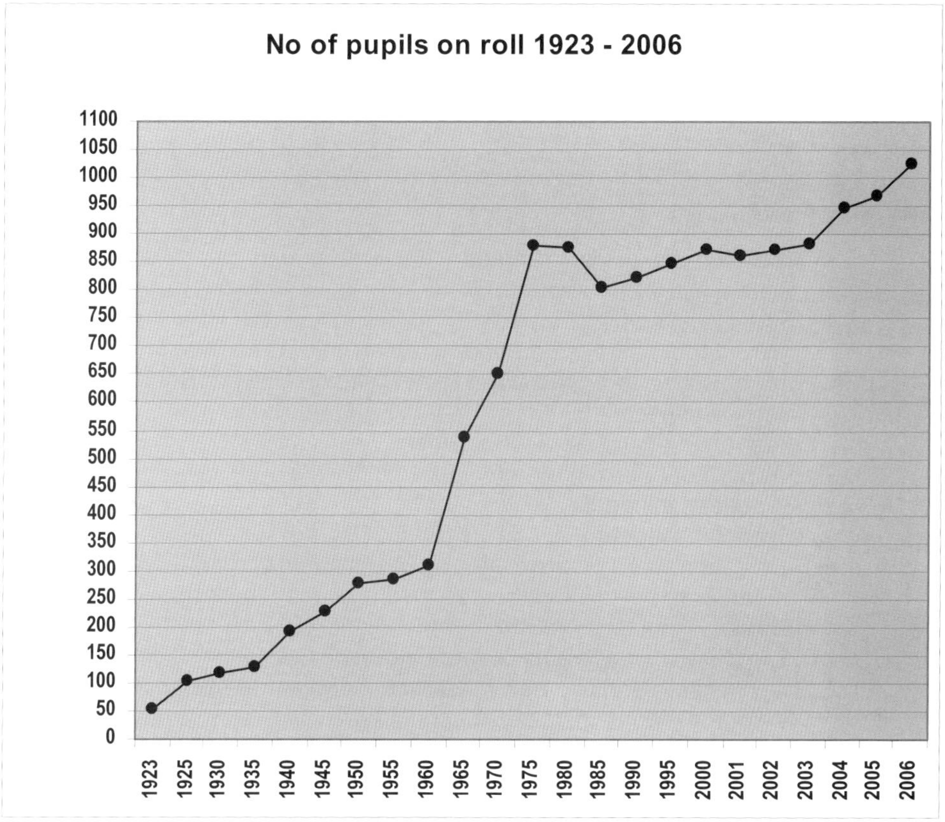

No of pupils on roll 1923 - 2006

Woodroffe students 2007

(Photograph from School Prospectus)

Appendix 10: Time Line 1923 to 2007

1923	Lyme Regis County Secondary School founded and Mr Greenfield appointed as Head, with Mr Woodroffe as Chairman of Governors
	Shaftesbury House and Woodroffe House formed
1925	School visited by HMI
1927	School renamed Lyme Regis Grammar School
	Mr Watton appointed as Head
	Old Boys Association formed
	School magazine started
1928	School visited by HMI
1931	In April foundation stone of new school laid by Mr Woodroffe
1932	In September School moved to new site on Uplyme Road
1933	School inspected
1934	Formation of Old Girls Association
1939	Preparatory Form opened
1940	Evacuees joined the school
1942	School inspected
1944	Education Act – Lord Butler – Selection according to age, ability and aptitude and also lifted the ban on women teachers marrying
	School inspected
	Twenty first anniversary of founding of LRGS
1945	New kitchen and two new classrooms opened at back of school
1946	Memorial plaque installed in school hall
	Mr Watton retired and Mr Pearn appointed
	Parents Association formed
	School Song and school motto introduced
1947	School Song first sung at Speech Day
	School leaving age raised to fifteen
	Preparatory Form closed
	Sixth Form introduced
	Introduction of ties and caps for boys, and gold tassels for prefects' hats
1948	School celebrated its Silver Jubilee and held its first Open Day
	Speech Day held at cinema due to numbers
1949	School inspected
	New laboratory opened for Physics and Technical Drawing
	Brass Lectern and large leather bound Bible presented to the school by the Old Boys' Association in memory of the Old Boys who had died in the Second World War
1950	Opening of St Andrews boarding house
	Two new rooms installed for Sixth Formers in the roof space over the Head's office
1952	First School Fete
	Opening of Harcombe House
1953	Speech Day moved to Marine Theatre
1954	School House formed for boarders
	General Certificate of Education introduced

1958	Grey flannel suits phased out for boys in favour of blazers and grey flannel trousers with gym slips replaced by skirts and blouses for girls
	New Biology lab and Technical Drawing room built on bank above school
	Start of Field Society
1959	School inspection
	Mr Woodroffe resigned as Chairman of Governors
1962	Transfer of pupils from Lyme Regis Junior School to Lyme Regis Senior School ceased with all pupils transferred to a newly built temporary classroom at LRGS
	Start of major building programme
	Speech Day in November at Marine Theatre with, for the first time, Juniors in the afternoon and Seniors in the evening
1963	Coram House formed and school renamed The Woodroffe School
	11+ abolished – Senior School in Lyme Regis closed
	First fifty mile walk took place in March
	Old Boys and Old Girls Associations disbanded and Woodroffe School Association formed for ex-pupils
1964	New buildings completed ie hall, gymnasium, changing rooms, three new laboratories and three prep rooms, art and crafts room and workshops plus new canteen
	Death of Mr Woodroffe
1965	Junior Speech Day moved to the end of the Summer Term
	Swimming pool opened
	Old school hall converted to the new Library, the Music Room enlarged and Domestic Science allocated a whole wing
1966	New CSE examination introduced
1969	Space under hall converted to two classrooms
	Hope Wright Fund started
	Rhode Hill opened as an additional boarding house
	Woodroffe, Shaftesbury, Coram and School House disbanded and new houses formed ie Blake, Lister and Somers
	First teams entered in Ten Tors
1970	Caps and berets no longer worn
1971	ROSLA block opened
1972	Mr and Mrs Pearn leave St Andrews
	Trousers introduced as an option for female pupils
	Raising of school leaving age to 16
1974	Additional temporary classroom installed
	Bus bay constructed and in use
1975	Inspectors visited the school
	Another temporary classroom installed
1976	Mr Pearn retires and Mr Butterworth appointed
1977	Homework diaries introduced
	Girls ran in the annual Cross Country Run for the first time
1979/1980	New build commenced with construction of facilities for Block A (Creative Arts) and Block B (Music and Modern Languages), plus the creation of car parking alongside the swimming pool

1980/1981	Major alterations/refurbishment to existing buildings including re-wiring, renovation of water tanks, installation of new boilers following the change over to gas and internal re-painting.
1981	Glass corridors now linking new build to old buildings ROSLA modified slightly and joined to main school building Re-build of £1.25k now complete Library moved to former Art rooms Work began on a footpath and footbridge extension beyond bus bay
1982	Open Day for parents 50th Anniversary of the school
1985	Retirement of Mr Butterworth and appointment of Mr Vittle Horizontal tutor groups introduced as opposed to vertical tutor groups
1986	Introduction of Certificate of Pre-Vocational Education (CPVE) and Technical, Vocational and Education Initiative (TVEI) First Lyme Regis Run Twenty fifth anniversary of Madrigal Group
1987	Woodroffe Parents' Association became Woodroffe Parent Teacher Association
1988	Education Reform Act – the most important legislation since the 1944 Education Act – outlined legislation for Local Management of Schools, Technology Colleges and Grant Maintained Schools Introduction of GCSE to replace GCE level and CSE
1989	First Dance Show held – Motion Commission Time Capsule buried outside hall First Staff/Pupil Cabaret Twenty fifth anniversary of comprehensive education
1990	Introduction of Local Management of Schools (LMS) Application made to "opt out"
1991	School became Grant Maintained School Shop opened School won a Sainsbury's Award valued at £3,000 School party travelled to Russia Harcombe House closed in October Renovation of school kitchens and installation of new equipment
1992	Combined Cadet Force started Former School Hall converted into offices and main reception area Conversion of old south wing into temporary Drama Studio and refurbishment of the adjacent Staff Room Reprographics area upgraded Mr Vittle resigned in November and Mr Cook took over as Acting Headteacher
1993	Mr Redman appointed as Head Renovation of School Hall St Andrews closed in July Lyme Regis Adventure Centre closed NVQs and GNVQs introduced
1994	New Science laboratory built over the old Biology lab Major repairs to flat roofs

	Governors made first unsuccessful application for Technology College status
1995	Erection of new sports store behind the gym
	Rugby tour to South Africa
	Madrigal Group tour to USA
	First links established with school in Slovakia
1996	Hockey tour to Canada
	Rhode Hill closed
	New IT room opened at the northern end of the quad
	School Inspection
1997	School week extended to twenty five hours
1998	The Schools Standards and Framework Act 1998 led to Grant Maintained schools being phased out with the introduction of Foundation/Community Schools
	Woodroffe becomes a foundation school
	Fair funding introduced
1999	Thornton Pearn Studio opened in October
	School Reunion held in Autumn Term
	Extension to Art and Design area to provide an additional room on C level and extensions to the Textiles and Ceramics areas
	Refurbishment of Science laboratories
	The timing of the school week was changed to twenty five one hour periods
2000	New Sports Hall was completed
	Basic toilet, changing and first aid facilities were established on top pitch
	OFSTED inspection
2001	Whole school computer network installed plus internet connection
	Barbados Hockey Tour
	Jazz Band tour to Barcelona
2002	First bid made for Arts College Status
	Introduction of embroidered polo shirts
2003	Curriculum at Key Stage 4 "freed up" with the only compulsory subjects being English, Maths, Science and RE.
	Retirement of Mr Redman and appointment of Dr Steward
	School achieved Arts College status
	School Reunion held in Autumn Term
	Woodroffe team won the Gold Medal in the European Science Olympiad
2004	Artsmark Gold Award achieved
	School achieved Investors in People Status
2005	Excellent OFSTED reported declared that the school was "good with some outstanding features".
2006	New literacy-based curriculum introduced for Year 7 pupils
2007	School Reunion held in October.

Appendix 11 – Staff Photograph – January 2007

(Photograph taken by Scott Robson)

Key to Staff Photograph

Back row:

Tracey Simpson, Jill Hall, Ian Snowling, David Manners, Jeremy Clulee, Michael Greenhough, Sophie Medd, Ruth Wason, Martin Grier, Richard Sloan, Simon Ransome-Williams, Nic Wootton, Peter Furzey, Nigel White, Peter Dawson

Next row:

Denise Tweddle, Susie Chesterton, Vicky Pearce, James Thomas, Alan Brown, Sarah Vincent, John Seabrook, Laurence Clarke, Alan Goddard, Simon Winward, Sheena Mandy, Martin Banfield, Hugh FitzGerald

Next row:

Gill Sleigh, Eddie Clark, Ian Wood, Neil Vincent, David Chambers, Jon Cullimore, Gary Wells, Chris Joyner, Chris Sweetland, Jean Shaw, Zahid Akram, Liz Corbett, Alex Wilson, Kathy Elliott, Tracey Curtis

Next row:

Anne Cruwys-Finnigan, Rebecca Barnes, Richard Vine, Jan Melvin, Mat Daly, Justin Loveland, Chrissie Robson, Chris Everidge, Zandra Russell, Rodney Perry, Pam Patterson, Cindy Creedon, Sally-Ann Mowbray, Ann Bruford, Gemma Davenport

Next row:

Lyn Lake, Hilary Warne, Claire Sweetland, Caroline Hill, Alison Bowskill, Linda Watts, Alison Brightwell, Sheila Larcombe, Kim Heffernan, Jenny Cowling, Carol Hyde, Gina Wooderson, Natalie David, Jackie Fletcher, Sheila Bland, Scott Robson

Front row:

Kathy Summers, Carys Lowe, Sharron Hutchings, Cherrill Ware, Jennie Golding, Gilly Warr, John Haylock, Richard Steward, Jo Culham, Dot Wood, Stephanie Humphries, Alison Edwards, Julia Lamb-Wilson

Absent on the day of the photograph: Karen Walker, Ellen Kumar, Sarah Ryerson, Claire Thornett, Stuart Ruffle, Anna Bugg, Vanessa Cropp, Diane FitzGerald, David Johnson, Julie Kabia, Kevin Griffiths, Mike Goodrick, Mary Ball, Emma Dixon, Tracey Humphries, Caroline Bush, Ros Moore, Linda Johnson, Trish Secrett, Sue Vine, Nicola Terry, Kath Townsend, Sue Chadney, Paula Bartlett, Hayley Cross, Carolann Allen, Nichola Pemberton and Helen Case

NB The photograph was taken on a Staff Training Day hence the casual attire

Appendix 12 - Maps

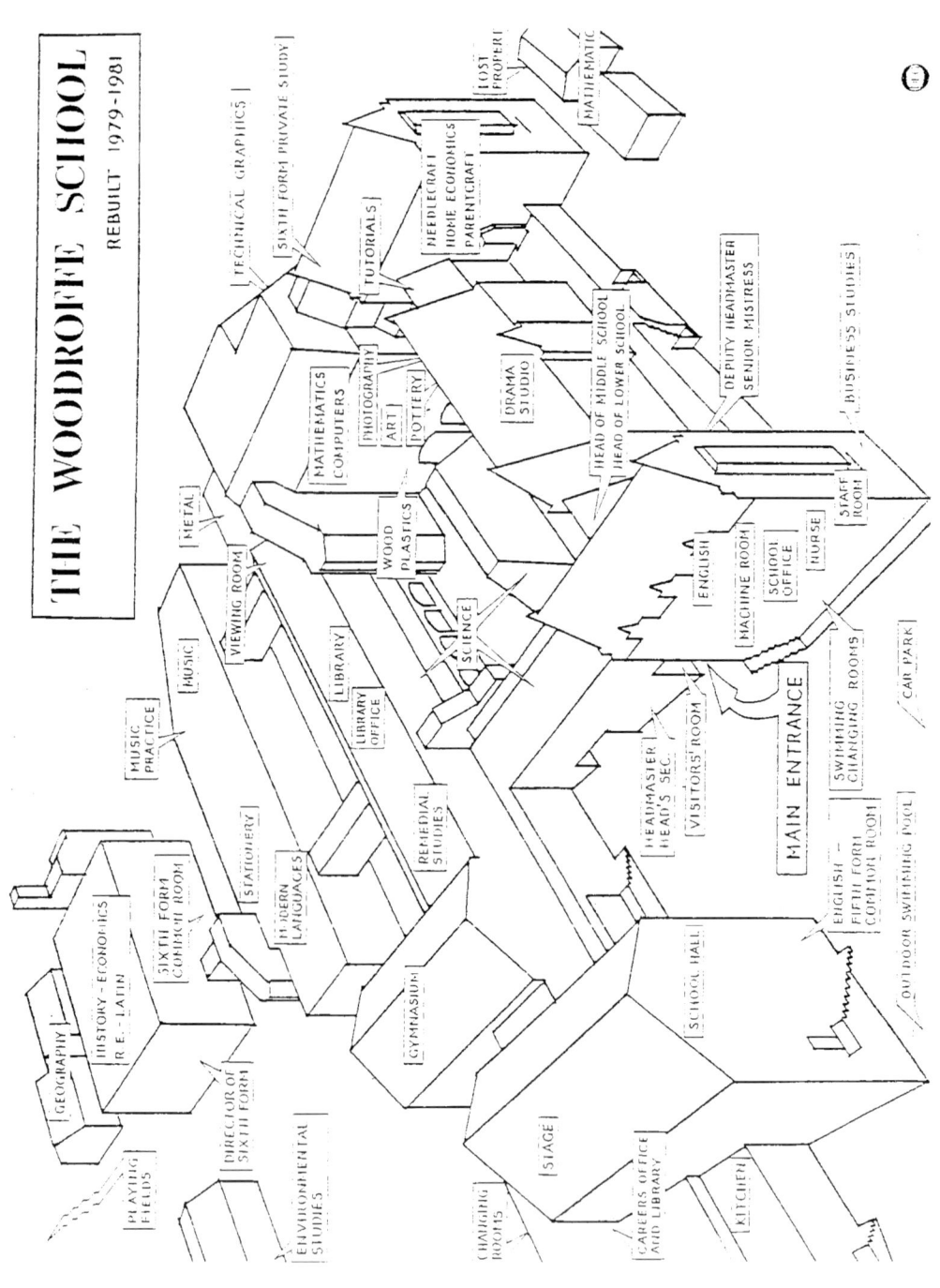

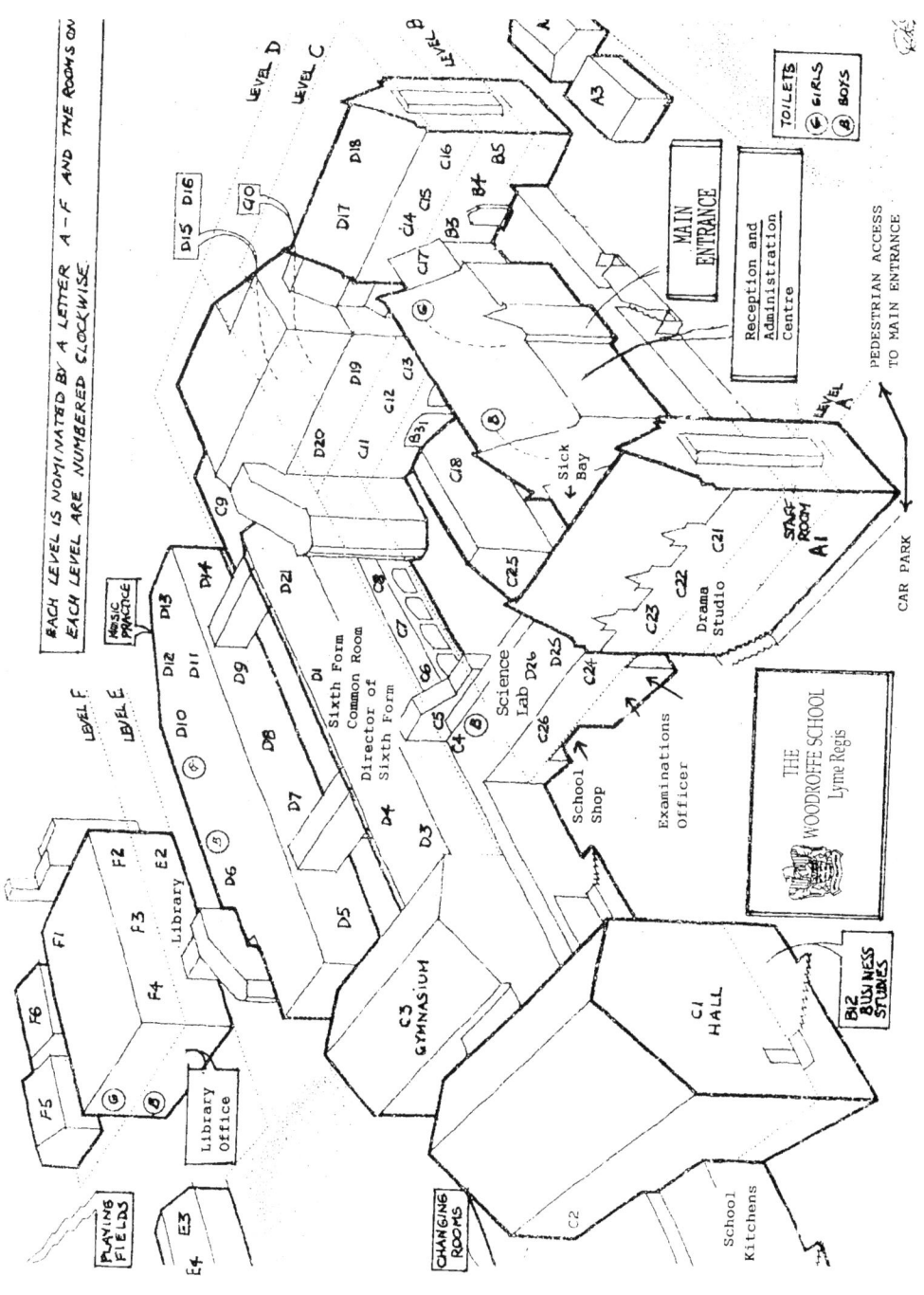

School Site 1992

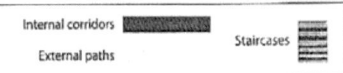
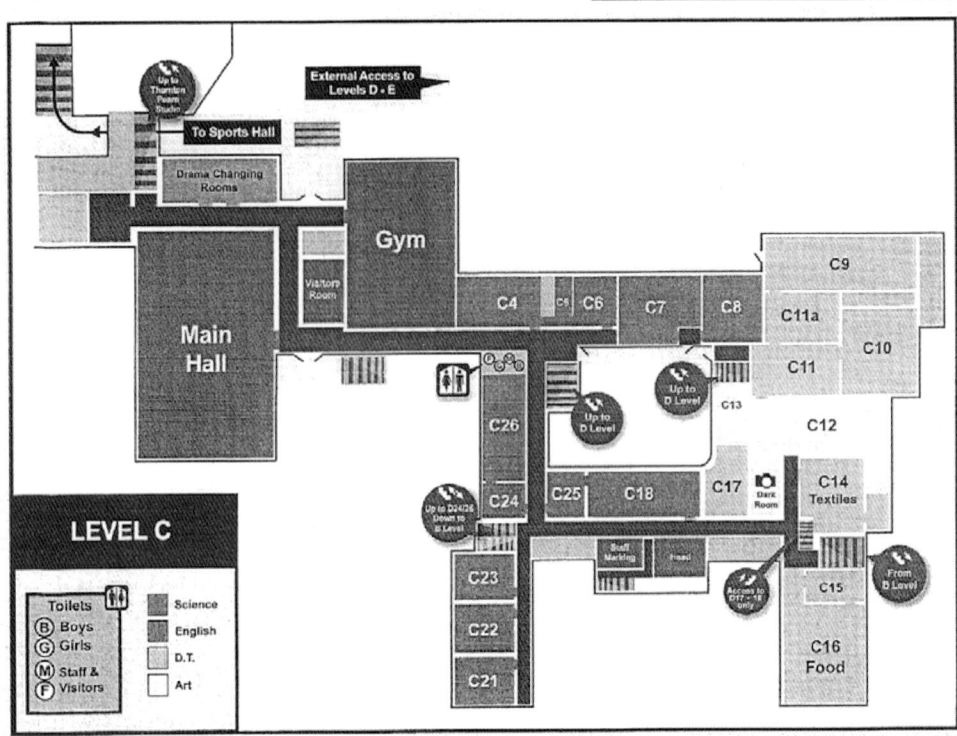
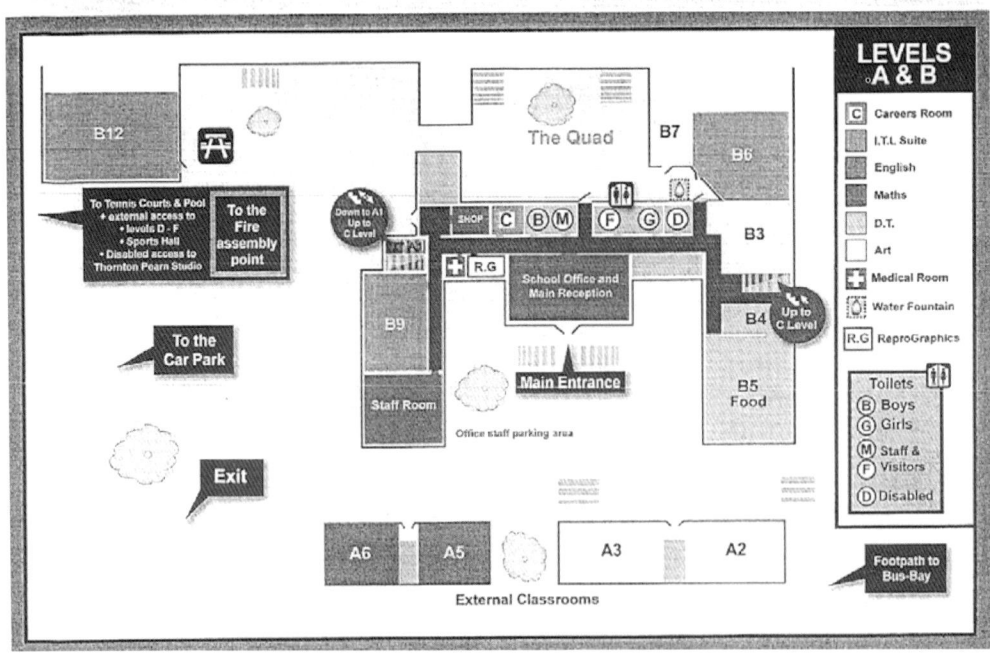

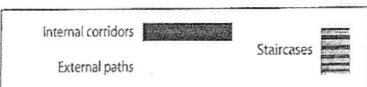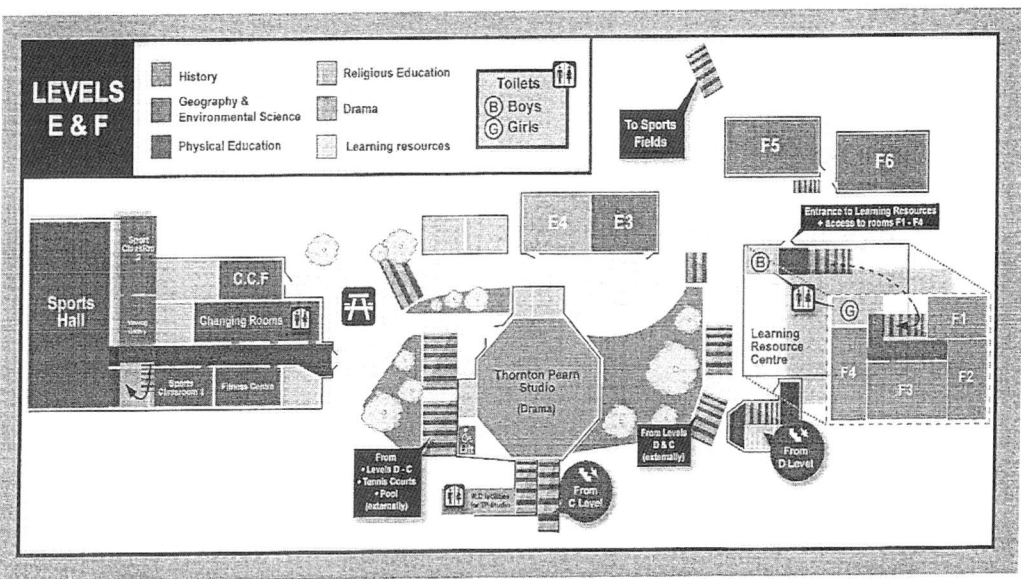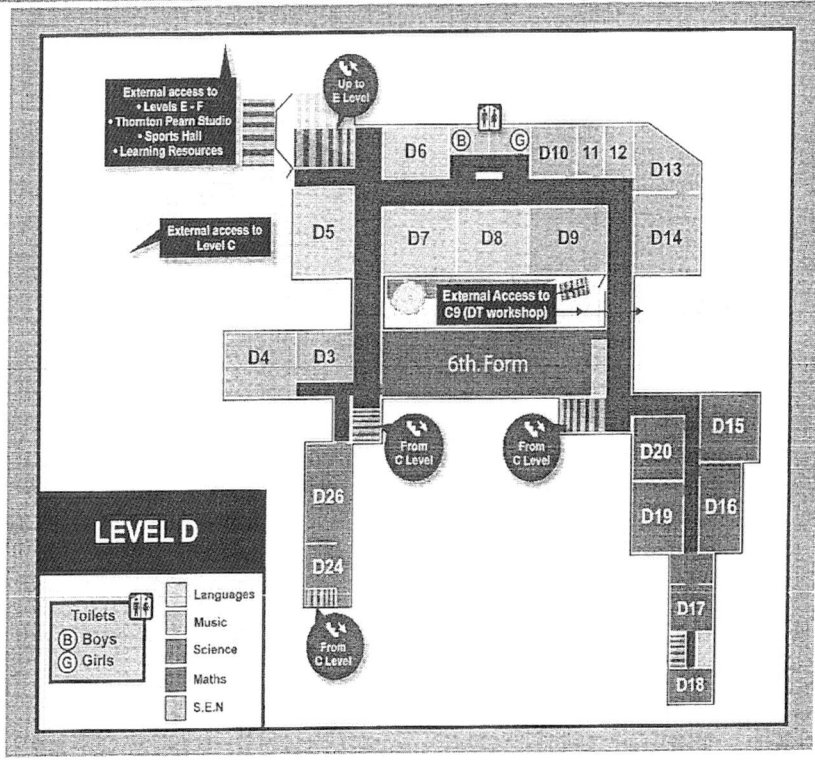

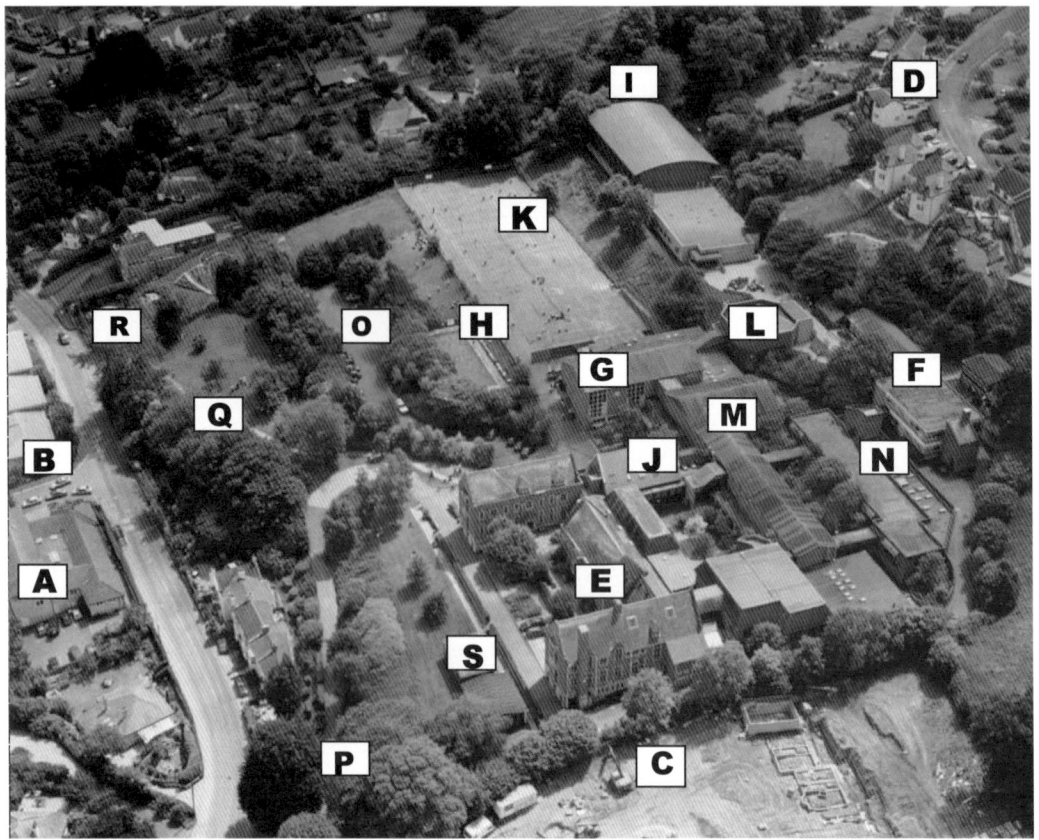

This recent aerial photograph of the school clearly shows how the site and the surrounding area has developed over the years.

A – Lyme Regis Community Care Centre
B – Small Industrial Estate
C – Housing development: Woodroffe Meadow
D – More housing: Somers Field.*
E – The original school buildings (1923)
F – ROSLA (Richards) block (1971)
G – School Hall (1964)
H – Swimming Pool (1965)
I – Sports Hall (2000)
J – Additional Science Laboratory (1994)
K – Tennis Courts
L – Thornton Pearn Studio (1999)
M – New Build (1964)
N – New Build (1980)
O – Staff Car Park
P – Main entrance
Q – Path to pedestrian access
R – Former Caretaker's Bungalow (now privately owned)
S – Mobile classrooms and two memorial trees

* The area between the school and the playing field is now completely developed.

Appendix 13
Education Terminology

AST	Advanced Skills Teacher
ATL	Association of Teachers and Lecturers
AWPU	Age weighted pupil unit – the sum of money allocated to the school for each student according to age. The main source of funding for schools
CATS	Cognitive Ability Tests
CEO	Chief Education Officer
Connexions	A support service for young people aged 13 – 19 years (includes giving advice on careers, health, housing, finance, relationships)
COP	Code of Practice
COSHH	Control of Substances Hazardous to Health
CPA	Child Protection Agency
CPD	Continuing Professional Development
CPVE	Certificate of Pre-Vocational Education
CRB	Criminal Records Bureau
CSE	Certificate of Secondary Education
DDA	Disability Discrimination Act
DEFRA	Department for Environment, Food and Rural Affairs
DfES	Department for Education and Skills – our DfES No. is 835/5401
DPA	Data Protection Act
DTI	Department of Trade and Industry
D & T	Design Technology
EBP	Education Business Partnership
EMA	Educational Maintenance Allowance – grant paid to young people in schools to keep them on beyond statutory school age
EOP	Equal opportunities Policy
EWO	Educational Welfare Officer
Extra Curricular Activities	Activities held outside normal lesson times ie clubs
FAS	Funding Agency for Schools
FE	Further Education
FOI	Freedom of Information Act
Foundation Subjects	English, Maths, Science, Technology, History, Geography and PE
GCE	General Certificate of Education
GCSE	General Certificate of Secondary Education National external qualification usually taken at age 16 after two years of study. Exams taken at the end of Key Stage 4
GNVQ	General National Vocational Qualification
GTC	General Teaching Council

GTP	Graduate Teacher Programme – trainee teachers in school all academic year
H & S	Health and Safety
HE	Higher Education
HMI	Her Majesty's Inspectors of Schools
HODS	Heads of Department
HSE	Health and Safety Executive
ICT	Information and Communication Technology
IEP	Individual Education Plan
IIP	Investors in People
INSET	In Service Education and Training
ISB	Individual Schools Budget – the total amount of money the LA has to distribute directly to schools after paying for central services
IT	Information Technology
ITT	Initial Teacher Training – programme run in conjunction with universities where student teachers come into school for a few weeks at a time to carry out their required placements
Key Stage 3	Years 7, 8 and 9
Key Stage 4	Years 10 and 11
Key Stage 5	Years 12 and 13
LA formerly LEA	Local Authority. LAs have a statutory duty to provide education in their area
Leadership Group	School Senior Management Team
Learning Centre	Targeted support for students with learning/behavioural issues
LIS	Library Information Service
LLL	Life Long Learning
LMS	Local Management of Schools
LSC	Learning and Skills Council
LSUs	Learning Support Units
MAs	Modern Apprenticeships
MidYis	Mid Years Information System (Key Stage 4)
MIS	Management Information Systems
NAHT	National Association of Headteachers
NASUWT	National Association of Schoolmasters Union Women Teachers
NC	National Curriculum
NGFL	National Grid for Learning
NOF	New Opportunities Fund
NOR	Number on Roll
NPQH	National Professional Qualification for Headteachers
NRA	National Record of Achievement
NUT	National Union of Teachers
NVQ	National Vocational Qualification

NQT	Newly Qualified Teacher
OCR, EDEXCEL, AQA, WJEC	Examination Boards
OFSTED	Office for Standards in Education. Responsible for managing the system of independent inspection introduced by the Education Act in 1992. Funded by the government
PAN	Planned Admission Number
PANDA	Performance and Assessment Documents
Pastoral Team	Organisation within school to ensure that students' social and emotional needs are met
PAT	Professional Association of Teachers
PFI	Private Finance Initiative
PGCE	Post-Graduate Certificate in Education
Post-16	The Sixth Form (Years 12 and 13)
PHSE	Personal, Health and Social Education. Includes personal relationships, communication, health education and sex education
PI	Performance Indicator
PLASC	Pupil Level Annual School Census
PRP	Performance Related Pay
PRUs	Pupil Referral Units
PTA	Parent Teacher Association
PTR	Pupil Teacher Ratio
QCA	Qualifications and Curriculum Authority
ROA	Record of Achievement
Reprographics	Team responsible for producing printed, word processed, desk top published material
SACRE	Standing Advisory Council for Religious Education
SAR	Strategic Area Review
SATs	Standard Assessment Tasks
SCAA	School Curriculum and Assessment Authority
SDP	School Development Plan
SENCO	The person responsible for leading the Learning Support Team (for students with special needs and learning difficulties eg health/social)
SEN	Special Educational Needs
SENCOP	Special Educational Needs Code of Practice
SIMS.net	Software used for students' and teachers' timetables and personal details
SIP	School Improvement Partner
SMT	Senior Management Team
SOW	Schemes of Work
STPCD	School Teachers' Pay and Conditions Document
STRB	School Teachers' Review Body
SWOT	Strengths Weaknesses Opportunities Threats – a planning tool

TA	Teaching Assistant
TEC	Training Enterprise Council (Replaced by Learning and Skills Council)
TES	Times Educational Supplement
Training Days	Teachers have five in-service training days or staff development days each year, in addition to the 190 days when students attend school
TTA	Teaching Training Agency
Tutorial/Tutor Time	This takes place daily from 8.40 am until 9.00 am and 1.25 pm until 1.35 pm. It is when registers are taken and provides an opportunity for tutors to relay any messages to students. Once a week each year group has a whole year assembly during morning tutor time
TVEI	The Technical and Vocational Education Initiative
UCAS	Universities and Colleges Admissions Service
UNISON	Union of Public Employees
UPN	Unique Pupil Number
VA	Voluntary Aided
VC	Voluntary Controlled
VI	Visual Impairment
VLE	Virtual Learning Environment
WAN	Wide Area Network
Yellis	Year 11 Information System (Key Stage 4)

Explanation re Forms/Year Groups		
1923 - 1990	1990 to date	Age
1st Form	Year 7 Key Stage 3	11
2nd Form	Year 8 Key Stage 3	12
3rd Form	Year 9 Key Stage 3	13
4th Form	Year 10 Key Stage 4	14
5th Form	Year 11 Key Stage 4	15
Lower Sixth	Year 12 Lower Sixth Post 16	16
Upper Sixth	Year 13 Upper Sixth Post 16	17

BIBLOGRAPHY

UNPUBLISHED SOURCES
Dorset History Centre
Lyme Regis Grammar School – Governors' Minutes 1923 - 1944 Ref: S184 1/1
Lyme Regis Grammar School – Governors' Minutes 1944 - 1962 Ref: S184 1/2
Lyme Regis Grammar School – Governors' Minutes 1962 - 1968 Ref: S184 1/3
Lyme Regis Grammar School – Governors' Minutes 1969 - 1972 Ref: S184 1/4
Lyme Regis Grammar School – Governors' Minutes 1972 - 1981 Ref: S184 1/5

PUBLISHED SOURCES
FOWLES John (1982) Short History of Lyme Regis
Published by Little, Brown and Company (Canada) Limited
LEGG Rodney (2003) The Book of Lyme Regis
Published by Halsgrove
LELLO John (1999) Lyme Regis Past
Published by Lello Publishing

- An article on the official opening of the Lyme Regis Secondary School dated September 1923 by kind permission of Pulmans Weekly News
- An article on Boarding Education dated 3rd October 1952 by kind permission of the Bridport and Lyme Regis News
- An abridged history of Lyme Regis Grammar School written by Mr Woodroffe in October 1956 for distribution at Speech Day
- "Lyme Regis Grammar School – The Post War Years" written in November 1956 by Major T B Pearn, Headmaster
- A transcript of a record made by Mr Woodroffe on Lyme Regis Grammar School, written and annotated by him dated 1961
- "The origins and brief history of St Michael's Senior School, Lyme Regis" written by Mr Ernest Wellings in June 1964 on the retirement of Mr Davies, Head of the Senior School, by kind permission of Mr Wellings
- The Lyme 1200 newspaper produced in 1974 to celebrate the Lyme 1200 celebrations
- Notes entitled "Alban J. Woodroffe, MBE, JP 1875 – 1964" written in 1975 by Mr Michael Fairley, History Master at the school
- School Magazines, Speech Day programmes and press cuttings from 1926 to date held in the school archive
- Papers on the school held at the Philpot Museum, Lyme Regis, by kind permission of the curator, Jo Draper.

Websites:

www.theaward.org for information relating to the Duke of Edinburgh Award Scheme.
www.events.ex.ac.uk/tentors/challenge for information relating to Ten Tors.
www.cwgc.org – The Commonwealth War Graves Commission
www.iwm.org – The Imperial War Museum

Gilly Warr née Williams was a pupil at Lyme Regis Grammar School from 1962 to 1969, during which time it changed its name to the Woodroffe School and became a comprehensive. Gilly attended the school with her twin sister, Jackie, and her three daughters have since been pupils. She has worked at the school in various support roles since 1988. Gilly is currently PA to the Head and Administration Manager. She is also a former Chairman and Secretary of Woodroffe Association, the organisation for ex-students which has organised many successful reunions at the school in recent years.